J H Cavinder
Nov 1 1790

THE LIBRARY
OF THE
UNIVERSITY OF ILLINOIS

THE OPEN POLAR SEA:

A

NARRATIVE OF A VOYAGE OF DISCOVERY
TOWARDS THE NORTH POLE,

IN THE

SCHOONER "UNITED STATES."

BY

Dr. I. I. HAYES.

NEW YORK:
PUBLISHED BY HURD AND HOUGHTON.
1867.

Entered according to Act of Congress, in the year 1866, by

I I HAYES,

in the Clerk's Office of the District Court for the Southern District of New York.

RIVERSIDE, CAMBRIDGE:
STEREOTYPED AND PRINTED BY
H O HOUGHTON AND COMPANY

919.8
H32a

I HAD INTENDED TO DEDICATE THIS BOOK TO

WILLIAM PARKER FOULKE,

Of Philadelphia,

To whom I am indebted
for all that a powerful intellect and
a generous friendship could do, to give practical
shape to my plans, and to insure success to an enterprise
in which I had embarked, with the simple advantage of an aim,
and with no better guide than the impulse of youth: but
since it is denied me to pay that tribute of my
admiration to one of the noblest of men,
I now inscribe it to his

MEMORY.

PREFACE.

THE design of this book may be briefly explained. I have attempted little more than a personal narrative, endeavoring to select from my abundant notes such scenes and incidents of adventure as seemed to me best calculated to bring before the mind of the reader, not merely the history of our voyage, but a general view of the Arctic regions, — its scenery and its life, with a cursory glance at those physical forces which, in their results, give characteristic expression to that remote quarter of the world. A day of months, followed by a night of months, where the mean annual temperature rises but little above zero, must necessarily clothe the air and the landscape with a sentiment difficult to appreciate, or, I might perhaps say, feel, without actual observation. I shall be abundantly rewarded if I have succeeded in impressing upon the reader's mind, with any degree of vividness, the wonders and the grandeur of Nature as unfolded to us under the Arctic sky.

I know it is usually thought that a book of travels should be simply a diary of events and incidents; but this, of necessity, involves a ceaseless repetition, and it seemed to me that I would do better to drop vi

PREFACE.

from my diary all that did not appear as immediately relevant to the scene; and, indeed, where the occasion appeared to require concentration, to abandon the diary altogether, and use the more concise form of descriptive narrative.

The reader will observe that I have not attempted, in any sense, to write a work of Science. True, the purpose of the voyage was purely a scientific one, — its chief object and aim being to explore the boundaries of the Open Polar Sea; at least to determine if such a sea did exist, as had been so often asserted; but while I have given a general discussion of the conditions of the Polar waters and the Polar ice, and have recorded many new facts in various departments of physical and natural science, yet I have desired to treat the subject in a manner which, as it seemed to me, would be most acceptable to the general reader, rather than to the scientific student, —preferring to direct the latter to those more strictly scientific channels where my materials have been or are about being published.

Soon after returning from the North, my principal records were placed at the disposal of the Smithsonian Institution at Washington; and I have employed such leisure as I could command in their elaboration and discussion, — the principal labor, however, falling upon Mr. Charles A. Schott, Assistant, United States Coast Survey, who brought to the task the best faculties of a well-stored mind, and unusual powers of patient investigation; and papers, giving a full

PREFACE. vii

analysis of the *magnetic, meteorological, astronomical, geographical, pendulum,* and *tidal* observations, were prepared, and were accepted for publication in the Smithsonian " Contributions to Knowledge." I regret to say that the publication of these papers has been much delayed. Deeming it desirable that some of the general conclusions to which we had arrived in our discussion of the observations should be given to the world without further postponement, I proposed to embody some leading facts in a short Appendix to this volume. Upon submitting the matter to the learned Secretary of the Institution, it was, however, claimed by him that, since I had intrusted the materials to his care, the Institution now possessed the exclusive right to whatever advantage was to be derived from their publication. To a proposition so eminently reasonable I readily assented, especially as I was informed that the papers were already in type and were to be published immediately; and, considering myself thus absolved from any further responsibility to the scientific world for the long delay, I accordingly abandoned the idea of the Appendix. The Chart exhibiting the track and discoveries of my voyage, and of my various sledge journeys, was claimed, in like manner, as the exclusive property of the Smithsonian Institution, and, like the papers, was to be published immediately. Hence it is that the small map which illustrates this volume is but a copy (reduced ten diameters) of my field chart, projected on the spot from my unrevised materials. It

viii PREFACE.

is perhaps needless for me to observe that entire accuracy was not attainable in the field, inasmuch as I had neither the leisure nor the facilities for reducing the magnetic variation, nor for obtaining the absolute time. I am happy to say, however, that no greater discrepancy exists than the one which places my highest latitude two minutes too far south on the field chart; but the reductions having been made, and a chart projected therefrom, I had confidently relied upon this source for the correct information which the Smithsonian Institution now alone possessed. This failing me, I was obliged to fall back upon my original resources, as the time was too short for a new reduction. I am glad to say, however, that the field chart is sufficiently accurate for every practical purpose, and differs chiefly from the one prepared, with greater carefulness, and of large size, for the Smithsonian "Contributions to Knowledge," in the unimportant feature of the names applied to newly discovered places, some of which were changed after my return. No list of these alterations having been preserved, and being unable to get the more accurate map again into my hands from the Secretary of the scientific institution in whose care it had been placed, as before observed, for publication, I have simply adopted the original nomenclature, and have used the names as they appear in my journal and on my field chart. This explanation is made in anticipation of the possible contingency of the Smithsonian Institution publishing the map, for some years

PREFACE.

ix

past in its possession, — an event which I think unlikely to happen, and which will now be unnecessary, the more especially as I am at present engaged in a new reduction of my materials, and the projection of a new map, the publication of which, in sufficiently large form to give it topographical as well as geographical value, has been proposed by my distinguished and very kind friend, Dr. Augustus Petermann, Gotha, in his Geographical Journal.

Papers descriptive of the *botanical* collection, prepared by Mr. Elias Durand; of the *algæ*, by Mr. Ashmead; of the *lichens*, by Professor James; of the *birds*, by Mr. John Cassin; of the *invertebrata*, by Dr. William Stimpson; of the *mammalia*, by Dr. J. H. Slack; of the *cetacea*, by Professor E. Cope; of the *infusoria*, by Dr. F. W. Lewis; of the *fishes*, by Dr. Theodore Gill; and of the *paleontology*, by Professor F. B. Meek, have appeared from time to time in the "Proceedings of the Academy of Natural Sciences of Philadelphia," excepting the last, which was published in the American "Journal of Arts and Sciences." Dr. J Atkin Meigs has in preparation a monograph on *ethnology*, based upon a collection of upward of one hundred and forty specimens, and I shall soon have completed a more elaborate discussion of the Greenland Glaciers and other collateral topics than has been allowed me by the limits and character of this work.

I should do great injustice to my own feelings, did I not here express the acknowledgment of my obligation to those societies, associations, and indi-

PREFACE.

viduals who united themselves with me in effecting the organization of the Expedition, and who liberally shared with me its expenses. My wishes were always promptly met by them, to the extent of their ability; and the enterprise was sustained with a zeal and interest rarely accorded to a purely scientific purpose. That I have not before published an account of my voyage, or presented any detailed statement of my discoveries to those who had a natural right to expect it, has been entirely owing to the circumstance that my time has been wholly occupied in the public service, from the period of my return until late last year; and they will, I trust, accept as a sufficient excuse for my silence during that period, the fact that the command of an army hospital, with from three to five thousand inmates, which devolved upon me during the greater part of the recent war, allowed me little leisure for literary or scientific work. It will also be understood that the temporary abandonment of the exploration was due to the same general cause.

October 23d, 1866.

LIST OF SUBSCRIBERS

TO THE

EXPEDITION.*

———

THROUGH A SPECIAL COMMITTEE OF THE AMERICAN GEOGRAPHI-
CAL AND STATISTICAL SOCIETY, NEW YORK   EGBERT L. VIELE,
Chairman; HENRY GRINNELL, *Treasurer*

Henry Grinnell.

A. D. Bache.

George Folsom.

Henry E. Pierrepont.

Benjamin H. Field.

M. de LeRoquette.

The " American Journal of
Arts and Sciences " —
Profs. Silliman and Dana.

Egbert L. Viele.

Cyrus W. Field.

J. L. Graham.

August Belmont.

Horace B. Clafflin.

George Opdyke.

Brown, Brothers & Co.

F. S. Stalknecht.

John Jay.

C. Godfrey Gunther.

Peter Cooper.

Wm. Remsen.

J. Carson Brevoort.

Lewis Rutherford.

C. P. Daly.

Hugh N. Camp.

W. A. White.

John D. Clute.

Marshall Lefferts.

Wolcott Gibbs.

John D. Jones.

Joseph Harsen.

Alexander H. Stevens.

John C. Green.

Samuel E. Barlow.

A. H. Ward.

James T. Hall.

* The author has reason to suppose that there are several persons to
whom the Expedition is indebted for support whose names, not having
been furnished him, do not appear in this list. Desiring to make it entirely complete, he will feel personally obliged to any one whose name is
omitted to notify him of the fact, through the agency by which the subscription was furnished.

LIST OF SUBSCRIBERS.

E. A. Stansbury.
W. T. Blodgett.
Dr. Samuel W. Francis.
Frank Moore.
H. M. Field.
Blakeman & Phinney.
Harpers Brothers.
John Austin Stevens.
George A. Woodward.
C. Detmold.
Z. T. Detmold.
Francis Lieber.
F. E. Church.
Bayard Taylor.
O. M. Mitchell.
Henrietta B. Haines.
Mary W. Talman.
Clarence A. Seward.

F. L. Hawks.
Robert B. Winthrop.
G. P. Putnam.
A. W. White.
A. H. Wood.
George L. Samson.
Henry A. Robbins.
Wm. H. Allen.
Albert Clark.
Joseph W. Orvis.
John D. Wing.
Grinnell & Bibby.
Simeon Holton, Jun.
Sheldon, Blakeman & Co.
American Desiccating Co.
Ruxton, Barker & Co.
G. Tagliabue.
Messrs. Nequs.

THROUGH COMMITTEES OF THE BOARD OF TRADE AND ACADEMY OF NATURAL SCIENCES, PHILADELPHIA FRANCIS COPE, *Treasurer.*

Wm. Parker Foulke.
Joseph Harrison, Jun.
Henry Cope.
Alfred Cope.
Wm. Bucknell.
John Rice.
North American Life Insurance Co.
Delaware Mutual Ins. Co.
Corn Exchange.
Cope Brothers.
Isaac Lea.
R. Pearsall.
C. Macalister.
Henry C. Carey.
John C. Cresson.
Wm. R. Lejeé.

Childs & Peterson.
Samuel J. Reeves.
Edward Trotter.
J. T. Alburger & Co.
M. J. Wickersham.
Thomas Sparks.
E. J. Lewis.
Joseph Leidy.
R. E. Rogers.
Jacob P. Jones.
J. B. Lippincott & Co.
M. W. Baldwin.
Samuel E. Stokes.
Dr. T. B. Wilson.
James C. Hand.
Henry C. Townsend.
Richard Price.

LIST OF SUBSCRIBERS. xiii

M. L. Dawson.
Samuel Coffin.
W. Haye.
Lodge 51, A. Y. M.
John Thompson.
John P. Crozer.
Joseph Jeanes.
E. J. Levis.
Edward A. Souder.
Geo. N. Tatham.
John A. Brown.
B. Marshall.
R. Marshall.
Thomas Richardson & Co.
D. Haddock, Jun.
J. B. Morris.
Israel Morris.
B. C. & R. A. Tilghman.
John W. Sexton.
John Grigg.
William Sellers & Co.
Tobias Wagner.
Warren Fisher.
Wm. S. Vaux.
Dr. James Bond.
Chas. Henry Fisher.
J. Edgar Thompson.
Charles E. Smith.
Frothingham, Wells & Co.
Fairman Rogers.
John L. Leconte.
J. C. Trautwine.
Edward Hayes.

Aubrey H. Smith.
C. Townsend.
E. C. Knight.
Buckman & Co.
E. Durar.
E. H. Butler.
Blair & Wyeth.
King & Baird.
Sharp & Brother.
Rowland & Irvin.
Henry Winsor.
David McConkey.
Wilson, Childs & Co.
A. Whitney & Son.
Townsend Sharpless.
David S. Brown.
Chas. Ellis.
Wm. M. Baird.
James H. Orne.
Joshua L. Bailey.
James Addicks.
Benj. Marsh.
Buzby & Co.
Weaver, Fitler & Co.
James Leslie & Co.
McAlister & Brother.
Bible Society.
John H. Cooper.
S. Hazard.
Isaac J. Williams.
Buckner & M'Connor.
Burley & Co.
Mrs. Dr. Bond.

THROUGH COMMITTEE OF CITIZENS, ALBANY, N. Y. D. V. N. RADCLIFFE, *Treasurer.*

J. H. Armsby.
Thomas W. Olcott.
Eli Perry.

D. V. N. Radcliffe.
Erastus Corning.
R. C. Davis.

xiv LIST OF SUBSCRIBERS.

Isaac W. Vosburg.
John T. Rathbone.
Alden Marsh.
A. B. Banks.
Charles L. Garfield.
David J. Boyd.
T. Rousell & Son.
W. Frothingham.
G. J. H. Thatcher.
Samuel Anable.

S. H. Ransom.
R. H. Wakeman.
J. O. Souner.
James Kidd.
A. A. Dunlap.
Alanson Sumner.
James W. Cook.
E. Owens.
John Tracy.
Cook & Palmer.

THROUGH THE CITIZENS' COMMITTEE AND COMMITTTEE OF THE ACADEMY OF ARTS AND SCIENCES, BOSTON. RICHARD BAKER, JUN, *Treasurer.*

Richard Baker, Jun.
Warren Sawyer.
John Stetson.
J. D. W. Joy.
O. W. Peabody.
S. A. Dix.
Theodore Lyman.
Richard P. Pope.
David Sears.
Thomas Lee.
Philip H. Sears.
B. W. Taggard.
Amos A. Lawrence.
Jacob Bigelow, M. D.
James M. Beebe.
A. W. Spencer.
S. H. Walley.
Wm. Gray.
H. A. Whitney.
Geo. R. Russell.
L. Agassiz.
B. A. Gould.
C. C. Felton.
Prof. J. Lovering.
Prof. E. N. Horsford.

James Lawrence.
Jonathan Phillips.
Nathan Appleton.
Joseph Whitney.
Abbott Lawrence.
George W. Lyman.
Edward Wigglesworth.
Francis Skinner.
George B. Blake.
Naylor & Co.
H. O. Houghton.
Columbia Lodge.
Woburn Lodge.
Mt. Lebanon Lodge.
Winslow Lewis Lodge.
Merchants' Insurance Co. (through Capt. Smith.)
Manufacturers' Ins. Co.
J. Sawyer & Co.
Wm. H. Kennard.
E. Hammer (Danish Con sul.)
D. N. Haskell.
Wm. Baker.
Daniel Paine.

LIST OF SUBSCRIBERS.

XV

H. Howard.
Wm. M. Parker.
Francis Kendall.
C. G. Kendall.
E. R. Mudge & Co.
Wilkinson, Stetson & Co.
Merrill & Co.
Allen, Whiting & Co.
Huntington, Wadsworth & Parks.
Fitchburg Woolen Co.
Macullum, Williams & Parker.
Edward Everett.
N. P. Banks.
Frederick W. Lincoln.
John Cummings, Jun.
John Clark.
James O. Safford.
S. S. Arnold.
Winslow Lewis, M. D.
Benj. French.
Black & Bacheller.
Wm. B. Boyd.
Wm. Furness, Jun.
John Paine.
James Sturgis.
Thornton K. Lothrop.
Caleb Curtis.
Chas. D. Homans, M. D.
George L. Pratt.
A. G. Smith.
Henry P. Kidder.
Henry Mulliken.
A. W. Stetson.
Chas. J. Sprague.
N. I. Bowditch.
Stone, Wood & Baldwin.

Messinger & Brothers.
Middlesex Co.
Oak Hall.
Fenno & Co.
F. A. Hawley & Co.
Andrew Pierce.
Burnham & Scott.
March Brothers.
William R. Lovejoy & Co.
Whiting, Galloupe & Co.
Kelley & Levin.
John A. Whipple.
Stetson, Kendall & Minot.
Isaac Fenno.
Charles E. Wiggin.
Joshua Blake.
Preston & Merrill.
Wm. Read & Son.
Richard Fay, Jun.
Redding & Co.
Hostetter & Smith, (Pittsburg, Pa.)
John Wilson.
Henry W. Poole.
Otis Norcross.
H. B. Walley.
Richard F. Bond.
L. Audenried & Co.
Noble, Hammott & Hall.
N. Sturtevant & Co.
Wm. F. Weld.
J. G. Bigelow.
Wm. D. Atkinson, Jun.
Jos. W. Wightman.
George H. Snelling.
J. C. Hoadley.
A. Loring.
H. Poor & Son.

LIST OF SUBSCRIBERS.

Thomas Thompson.
Wm. Bond & Son.
Pierce & Co.
Joshua Stetson.
Chas. W. Freeland & Co.
Burrough, Bro. & Co.
Frost & Kimball.
Washington Mills.
Hunt & Goodwin.
Geo. W. Simmons.
Nevin, Sawyer & Co.
George Osgood.
Theodore H. Bell.
Brown & Taggard.
Winsor & Whitney.
Richard Morris Hunt.
Edward J. Thomas.
Wm. B. Hayden.
E. H. Blake.
Lewis R. Reynolds.
Swann, Brewer & Tileston.
E. B. Moore.
John E. Hayes.
Ballard & Prince.
Dana, Farrar & Hyde.
Solo. Piper.
Jacob Stanwood.
E. P. Tileston.
Isaac Rich.
Salem T. Lamb.
Daniel D. Kelley.
Wm. M. Jacobs & Son.

Mrs. Pratt.
Mrs. E. Thompson.
W. Clafflin & Co.
Day, Wilcox & Co.
J. J. Adams & Co.
Alex. Williams & Co.
E. Paige & Co.
D. P. Ives & Co.
Max, White & Bartlett.
J. B. Kendall.
Sewall, Day & Co.
E. A. & W. Winchester.
Seth Adams.
J. & J. F. Samson & Co.
Wilder & Eastbrook.
Maynard & Noyes.
Winn, Eaton & Co.
J. H. Poole.
Fogg, Houghton & Co.
Brown & Stanley.
J. Childs, Jun.
Doan & Skilton.
Parker, Gannett & Osgood.
Denton & Wood.
Foster & Smith.
Wm. K. Lewis & Co.
Thomas W. Pierce.
Joseph B. Glover.
Addison Gage.
I. N. Brown.
New Bedford Cordage Co.
C. B. Bryant.

LIST OF ILLUSTRATIONS.

	PAGE
1 MAP OF THE POLAR REGIONS	1
Drawn by C. A. Schott. Engraved by J Schedler.	
2 MAP OF SMITH SOUND, SHOWING DR. HAYES' TRACK AND DISCOVERIES	72
Drawn by Dr Hayes. Engraved by J. Schedler	
3. MAP OF PORT FOULKE, THE WINTER QUARTERS OF THE EXPEDITION	96
Drawn by Dr. Hayes. Engraved by J. Schedler	
4 AN ARCTIC TEAM	104
Drawn by G. G. White, from a Sketch by Dr. Hayes. Engraved by J. A. Bogert.	
5. A BEAR-HUNT	174
Drawn by Darley, from Description. Engraved by J A. Bogert.	
6. CROSSING THE HUMMOCKS	322
Drawn by G. G. White, from a Sketch by Dr. Hayes. Engraved by J. A Bogert	
7. THE SHORES OF THE POLAR SEA	346
Drawn by H. Fenn, from a Sketch by Dr Hayes. Engraved by Fay & Cox.	
8. A WALRUS-HUNT	408
Drawn by Darley, from Description. Engraved by J. A. Bogert.	
9. TYNDALL GLACIER, WHALE SOUND	438
Drawn by H. Fenn, from a Photograph by Dr Hayes. Engraved by Kingdon & Boyd.	

EXPLANATION OF TAIL–PIECES.

Drawn on wood by G. G. White from Photographs and Sketches by Dr. Hayes. Engraved mostly by J. A. Bogert.

		PAGE
1	ANCHOR	15
2.	ARCHED ICEBERG	27
3.	GREENLANDER IN HIS KAYAK	34
4	UPERNAVIK	43
5.	SNOWFLAKE (magnified three diameters)	56
6.	SEAL ON CAKE OF ICE	67
7.	HEAD OF A REINDEER	91
8	PORT FOULKE	100
9.	SNOWFLAKE (same as No 5)	126
10.	CHESTER VALLEY, SHOWING ALIDA LAKE AND THE GLACIER	136
11	"MY BROTHER JOHN'S GLACIER," FROM FIRST CAMP.	148
12	GROUP OF REINDEER	164
13.	SCHOONER IN WINTER QUARTERS	211
14	THE ESQUIMAU HUT AT ETAH.	235
15	HEAD OF WALRUS	247
16	PORTRAIT OF BIRDIE, THE ARTIC FOX	250
17.	SONNTAG'S GRAVE	276
18.	SNOWFLAKE (same as No. 5)	296
19.	CAMPING IN A SNOW-BANK	306
20	POLAR BEAR	314
21.	DOG SLEDGE	321
22	HEAD OF THE ESQUIMAU DOG OOSISOAK	332
23	CAPE UNION	352
24.	A SKETCH	362
25.	OBSERVATORY AT PORT FOULKE.	375
26.	SNOWFLAKE (same as No. 5)	380
27.	KALUTUNAH AND HIS FAMILY	395
28.	HEAD OF ARCTIC HARE	425
29.	A SKETCH	438
30.	"END"	454

CONTENTS.

INTRODUCTION.

Plan of the Expedition. — First Announcement — Appeal to Scientific Societies — Aid solicited. — Public Lectures. — Liberality of various Societies and Individuals — Vessel purchased in Boston. — Interest manifested in that City. — Difficulty in obtaining a proper Crew. — Organization of the Party. — Scientific Outfit. — Abundant Supplies 1

CHAPTER I.

Leaving Boston. — At Anchor in Nantasket Roads. — At Sea... ... 13

CHAPTER II.

Passage to the Greenland Coast. — Discipline. — The Decks at Sea. — Our Quarters. — The First Iceberg. — Crossing the Arctic Circle — The Midnight Sun. — The Endless Day. — Making the Land — A Remarkable Scene among the Bergs. — At Anchor in Pröven Harbor 16

CHAPTER III.

The Colony of Proven. — The Kayak of the Greenlander. — Scarcity of Dogs. — Liberality of the Chief Trader. — Arctic Flora 28

CHAPTER IV.

Upernavik. — Hospitality of the Inhabitants. — Death and Burial of Gibson Caruthers. — A Lunch on Board. — Adieu 35

CHAPTER V.

Among the Icebergs. — Dangers of Arctic Navigation. — A Narrow Escape from a Crumbling Berg. — Measurement of an Iceberg 44

CHAPTER VI.

Entering Melville Bay. — The Middle Ice. — The Great Polar Current. — A Snow-Storm. — Encounter with an Iceberg — Making Cape York. — Rescue of Hans 57

XX   CONTENTS.

CHAPTER VII.

PAGE

Hans and his Family. — Petowak Glacier. — A Snow-Storm. — The
Ice-Pack. — Entering Smith Sound. — A Severe Gale. — Collision
with Icebergs. — Encounter with the Ice-Fields. — Retreat from the
Pack. — At Anchor in Hartstene Bay. — Entering Winter Quar-
ters 68

CHAPTER VIII.

Our Winter Harbor. — Preparing for Winter. — Organization of Duties. — Scientific Work — The Observatory. — Schooner Driven
Ashore. — The Hunters — Sawing a Dock. — Frozen up. — Sun-
set 92

CHAPTER IX.

Sunset. — Winter Work. — My Dog-Teams. — "My Brother John's
Glacier." — Hunting. — Peat Beds. — Esquimau Graves. — Putre-
faction at Low Temperatures. — Sonntag climbs the Glacier. —
Hans and Peter. — My Esquimau People. — The Esquimau Dog
— Surveying the Glacier — The Sailing-Master. — His Birthday
Dinner.. 101

CHAPTER X

Journey on the Glacier — The First Camp. — Scaling the Glacier —
Character of its Surface. — The Ascent. — Driven back by a Gale
— Low Temperature. — Dangerous Situation of the Party — A
Moonlight Scene 127

CHAPTER XI.

Important Results of the recent Journey. — The Glacier System of
Greenland. — General Discussion of the Subject. — Illustrations
drawn from the Alpine Glaciers. — Glacier Movement. — Outline
of the Greenland *Mer de Glace* 137

CHAPTER XII

My Cabin. — Surveying. — Castor and Pollux. — Concerning Scurvy.
— Dangers of eating Cold Snow. — Knorr and Starr. — Frost-Bites.
— Hans, Peter, and Jacob again. — Coal Account. — The Fires —
Comfort of our Quarters. — The House on Deck. — Mild Weather.
— Jensen. — Mrs. Hans. — John Williams, the Cook. — A Cheer-
ful Evening 149

CHAPTER XIII

Increasing Darkness. — Daily Routine. — The Journal. — Our Home.
— Sunday. — Return of Sonntag. — A Bear-Hunt. — The Open
Water. — Accident to Mr. Knorr. — A Thaw. — " The Port Foulke

CONTENTS.   xxi

PAGE

Weekly News." — The Tide-Register. — The Fire-Hole. — Hunting Foxes. — Peter.. 165

CHAPTER XIV.

Midwinter. — The Night of Months. — Brilliancy of the Moonlight. — Mild Temperatures. — Remarkable Weather. — A Shower. — Depth of Snow — Snow Crystals. — An Epidemic among the Dogs. — Symptoms of the Disorder. — Great Mortality. — Only one Team left. — New Plans. — Schemes for reaching the Esquimaux in Whale Sound 192

CHAPTER XV.

The Arctic Midnight. — Sonntag starts for Whale Sound — Effects of Darkness on the Spirits. — Routine of Duties. — Christmas Eve. — Christmas Day. — The Christmas Dinner. 200

CHAPTER XVI.

The New Year. — Looking for Sonntag. — The Aurora Borealis. — A Remarkable Display. — Depth of Snow — Strange Mildness of the Weather. — The Open Sea. — Evaporation at Low Temperatures. — Looking for the Twilight. — My Pet Fox............... 212

CHAPTER XVII.

The Arctic Night 222

CHAPTER XVIII.

Prolonged Absence of Mr. Sonntag. — Preparing to look for him. — Arrival of Esquimaux. — They report Sonntag dead. — Arrival of Hans. — Condition of the Dogs. — Hans's Story of the Journey... 227

CHAPTER XIX.

Sonntag. — Twilight increasing — A Deer-Hunt. — The Arctic Foxes. — The Polar Bear. — Adventures with Bears — Our New Esquimaux. — Esquimau Dress. — A Snow House. — Esquimau Implements. — A Walrus Hunt 236

CHAPTER XX.

Looking for the Sun — The Open Sea. — Birds 248

CHAPTER XXI.

Sunrise 251

CHAPTER XXII.

Spring Twilight. — Arrival of Esquimaux. — Obtaining Dogs. — Kalutunah, Tattarat, Myouk, Amalatok and his Son. — An Arctic Hospital. — Esquimau Gratitude......... 255

xxii CONTENTS.

CHAPTER XXIII

Kalutunah returns — An Esquimau Family. — The Family Property — The Family Wardrobe. — Myouk and his Wife. — Peter's Dead Body found. — My New Teams. — The Situation — Hunting. — Subsistence of Arctic Animals. — Pursuit of Science under Difficulties. — Kalutunah at Home — An Esquimau Feast. — Kalutunah in Service. — Recovering the Body of Mr. Sonntag. — The Funeral. — The Tomb 265

CHAPTER XXIV.

Starting on my First Journey. — Object of the Journey. — A Mishap. — A Fresh Start. — The First Camp. — Hartstene's Cairn. — Exploring a Track. — A New Style of Snow-Hut. — An Uncomfortable Night. — Low Temperature. — Effect of Temperature on the Snow — Among the Hummocks. — Sighting Humboldt Glacier — The Track impracticable to the Main Party. — Van Rensselaer Harbor. — Fate of the *Advance.* — A Drive in a Gale 277

CHAPTER XXV.

Sending forward Supplies. — Kalutunah as a Driver. — Kalutunah civilized. — Mr. Knorr. — Plan of my Proposed Journey. — Preparing to set out — Industrious Esquimau Women. — Death and Burial of Kablunet. — The Start 290

CHAPTER XXVI.

The First Day's Journey. — A Fall of Temperature. — Its Effect upon the Men — Camped in a Snow-Hut. — The Second Day's Journey. — At Cairn Point — Character of the Ice. — The Prospect — Storm-stayed. — The Cooks in Difficulty. — Snow-Drift. — Violence of the Gale. — Our Snow-Hut 297

CHAPTER XXVII.

The Storm continues. — At Work. — Among the Hummocks — Difficulties of the Track. — The Snow-Drifts. — Slow Progress. — The Smith Sound Ice. — Formation of the Hummocks. — The Old Ice-Fields. — Growth of Ice-Fields. — Thickness of Ice — The Prospect 307

CHAPTER XXVIII.·

The Difficulties multiplying. — Sledge broken. — Reflections on the Prospect. — The Men breaking down. — Worse and Worse — The Situation. — Defeat of Main Party. — Resolve to send the Party back and continue the Journey with Dogs. 315

CONTENTS.

xxiii

CHAPTER XXIX.

PAGE

The Main Party sent back. — Plunging into the Hummocks again. — Advantages of Dogs. — Camp in an Ice-Cave. — Nursing the Dogs. — Snow-Blindness. — A Chapter of Accidents. — Cape Hawks. — Cape Napoleon — Storm-stayed. — Grinnell Land looming up — Discovering a Sound. — Ravenous Disposition of Dogs — A Cheerless Supper. — Camping in the Open Air. — Prostration of Men and Dogs. — Making the Land at last 322

CHAPTER XXX.

The Prospect Ahead. — To Cape Napoleon. — To Cape Frazer — Traces of Esquimaux. — Rotten Ice. — Kennedy Channel. — Mildness of Temperature. — Appearance of Birds. — Geological Features of Coast. — Vegetation. — Accident to Jensen 333

CHAPTER XXXI.

A New Start. — Speculations. — In a Fog. — Polar Scenery. — Stopped by Rotten Ice. — Looking Ahead. — Conclusions. — The Open Sea. — Climax of the Journey. — Returning South 343

CHAPTER XXXII

The Open Polar Sea. — Width of the Polar Basin. — Boundaries of the Polar Basin. — Polar Currents. — Polar Ice. — The Ice-Belt — Arctic Navigation and Discovery. — The Russian Sledge Explorations. — Wrangel's Open Sea. — Parry's Boat Expedition. — Dr. Kane's Discoveries. — Expansion of Smith Sound — General Conclusions drawn from my own Discoveries and those of my Predecessors 353

CHAPTER XXXIII.

On Board the Schooner. — Review of the Journey. — The Return down Kennedy Channel. — A Severe March in a Snow-Storm. — Rotten Ice. — Effects of a Gale. — Returning through the Hummocks. — The Dogs breaking down. — Adrift on a Floe at Cairn Point. — The Open Water compels us to take to the Land. — Reaching the Schooner. — Projecting a Chart. — The New Sound. — My Northern Discoveries 363

CHAPTER XXXIV.

Inspection of the Schooner. — Method of Repairing. — The Serious Nature of the Injury. — The Schooner unfit for any further Ice-Encounters. — Examination of my Resources. — Plans for the Future ....·.......... 376

xxiv CONTENTS.

CHAPTER XXXV.

The Arctic Spring. — Snow disappearing. — Plants show Signs of Life. — Return of the Birds. — Change in the Sea. — Refitting the Schooner. — The Esquimaux. — Visit to Kalutunah. — Kalutunah's Account of the Esquimau Traditions. — Hunting-Grounds contracted by the Accumulation of Ice. — Hardships of their Life. — Their Subsistence. — The Race dwindling away. — Visit to the Glacier. — Re-survey of the Glacier. — Kalutunah catching Birds. — A Snow-Storm and a Gale. — The Mid-day of the Arctic Summer . . 381

CHAPTER XXXVI.

The Arctic Summer. — The Flora. — The Ice dissolving — A Summer Storm of Rain, Hail, and Snow. — The Terraces — Ice Action — Upheaval of the Coast. — Geological Interest of Icebergs and the Land-Ice — A Walrus Hunt. — The " Fourth " — Visit to Littleton Island. — Great Numbers of Eider-Ducks and Gulls. — The Ice breaking up. — Critical Situation of the Schooner. — Taking Leave of the Esquimaux. — Adieu to Port Foulke 396

CHAPTER XXXVII.

Leaving Port Foulke. — Effort to reach Cape Isabella. — Meet the Pack and take Shelter at Littleton Island. — Hunting. — Abundance of Birds and Walrus. — Visit to Cairn Point — Reaching the West Coast. — View from Cape Isabella. — Plans for the Future. — Our Results. — Chances of reaching the Polar Sea discussed. — The Glaciers of Ellesmere Land 416

CHAPTER XXXVIII

Leaving Smith Sound. — Crossing the North Water. — Meeting the Pack. — The Sea and Air teeming with Life. — Remarkable Refraction. — Reaching Whale Sound. — Surveying in a Boat. — The Sound traced to its Termination. — Meeting Esquimaux at Iteplik. — Habits of the Esquimaux. — Marriage Ceremony — The Decay of the Tribe. — View of Barden Bay. — Tyndall Glacier 426

CHAPTER XXXIX.

Homeward Bound. — Entering Melville Bay. — Encounter with a Bear. — Meeting the Pack. — Making the " South Water. " — Reaching Upernavik. — The News. — To Goodhaven. — Liberality of the Danish Government and the Greenland Officials — Driven out of Baffin Bay by a Gale. — Crippled by the Storm and forced to take Shelter in Halifax. — Hospitable Reception. — Arrival in Boston. — Realize the State of the Country. — The Determination. — Conclusion 439

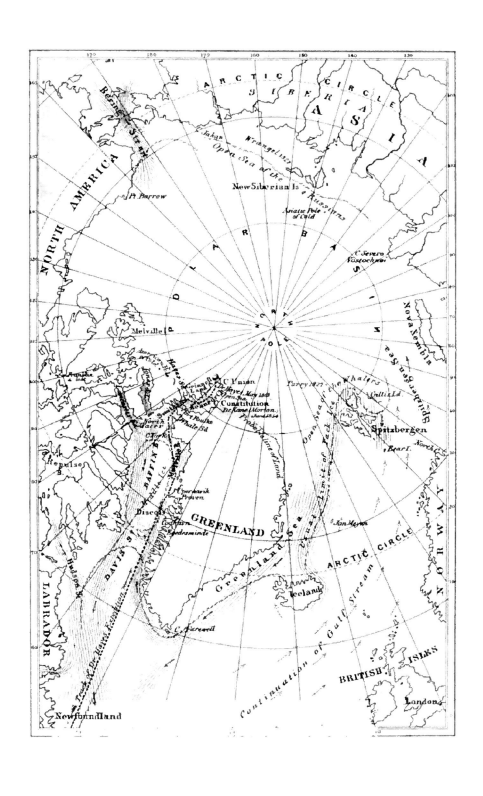

INTRODUCTION.

PLAN OF THE EXPEDITION. — FIRST ANNOUNCEMENT. — APPEAL TO SCIENTIFIC SOCIETIES — AID SOLICITED — PUBLIC LECTURES — LIBERALITY OF VARIOUS SOCIETIES AND INDIVIDUALS. — VESSEL PURCHASED IN BOSTON — INTEREST MANIFESTED IN THAT CITY. — DIFFICULTY IN OBTAINING A PROPER CREW — ORGANIZATION OF THE PARTY. — SCIENTIFIC OUTFIT. — ABUNDANT SUPPLIES.

I PURPOSE to record in this Book the events of the Expedition which I conducted to the Arctic Seas.

The plan of the enterprise first suggested itself to me while acting as Surgeon of the Expedition commanded by the late Dr. E K. Kane, of the United States Navy. Although its execution did not appear feasible at the period of my return from that voyage in October, 1855, yet I did not at any time abandon the design. It comprehended an extensive scheme of discovery. The proposed route was that by Smith's Sound My object was to complete the survey of the north coasts of Greenland and Grinnell Land, and to make such explorations as I might find practicable in the direction of the North Pole.

My proposed base of operations was Grinnell Land, which I had discovered on my former voyage, and had personally traced beyond lat. 80°, far enough to satisfy me that it was available for my design.

Accepting the deductions of many learned physicists that the sea about the North Pole cannot be frozen, that an open area of varying extent must be found within the Ice-belt which is known to invest it, I desired to add to the proofs which had already been

2 PLAN OF THE EXPEDITION.

accumulated by the early Dutch and English voyagers, and, more recently, by the researches of Scoresby, Wrangel, and Parry, and still later by Dr. Kane's expedition.

It is well known that the great difficulty which has been encountered, in the various attempts that have been made to solve this important physical problem, has been the inability of the explorer to penetrate the Ice-belt with his ship, or to travel over it with sledges sufficiently far to obtain indisputable proof. My former experience led me to the conclusion that the chances of·success were greater by Smith's Sound than by any other route, and my hopes of success were based upon the expectation which I entertained of being able to push a vessel into the Ice-belt, to about the 80th parallel of latitude, and thence to transport a boat over the ice to the open sea which I hoped to find beyond. Reaching this open sea, if such fortune awaited me, I proposed to launch my boat and to push off northward. For the ice-transportation I expected to rely, mainly, upon the dog of the Esquimaux.

How far I was able to execute my design these pages will show.

It will be remembered that the highest point reached by Dr. Kane with his vessels was Van Rensselaer Harbor, latitude 78° 37', where he wintered. This was on the eastern side of Smith's Sound It seemed to me that a more favorable position could be attained on the western side; and from personal observations made in 1854, while on a sledge journey from Van Rensselaer Harbor, it appeared to me probable that the degree of latitude already indicated might be secured for a winter station and a centre of observation

ANTICIPATED RESULTS

It would be needless for me to attempt to illustrate the value of such a centre for the purpose of scientific inquiry. It was not alone the prospect of the satisfaction to be achieved by completing our geographical knowledge of that portion of the globe, nor that of solving definitely the problem of an Open Polar Sea, that encouraged me in the task which I had undertaken. There were many questions of physical science to be settled, and I hoped to take with me a corps of well-instructed observers. The movements of the currents of the air and water, the temperature of these elements, the pressure of the former and the tides of the latter, the variations of gravity, the direction and intensity of the "magnetic force," the Aurora Borealis, the formation and movement of the glaciers, and many important features of Natural History remained to be solved by observations about the centre indicated. Years of profitable labor might indeed be expended in that locality by an enterprising force of skilled workers.

With these objects in view, I applied with great confidence to the scientific men of the world and to the enlightened public sentiment of my countrymen.

The response, although in the end highly gratifying, was more tardy in its coming than had been at first anticipated. There were indeed many circumstances of discouragement, not the least of which was an impression which then had possession of the public judgment, that any further efforts toward the North Pole must be fruitless, and must involve an unjustifiable loss of life. It was only after many endeavors that here and there the influences favorable to the design began to affect the community. The most important of these was, of course, the sanction given to the project by those associations whose opinions govern the mass of men in relation to scientific matters.

The first public announcement of it was made to the American Geographical and Statistical Society, before which body I read a paper in December, 1857, setting forth the plan, and the means proposed for its accomplishment. It was on this occasion that I first experienced the discouragement to which I have already referred, and it became evident to all who had thus far interested themselves in the subject, that it would be necessary to instruct the public mind in relation to the practicability of the proposed exploration, and its comparative freedom from danger, before any earnest support could be anticipated.

To this task I at once addressed myself, although, indeed, I might with some show of reason have abandoned the undertaking altogether; but at twenty-five one is not easily discouraged. In concert with the friends of the enterprise, I caused it to be understood that I was open to invitations from any of the numerous literary societies and clubs who were organizing popular courses of lectures for the winter. Such lectures were at that time quite the fashion, and almost every little town in the country could boast of its "course." The invitations which reached me were very numerous, and I availed myself of them to the full limit of my time. The scientific and literary journals and the press, ever ready to aid in the advancement of liberal and enlightened purposes, gave very cordial support; and, when the spring of 1858 opened, we had the satisfaction to perceive that we had dispelled some of the popular illusions respecting the dangers of Arctic exploration. Among the most im-

SCIENTIFIC INTEREST. 5

portant of the lectures given at this period was a course which I delivered at the instance of Professor Joseph Henry, in the fine lecture-room of the Smithsonian Institution at Washington. These lectures were the more important, in that they secured to the undertaking the friendship and support of Professor A. D. Bache, the learned and efficient chief of the United States Coast Survey.

In April, 1858, I brought the subject before the American Association for the Advancement of Science, at its annual meeting held in Baltimore; and that body of representative men, at the suggestion of Professor Bache, appointed sixteen of its leading members a committee on "Arctic Exploration."

It remained now only to secure the necessary material aid. With this object in view, committees were promptly appointed by the American Philosophical Society, the Academy of Natural Sciences of Philadelphia, the American Geographical Society, the Lyceum of Natural History of New York, the American Academy of Arts and Sciences, and the Boston Society of Natural History.

Subscription lists were at once opened by these several committees, and Professor Bache, at all times foremost to promote scientific discovery, headed the list with his powerful name.

The learned Secretary of the Smithsonian Institution, Professor Joseph Henry, further strengthened the cause by the proffer of scientific instruments, and this was followed by the earnest support of Mr. Henry Grinnell, whose zealous efforts and sacrifices in behalf of Arctic exploration are too well known to gain any thing from my commendation.

At a subsequent period I addressed the Chamber

PUBLIC LECTURES

of Commerce in New York, and the Board of Trade in Philadelphia. The latter promptly appointed a committee with the same objects as those previously appointed by the scientific societies. Still later I spoke to a large audience in the lecture-room of the Lowell Institute, Boston, assembled under the auspices of the committee of the Academy of Arts and Sciences, on which occasion, after eloquent addresses by the chairman, the late Hon. Edward Everett, and Professors Agassiz and W. B. Rogers, a committee of citizens was appointed to coöperate with the committees already named.

The system of public lecturing which had been improved with such satisfactory advantage in the beginning, was continued, and, in addition to the increased public interest which the lectures created, they proved a source of more substantial benefit. Two of them were delivered under the auspices of the American Geographical Society. The value of these last was derived from the circumstance that public support was given to the project by Dr. Francis Lieber, the late Rev. Dr Bethune, Rev. J. P. Thompson, the late Professor (afterward Major-General) O M. Mitchel, and Mr. (now Brigadier-General) Egbert L. Viele, who spoke on the occasion. The principal address was made by Dr. Lieber, and it was characteristic of that able and learned writer.

The interest manifested among geographers abroad was scarcely less than that shown by scientific men at home. The eminent President of the Geographical Society of London, Sir Roderick Impey Murchison, in announcing the proposed renewal of Arctic discovery to that distinguished body, expressed the earnest desire of the society for the success of the undertaking;

and the enlightened Vice-President of the Geographical Society of Paris, M. de la Roquette, promptly offered, as an earnest of his good will, a liberal contribution to the fund.

The Masonic Fraternity in New York, Boston, and Philadelphia also gave their assistance, and it was not the less appreciated that it was spontaneous and unexpected.

Notwithstanding the unceasing efforts which were thus made in every quarter, and the almost universal interest which the undertaking at length excited, it was not until the beginning of June, 1860, that I was able to commence my preparations. My plans of exploration had been based upon the expectation of being able to start with two vessels,—one a small steamer, to be taken out under sails, and the steam-power only to be used when actually among the ice; —the other a sailing vessel, to be employed as a tender or store-ship.

It now became evident to us that if my departure was deferred to another year, the chances of my sailing at all would be diminished rather than increased; and we therefore determined to do the best we could with the means at hand. These means would enable us to fit out and man only one small sailing vessel.

To Mr. Richard Baker, Jr., the energetic chairman of the Boston Committee, (aided by a sub-committee consisting of Mr. Warren Sawyer, Mr. John Stetson, Mr. O. W. Peabody, and Mr. J. D. W. Joy,) was intrusted the selection and purchase of such a craft as would best compromise between the services to be performed and the state of our finances; and the duty was accomplished with characteristic sagacity. When I reached Boston, a few days after the purchase

VESSEL PURCHASED.

had been made, I found the vessel lying at a wharf, heavily laden with a cargo brought from the West Indies. She was a strong, snug, jaunty looking craft, and appeared to be well adapted for the peculiar service to which she was destined. Her "register" quaintly set forth that she was "A 1," that she measured one hundred and thirty-three tons burden, that she was a fore-and-aft schooner, drew eight feet of water, and was named *Spring Hill.* For this name we at once substituted *United States,* which change was, upon my memorial, subsequently confirmed by act of Congress.

The season was now growing very late. Before the vessel had been purchased it was fully time that I should have been upon my voyage, and every day's delay added to my anxiety lest I should be unable to penetrate the Baffin's Bay ice, and secure a harbor before the winter had shut out all access to the land. It was therefore with no small degree of satisfaction that I saw the schooner on the ways in the shipyard of Mr. Kelly in East Boston, and the work of refitting her going rapidly forward.

As a protection against the wear and pressure of the ice, a strong sheathing of two and a half inch oak planking was spiked to her sides, and the bows were cased with thick iron plates as far aft as the fore-chains. Internally she was strengthened with heavy beams, crossing at intervals of twelve feet a little below the water-line, which, as well as the deck-timbers, were supported by additional knees and diagonal braces. For convenience of working among the ice, her rig was changed from a fore-and-aft to a foretop-sail schooner.

Owing to many unavoidable delays, the month of

PREPARATION. 9

June had almost passed before the schooner was brought to the wharf in Boston to receive her cargo. Much of this cargo was made up of voluntary gift offerings, "in the cause of science," and came from various places, and, as these "offerings" arrived irregularly, there was naturally much confusion in the storage. It will not therefore appear surprising that our departure was several days delayed. One month was indeed a short time, even under the most favorable circumstances, to fit a vessel, purchase and store a complicated cargo, construct and get together sledges, boats, and other equipments for travelling, obtain instruments and all the requisite materials for scientific exploration, — in short, to accumulate the various odds and ends necessary for so unusual and protracted a voyage. It was a busy month, and into no equal period of my life did I ever crowd so much labor and anxiety.

The selection of my ship's company gave me not a little concern. Of material from which to choose there was quite an ample supply. In numbers there were indeed enough to have fitted out a respectable squadron; but it was not easy to find those whose constitutions and habits of life fitted them for the service. The greater number of the volunteers had never been to sea, and most of them were eager "to serve in any capacity," — a declaration which, too often on this, as on other occasions, I have found to signify the absence of any capacity at all.

I esteemed myself fortunate in securing the services of my former companion and friend in the Grinnell Expedition, Mr. August Sonntag, who early volunteered to join me from Mexico, in which country he was engaged in conducting some important scientific

10 OFFICERS AND CREW.

explorations. He even proposed to me that he should abandon the work upon which he was then employed, in order to aid me in the preliminary preparations. Returning to the United States in 1859, he was appointed to the Dudley Observatory, Albany, and, to accompany me, he sacrificed the fine position of Associate Director of that institution.

My party, when at length completed, numbered fourteen persons all told, as follows: —

AUGUST SONNTAG,	Astronomer, and second in command.
S. J. McCORMICK,	Sailing Master.
HENRY W. DODGE,	Mate.
HENRY G. RADCLIFFE,	Assistant Astronomer.
GEORGE F. KNORR,	Commander's Secretary.
COLLIN C. STARR,	Master's Mate.
GIBSON CARUTHERS,	Boatswain and Carpenter.
FRANCIS L. HARRIS,	Volunteer.
HARVEY HEYWOOD,	Volunteer.
JOHN McDONALD,	Seaman.
THOMAS BARNUM,	Seaman.
CHARLES McCORMICK,	Seaman.
WILLIAM MILLER,	Seaman.
JOHN WILLIAMS,	Seaman.

Our equipment for scientific observations was reasonably perfect. The Smithsonian Institution furnished a good supply of barometers and thermometers, besides other apparatus not less important, and also spirits, cans, and other materials for the collection and preservation of specimens of Natural History. In this latter department I owe especial obligations to the Academy of Natural Sciences of Philadelphia, and also to the Cambridge Museum. From the skilful maker, Mr. John Tagliabeau, of New York, I had a handsome present of spirit thermometers. From the Topographical Bureau at Washington, through the

SCIENTIFIC OUTFIT. 11

courtesy of its chief, I was supplied with two pocket-sextants, instruments which could not have been obtained either by purchase or loan elsewhere. I had hoped to secure from the National Observatory the use of a deep-sea sounding apparatus, until it was made known to me that the concession was not provided for by act of Congress. Outside of the limits of nautical routine I fared better. The Chief of the Coast Survey furnished me with a vertical circle, which contained the double advantage of a transit and theodolite, a well-tested unifilar magnetometer, a reflecting circle, a Wurdeman compass, and several other valuable instruments. We had five chronometers, — three box and two pocket, which last were intended for use in sledge travelling. We had an excellent telescope, with a four and a half inch object-glass; and, under the joint superintendence of the late Professor Bond, of Cambridge, and Mr. Sonntag, I caused to be constructed a pendulum apparatus after the plan of Foster's instrument.

I lacked not instruments, but men. My only well-instructed associate was Mr. Sonntag.

Our outfit was altogether of the very best description, and our larder contained every thing that could reasonably be desired. An abundant supply of canned meats, vegetables, and fruits insured us against scurvy, and a large stock of desiccated beef, beef soup, (a mixture of meat, carrots, onions, &c.,) and potatoes, prepared expressly for me by the American Desiccating Company of New York, gave us a light and portable food for the sledge journeys. I preferred the food in this form to the ordinary pemican. We were amply provided with good warm woollen clothing, and four large bales of buffalo-skins promised each of us

12   READY TO SAIL.

the materials for a coat and protection against the Arctic winds. A good stock of rifles and guns, and a plentiful supply of ammunition, finished our guarantees against want. We had forty tons of coal and wood in the hold, and a quantity of pine boards, intended for housing over the upper deck when in winter quarters.

Our sledges were constructed after a pattern furnished by myself, and the tents, cooking-lamps, and other camp fixtures, were manufactured under my personal supervision. From numerous friends, whose names I cannot here mention without violating the obligations of confidence, we received books and a great quantity of "small stores" which were afterward greatly appreciated during our winter imprisonment in the ice.

We had expected to sail on the 4th of July, and the friends of the Expedition were invited by the Boston Committee, through its secretary, Mr. O. W. Peabody, to see us off. Although the day was dark and drizzly many hundreds of persons were present. Through some unavoidable accident we did not get away. The guests, however, made us the recipients of their best wishes, and when the members of my little command (assembled together on that day for the first time) found themselves addressed in turn by the Governor of the State, the Mayor of the City, and the President of Harvard, and by renowned statesmen, orators, divines and merchants of Boston, and by *savans* of Cambridge, the measure of their happiness was full. Inspired by the interest thus so conspicuously manifested in their fortunes, they felt ready for any emergency.

THE OPEN POLAR SEA.

CHAPTER I.

LEAVING BOSTON — AT ANCHOR IN NANTASKET ROADS. — AT SEA.

LATE in the evening of July 6th, 1860, the schooner *United States* was hauled into the stream, prepared to leave port the following morning.

The morning dawned clear and auspicious. Upon going on board, I found that a number of friends whom I had invited to accompany us down the bay had preceded me by half an hour. Among them were His Excellency the Governor of the State, and representatives of the Boston, New York and Philadelphia committees.

The fine, large steam-tug *R. B. Forbes* soon came alongside, alive with a gay party of well-wishers, and, taking the end of our hawser, started us from our anchorage. As we passed Long Wharf we were honored with a salute from a battery which the Mayor of the city had sent down for that purpose, and numerous parting cheers greeted us as we steamed down the bay.

The wind being unfavorable, we dropped anchor for the night in Nantasket Roads. The tug took most of our friends back to Boston, and I was left in my cabin with the official representatives of the promoters of the enterprise, engaged in the last of our

14 LEAVING BOSTON.

numerous consultations. A handful of papers were put into my possession, and I became the sole owner of the schooner *United States* and the property on board of her. The sun had set before our conference ended, and the wind promising to hold from the eastward during the night, I returned to Boston with Mr. Baker, in his yacht.

Upon arriving at the schooner next morning, I found that the executive officer had availed himself of the delay to break out the ship's hold and effect a better stowage of the deck cargo. Indeed, we were in no condition for going to sea. Many of the stores were hurried on board at the last moment, and the deck was literally covered with boxes and bales, which, in the haste of departure, could not be stowed away. It was long after nightfall when the hatches were closed and every thing secured; but as the pilot did not come on board, we were compelled to wait until daylight.

I passed the night on Mr. Baker's yacht, which lay near by, with some kind friends who would not quit us until they saw us fairly off. The pretty yachts *Stella* and *Howard*, to whose gentlemanly owners I was indebted for courteous attentions, also kept us company.

With the first gray streak of the dawning day, this little fleet tripped their anchors and glided home, bearing our last good-byes, while we, with a fair wind, stood out to sea.

Before the night closed in, the coast had sunk out of sight, and I was once more tossing on the waves of the broad Atlantic. Again I saw the sun sink beneath the line of waters, and I watched the changing clouds which hung over the land I had left behind me, until the last faint flush of gold and crimson had melted away into the soft twilight. Creeping then into my damp, narrow bunk, I slept the first long, unbroken sleep I had had for weeks. The expedition which had absorbed so much of my attention during the past five years was now fairly on its way. Trusting in Providence and my own energy, I had faith in the future.

CHAPTER II.

PASSAGE TO THE GREENLAND COAST.—DISCIPLINE —THE DECKS AT SEA — OUR QUARTERS —THE FIRST ICEBERG —CROSSING THE ARCTIC CIRCLE — THE MIDNIGHT SUN —THE ENDLESS DAY.— MAKING THE LAND.—A REMARK-ABLE SCENE AMONG THE BERGS —AT ANCHOR IN PRÖVEN HARBOR

I WILL not long detain the reader with the details of our passage to the Greenland coast. It was mainly devoid of interest.

My first concern was to regulate the domestic affairs of my little company; my second, to make the schooner as tidy and comfortable as possible. The former was much more easily managed than the latter. Calling the officers and crew together, I explained to them that, inasmuch as we would for a long time constitute our own little world, we must all recognize the obligations of a mutual dependence and the ties of mutual safety, interest, and ambition. Keeping this in view, we would find no hardship in making all selfish considerations subordinate to the necessities of a mutual accommodation. The response was highly gratifying to me, and I had afterward abundant reason to congratulate myself upon having at the outset established the relations of the crew with myself upon such a satisfactory footing. To say nothing of its advantages to our convenience, this course saved much trouble. From the beginning to the end of the cruise I had no occasion to record a breach of discipline; and I did not find it necessary to establish

THE DECKS. 17

any other rules than those which are usual in all well disciplined ships.

To make the schooner comfortable was impracticable, and to make her tidy equally so. I found myself rocking about on the Atlantic with decks in a condition to have sorely tried the patience of the most practised sailor. Barrels, boxes, boards, boats, and other articles were spiked or lashed to the bulwarks and masts, until all available space was covered, and there was left only a narrow, winding pathway from the quarter to the forecastle deck, and no place whatever for exercise but the top of the trunk cabin, which was just twelve feet by ten; and even this was partly covered, and that too with articles which, if they have existence, should at least never be in sight on a well-regulated craft. But this was not to be helped, — there was no room for any thing more below hatches ; every nook and cranny in the vessel was full, and we had no alternative but to allow the decks to be "lumbered up" until some friendly sea should come and wash the incumbrance overboard. (We were entirely too prudent to throw any thing away.) That such an event would happen seemed likely enough, for we were loaded down until the deck, in the waist, was only a foot and a half above the water; and, standing in the gangway, you could at any time lean over the monkey-rail and touch the sea with your fingers. The galley filled up the entire space between the fore hatch and the mainmast; and the water, coming in over the gangway, poured through it frequently without restraint. The cook and the fire were often put out together, and the regularity of our meals was a little disturbed in consequence.

THE CABIN.

My cabin occupied the after-half of the "trunk," (which extended two feet above the quarter-deck,) and was six feet by ten. Two "bull's-eyes" gave me a feeble light by day, and a kerosene lamp, which creaked uneasily in its gimbals, by night. Two berths let, one into either side, furnished commodious receptacles for ship's stores. The carpenter, however, fixed up a narrow bunk for me; and when I had covered this with a brilliant afghan, and enclosed it with a pair of crimson curtains, I was astonished at the amount of comfort which I had manufactured for myself.

The narrow space in front of my cabin contained the companion ladder, the steward's pantry, the stove-pipe, a barrel of flour, and a "room" for Mr. Sonntag. Forward of this, two steps down in the hold, was the officers' cabin, which was exactly twelve feet square by six feet high. It was oak-panelled, and had eight bunks, happily not all occupied. It was not a commodious apartment. The men's quarters were under the forecastle deck, close against the "dead-wood" of the "ship's eyes." They, too, were necessarily crowded for room.

Our course from Boston lay directly for the outer capes of Newfoundland, inside of Sable Island. Every one who has sailed down the coast of Nova Scotia knows the nature of the fogs which hang over the banks, especially during the warm season of the year; and we had our full measure of the embarrassing fortune which usually befalls the navigator of those waters.

We ran into a fog-bank on the second day out from Boston, and for seven days thereafter were enveloped in an atmosphere so dense as completely to obscure the sun and horizon. We could, of course,

"BREAKERS AHEAD."

19

obtain no "sights," and, during that period, were obliged in consequence to rely for our position upon the lead line and our dead reckoning. Uncertain currents made this last a method of doubtful dependence.

On the sixth day of this seemingly endless fog I grew rather more than usually uneasy; but the sailing-master assured me that he was certain of our position; and, with the map before us on the table, he *proved* it by the soundings. We would clear Cape Race in the morning watch.

The morning watch found me on deck, and, as before, our position was shown by the record of the lead. The lead was a false prophet, for instead of running outside we were rushing squarely upon the cape. Satisfied, however, by the assurances which I had received, I went below to breakfast, and had scarcely been seated when that most disagreeable of all cries, — once heard, never to be forgotten, — "Breakers ahead!" startled us. Upon reaching the deck, I found the sails shivering in the wind, and almost within pistol-shot rose a great black wall, against which the sea was breaking in a most threatening manner. Fortunately the schooner came quickly to the wind and held in stays, otherwise we must have struck in a very few minutes. As it was, we settled close upon the rocks before the sails filled and we began to crawl slowly off. The spray, thrown back from the sullen cliff, actually fell upon the deck, and it seemed as if I could almost touch the rocks with my hand. We were soon relieved by seeing the dark fog-veil drawn between us and danger. But the danger was, apparently, not yet passed. In half an hour the wind died away almost to a calm, leaving us a heavy sea to fight

20 ACROSS THE ARCTIC CIRCLE

with, while out of the blackness came the wail of the angry surf bemoaning the loss of its prey.

The wind increased toward noon, and freed us from suspense. Resolved this time to give Cape Race a wide berth, we ran off E. S. E., and not until I was sure, by the color of the water, that Newfoundland was at a safe distance, did I let the schooner fill away on her course toward Cape Farewell. By this time a stiff breeze was blowing from the south, and as the night closed in we were running before the wind under a close-reefed topsail.

A succession of southerly gales now chased us northward, and we hauled in our latitude with gratifying rapidity. In a few days we were ploughing the waters which bathe the rock-bound coasts of Greenland.

On the 30th of July I had the satisfaction of being once more within the Arctic Circle. That imaginary line was crossed at eight o'clock in the evening, and the event was celebrated by a salute from our signal-gun and a display of bunting.

We now felt that we had fairly entered upon our career.

We were twenty days out from Boston, and had made throughout an average run of a hundred miles a day. The schooner had proved herself an excellent sea-boat. The coast of Greenland was about ten leagues away, obscured by a cloud; we had Cape Walsingham on the port beam, and the lofty Suckertoppen would have been visible over the starboard quarter had the air been clear. We had not yet, however, sighted the land, but we had made our first iceberg, we had seen the "midnight sun," and we had come into the endless day. When the hour-

THE FIRST ICEBERG.

hand of the Yankee clock which ticked above my head pointed to XII., the sunlight still flooded the cabin. Accustomed to this strange life in former years, the change had to me little of novelty; but the officers complained of sleeplessness, and were lounging about as if waiting for the old-fashioned darkness which suggests bed-time.

The first iceberg was made the day before we passed the Arctic Circle. The dead white mass broke upon us out of a dense fog, and was mistaken by the lookout for land when he first caught the sound of breakers beating upon it. It was floating directly in our course, but we had time enough to clear it. Its form was that of an irregular pyramid, about three hundred feet at its base, and perhaps half as high. Its summit was at first obscured, but at length the mist broke away, disclosing the peak of a glittering spire, around which the white clouds were curling and dancing in the sunlight. There was something very impressive in the stern indifference with which it received the lashings of the sea. The waves threw their liquid arms about it caressingly, but it deigned not even a nod of recognition, and sent them reeling backward, moaning and lamenting.

We had some rough handling in Davis' Strait. Once I thought we had surely come ingloriously to grief. We were running before the wind and fighting a wretched cross-sea under reefed fore and mainsail and jib, when the fore fife-rail was carried away; — down came every thing to the deck, and there was left not a stitch of canvas on the schooner but the lumbering mainsail. It was a miracle that we did not broach to and go to the bottom. Nothing saved us but a steady hand at the helm.

22 A LAND-FALL.

The following entry in my journal, made at this period, will exhibit our condition and the temper of the crew : —

"Notwithstanding all this knocking about, every body seems to take it for granted that this sort of thing is very natural and proper, and a part of the engagement for the cruise. It is at least gratifying to see that they take kindly to discomfort, and receive every freak of fortune with manly good nature. I really believe that were affairs otherwise ordered they would be sadly disappointed. They are "the small band of brave and spirited men" they read about in the newspapers, and they mean to show it. The sailors are sometimes literally drowned out of the forecastle. The cabin is flooded at least a dozen times a day. The skylight has been knocked to pieces by the head of a sea, and the table, standing directly under it, has been more than once cleared of crockery and eatables without the aid of the steward. My own cabin gets washed out at irregular intervals, and my books are half of them spoiled by tumbling from their shelves in spite of all I can do to the contrary. Once I caught the whole library tacking about the deck after an unusually ambitious dive of the schooner, and the advent of a more than ordinarily heavy rush of water through the 'companion-way.'"

It had been my intention to stop at Egedesmindie, or some other of the lower Danish stations, on the Greenland coast, to obtain a stock of furs, and at the upper settlements to procure the needful supply of dogs for sledge travelling ; but, the wind being fair, I resolved to hold on and trust to obtaining every thing required at Pröven and Upernavik.

We made our first land-fall on the 31st. It proved

to be the southern extremity of Disco Island. The lofty mountains broke suddenly through the thick mist, and exposed their hoary heads, not a little to our astonishment; but they vanished again as quickly as they had appeared. But we had got a clutch upon the land, and found that, befogged though we were, we had calculated our position to a nicety. From this moment the interest of our cruise was doubled.

The next day we were abreast the Nord Fiord of Disco, in latitude 70°, and, gliding on with a light wind, the Waigat and Oominak Fiord were soon behind us; and on the evening of August 2d we were approaching the bold promontory of Svarte Huk, which is only forty miles from Pröven, whither we were bound.

"A man's heart deviseth his way, but the Lord directeth his steps." Just as we were congratulating ourselves upon the prospect of getting an appetite for breakfast among the Greenland hills, the wind began to show decided symptoms of weakness; and, after a succession of spasmodic efforts to recover itself, prolonged through the next four and twenty hours, it at length died away completely, and left us lying on the still waters, impatient and ill at ease. We were sadly disappointed; but the sun scattered the vapors which had hung so long about us, and, in the scene which broke out of the dissolving mist, we buried our vexation.

Greenland had been for some time regarded by my companions as a sort of myth; for, although frequently only a few miles from its coast, so thick and constant had been the clouds and fogs, that, except for a few brief minutes, it had been wholly hidden from our view. Here, however, it was at last, shaking

24 AMONG THE ICEBERGS.

off its cloud mantle, and standing squarely out before us in austere magnificence, — its broad valleys, its deep ravines, its noble mountains, its black, beetling cliffs, its frowning desolation.

As the fog lifted and rolled itself up like a scroll over the sea to the westward, iceberg after iceberg burst into view, like castles in a fairy tale. It seemed, indeed, as if we had been drawn by some unseen hand into a land of enchantment, rather than that we had come of our own free will into a region of stern realities, in pursuit of stern purposes; — as if the elves of the North had, in sportive playfulness, thrown a veil about our eyes, and enticed us to the very "seat eternal of the gods." Here was the Valhalla of the sturdy Vikings; here the city of the sun-god Freyer, — Alfheim, with its elfin caves, — and Glitner, with its walls of gold and roofs of silver, and Gimle, more brilliant than the sun, — the home of the happy; and there, piercing the clouds, was Himinborg, the Celestial Mount, where the bridge of the gods touches Heaven.

It would be difficult to imagine a scene more solemnly impressive than that which was disclosed to us by the sudden change in the clouded atmosphere. From my diary I copy the following brief description of it: —

"MIDNIGHT. — I have just come below, lost in the wondrous beauty of the night. The sea is smooth as glass; not a ripple breaks its dead surface, not a breath of air stirring. The sun hangs close upon the northern horizon; the fog has broken up into light clouds; the icebergs lie thick about us; the dark headlands stand boldly out against the sky; and the clouds and sea and bergs and mountains are bathed in

BEAUTY OF THE ICEBERGS. 25

an atmosphere of crimson and gold and purple most singularly beautiful."

In all my former experience in this region of startling novelties I had never seen any thing to equal what I witnessed that night. The air was warm almost as a summer's night at home, and yet there were the icebergs and the bleak mountains, with which the fancy, in this land of green hills and waving forests, can associate nothing but cold repulsiveness. The sky was bright and soft and strangely inspiring as the skies of Italy. The bergs had wholly lost their chilly aspect, and, glittering in the blaze of the brilliant heavens, seemed, in the distance, like masses of burnished metal or solid flame. Nearer at hand they were huge blocks of Parian marble, inlaid with mammoth gems of pearl and opal. One in particular exhibited the perfection of the grand. Its form was not unlike that of the Coliseum, and it lay so far away that half its height was buried beneath the line of blood-red waters. The sun, slowly rolling along the horizon, passed behind it, and it seemed as if the old Roman ruin had suddenly taken fire.

Nothing indeed but the pencil of the artist could depict the wonderful richness of this sparkling fragment of Nature. Church, in his great picture of "The Icebergs," has grandly exhibited a scene not unlike that which I would in vain describe.

In the shadows of the bergs the water was a rich green, and nothing could be more soft and tender than the gradations of color made by the sea shoaling on the sloping tongue of a berg close beside us. The tint increased in intensity where the ice overhung the water, and a deep cavern near by exhibited the solid color of the malachite mingled with the transpa-

NEARING HARBOR.

rency of the emerald; while, in strange contrast, a broad streak of cobalt blue ran diagonally through its body.

The bewitching character of the scene was heightened by a thousand little cascades which leaped into the sea from these floating masses, — the water being discharged from lakes of melted snow and ice which reposed in quietude far up in the valleys separating the high icy hills of their upper surface. From other bergs large pieces were now and then detached, — plunging down into the water with ·deafening noise, while the slow moving swell of the ocean resounded through their broken archways.

I had been watching this scene for hours, lost in reverie and forgetfulness, when I was brought suddenly to my senses by the master's mate, who came to report, "Ice close aboard, sir." We were drifting slowly upon a berg about the height of our topmasts. The boats were quickly lowered to pull us off, and, the schooner once more in safety, I went to bed.

I awoke after a few hours, shivering with ·the cold. The "bull's-eye" above my head was open, and a chilly fog was pouring in upon me. Hurrying on deck, I found the whole scene changed. A dense gray mist had settled over the waters and icebergs and mountains, blending them all in chaotic gloom.

Twenty-four days at sea had brought the water very low in our casks, and I took advantage of the delay to send off to a neighboring iceberg for a fresh supply. The water of these bergs is pure and clear as crystal.

Getting at last a slant of the wind, we ran in among the low islands which line the coast above Svarte Huk; and Sonntag, who had gone ahead in·a boat to

Pröven, having sent off to us a swarthy-looking pilot, we wound our way slowly through the tortuous passage, and at a little after midnight of August 6th we dropped anchor in the snuggest of little harbors. The loud baying of dogs, and an odor, baffling description, — "a very ancient and fish-like smell," — first warned us of our approach to a Greenland settlement.

CHAPTER III.

THE COLONY OF PRÖVEN. — THE KAYAK OF THE GREENLANDER. — SCARCITY
OF DOGS. — LIBERALITY OF THE CHIEF TRADER. — ARCTIC FLORA.

WE were escorted into the harbor of Pröven by the strangest fleet of boats and the strangest-looking boatmen that ever convoyed a ship. They were the far-famed kayakers of Greenland, and they deserve a passing notice.

The *kayak* of the Greenlander is the frailest specimen of marine architecture that ever carried human freight. It is eighteen feet long and as many inches wide at its middle, and tapers, with an upward curving line, to a point at either end. The skeleton of the boat is made of light wood; the covering is of tanned seal-skin, sewed together by the native women with sinew thread, and with a strength and dexterity quite astonishing. Not a drop of water finds its way through their seams, and the skin itself is perfectly water-proof. The boat is about nine inches deep, and the top is covered like the bottom. There is no opening into it except a round hole in the centre, which admits the hunter as far as his hips. This hole is surrounded with a wooden rim, over which the kayaker laces the lower edge of his water-tight jacket, and thus fastens himself in and keeps the water out. He propels himself with a single oar about six feet long, which terminates in a blade or paddle at either end. This instrument of locomotion is grasped in the

THE KAYAK OF THE GREENLANDER.   29

centre, and is dipped in the water alternately to right and left. The boat is graceful as a duck and light as a feather. It has no ballast and no keel, and it rides almost on the surface of the water. It is therefore necessarily top-heavy. Long practice is required to manage it, and no tight-rope dancer ever needed more steady nerve and skill of balance than this same savage kayaker. Yet, in this frail craft, he does not hesitate to ride seas which would swamp an ordinary boat, or to break through surf which may sweep completely over him. But he is used to hard battles, and, in spite of every fortune, he keeps himself upright.

I watched their movements with much interest as they collected about the schooner. Among the benefits which they had derived from civilization was an appreciation of the value of rum, coffee, and tobacco; and they were not overly modest in their demands for these articles. Most of them had, however, something to trade, and went home with their reward. One old fellow who had managed to pick up a few words of English, without being particularly clear as to their meaning, was loud in his demands for a "pound rum, bottle sugar," offering in exchange a fine salmon.

I had intended to remain at Pröven only a single day, and then to hasten on with all possible speed; but our stay was prolonged by circumstances to which I was forced to submit with as good a grace as possible. It was idle for me to leave without a supply of dogs, for my plans and preparations were entirely based upon them; and the prospect of accomplishing my design in this respect appeared, from the first, very feeble. In order to save time, Sonntag had gone to the vil-

SCARCITY OF DOGS.

lage when we lay becalmed off Svarte Huk, and he returned on board with the most discouraging accounts of the poverty of the settlements in that which was such an essential addition to our equipment. A disease which had prevailed among the teams, during the past year, had diminished the stock to less than half of what was required for the prosperity of the people; and all our offers to purchase, either with money or provisions, were at first flatly refused, and were in the end only partially successful.

Mr. Sonntag had called upon the Assistant Trader immediately after his arrival, and was at once informed by that official of the unfortunate state of affairs. He would, however, personally interest himself in the matter, and advised that we should await the arrival of the Chief Trader, Mr. Hansen, who resided at Upernavik, which is forty miles to the north, and would be in Pröven in a day or so. It was evident that nothing could be done without the aid of this all-powerful public functionary, for whose arrival we had no alternative but to wait. If we went on to Upernavik we ran the hazard of missing him; and, by not seeing him until his return to that settlement from his southern tour, of losing the advantage of his prompt coöperation.

Mr. Hansen arrived the following day, and assured me that he would do what was in his power; but he feared that he should have little success. As an earnest of his good-will, he informed me, with a delicate courtesy which made me for the moment wonder if a lordly son of Castile had not wandered to this land of ice, and disguised himself in a seal-skin coat, that his own teams were at my disposal. Beyond this, however, he could neither advise nor command. There

LIBERALITY OF THE CHIEF TRADER. 31

was no public stock from which to supply my wants; and so great and universal had been the ravages of disease among the animals, that many hunters were wholly destitute, and none were in possession of their usual number. He however at once dispatched a courier to Upernavik, and others to various small settlements, and thus heralded the news that any hunter who had an extra dog would find a market for it by bringing it forthwith to Pröven or Upernavik.

This action of the Chief Trader was the more appreciated that it was disinterested, and was uncalled for either by any official demands which were laid upon him, or by any special show of dignity or importance with which the insignificant schooner lying in the harbor could back up my claims. The State Department at Washington had, at my solicitation, requested from the Danish Government such recognition for me as had been hitherto accorded to the American and English naval expeditions; but the courteous response which came in the form of a command to the Greenland officials to furnish me with every thing in their power did not reach the settlements until the following year. The commands of his Majesty the King could not, however, have stood me in better stead than the gentlemanly instincts of Mr. Hansen.

There is little in the history of Pröven, either past or present, that will interest the readers of this narrative. What there is of it stands on the southern slope of a gneissoid spur which forms the terminus of one of the numerous islands of the vast archipelago lying between the peninsula of Svarte Huk and Melville Bay. A government-house, one story high and plastered over with pitch and tar, is the most conspic-

THE SETTLEMENT.

uous building in the place. A shop and a lodging-house for a few Danish employees stands next in importance. Two or three less imposing structures of the pitch and tar description, inhabited by Danes who have married native women; a few huts of stone and turf, roofed with boards and overgrown with grass; about an equal number of like description, but without the board roof, and a dozen seal-skin tents, all pitched about promiscuously among the rocks, make up the town. There is a blubber-house down by the beach, and a stunted flag-staff on the hill, from which the Danish Flag gracefully waving in the wind, gave the place a show of dignity. The dignity of civilization was further preserved by an old cannon which lay on the grass under the flag, and whose rusty throat made the welkin ring as our anchor touched the Greenland rocks.

The settlement, or *Colonien*, as the Danes distinguish it, dates back almost to the days of good old Hans Egede, and its name, as nearly as can be interpreted, signifies " Experiment;" and, after the Greenland fashion, a successful experiment it has been. Its people live, chiefly, by hunting the seal; and, of all the northern colonies, few have been as prosperous. The collections of oil and skins during some years are sufficient to freight a brig of three hundred tons.

The place bears ample evidence of the nature of its business. Carcasses of seals and seal's offal lay strewn along the beach, and over the rocks, and among the huts, in every stage of decomposition; and this, added to every other conceivable accumulation that could exhibit a barbarous contempt for the human nose, made the first few hours of our stay there any thing but comfortable.

ARCTIC FLORA. 33

A better prospect, however, greeted us behind the town. A beautiful valley lay there, nestling between the cliffs, and rich in Arctic vegetation. It was covered with a thick turf of moss and grasses, among which the *Poa Arctica, Glyceria Arctica,* and *Alopecurus Alpinus* were most abundant. In places it was, indeed, a perfect marsh. Little streams of melted snow meandered through it, gurgling among the stones, or dashing wildly over the rocks. Myriads of little golden petaled poppies (*Papaver nudicaule*) fluttered over the green. The dandelion (*Leontodon palustre*), close kindred of the wild flower so well known at home, kept it company; the buttercup (*Ranunculus nivalis*), with its smiling, well-remembered face, was sometimes seen; and the less familiar *Potentilla* and the purple *Pedicularis* were dotted about here and there. The saxifrages, purple, white, and yellow, were also very numerous. I captured not less than seven varieties. The birch and crowberry, and the beautiful *Andromeda*, the heather of Greenland, grew matted together in a sheltered nook among the rocks; and, in strange mimicry of Southern richness, the willows feebly struggled for existence on the spongy turf. With my cap I covered a whole forest of them.

I had been in Pröven in 1853, and the place had not changed in the interval. The old ex-trader Christiansen was there, a little older, but not less frugal than before. He complained bitterly of Dr. Kane not having kept his promises to him, and I endeavored to mollify his wrath by assuring him that Dr. Kane had lost his vessel and could not return; but his life had been made unhappy during seven long years by visions of a barrel of American flour, and he would not be comforted. He was scarcely able to crawl about; but, when I sent ashore to him the coveted treasure, he found strength to break the head out of the cask, to feast his eyes on the long-expected gratuity. His sons, each with a brood of Esquimaux visaged, though flaxen-haired children, crowded around the present. My diary records that they were the best hunters in the settlement, and that they had the best teams of dogs; and it also mentions, with a little chagrin, that they would not sell one of them. I attributed this obstinacy, at the time, to their cross old paternal relative; but there were better reasons than this. They knew by bitter experience the risks of going into the long winter without an ample supply of dogs to carry them over the ice upon the seal hunt, and to part with their animals was to risk starvation. I offered to give them pork and beef and canned meats, and flour and beans; but they preferred the seal and the excitement of the hunt, and refused to trade.

At last the couriers had all come in, bringing unwelcome news. A half-dozen old dogs and a less number of good ones were all that I had to console myself for the delay; but the Chief Trader had returned to Upernavik, from which place I had received more encouraging accounts than from the lower stations.

CHAPTER IV.

UPERNAVIK.—HOSPITALITY OF THE INHABITANTS.—DEATH AND BURIAL OF
GIBSON CARUTHERS.—A LUNCH ON BOARD.—ADIEU.

WE put to sea early in the morning of the 12th, and in the evening of the same day were at Upernavik. The entrance to the harbor is somewhat unsafe, owing to a reef which lies outside the anchorage; but we were fortunate in obtaining a native pilot at Pröven, and ran in without accident. This pilot was a character in his way. It seems that he had been converted from his heathen ways, and rejoiced in the benefits of baptism and the name of Adam. Dressed in a well-worn suit of seal-skins, Adam had about him little of the sailor trigness; yet, though not a Palinurus, no pilot in all the world had ever a higher appreciation of his personal importance. His appearance, however, was not calculated to inspire any great degree of confidence in his skill; and the sailing-master plied him so incessantly with questions that he at length grew impatient; and, concentrating his vanity and knowledge into one short sentence, which signified plainly, "I am master of the situation," he informed that officer that there was "plenty water all de times, no rocks altogeder," and retired with every mark of offended dignity. He was correct in his information, if not in his English.

We found the Danish brig *Thialfe* lying snugly

36 UPERNAVIK.

moored in the harbor, and we anchored close beside her. This was the first vessel we had seen since leaving the fishing-smacks off Cape Cod. She was taking in oil and skins for Copenhagen, and her commander, Mr. Bordolf, informed me that he expected to sail in a few days,—a chance, at last, for letters to the anxious ones at home.

The people of the Colony were already much excited over the arrival of the "Danske skip," and two vessels in the port at once was a sight which they had not for a long time witnessed. The moss-covered hill which slopes from the town to the beach was covered with a motley group of men, women, and children, presenting quite a picturesque appearance as we approached the anchorage.

Mr. Hansen received me with true Scandinavian heartiness; and, escorting me to the government-house, introduced me to the retiring Chief Trader, Dr. Rudolph, a very gentlemanly representative of the Danish Army, who was about returning home in the *Thialfe*. Over a jug of home-brewed beer and a Dutch pipe, we were soon discussing the prospect of obtaining dogs and the state of the ice to the northward.

Upernavik differs but little in its general appearance from Pröven. There are a few more huts and a few more inhabitants; and, from being the residence of the Chief Trader for the "Upernavik district," which includes Pröven and its dependencies, it has attached to it something more of importance. Perhaps this is, in a measure, due to a quaint little church and a parsonage. To the parsonage I quickly found my way, for I fancied that from behind the neat muslin curtains of its odd little windows I detected a

THE PARSONAGE. 37

female face. I tapped at the door, and was ushered into a cosy little apartment, (the fastidious neatness of which left no doubt as to the sex of its occupants,) by the oddest specimen of woman-kind that ever answered bell. She was a full-blown Esquimau, with coppery complexion and black hair, which was twisted into a knot on the top of her head. She wore a jacket which extended to her waist, seal-skin pantaloons, and boots reaching above the knees, dyed scarlet and embroidered in a manner that would astonish the girls of Dresden. The room was redolent of the fragrant rose and mignonette and heliotrope, which nestled in the sunlight under the snow-white curtains. A canary chirped on its perch above the door, a cat was purring on the hearth-rug, and an unmistakable gentleman put out a soft white hand to give me welcome. It was the Rev. Mr. Anton, missionary of the place. Mrs. Anton soon emerged from a snug little chamber adjoining. Her sister came in immediately afterward, and we were soon grouped about a home-like table; a genuine bottle of Lafitte, choice coffee, Danish fare, and Danish heartiness, quickly made us forget the hardships of our cramped life in the little tempest-tossed schooner.

My visit to Mr. Anton had, however, an association of much sadness. A valued member of my party, Mr. Gibson Caruthers, had died during the previous night, and I called to ask the missionary to officiate at the funeral service. His consent was promptly given, and the hour of burial was fixed for the following day.

The burial of a companion, at any time painful, was doubly so to us, isolated as we were from the world. The deceased had endeared himself to all on board by

38   AN ARCTIC SEPULCHRE.

his excellent qualities of head and heart; and the suddenness of his death made the impression upon his late associates all the more keenly felt. He had retired the night before in perfect health, and was found dead in his berth next morning. To the expedition he was a serious loss. Besides Mr. Sonntag, he was the only member of my party who had been in the Arctic seas, and I had counted much upon his knowledge and intelligence. He had served under De Haven in the First Grinnell Expedition of 1850–51, and had brought home an excellent record for fortitude and daring.

The burial-ground at Upernavik is a sad place for human sepulture. It lies on the hill-side above the town, and is dreary and desolate past description. It is made up of a series of rocky steps, on which lie, covered over with piles of stones, (for there is no earth,) a few rude coffins, — mournful resting-place for those who sleep here their last sleep in the everlasting winter. The body of poor Caruthers lies upon a ledge overlooking the sea, which he loved so well, and the beating surf will sing for him an eternal requiem.

We were detained four days at Upernavik, collecting dogs and accumulating the elements of an Arctic wardrobe. This last consisted of reindeer, seal, and dog skins, a quantity of which had been obtained at Pröven, and placed in the hands of the native women, to be converted into suitable garments. The boots required the longest time to manufacture. They are made of tanned seal-skin, sewed with sinew, and are "crimped" and fitted to the foot in a very ingenious manner. When properly made they are perfectly water-proof. The boot worn by the half-civilized native women is really a pretty as well as serviceable

POPULATION OF UPERNAVIK. 39

piece of cunning needlework. The tanned seal-skin, by alternate freezing and thawing, and exposure to the sun, becomes perfectly bleached, and in that condition is readily stained with any color which woman's caprice may suggest, or the Chief Trader may happen to have in his store-room. The women of Greenland are not exempt from the graceful vanities of other lands. They are fond of gay colors, and do not disdain admiration. Red boots, or white, trimmed with red, seemed to be most in vogue, though, indeed, there is no more an end to the variety than there is to the strangeness of the fancy which suggests it. It would be difficult to imagine a more ludicrous sight than was presented by the crowd of red and yellow and white and purple and blue legged women who crowded along the beach as we entered the harbor.

The population of Upernavik numbers about two hundred souls, comprising about twenty Danes, and a larger number of half-breeds, the remainder being native Greenlanders, that is, Esquimaux. I shall have more to say of them hereafter, my purpose now being to carry the reader as rapidly as possible to the scene of our explorations. He may indeed have as much anxiety to get away from Upernavik as I had.

Through the kindness of Mr. Hansen, I obtained here three native hunters, and also an interpreter. This latter had taken passage by the *Thialfe* for Copenhagen, but he could not withstand the tempting offer which I made him, and he quickly transferred himself from the Danish brig to our crowded cabin. He was a hearty, strong man, had lived in Greenland for ten years; and, being more than usually intelligent, had picked up on board the English whaleships a sufficient knowledge of the English language

40 NEW RECRUITS.

to insure his being a very useful member of my party in the event of our falling in with Esquimaux, with whose language he was perfectly familiar. Besides, he was an excellent hunter and dog-driver; and, by joining me, I secured his team of dogs, the finest in all North Greenland. But unfortunately this involved another halt, for they were sixty miles up the coast, at Tessuissak, a small hunting station of which he was Trader at the time of obtaining his leave of absence to go home for the year. I also shipped two Danish sailors, thus increasing my party to twenty souls. As the new recruits will figure frequently in these pages, I give their names: —

PETER JENSEN,	Interpreter and dog-manager.
CARL EMIL OLSWIG,	Sailor.
CARL CHRISTIAN PETERSEN,	Sailor and Carpenter.
PETER (converted Esquimau),	Hunter and dog-driver.
MARCUS, " "	" "
JACOB, " "	" "

I owe much to the kindly disposition of the inhabitants of Upernavik. Their simple though cordial hospitality was a refreshing incident of our cruise; and the constant desire to supply my wants, and the pains which they took to furnish what I so much needed, is gratefully remembered. If those in authority had allowed me to shift for myself I should have been badly off indeed. I mention it to their credit that they refused compensation of every kind; and it was not without great effort that I could prevail upon any of them to accept so much as a barrel of flour or a box of canned food. "You will want them more than we," was the uniform answer. The Chief Trader actually sent aboard a present I had made him in return for the fine team of dogs which I owed to his generosity.

It was in some measure to show my appreciation of the spirit which prompted these warm-hearted people that I resolved to signalize our departure with a *lunch* to the representatives of King Frederick the Seventh, at this most northern outpost of Christian settlement. Accordingly I sent my secretary, Mr. Knorr, out with some formal-looking invitations, gotten up in all the dignity of Parisian paper and rose-scented wax. He came back in a few hours with three couples. Two of the ladies were from the parsonage; the other was the wife of the Chief Trader. Dr. Rudolph, Mr. Hansen, and the missionary, were their escorts. The master of the *Thialfe* was already on board.

Meanwhile our old Swedish cook had gone half crazy, and the steward kept him company. To prepare a lunch for ladies in these high latitudes was not within their conception of the hard-fisted requirements of exploration dignity. They "could *not* understand it." The steward contrived, however, to stow away in the bunks the seal-skins which encumbered the cabin, and thus got rid of all our Greenland rubbish but the odor. But it was not until the clean white table-cloth, which he produced from some out-of-the-way locker, was covered with the smoking dishes which his ingenuity had contrived, that his face was lit up with any thing approaching the kindly. Being, however, in a general way a mild-mannered man, his ferocious looks did not materially affect the progress of the preparations; and the solemn face with which he predicted, in great confidence, to the cook that "such folly would bring us all to ruin, indeed it would," at length wore a ghastly smile, and finally exhibited decided manifestations of a forgiving dis-

42 A LUNCH ON BOARD.

position. Indeed, he was in the end very proud of his "spread."

In truth, the spread was a very creditable affair. The contents of our hermetically sealed cans furnished a welcome variety to these dwellers in the land of seals; the lakes of Greenland supplied some noble salmon, and my lockers contributed something from sunny France and golden Italy, and the materials for an excellent punch from Santa Cruz. At first we got on badly with the conversation, but by and by English, Danish, German, and bad Latin became mixed harmoniously together like the ingredients of the punch; healths were drunk, — to the King, to the President, to all good fortune, to ourselves, and speeches were made, in which were duly set forth the glorious memories of the children of Odin. The merriment was waxing warm. Some one, stimulated perhaps by a recent tribute of praise to the valiant Harold and the Russian Maiden, and the fights and loves of the vikings generally, had just proposed that best toast of the sailor, "sweethearts and wives," and obtained a fitting response, when the heavy thump of a pair of mammoth sea-boots was heard on the companion-ladder, and the master's mate broke in upon us like the ghost of Banquo.

"The officer of the deck directs me to report, sir, that the dogs are all aboard, sir, and that he is hove short on the anchor, as ordered, sir."

"How 's the wind?"

"Light, and southerly, sir."

There was no help for it. The guests must be got away. The ladies' "things" were hunted up; the ladies themselves were hurried over the gangway into the boat; Dr. Rudolph took charge of our letters, promising to deliver them to the American consul at Copenhagen; "click, click," went the windlass; up went our white wings, and the last link which bound us to the world — the world of love and warm skies and green meadows — was fairly broken, when we caught from the hill-top the last glimpse of a gay ribbon and the last flutter of a white handkerchief.

CHAPTER V.

AMONG THE ICEBERGS. — DANGERS OF ARCTIC NAVIGATION. — A NARROW ESCAPE FROM A CRUMBLING BERG. — MEASUREMENT OF AN ICEBERG.

UPERNAVIK is not less the limit of safe navigation than the remotest boundary of civilized existence. The real hardships of our career commenced before its little white gabled church was fairly lost against the dark hills behind it. A heavy line of icebergs was discovered to lie across our course; and, having no alternative, we shot in among them. Some of them proved to be of enormous size, upwards of two hundred feet in height and a mile long; others were not larger than the schooner. Their forms were as various as their dimensions, from solid wall-sided masses of dead whiteness, with waterfalls tumbling from them, to an old weather-worn accumulation of gothic spires, whose crystal peaks and sharp angles melted into the blue sky. They seemed to be endless and numberless, and so close together that at a little distance they appeared to form upon the sea an unbroken canopy of ice; and when fairly in among them the horizon was completely obliterated. Had we been in the centre of the Black Forest, we could not have been more absolutely cut off from "seeing daylight." As the last streak of the horizon faded from view between the lofty bergs behind us, the steward (who was of a poetical turn of mind) came from the galley, and halting

AMONG THE ICEBERGS. 45

for an instant, cast one lingering look at the opening, and then dropped through the companion scuttle, repeating from the "Inferno" : —

"They who enter here leave hope behind."

The officers were calling from below for their coffee, and it was never discovered whether the steward was thinking of the cabin or the icebergs.

During four days we continued threading our way through this apparently interminable labyrinth. The days passed wearily away, for the wind, at best but a "cat's paw," often died away to a dead calm, leaving us to lounge through the hours in a chilly fog or in the broad blaze of the constant daylight. If this state of things had its novelty, it had too its dangers and anxieties.

The bergs, influenced only by the under-currents, were, to us, practically stationary; and the surface flow of the water which drifted us to and fro, when we lost our steerage-way, rendered our situation any thing but safe. They soon came to be looked upon as our natural enemies, and were eyed with suspicion. We were often drifted upon them, and escaped not without difficulty and alarm; and many times more we saved ourselves from collision by the timely lowering of the boats and taking the schooner in tow, or by planting an ice-anchor in another berg and warping ourselves into greater security. Sometimes we tied up to a berg and waited for the wind. We had hard work, and made little progress. I found consolation, however, in my sketch-book, which was in constant use; and one fine day I got out my photographic apparatus. Landing on a neighboring island, with the aid of my two young assistants, Radcliffe and

PHOTOGRAPHING.

Knorr, I made my first trial at this new business. It was altogether unsatisfactory, except to convince me that, with perseverance, we might succeed in obtaining at least fair pictures.

Practically I knew nothing whatever of the art. It was a great disappointment to me that I could not secure for the expedition the services of a professional photographer; but this deficiency did not, I am happy to say, prevent me, in the end, from obtaining some views characteristic of the rugged beauties of the Arctic landscape. We had, however, only books to guide us. With our want of knowledge and an uncomfortable temperature to contend with, we labored under serious disadvantages.

Sonntag went ashore with me, and obtained good sextant sights for our position, and some useful results with the magnetometer. Knorr added to my collection some fine specimens of birds. The gulls, mollimuks and burgomeisters, the chattering kittiwake and the graceful tern were very numerous. They fairly swarmed upon the bergs. The hunters were often out after eider-ducks, large flocks of which congregate upon the islands, and sweep over us in long undulating lines. Seals, too, were sporting about the vessel, bobbing their intelligent, almost human-looking faces up and down in the still water, marks for the fatal rifles of our sportsmen. They looked so curiously innocent while making their inspections of us that I would not have had the heart to kill them, were it not that they were badly needed for the dogs.

We led a strange weird sort of life, — a spice of danger, with much of beauty and a world of magnificence. I should have found pleasure in the lazy hours, but that each hour thus spent was one taken from my

IN DANGER. 47

more serious purposes, and this reflection made the days irksome to me.

Four days of almost constant calm would tax the patience of even Job-like resignation. We had a breath of wind now and then to tantalize us, treacherous currents to keep us ever anxious, icebergs always threatening us; now at anchor, then moored to a berg, and again keeping free from danger through a hard struggle with the oars. We had many narrow escapes, one of which, as illustrating a peculiar feature of Arctic navigation, is perhaps worthy of more particular record.

We had made a little progress during the night, but soon after breakfast the wind died away, and the schooner lay like a log upon the water. Giving too little heed to the currents, we were eagerly watching the indications of wind which appeared at the south, and hoping for a breeze, when it was discovered that the tide had changed, and was stealthily setting us upon a nest of bergs which lay to leeward. One of them was of that description known among the crew by the significant title of "Touch me not," and presented that jagged, honey-combed appearance indicative of great age. They are unpleasant neighbors. The least disturbance of their equilibrium may cause the whole mass to crumble to pieces, and woe be unto the unlucky vessel that is caught in the dissolution.

In such a trap it seemed, however, that we stood a fair chance of being ensnared. The current was carrying us along at an uncomfortably rapid rate. A boat was lowered as quickly as possible, to run out a line to a berg which lay grounded about a hundred yards from us. While this was being done, we grazed

48 FIGHTING AN ICEBERG

the side of a berg which rose a hundred feet above our topmasts, then slipped past another of smaller dimensions. By pushing against them with our ice-poles we changed somewhat the course of the schooner; but when we thought that we were steering clear of the mass which we so much dreaded, an eddy changed the direction of our drift, and carried us almost broadside upon it.

The schooner struck on the starboard quarter, and the shock, slight though it was, disengaged some fragments of ice that were large enough to have crushed the vessel had they struck her, and also many little lumps which rattled about us; but fortunately no person was hit. The quarter-deck was quickly cleared, and all hands, crowding forward, anxiously watched the boat. The berg now began to revolve, and was settling slowly over us; the little lumps fell thicker and faster upon the after-deck, and the forecastle was the only place where there was the least chance of safety.

At length the berg itself saved us from destruction. An immense mass broke off from that part which was beneath the surface of the sea, and this, a dozen times larger than the schooner, came rushing up within a few yards of us, sending a vast volume of foam and water flying from its sides. This rupture arrested the revolution, and the berg began to settle in the opposite direction. And now came another danger A long tongue was protruding immediately underneath the schooner; already the keel was slipping and grinding upon it, and it seemed probable that we should be knocked up into the air like a foot-ball, or at least capsized. The side of our enemy soon leaned from us, and we were in no danger from the worse than hail-

PULLING FOR LIFE. 49

stone-showers which had driven us forward; so we sprang to the ice-poles, and exerted our strength in endeavoring to push the vessel off. There were no idle hands. Danger respects not the dignity of the quarter-deck.

After we had fatigued ourselves at this hard labor without any useful result, the berg came again to our relief. A loud report first startled us; another and another followed in quick succession, until the noise grew deafening, and the whole air seemed a reservoir of frightful sound. The opposite side of the berg had split off, piece after piece, tumbling a vast volume of ice into the sea, and sending the berg revolving back upon us. This time the movement was quicker; fragments began again to fall; and, already sufficiently startled by the alarming dissolution which had taken place, we were in momentary expectation of seeing the whole side nearest to us break loose and crash bodily upon the schooner, in which event she would inevitably be carried down beneath it; as hopelessly doomed as a shepherd's hut beneath an Alpine avalanche.

By this time Dodge, who had charge of the boat, had succeeded in planting an ice-anchor and attaching his rope, and greeted us with the welcome signal, "Haul in." We pulled for our lives, long and steadily. Seconds seemed minutes, and minutes hours. At length we began to move off. Slowly and steadily sank the berg behind us, carrying away the mainboom, and grazing hard against the quarter. But we were safe. Twenty yards away, and the disruption occurred which we had all so much dreaded. The side nearest to us now split off, and came plunging wildly down into the sea, sending over us a shower of spray,

50   CRUMBLING ICEBERGS.

raising a swell which set us rocking to and fro as if in
a gale of wind, and left us grinding in the *débris* of the
crumbling ruin.

At last we succeeded in extricating ourselves, and
were far enough away to look back calmly upon the
object of our terror. It was still rocking and rolling
like a thing of life. At each revolution fresh masses
were disengaged; and, as its sides came up in long
sweeps, great cascades tumbled and leaped from them
hissing into the foaming sea. After several hours it
settled down into quietude, a mere fragment of its former greatness, while the pieces that were broken from
it floated quietly away with the tide.

Whether it was the waves created by the dissolution which I have just described, or the sun's warm
rays, or both combined, I cannot pretend to say, but
the day was filled with one prolonged series of reports
of crumbling icebergs. Scarcely had we been moored
in safety when a very large one about two miles distant from us, resembling in its general appearance the
British House of Parliament, began to go to pieces.
First a lofty tower came plunging into the water,
starting from their inhospitable perch an immense
flock of gulls, that went screaming up into the air;
over went another; then a whole side settled squarely
down; then the wreck capsized, and at length after
five hours of rolling and crashing, there remained of
this splendid mass of congelation not a fragment that
rose fifty feet above the water. Another, which appeared to be a mile in length and upwards of a hundred feet in height, split in two with a quick, sharp,
and at length long rumbling report, which could
hardly have been exceeded by a thousand pieces of
artillery simultaneously discharged, and the two frag-

EFFECTS OF DISSOLUTION. 51

ments kept wallowing in the sea for hours before they came to rest. Even the berg to which we were moored chimed in with the infernal concert, and discharged a corner larger than St. Paul's Cathedral.

No words of mine can adequately describe the din and noise which filled our ears during the few hours succeeding the encounter which I have narrated, and therefore I borrow from the " Ancient Mariner " : —

> " The ice was here,
>   The ice was there,
>   The ice was all around ;
>   It creaked and growled,
>   And roared and howled
>   Like demons in a swound."

It seemed, indeed, as if old Thor himself had taken a holiday, and had come away from his kingdom of Thrudwanger and his Winding Palace of five hundred and forty halls, and had crossed the mountains with his chariot and he-goats, armed with his mace of strength, and girt about with his belt of prowess, and wearing his gauntlets of iron, for the purpose of knocking these Giants of the frost to right and left for his own special amusement.

It is, however, only at this season of the year that the bergs are so unneighborly. They are rarely known to break up except in the months of July and August. It must be then owing to an unevenly heated condition of the interior and exterior, caused by the sun's warm rays playing upon them. From the sunny side of a berg I have not unfrequently seen pieces discharged in a line almost horizontal, with great force, and with an explosive report like a quarryman's blast. These explosions and the crumbling of the ice are always attended with a cloud of vapor,

52   BEAUTIES OF THE ICEBERGS.

no doubt caused by the colder ice of the interior being brought suddenly in contact with the warmer air. The effect is often very remarkable as well as beautiful, especially when the cloud reflects the rays of the sun.

If, however, my pen cannot convey a picture of these icebergs in their more terrible aspects, it will, I fear, be equally impotent to portray their wondrous beauties. I have tried it once before, and was much dissatisfied with the result. I had then, however, a soft sky, when the whole heavens were a mass of rich, warm color, the sea a dissolved rainbow, and the bergs great floating monoliths of malachite and marble bathed in flame. Now the sky was gray, the air clear, and the ice everywhere a dead white or a cold transparent blue.

I clambered up the sloping side of the berg to which we were tied, and, from an elevation of nearly two hundred feet, obtained a view which well repaid me for the trouble of the venture. I am glad to say, however, that I came down again before St. Paul's Cathedral tumbled from its corner; an event which sent us drifting away to a less uncomfortable neighborhood, at the expense of an ice-anchor and eighty fathoms of manilla line.

As I approached the berg, I was struck with the remarkable transparency of the water. Looking over the gunwale of the boat, I could trace the ice stretching downward apparently to an interminable distance. Looking back at the schooner, its reflection was a perfect image of itself, and it required only the separation of it from the surrounding objects to give to the mind the impression that two vessels, keel to keel, were floating in mid-air. This singular transparency of the water

VIEW FROM AN ICEBERG. 53

was further shown when I had reached the top of the berg. Off to the southeast a high rocky bluff threw its dark shadow upon the water, and the dividing line between sunlight and shade was so marked that it required an effort to dispel the illusion that the margin of sunlight was not the edge of a fathomless abyss.

It is difficult for the mind to comprehend the immense quantity of ice which floated upon the sea around me. To enumerate the separate bergs was impossible. I counted five hundred, and gave up in despair. Near by they stood out in all the rugged harshness of their sharp outlines; and from this, softening with the distance, they melted away into the clear gray sky; and there, far off upon the sea of liquid silver, the imagination conjured up effigies both strange and wonderful. Birds and beasts and human forms and architectural designs took shape in the distant masses of blue and white. The dome of St. Peter's loomed above the spire of Old Trinity; and under the shadow of the Pyramids nestled a Byzantine tower and a Grecian temple.

To the eastward the sea was dotted with little islets, — dark specks upon a brilliant surface. Icebergs, great and small, crowded through the channels which divided them, until in the far distance they appeared massed together, terminating against a snow-covered plain that sloped upward until it was lost in a dim line of bluish whiteness. This line could be traced behind the serrated coast as far to the north and south as the eye would carry. It was the great *mer de glace* which covers the length and breadth of the Greenland Continent. The snow-covered slope was a glacier descending therefrom, — the parent stem from which had been discharged, at irregular intervals,

54 TESSUISSAK.

many of the icebergs which troubled us so much, and which have supplied materials for this too long description.

At length a strong breeze came moaning among the bergs, and sent us on our way rejoicing. In the evening of August 21st we were moored in a little harbor scarcely large enough for the schooner to turn round. We lay abreast of a rocky slope on which were pitched a few seal-skin tents, inhabited by a set of well-to-do-looking Esquimaux. I noticed two or three native huts, overgrown with moss and grass, and one, better looking than the rest, in which Jensen, my interpreter, informed me that he had resided. The place is called Tessuissak, which means "the place where there is a bay." Sonntag went ashore with his sextant and "horizon," to find out its exact position in the world, an event which had not before come to pass in its history, and which I fear was not duly appreciated by its inhabitants.

We should have been away in a couple of hours; but Jensen discovered that his team was scattered, and many of the animals could not be found until after much searching. Meanwhile some ice drifted across the mouth of the harbor, and hermetically sealed us up.

At last the dogs were all aboard, something over thirty in number. The poor ones I had either given away or exchanged, and we had four superb teams. Thirty wild beasts on the deck of a little schooner! Think of it, ye who love a quiet life and a tidy ship! Some of them were in cages arranged along the bulwarks; others running about the deck; all of them badly frightened, and most of them fighting. They made day and night hideous with their incessant howling.

MEASUREMENT OF AN ICEBERG.

We were all ready for sea, and impatient to be off. Our Arctic wardrobe was complete with a few purchases made of the natives in exchange for pork and beans. We were thoroughly prepared for the ice encounters. The lines were all neatly and carefully coiled; the ice-anchors and ice-hooks and ice-saws and ice-chisels and ice-poles were all so placed that they were within easy reach when wanted. The capstan and windlass were free, and Dodge, who had not forgotten his naval experience, reported "the decks cleared for action." Would the tide float away the ice and let us out?

I was growing very restless. The season was moving on; already ice began to form; the temperature was below freezing. The nights made a decided scum on the fresh-water pools. I could count upon only fifteen days of open season. The *Fox* was frozen up in the "pack" on the 26th of August, 1857, only four days later, notwithstanding her advantage of steampower.

I did every thing I could to while away the tedium of this detention. I tried the photographic apparatus, and with less satisfactory results than before. I tried dredging, without much to show for it; botanizing, and found nothing which I had not already in my Pröven and Upernavik collections. The flowers warned me of the approach of winter. The petals had begun to fall, and their drooping heads wore a melancholy look. They seemed to be pleading with the chilly air for a little longer lease of life.

One thing only was satisfactorily done. An immense iceberg lay off the harbor, and I had the measurement of it in my note-book, and a sketch of it in my portfolio. The square wall which faced toward my base of measurement was three hundred and fifteen feet high, and a fraction over three quarters of a mile long. The natives told me that it had been grounded for two years. Being almost square-sided above the sea, the same shape must have extended beneath it; and since, by measurements made two days before, I had discovered that fresh-water ice floating in salt water has above the surface to below it the proportion of one to seven, this crystalized piece of Eric's Greenland had stranded in a depth of nearly half a mile. A rude estimate of this monster, made on the spot, gave me in cubical contents about twenty-seven thousand millions of feet, and in weight something like two thousand millions of tons. I leave the reader to calculate for himself its equivalent in dollars and cents, were it transported to the region of ice-creams and sherry-cobblers, and how much of it would be required to pay off the national debt, and how much more than half a century it would withstand the attacks of the whole civilized world upon it, for all those uses to which luxury-loving man puts the skimmings of the Boston ponds.

The tide at length carried off the ice which imprisoned us, and in the evening of the 22d we were again threading our way among the bergs and islands. Cape Shackleton and the Horse's Head lay off the starboard bow, and we were shaping our course for Melville Bay.

CHAPTER VI.

ENTERING MELVILLE BAY. — THE MIDDLE ICE — THE GREAT POLAR CURRENT
— A SNOW STORM. — ENCOUNTER WITH AN ICEBERG. — MAKING CAPE YORK
— RESCUE OF HANS.

THE sun was now no ·longer above the horizon at midnight, and the nights were growing gloomy, a circumstance which warned us to additional carefulness.

Notwithstanding our precautions, we narrowly escaped running upon a· sunken reef which lies off the Horse's Head, and is not laid down on the chart. We came also among some ice-fields, the first that we had yet encountered. The waves were rolling in threateningly from the southwest, and the ice, tossing madly upon them, gave us an uncomfortable sense of insecurity; but we escaped into clear water after receiving a few thumps which did no material damage to our solid bows.

By eight o'clock in the morning we had Wilcox Point clearly in view, and the Devil's Thumb loomed above a light cloud which floated along its base. Before us lay Melville Bay. Climbing to the fore-yard, I swept the horizon with my glass; — there was no ice in sight except here and there a vagrant berg. To the westward an "ice-blink" showed us that the "pack" lay there; but before us all was clear, — nothing in sight but the "swelling and limitless billows."

No discovery of my life ever gave me greater gratification. The fortunes of the expedition were, at

58   MELVILLE BAY.

least for the present year, dependent upon an open season, and my most sanguine anticipations did not equal the apparent reality.

In order that the reader may appreciate, in some measure, the satisfaction which I took in the prospect that opened before me, it is necessary that I should here pause to give a general description of the region we were about to traverse, and an explanation of the physical conditions which made this portion of the Greenland waters of such conspicuous importance in the destinies of our voyage.

The shores of Melville Bay, as laid down on the maps, appear as a simple curved line of the Greenland coast; but the Melville Bay of the geographer comprehends much less than that of the mariner. The whalers have long called by that name the expansion of Baffin Bay which begins at the south with the "middle ice," and terminates at the north with the "North Water." The North Water is sometimes reached near Cape York, in latitude 76°, but more frequently higher up; and the "middle ice," which is more generally known as "the pack," sometimes stretches down to the Arctic Circle. This pack is made up of drifting ice-floes, varying in extent from feet to miles, and in thickness from inches to fathoms. These masses are sometimes pressed close together, having but little or no open space between them; and sometimes they are widely separated, depending upon the conditions of the wind and tide. They are always more or less in motion, drifting to the north, south, east, or west, with the winds and currents. The penetration of this barrier is usually an undertaking of weeks or months, and is ordinarily attended with much risk.

THE MIDDLE ICE. 59

Since the days when Baffin first penetrated these waters, in the *Discovery*, a vessel of fifty-eight tons burden, (it was in the year 1616,) a fleet of whale-ships has annually run this gauntlet. The fleet was once large, numbering upwards of a hundred sail; but of latter years it has been reduced to less than one tenth of its former magnitude. Great though the danger, it has always been a favorite route of the whale fishers. Many a stout ship has gone down with her sides mercilessly crushed in by the "thick-ribbed ice;" but those vessels which escape disaster almost uniformly return home with holds well filled with the blubber and oil of unlucky whales whose evil destiny led them to frequent the waters about Lancaster Sound, Pond's Bay, and the coasts below.

The "middle ice" is always more or less in motion, and is never tightly closed up, even in midwinter. Of this we have abundant proof in the fate of the Steamer *Fox*, which was caught towards the close of the autumn, and released in the spring, after a perilous winter drift, down near the Arctic Circle.

As the summer advances, it becomes more and more broken up; and, little by little, the solid land-belt, which is known as the "fast" or "land-ice," is encroached upon. Of this, however, there usually remains a narrow strip up to the close of the season. To it the whalers cling most tenaciously, and the exploring vessels have usually followed their example, taking always the last crack that has opened, or, as they call it, the "in-shore lead." They have naturally a great horror of being caught in the "pack." The "fast" gives them security if the wind brings the ice down upon them from the westward, for they can always saw a dock for their ships in the solid ice, or find a

THE GREAT POLAR CURRENT.

bight in which to moor the vessel. They have always, too, the advantage of being able, when the ice is loose and there is no wind, to tow their vessel along its margin with the crew, steam being rarely used by the whalers.

The currents have much to do with the formation of this barrier. The great Polar Current coming down through the Spitzbergen Sea along the eastern coast of Greenland, laden with its heavy freight of ice, and bringing from the rivers of Siberia a meagre supply of drift-wood to the Greenlanders, sweeps around Cape Farewell and flows northward as far as Cape York, where it is deflected to the westward. Joining here the ice-encumbered current which comes from the Arctic Ocean through Smith, Jones, and Lancaster Sounds, it flows thence southward, past Labrador and Newfoundland, receives on its way an accession of strength from Hudson Strait, wedges itself in between the Gulf Stream and the shore, gives cool, refreshing waters to the bathers of Newport and Long Branch, and is finally lost off the Capes of Florida.

Now it will readily be seen, by the most casual glance at any map of Baffin Bay, that this movement of the current forms, where the middle ice is found, a sort of slow-moving whirlpool, and this it is which locks up the ice and prevents its more rapid movement southward. It will also be readily understood that, by the end of August, the pack has been very materially shorn of its dimensions. The sun above and the waters beneath have both eaten it away, until much of it has disappeared altogether, and all of it has become more or less rotten. The month of August is necessarily the most favorable period of the year for the navigation of this sea, so far as concerns the ice ; but the winter is then near at hand, and presents a serious source of danger ; for if the ice once closes around you, the first fall of temperature may glue you fast for the next ten months to come. The whalers usually take the pack in May or June, and even sometimes earlier, when the ice is hard and is just beginning to break up.

When we entered Melville Bay there were but eight days remaining to us of the month of August. I had to regret the loss of time at the settlements ; but this was unavoidable. Before leaving Upernavik I had resolved upon the course which I would pursue, — to take the pack whenever we should find it, enter it at the most favorable opening, and, without looking for the land ice, to make the most direct line for Cape York. It was much in our favor that the wind had prevailed for many days from the eastward, and had apparently pushed the whole pack over toward the American side, opening for us a clear, broad expanse of water. Would it so remain, and give us a free passage to Cape York ? I have already said that I saw its reflection over the clouds, — the "ice-blink" to the westward. It was not far away. Would it remain so ?

While reflecting upon the chances ahead the wind rose, and blew half a gale. A heavy sea was getting up behind us. A dark cloud, which had hung upon the southern horizon for some time, came climbing up the sky, and at length spreading itself out in flying fragments, it shook over us a shower of frozen vapor, and then settled into a regular snow storm. Unable to see fifty yards on either side, I came down from my uncomfortable perch on the fore-yard.

It became now a subject for serious consideration

62 AN ANXIOUS NIGHT.

whether we should continue on in our course, or heave to and wait for better weather. In either case we were exposed to much risk. By heaving to, the vessel would not be under command ; and, drifting through the gloom, we stood a fair chance of settling upon a stray berg or upon the ice-fields which we had every reason to suppose would, sooner or later, obstruct our progress ; besides, and it was not an unimportant consideration, we lost a fine wind. On the other hand, by holding on, although we had the vessel under control, there was an even chance that, in the event of ice lying in our course, we would not be able to see it through the thick atmosphere in time to avoid it. The question was, however, quickly decided. Preferring that danger which had some energy in it, I reefed every thing down, pointed the schooner's head for Cape York, and went at it.

I paced the deck in much anxiety of mind. We were traversing a sea which no keel had ever plowed before without meeting ice, and why should better fortune be in store for our little craft. The air was so thick that I could sometimes barely see the lookout on the forecastle ; then again it would lighten up, and, underneath the broad canopy of dark vapors, which seemed to be supported by the icebergs that here and there appeared, I could see a distance of several miles. Then again the air became thick with the falling snow and rattling hail ; the wind whistled through the rigging, and all the while the heavy waves were rolling up behind us, deluging the decks, and threatening to swallow us up I shall not soon forget our first ten hours in Melville Bay.

At length, after a few hours of this wild running, my ear, which was keenly alive to every impression,

ENCOUNTER WITH AN ICEBERG. 63

caught the sound of breakers. The lookout gave the alarm a moment afterward.

"Where away?"

"I can't make out, sir."

The sound came from an object which was evidently near at hand, but no one could tell where. A few moments more, and the loom of an iceberg appeared in our course. There was no time for reflection, and it was too late for action. To haul the schooner by the wind was to insure our plunging broadside upon it; and so indistinct was the object that we knew not which way to steer. We could not see either end of it or its top, — nothing but a white shimmer and a line of angry surf.

I have always found inaction to be a safe course when one does not know what to do; and in the present case that course saved us. Had I obeyed my first impulse, and put the helm up, we should have gone straight to ruin; as it was, we slipped past the ugly monster, barely escaping a collision which, had it occurred, would have been instantly fatal to the vessel, and of course to every one on board. The fore-yard actually grazed its side, and the surf was thrown back upon us from the white wall. In a few moments the berg was swallowed up in the gloom from which it had so suddenly emerged.

"A close shave, that!" said cool-headed Dodge.

"Ver—very close," answered Starr, much as if he had just received the first shock of a shower-bath.

The old cook was called out of his galley to lend a hand, and in the midst of the excitement he was heard to growl out, "I don't see how I's to get de gentlemens' dinner ready if I's to be called out of my galley

64 CAPE YORK IN SIGHT.

in dis way to pull and haul on de ropes." He did not seem to have a thought that there was, a moment before, very little expectation on the part of "de gentlemens" that any of them would have further occasion for his services.

This adventure inspired the crew with greater confidence. I suppose they thought that, as two cannon-balls never strike in the same spot, another iceberg would not very likely lay in our course ; and so it fell out. The cry of "breakers" was often heard from the forecastle-deck, but in the end the sound proved to come from off the bow, and we passed on unharmed.

At length the wind blew itself out, the snow ceased falling, the clouds broke, the sun shone out brightly, and we lay becalmed not far from the centre of Melville Bay. The snow and ice were shovelled from the deck and beaten from the rigging. I went aloft again with my glass. There were no ice-fields in sight, but the reflection of them was still visible in the sky to the westward.

The sea was dotted over with icebergs, and it seemed wonderful that we should have passed safely between them. One near by particulary excited my admiration. It was a perfect " triumphal arch," through which the schooner might have passed with perfect ease.

The schooner lay motionless during the night, but early in the morning a fair wind sent us again upon our course, and this wind held steadily through the day. Icebergs rose before us and set behind us in solemn procession. My journal designates them as "milestones of the ocean." The lofty, snow-crowned highlands behind Cape York rose at length above the

IN THE NORTH WATER. 65

horizon, and the bold, dark-sided cape itself was, after a while, seen "advancing in the bosom of the sea."

We did not meet any field-ice until near noon of the 25th. I had been aloft in anxious watching during almost all of the whole preceding day and night; but when I had made up my mind that we should clear Melville Bay without a single brush with the enemy, a line of whiteness revealed itself in the distance. We were not long in reaching it, and, selecting the most conspicuous opening, forced our way through. It proved to be only a loose "pack" about fifteen miles wide, and, under a full pressure of canvas, we experienced little difficulty in "boring" it.

And now we were in the "North Water." We had passed Melville Bay in fifty-five hours.

Standing close in under Cape York, I kept a careful lookout for natives. The readers of the narrative of Dr. Kane may remember that that navigator took with him from one of the southern settlements of Greenland a native hunter, who, after adhering to the fortunes of the expedition through nearly two years, abandoned it, (as reported,) for a native bride, to live with the wild Esquimaux who inhabit the shores of the headwaters of Baffin Bay. This boy was named Hans. Anticipating that, growing tired of his self-imposed banishment, he would take up his residence at Cape York, with the hope of being picked up by some friendly ship, I ran in to seek him. Passing along the coast at rifle-shot I soon discovered a group of human beings making signs to attract attention. Heaving the vessel to, I went ashore in a boat, and there, sure enough, was the object of my search. He quickly recognized Sonntag and myself, and called us by name.

AN ESQUIMAU FAMILY.

Six years' experience among the wild men of this barren coast had brought him to their level of filthy ugliness. His companions were his wife, who carried her first-born in a hood upon her back; her brother, a bright-eyed boy of twelve years, and "an ancient dame with voluble and flippant tongue," her mother. They were all dressed in skins, and, being the first Esquimaux we had seen whose habits remained wholly uninfluenced by contact with civilization, they were, naturally, objects of much interest to us all.

Hans led us up the hill-side, over rough rocks and through deep snow-drifts, to his tent. It was pitched about two hundred feet above the level of the sea, in a most inconvenient position for a hunter; but it was his "lookout." Wearily he had watched, year after year, for the hoped-for vessel; but summer after summer passed and the vessel came not, and he still sighed for his southern home and the friends of his youth.

His tent was a sorry habitation. It was made after the Esquimau fashion, of seal-skins, and was barely large enough to hold the little family who were grouped about us.

I asked Hans if he would go with us.

"Yes!"

Would he take his wife and baby.

"Yes!"

Would he go without them.

"Yes!"

Having no leisure to examine critically into the state of his mind, and having an impression that the permanent separation of husband and wife is regarded as a painful event, I gave the Esquimau mother the benefit of this conventional suspicion, and brought them both aboard, with their baby and their tent and all their household goods. The old woman and bright-eyed boy cried to be taken along; but I had no further room, and we had to leave them to the care of the remainder of the tribe, who, about twenty in number, had discovered the vessel, and came shouting gleefully over the hill. After distributing to them some useful presents, we pushed off for the schooner.

Hans was the only unconcerned person in the party. I subsequently thought that he would have been quite as well pleased had I left his wife and child to the protection of their savage kin; and had I known him as well then as, with good reason, I knew him afterward, I would not have gone out of my way to disturb his barbarous existence.

CHAPTER VII.

HANS AND HIS FAMILY — PETOWAK GLACIER — A SNOW-STORM — THE ICE-PACK — ENTERING SMITH'S SOUND — A SEVERE GALE — COLLISION WITH ICEBERGS — ENCOUNTER WITH THE ICE-FIELDS — RETREAT FROM THE PACK — AT ANCHOR IN HARTSTENE BAY. — ENTERING WINTER QUARTERS.

IT was five o'clock in the evening when I reached the schooner. The wind had freshened during our absence; and, unwilling to lose so favorable an opportunity for pushing on, I had hastened on board. Otherwise I should gladly have given some time to an examination of the native village which lies a few miles to the eastward of the cape, on the northern side of a conspicuous bay, near a place called Kíkertait, — "The Place of Islands."

In anticipation of a heavy blow and a dirty night, McCormick had, during my absence, taken a reef in the sails, and the little schooner, with her canvas shivering in the wind, seemed impatient as a hound in the leash. When the helm went up, she wheeled round to the north with a graceful toss of her head, and, after steadying herself for an instant, as if for a good start, she shot off before the wind at ten knots an hour. Capes, bays, islands, glaciers, and icebergs sank rapidly behind us; and, rejoicing over their extraordinary fortune, the ship's company were in the best of spirits. As we dashed on through nest after nest of icebergs, it was curious to observe the evidences of reckless daring which inspired their thoughts. Dodge

A HAZARDOUS PASSAGE. 69

had the deck, and Charley, as dare-devil an old sailor as ever followed the fortunes of the sea, had the helm; and it seemed to me, as I sat upon the fore-yard, that there was some quiet understanding between the two to see how near they could come to the icebergs without hitting them. We passed through many narrow places; but instead of finding the schooner in the middle of the channel, she generally managed to fall off to one side or the other at the critical moment (of course, by mere accident); and when I shouted a remonstrance at the lubberly steering, I was answered with the assurance that the schooner would not obey her helm with so much after-sail on, when running before the wind; so I accordingly hove the schooner to, and close-reefed the mainsail; and now, either from the want of a reasonable excuse for doing otherwise, or from a real difficulty being overcome, the vessel was made to keep somewhat nearer to a straight course; and we dashed on through the waveless waters with a celerity which, in view of our surroundings, fairly made one's head swim.

I was once not a little alarmed. Before us lay what appeared to be two icebergs separated by a distance of about twenty fathoms. To go around them was to deviate from our course, and I called to Dodge to know if he could steady the schooner through the narrow passage. Ever ready when there was a spice of danger, he willingly assumed the responsibility of the schooner's behavior, and we approached the entrance; but, when it was too late to turn either to the right or left, I discovered, much to my amazement, that the objects which I had supposed to be two bergs were in fact but portions of the same mass, connected together by a link which was only a few feet below

70 HANS AND HIS FAMILY.

the surface of the water. The depth of water proved,
however, to be greater than at first appeared, but the
keel actually touched twice as we shot through the
opening ; and while the schooner was, with some hes-
itancy and evident reluctance, doing this sledge duty,
I must own that I wished myself anywhere else than
on her fore-yard.

The officers and men amused themselves with our
new allies. Hans was delighted, and he expressed
himself with as much enthusiasm as was consistent
with his stolid temperament. His wife exhibited a
mixture of bewilderment and pride ; and, apparently
overwhelmed with the novelty of the situation in
which she so suddenly found herself, seemed to have
contracted a chronic grin ; while her baby laughed
and crowed and cried as all other babies do.

The sailors set to work at once with tubs of warm
water and with soap, scissors, and comb, to prepare
them for red shirts and other similar luxuries of civilization. At this latter they were overjoyed, and strut-
ted about the deck with much the same air of exalted
consequence as that of a boy who has been freshly promoted from frock and shoes to pantaloons and boots ;
but it must be owned that the soap-and-water arrangement was not so highly appreciated ; and well they
might object, for they were not used to it. At first
the whole procedure seemed to be great sport, but at
length the wife began to cry, and demanded of her
husband to know whether this was a white man's re-
ligious rite, with an expression of countenance which
appeared to indicate that it was regarded by her as a
refined method of Christian torture. The family were
finally stowed away for the night down among the
ropes and sails in the "ship's eyes;" and one of the

PETOWAK GLACIER. 71

sailors who played chamberlain on the occasion, and who appeared to be not overly partial to this increase of our family, remarked that, "If good for nothing else, they are at least good lumber for strengthening the schooner's bows against the ice."

The coast which we were passing greatly interested me. The trap formation of Disco Island reappears at Cape York, and the land presents a lofty, ragged front, broken by deep gorges which have a very picturesque appearance, and the effect was much heightened by numerous streams of ice which burst through the openings. One of these figures on the chart as Petowak Glacier. Measuring it as we passed with log-line and chronometer, it proved to be four miles across. The igneous rocks are interrupted at Cape Athol, on the southern side of Wolstenholme Sound, and the lines of calcareous sandstone and greenstone which meet the eye there and at Saunders Island and the coast above, toward Cape Parry, brought to my recollection many a hard struggle of former years. They were familiar landmarks.

At eight o'clock in the evening we were abreast of Booth Bay, the winter quarters in my boat journey of 1854. I could distinguish through my glass the rocks among which we had built our hut. They were suggestive of many unpleasant memories.

Soon afterward the sky became overcast, and a heavy snow began to fall. The wind dying away to a light breeze, we jogged on through the day, and, passing Whale Sound, outside of Hakluyt Island, were, at five o'clock in the evening, within thirty miles of Smith's Sound. Here we came upon an ice-pack which appeared to be very heavy and to stretch off to the southwest; but the air being too thick to warrant us

MEETING THE ICE PACK.

in approaching near enough to inspect its character, we began to beat to windward with the hope of reaching the lee side of Northumberland Island, there to await better weather. In this purpose we were, however, defeated, for, the wind falling almost to calm, we were forced to grope about in the gloom, seeking an iceberg for a mooring; but the waves proved to be running too high to admit of our landing from a boat, and we passed the night in much uneasiness, drifting northward. Fortunately the pack was moving in the same direction, otherwise we should have been carried upon it. The breakers could be distinctly heard all the time, and on several occasions we caught sight of them; but, by availing ourselves of every puff of wind to crawl off, we escaped without collision. Once I was satisfied that we had no alternative but to wear round and plunge head foremost into the danger, rather than await the apparent certainty of drifting broadside upon it; but at the critical moment the wind freshened, and, continuing for a few hours, we held our own while the pack glided slowly away from us.

Our dogs had made a heavy drain upon our water-casks, and the watch was engaged during the night in melting the snow which had fallen upon the deck. We also fished up from the sea some small fragments of fresh ice with a net. By these means we obtained a supply of water sufficient to last us for several days.

The wind hauled to the northeast as the morning dawned, and the clouds broke away, disclosing the land. Cape Alexander, whose lofty walls guard the entrance to Smith's Sound, appeared to be about twenty miles away, and Cape Isabella, thirty-five miles distant from it, was visible on the opposite side. Hold-

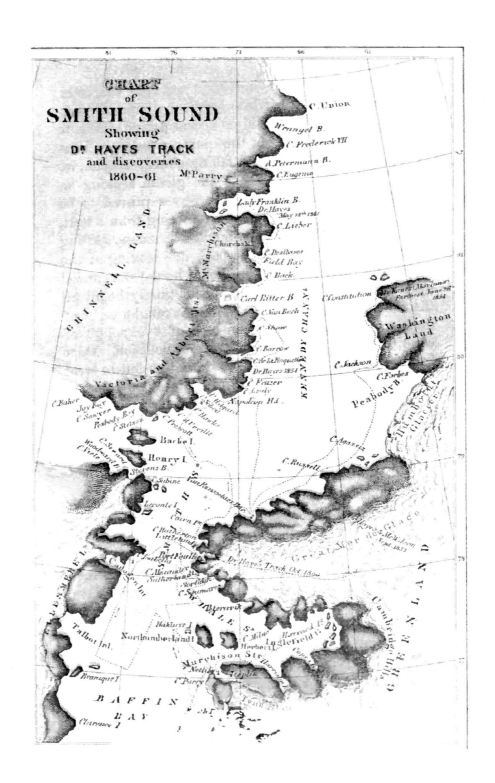

ENTERING SMITH'S SOUND.

ing to the eastward toward Cape Saumarez, we found a passage through the pack near the shore, but afterward the greater part of the day was passed in a provoking calm, during which, being embarrassed by a strong tidal-current that set us alternately up and down the coast, we were obliged almost constantly to use the boats to keep ourselves clear of the bergs, which were very numerous, and many of them of immense size. We were, however, at length gratified to find ourselves passing with a fair wind into Smith's Sound, the field of our explorations. Standing over toward Cape Isabella, we had for a time every prospect of good fortune before us, but a heavy pack was, after a while, discovered from the mast-head, and this we were not long in reaching.

This pack was composed of the heaviest ice-fields that I had hitherto seen, and its margin, trending to the northeast and southwest, arrested our further progress toward the western shore. Many of the floes were from two to ten feet above the water, thus indicating a thickness of from twenty to a hundred feet. Had they been widely separated, I should have attempted to force a passage; but they were too closely impacted to allow of this being done with any chance of safety to the schooner.

The ice appeared to be interminable. No open water could be discovered in the direction of Cape Isabella. The wind, being from the northeast, did not permit of an exploration in that direction; so we ran down to the southwest, anxiously looking for a lead, but without discovering any thing to give us encouragement.

We were not, however, permitted to come to any conclusions of our own as to what course we should

74   STOPPED BY THE PACK.

pursue, for the most furious gale that it has ever
been my fortune to encounter broke suddenly upon
us, and left us no alternative but to seek shelter under
the coast.   Our position was now one of great danger.
The heavy pack which we had passed the night previous lay to leeward of us, and was even visible from
the mast-head, thus shutting off retreat in that direction, even should our necessities give us no choice but
to run before the wind.

The entries of my diary will perhaps best exhibit
the ineffectual struggle which followed : —

August 28th, 3 o'clock, P. M.

Blowing frightfully.   We have run in under the
coast, and are partly sheltered by it, and trying hard
to find an anchorage.   But for the protection of the
land we could not show a stitch of canvas.   We are
about three miles from Sutherland Island, which lies
close to Cape Alexander, on its south side, but we
have ceased to gain any thing upon it.   We can carry
so little sail that the schooner will not work to windward ; besides, here under the coast, the wind comes
only in squalls.   If we can only get in between the
island and the mainland we shall be all right.   I have
not been in bed since the day before leaving Tessuissak, and during these six days I have snatched only
now and then a little sleep.   If our anchor once gets
a clutch on the bottom I shall make up for lost time.

I ought to have been more cautious, and sought
shelter sooner.   A heavy white cloud hanging over
Cape Alexander (Jensen calls it a "table-cloth")
warned me of the approaching gale, but then I did
not think it would come upon us with such fury.

It is a perfect hurricane.   My chief fear is that we

A SEVERE GALE. 75

will be driven out to sea, which is everywhere filled with heavy ice.

August 29th, 12 o'clock, M.

There has been a dead calm under the coast for an hour. The "table-cloth" has lifted from the cape, and there is a decided change in the northern sky. The light windy clouds are disappearing, and stratus clouds are taking their place. The neck of the gale appears to be broken.

2 o'clock, P. M.

My calculations of the morning were quite wrong. The gale howls more furiously than ever. We are lying off Cape Saumarez, about two miles from shore. Failing to reach Sutherland Island, we were forced to run down the coast with the hope of finding shelter in the deep bay below; but the wind, sweeping round the cape, drove us back, and we are now trying to crawl in shore and get an anchor down in a little cove near by, and there repair our torn sails. We are a very uncomfortable party. The spray flies over the vessel, sheathing her in ice. Long icicles hang from the rigging and the bulwarks. The bobstays and other head-gear are the thickness of a man's body; and, most unseamanlike procedure, we have to throw ashes on the deck to get about.

I can now readily understand how Inglefield was forced to fly from Smith's Sound. If the gale which he encountered resembled this one, he could not, with double the steam-power of the *Isabella*, have made headway against it. Were I to leave the shelter of these friendly cliffs I should have to run with even greater celerity; — and, very likely, to destruction.

The squalls which strike us are perfectly terrific, and the calms which follow them are suggestive of

SEEKING SHELTER.

gathering strength for another stroke. Fortunately the blows are of short duration, else our already damaged canvas, which is reduced to the smallest possible dimensions, would fly into ribbons.

The coast which gives us this spasmodic protection is bleak enough. The cliffs are about twelve hundred feet high, and their tops and the hills behind them are covered with the recent snows. The wind blows a cloud of drift over the lofty wall, and, after whirling it about in the air, in a manner which, under other circumstances, would no doubt be pretty enough, drops it upon us in great showers. The winter is setting in early. At this time of the season in 1853–54 these same hills were free from snow, and so remained until two weeks later.

10 o'clock, P. M.

We have gained nothing upon the land, and are almost where we were at noon. The gale continues as before, and hits us now and then as hard as ever. The view from the deck is magnificent beyond description. The imagination cannot conceive of a scene more wild. A dark cloud hangs to the northward, bringing the white slopes of Cape Alexander into bold relief. Over the cliffs roll great sheets of drifting snow, and streams of it pour down every ravine and gorge. Whirlwinds shoot it up from the hilltops, and spin it through the air. The streams which pour through the ravines resemble the spray of mammoth waterfalls, and here and there through the fickle cloud the dark rocks protrude and disappear and protrude again A glacier which descends through a valley to the bay below is covered with a broad cloak of revolving whiteness The sun is setting in a black and ominous horizon. But the wildest scene is upon

A WILD SCENE.

77

the sea. Off the cape it is one mass of foam. The water, carried along by the wind, flies through the air and breaches over the lofty icebergs. It is a most wonderful exhibition. I have tried in vain to illustrate it with my pencil. My pen is equally powerless. It is impossible for me to convey to this page a picture of that vast volume of foam which flutters over the sea, and, rising and falling with each pulsation of the inconstant wind, stands out against the dark sky, or of the clouds which fly overhead, rushing, wild and fearful, across the heavens, on the howling storm. Earth and sea are charged with bellowing sounds. Upon the air are borne shrieks and wailings, loud and dismal as those of the infernal blast which, down in the second circle of the damned, appalled the Italian bard ; and the clouds of snow and vapor are tossed upon the angry gusts, — now up, now down, — as spirits, condemned of Minos, wheel their unhappy flight in endless squadrons,

"Swept by the dreadful hurricane along."

In striking contrast to the cold and confusion above is the warmth and quiet here below. I write in the officers' cabin. The stove is red-hot, the tea-kettle sings a homelike song. Jensen is reading. McCormick, thoroughly worn out with work and anxiety, sleeps soundly, and Knorr and Radcliffe keep him company. Dodge has the deck ; and here comes the cook staggering along with his pot of coffee. I will fortify myself with a cup of it, and send Dodge below for a little comfort.

The cook had no easy task in reaching the cabin over the slippery decks.

78   A CABIN SCENE.

"I falls down once, but de Commander see I keeps de coffee. It's good an' hot, and very strong, and go right down into de boots."

"Bad night on deck, cook."

"Oh, it's awful, sar! I never see it blow so hard in all my life, an' I's followed de sea morn 'n forty year. And den it's so cold. My galley is full of ice, and de water it freeze on my stove."

"Here, cook, is a guernsey for you; that will keep you warm."

"Tank you, sar!" — and he starts off with his prize; but, encouraged by his reception, he stops to ask, "Would de Commander be so good as to tell me where we is? De gentlemens fool me."

"Certainly, cook. The land over there is Greenland. That big cape is Cape Alexander; beyond that is Smith's Sound, and we are only about eight hundred miles from the North Pole."

"De Nort' Pole, vere's dat?"

I explained the best I could.

"Tank you, sar. Vat for we come — to fish?"

"No, not to fish, cook; for science."

"Oh, dat it? Dey tell me we come to fish. Tank you, sar." And he pulls his greasy cap over his bald head, and does not appear to be much wiser as he tumbles up the companion-ladder into the storm. Somebody has hoaxed the old man into the belief that we have come out to catch seals.

August 30th, 1 o'clock, A. M.

The wind is hauling to the eastward, and the squalls come thicker and faster. We are drifting both up and from the coast, and I fear that if we recede much further we shall be sent howling to sea under

AT ANCHOR. 79

bare poles. It is not a pleasing reflection — a "pack" and a thousand icebergs to leeward, and an unmanageable vessel under foot. McCormick is struggling manfully for the shore.

10 o'clock, A. M.

We reached the shore this morning at 3 o'clock, and anchored in four fathoms water. The stern of the schooner was swung round and moored with our stoutest hawser to a rock; but a squall fell upon us soon afterward with such violence that, although the sails were all snugly stowed, the hawser was parted like a whip-cord; and we now lie to our "bower" and "kedge," with thirty fathoms chain.

And now, in apparent security, the ship's company abandon themselves to repose. Weary and worn with the hard struggle and exposure, we were all badly in need of rest. An abundant supply of hot coffee was our first refreshment. But, notwithstanding their fatigue, some of the more enthusiastic members of the party went ashore, so anxious were they to touch this far-north land.

8 o'clock, P. M.

I have just returned from a tedious climb to the top of the cliffs. At an elevation of twelve hundred feet I had a good view. The sea is free from ice along the shore apparently up to Littleton Island, from which the pack stretches out over the North Water as far as the eye will carry. There appears to be much open water about Cape Isabella, but I could not of course see the shore line. Above the cape the ice appeared to be solid. Although the prospect is discouraging, I have determined to attempt a passage with the first favorable wind.

The journey was a very difficult one, and when I

VIEW FROM THE CLIFFS.

had reached the summit of the cliff I was almost blown over it. The force of the wind was so great that I was obliged to steady myself against a rock while making my observations. Knorr, who accompanied me, lost his cap, and it went sailing out over the sea as if a mere feather. The scene was but a broader panorama of that which I described in this journal yesterday. It was a grand, wild confusion of the elements. The little schooner, far down beneath me, was writhing and reeling with the fitful gusts, and straining at her cables like a chained wild beast. The clouds of drifting snow which whirled through the gorges beneath me, now and then hid her and the icebergs beyond from view; and when the air fell calm again the cloud dropped upon the sea, and the schooner, after a short interval of unrest, lay quietly on the still water, nestling in sunshine under the protecting cliffs.

There are yet some lingering traces of the summer. Some patches of green moss and grass were seen in the valleys, where the snow had drifted away; and I plucked a little nosegay of my old friends the poppies and the curling spider-legged *Saxifraga flagelaris*. The frost and snow and wind had not robbed them of their loveliness and beauty. The cliffs are of the same sandstone, interstratified with greenstone, which I have before remarked of the coast below.

McCormick has replaced the old foresail which was split down the centre, with the new one, and has patched up the mainsail and jib, both of which were much torn.

An immense amount of ice has drifted past us, but we are too far in-shore for any masses of considerable

DRIVEN FROM SHELTER.   81

size to reach the vessel. Three small bergs have,
however, grounded in a cluster right astern of us,
and if we drag our anchors we shall bring up against
them. A perfect avalanche of wind tumbles upon us
from the cliffs; and instead of coming in squalls, as
heretofore, it is now almost constant. The temperature is 27°.

I made a trial to-day with the dredge, but nothing
was brought up from the bottom except a couple of
echinoderms (*Asterias Grœnlandica* and *A. Albula*). The
sea is alive with little shrimps, among which the *Cran-
gon Boreas* is most abundant. The full-grown ones are
an inch long, and their tinted backs give a purplish
hue to the water.

August 31st, 8 o'clock, P. M.

Night closes upon a day of disaster, — a day, I
fear, of evil omen. My poor little schooner is terribly cut up.

Soon after making my last entry yesterday I lay
down for a little rest, but was soon aroused with the
unwelcome announcement that we were dragging our
anchors. McCormick managed to save the bower,
but the kedge was lost. It caught a rock at a critical moment, and, the hawser parting, we were driven
upon the bergs, which, as before stated, had grounded
astern of us. The collision was a perfect crash. The
stern boat flew into splinters, the bulwarks over the
starboard-quarter were stove in, and, the schooner's
head swinging round with great violence, the jib-
boom was carried away, and the bowsprit and foretop-
mast were both sprung. In this crippled condition
we at length escaped most miraculously, and under
bare poles scudded before the wind. A vast number
of icebergs and the " pack " coming in view, we were

6

BACK IN SMITH'S SOUND

forced to make sail. The mainsail went to pieces as soon as it was set, and we were once more in great jeopardy; but fortunately the storm abated, and we have since been threshing to windward, and are once more within Smith's Sound. Again the gale appears to have broken; the northern sky is clear. Our spars will not allow us to carry jib and topsail; — bad for entering the pack.

The temperature is 22°, and the decks are again slippery with ice. Forward, the ropes, blocks, stays, halyards, and every thing else, are covered with a solid coating, and icicles a foot long hang from the monkey-rail and rigging. If they look pretty enough in the sunlight, they have a very wintry aspect, and are not at all becoming to a ship.

I tried this morning to reach Cape Isabella, but met the pack where it had obstructed us before. Some patches of open water were observed in the midst of it; but we found it impossible to penetrate the intervening ice. My only chance now is to work up the Greenland coast, get hold of the fast ice, and, through such leads as must have been opened by the wind higher up the Sound, endeavor to effect a passage to the opposite shore. Of reaching that shore I do not yet despair, although the wind has apparently packed the ice upon it to such a degree that it looks like a hopeless undertaking. I have already an eye upon Fog Inlet, twenty miles above Cape Alexander on the Greenland coast, and I shall now try to reach that point for a new start.

While I write the wind is freshening, and under close-reefed sails we are making a little progress. My poor sailors have a sorry time of it, with the stiffened ropes. The schooner, everywhere above the water, is

ENTERING THE PACK   83

coated with ice. The dogs are perishing with cold
and wet. Three of them have already died.

September 1st, 8 o'clock, P. M.

We have once more been driven out of the Sound.
The gale set in again with great violence, and in the
act of wearing the schooner, to avoid an iceberg, the
fore-gaff parted in the middle; and, unable to carry
any thing but a close-reefed staysail, we were forced
again to seek shelter behind our old protector, Cape
Alexander. McCormick is patching up the wreck and
preparing for another struggle.

The next two days were filled with dangerous adventure. The broken spar being repaired, we had
another fight for the Sound, and got again inside. The
pack still lay where it was before, and again headed us
off. There was a good deal of open water between
Littleton Island and Cape Hatherton, and apparently
to the northwest of that cape; but there was much
heavy ice off the island, with tortuous leads separating
the floes. I determined, however, to enter the pack
and try to reach the open water above. Taking the
first fair opening, we made a northwest course for
about ten miles, when, finding that we were unable to
penetrate any further in that direction, we tacked
ship, hoping to reach the clear water that lay above
the island.

We were now fairly in the fight. The current was
found to be setting strongly against us, and it was soon
discovered that the ice was coming rapidly down the
Sound, and that the leads were already slowly closing
up. We worked vigorously, crowding on all the sail
we could; but we did not make our point, and soon

84 IN THE PACK.

had to go about again; or rather, we tried to; for the schooner, never reliable without her topsail, which we could not carry owing to the accident to the topmast, missed in stays; and, fearful of being nipped between the fields which were rapidly reducing the open water about us, we wore round; and, there not being sufficient room, we were on the eve of striking with the starboard-bow a solid ice-field a mile in width. There was little hope for the schooner if this collision should happen with our full headway; and being unable to avoid it, I thought it clearly safest to take the shock squarely on the fore-foot; so I ordered the helm up, and went at it in true battering-ram style. To me the prospect was doubly disagreeable. For the greater facility of observation I had taken my station on the foretop-yard; and the mast being already sprung and swinging with my weight, I had little other expectation than that, when the shock came, it would snap off and land me with the wreck on the ice ahead. Luckily for me the spar held firm, but the cut-water flew in splinters with the collision, and the iron sheathing was torn from the bows as if it had been brown paper.

And now came a series of desperate struggles. No topsail-schooner was ever put through such a set of gymnastic feats. I had been so much annoyed by the detentions and embarrassments of the last few days that I was determined to risk every thing rather than go back. As long as the schooner would float I should hope still to get a clutch on Cape Hatherton.

Getting clear of the floe, the schooner came again to the wind, and, gliding into a narrow lead, we soon emerged into a broad space of open water. Had this continued we should soon have been rewarded with

BESET. 85

success, but in half an hour the navigation became so tortuous that we were compelled again to go about and stand in-shore. And thus we continued for many hours, tacking to and fro, — sometimes gaining a little, then losing ground by being forced to go to leeward of a floe, which we could not weather.

The space in which we could manœuvre the schooner became gradually more and more contracted; the collisions with the ice became more frequent. We were losing ground. The ice was closing in with the land, and we were finally brought to bay. There was no longer a lead. And it was now too late to retreat, had we been even so inclined. The ice was as closely impacked behind us as before us. With marvelous celerity the scene had shifted. An hour later, and there was scarcely a patch of open water in sight from the deck, and the floes were closing upon the schooner like a vice. Utterly powerless within its jaws, we had no alternative but to await the issue with what calmness we could.

The scene around us was as imposing as it was alarming. Except the earthquake and volcano, there is not in nature an exhibition of force comparable with that of the ice-fields of the Arctic Seas. They close together, when driven by the wind or by currents against the land or other resisting object, with the pressure of millions of moving tons, and the crash and noise and confusion are truly terrific.

We were now in the midst of one of the most thrilling of these exhibitions of Polar dynamics, and we became uncomfortably conscious that the schooner was to become a sort of dynamometer. Vast ridges were thrown up wherever the floes came together, to be submerged again when the pressure was exerted in

86   FORCE OF THE ICE-FIELDS.

another quarter; and over the sea around us these pulsating lines of uplift, which in some cases reached an altitude of not less than sixty feet, — higher than our mast-head, — told of the strength and power of the enemy which was threatening us.

We had worked ourselves into a triangular space formed by the contact of three fields. At first there was plenty of room to turn round, though no chance to escape We were nicely docked, and vainly hoped that we were safe ; but the corners of the protecting floes were slowly crushed off, the space narrowed little by little, and we listened to the crackling and crunching of the ice, and watched its progress with consternation

At length the ice touched the schooner, and it appeared as if her destiny was sealed. She groaned like a conscious thing in pain, and writhed and twisted as if to escape her adversary, trembling in every timber from truck to kelson. Her sides seemed to be giving way. Her deck timbers were bowed up, and the seams of the deck planks were opened. I gave up for lost the little craft which had gallantly carried us through so many scenes of peril ; but her sides were solid and her ribs strong ; and the ice on the port side, working gradually under the bilge, at length, with a jerk which sent us all reeling, lifted her out of the water ; and the floes, still pressing on and breaking, as they were crowded together, a vast ridge was piling up beneath and around us ; and, as if with the elevating power of a thousand jack-screws, we found ourselves going slowly up into the air.

My fear now was that the schooner would fall over on her side, or that the masses which rose above the bulwarks would topple over upon the deck, and bury us beneath them.

THE SCHOONER IN DANGER. 87

We lay in this position during eight anxious hours.

At length the crash ceased with a change of wind and tide. The ice exhibited signs of relaxing. The course of the monster floes which were crowding down the Sound was changed more to the westward. We beheld the prospect of release with joy.

Small patches of open water were here and there exhibited among the hitherto closely impacted ice. The change of scene, though less fearful, was not less magical than before. By and by the movement extended to the floes which bound us so uncomfortably, and with the first cessation of the pressure the blocks of ice which supported the forward part of the schooner gave way, and, the bows following them, left the stern high in the air. Here we rested for a few moments quietly, and then the old scene was renewed. The further edge of the outer floe which held us was caught by another moving field of greater size, when the jam returned, and we appeared to be in as great danger as before; but this attack was of short duration. The floe revolved, and, the pressure being almost instantly removed, we fell into the water, reeling forward and backward and from side to side, as the ice, seeking its own equilibrium, settled headlong and in wild confusion beneath us from its forced elevation.

Freed from this novel and alarming situation, we used every available means to disengage ourselves from the ruins of the frightful battle which we had encountered; and, as speedily as possible, got into a position of greater safety. Meanwhile an inspection was made to ascertain what damage had been done to the schooner. The hold was rapidly filling with water, the rudder was split, two of its pintles were broken off,

88 THE SCHOONER CRIPPLED.

the stern-post was started, fragments of the cut-water and keel were floating alongside of us in the sea, and, to all appearances, we were in a sinking condition.

Our first duty was to man the pumps.

We were many hours among the ice, tortured with doubt and uncertainty. We had to move with great caution. The crippled condition of the schooner warned us to use her gently. She would bear no more thumps. Forward we could not go, because of the ice; retreat we must, for it was absolutely necessary that we should get to the land and find shelter somewhere. The rudder was no longer available, and we were obliged to steer with a long "sweep."

The wind hauled more and more to the eastward, and spread the ice. Although at times closely beset and once severely "nipped," yet, by watching our opportunity, we crept slowly out of the pack, and, after twenty anxious hours, got at last into comparatively clear water, and headed for Hartstene Bay, where we found an anchorage.

The damage to the schooner was less than we had feared. A more careful examination showed that no timbers were broken, and the seams in a measure closed of themselves. Once at anchor, and finding that we were in no danger of sinking, I allowed all hands to take a rest, except such as were needed at the pumps. They were all thoroughly worn out.

On the following day a still further inspection of the vessel was made; and, although apparently unfit for any more ice-encounters, she could still float with a little assistance from the pumps. One hour out of every four kept the hold clear.

Such repairs as it was in our power to make were at once begun We could do very little without

ANOTHER TRIAL.

beaching the vessel, and this, in the uncertain state of the ice and weather, was not practicable. The rudder hung by one pintle, and after being mended was still unreliable.

While McCormick was making these repairs I pulled up to Littleton Island in a whale-boat, to see what the ice had been doing in our absence. The wind was dead ahead, and we had a hard struggle to reach our destination; but, once there, I found some encouragement. There was much open water along the coast up to Cape Hatherton, but the pack was even more heavy at the west and southwest than it had been before. To enter it would be folly, even with a fair wind and a sound ship. There was clearly no chance of getting to the west coast, except by the course which I had attempted with such unhappy results two days previous.

We were not a little surprised to discover on Littleton Island a reindeer. He was sound asleep, coiled up on a bed of snow. Dodge's rifle secured him for our larder and deprived the desolate island of its only inhabitant.

During our absence, Jensen had been out with Hans, and had also discovered deer   They had found a herd numbering something like a dozen. Two of them were captured, but the rest, taking alarm, escaped to the mountains.

The wind falling away to calm, we got to sea next day under oars, and again entered the pack. More ice had come down upon the island, and all our efforts to push up the coast were unavailing. The air had become alarmingly quiet, considering that the temperature was within twelve degrees of zero, and there was much fear that we should be frozen up at sea.

90 RETREAT FROM THE PACK.

A snow-storm came to add to this danger; but still we kept on at the cold and risky work of "warping" with capstan and windlass, whale-line and hawser, sometimes making and sometimes losing, and often pretty severely nipped.

At length we were once more completely "beset." The young ice was making rapidly, and I was forced reluctantly to admit that the navigable season was over. To stay longer in the pack was now to insure of being frozen up there for the winter, and accordingly, after having exhausted two more days of fruitless labor, we made what haste we could to get back again into clear water. This was not, however, an affair to be quickly accomplished. He who navigates these polar seas must learn patience.

Our purpose was, however, in the end safely accomplished, and, a breeze springing up, we put back into Hartstene Bay; and, steering for a cluster of ragged-looking islands which lay near the coast at its head, we came upon a snug little harbor behind them, and dropped our anchors. Next morning I had the schooner hauled further in-shore, and moored her to the rocks.

Meanwhile the crew were working with anxious uncertainty; and when I finally announced my intention to winter in that place they received the intelligence with evident satisfaction. Their exposure had been great, and they needed rest; but, notwithstanding this, had there been the least prospect of serviceable result following any further attempt to cross the Sound, they would, with their customary energy and cheerfulness, have rejoiced in continuing the struggle. But they saw, as their faces clearly told, even before I was willing to own it, that the season was over. I record it to their credit, that throughout a voyage of unusual peril and exposure they had never quailed in the presence of danger, and they had to a man exhibited the most satisfactory evidence of manly endurance.

The reader will readily understand that to me the failure to cross the Sound was a serious disappointment. Hoping, as heretofore stated, to reach the west coast, and there secure a harbor in some convenient place between latitude 79° and 80°, it was evident to me that in failing to do this my chances of success with sledges during the following spring were greatly jeopardized. Besides — and this to me was the most painful reflection — my vessel was, apparently, so badly injured as to be unfit for any renewal of the attempt the next year.

CHAPTER VIII.

OUR WINTER HARBOR. — PREPARING FOR WINTER. — ORGANIZATION OF DUTIES. — SCIENTIFIC WORK. — THE OBSERVATORY. — SCHOONER DRIVEN ASHORE. — THE HUNTERS. — SAWING A DOCK. — FROZEN UP.

I NAMED our harbor Port Foulke, in honor of my friend, the late William Parker Foulke, of Philadelphia, who was one of the earliest, and continued to be throughout one of the most constant advocates of the expedition.

It was well sheltered except from the southwest, toward which quarter it was quite exposed; but, judging from our recent experience, we had little reason to fear wind from that direction; and we were protected from the drift-ice by a cluster of bergs which lay grounded off the mouth of the harbor.

Our position was, even for the Greenland coast, not so satisfactory as I could have wished. Had I reached Fog Inlet we should have gained some advantages over our present location, and would have been indeed better situated than was Dr. Kane at Van Rensselaer Harbor; and we would then be as sure of an early liberation as we were likely to be at Port Foulke. In truth, the principal advantage which it possessed was that we would not be held very late the next summer, and there was no possible risk of my vessel being caught in a trap like that of the *Advance*. Besides this prospect of a speedy liberation to recommend it, there seemed to be a fair chance of an abundant supply of game.

From Dr. Kane's winter quarters we were not very remote, the distance being about twenty miles in latitude, and about eighty by the coast. We were eight nautical miles in a northeasterly direction from Cape Alexander, and lay deep within the recesses of a craggy, cliff-lined bight of dark, reddish-brown sienitic rock, which looked gloomy enough. This bight is prolonged by three small islands which figure in my journal as "The Youngsters," and which bear on my chart the names of Radcliffe, Knorr, and Starr. At the head of the bight there is a series of terraced beaches composed of loose shingle.

The ice soon closed around us.

My chief concern now was to prepare for the winter, in such a manner as to insure safety to the schooner and comfort to my party. While this was being done I did not, however, lose sight of the scientific labors; but, for the time, these had to be made subordinate to more serious concerns. There was much to do, but my former experience greatly simplified my cares.

Mr. Sonntag, with Radcliffe, Knorr, and Starr to assist him, took general charge of such scientific work as we found ourselves able to manage; and Jensen, with Hans and Peter, were detailed as an organized hunting force. Mr. Dodge, with the body of the crew, discharged the cargo, and, carrying it to the shore, swung it with a derrick up on the lower terrace, which was thirty feet above the tide, and there deposited it in a store-house made of stones and roofed with our old sails. This was a very laborious operation. The beach was shallow, the bank sloping, and the ice not

PREPARING FOR WINTER.

being strong enough to bear a sledge, a channel had to be kept open for the boats between the ship and the shore. The duty of preparing the schooner for our winter home devolved upon Mr. McCormick, with the carpenter and such other assistance as he required. After the sails had been unbent, the yards sent down, and the topmasts housed, the upper deck was roofed in, — making a house eight feet high at the ridge and six and a half at the side. A coating of tarred paper closed the cracks, and four windows let in the light while it lasted, and ventilated our quarters. Between decks there was much to do. The hold, after being floored, scrubbed, and whitewashed, was converted into a room for the crew; the cook-stove was brought down from the galley and placed in the centre of it under the main hatch, in which hung our simple apparatus for melting water from the snow or ice. This was a funnel-shaped double cylinder of galvanized iron connecting with the stove-pipe, and was called the "snow melter." A constant stream poured from it into a large cask, and we had always a supply of the purest water, fully ample for every purpose.

Into these quarters the crew moved on the first of October, and the out-door work of preparation being mainly completed, we entered then, with the ceremony of a holiday dinner, upon our winter life. And the dinner was by no means to be despised. Our soup was followed by an Upernavik salmon, and the table groaned under a mammoth haunch of venison, which was flanked by a ragout of rabbit and a venison pasty.

Indeed, we went into the winter with a most encouraging prospect for an abundant commissariat. The carcasses of more than a dozen reindeer were

OUR COMMISSARIAT. 95

hanging in the shrouds, rabbits and foxes were suspended in clusters from the rigging, and the hearty appetites and vigorous digestions which a bracing air and hard work had given us, were not only amply provided for in the present, but seemed likely to be supplied in the future. The hunters rarely came home empty-handed. Reindeer in herds of tens and fifties were reported upon every return of the sportsmen. Jensen, who had camped out several days on the hunting-grounds, had already cached the flesh of about twenty animals, besides those which had been brought on board. In a single hour I had killed three with my own hands. Both men and dogs were well provided. The dogs, which, according to Esquimau custom, were only fed every second day, often received an entire reindeer at a single meal. They were very ravenous, and, having been much reduced by their hard life at sea, they caused an immense drain upon our resources.

My journal mentions, with daily increasing impatience, the almost constant prevalence of strong northeast winds, which embarrassed us during this period; but at length the wind set in from the opposite direction, and, breaking up the young ice about us, jammed us upon the rocks. If there was little consolation in the circumstance of our situation being thus altered for the worse, there was at least novelty in the caprice of the weather. For once, at least, the uniform "N. E." had been changed in the proper column of the log-book. It was not without difficulty that we succeeded in relieving the schooner from the unpleasant predicament.

While these preparations for the winter were being made, I must not forget the astronomer and his little

THE OBSERVATORY.

corps. Between him and the executive officer there sprung up quite a rivalry of interest. While the one desired a clean ship moored in safety and a well-fed crew, he was naturally jealous of any detail of men for the other; and it must be owned that the men worked with much greater alacrity for the follower of Epicurus than the disciple of Copernicus. An appeal to head-quarters, however, speedily settled the question as to where the work was most needed; and by a judicious discrimination as to what was due to science and what to personal convenience, we managed, while the daylight lasted, to lay the foundation of a very clever series of observations, while at the same time our comfort was secured.

A neat little observatory was erected on the lower terrace, not far from the store-house, and it was promptly put to use; and an accurate survey of the harbor and bay, with soundings, was made as soon as the ice was strong enough to bear our weight. The observatory was a frame structure eight feet square and seven high, covered first with canvas and then with snow, and was lined throughout with bear and reindeer skins. In it our fine pendulum apparatus was first mounted, and Sonntag and Radcliffe were engaged for nearly a month in counting its vibrations. It was found to work admirably. Upon removing this instrument, the magnetometer was substituted in its place, upon a pedestal which was not less simple than original. It was made of two headless kegs, placed end to end upon the solid rock beneath the floor, and the cylinder thus formed was filled with the only materials upon which the frost had not laid hold, namely, beans. Water being poured over these, we had soon, at ten degrees below zero, a neat and perfectly solid

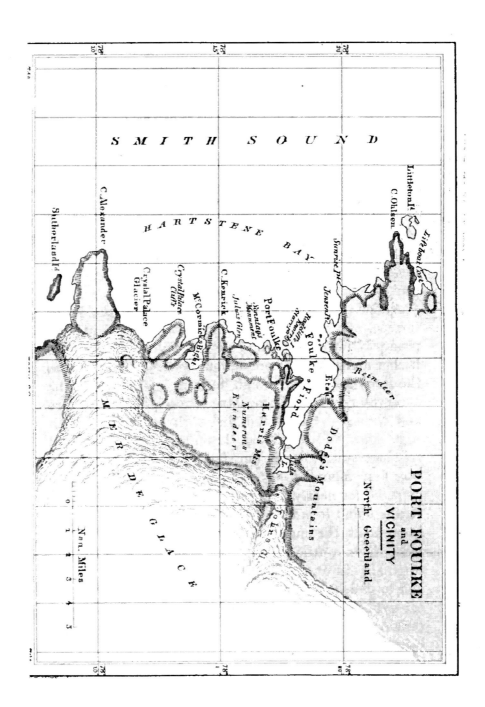

SCIENTIFIC WORK. 97

column ; and it remained serviceable throughout the winter, as no fire of any kind was allowed in this abode of science.[1]

In order to obtain an accurate record of temperature, we erected near the Observatory a suitable shelter for the thermometers. In this were placed a number of instruments, mostly spirit, which were read hourly every seventh day, and three times daily in the interval.[2] In addition to this, we noted the temperature every second hour with a thermometer suspended to a post on the ice. Mr. Dodge undertook for me a set of ice measurements, and the telescope was mounted alongside the vessel, in a dome made with blocks of ice and snow.

But the wind would still give us no rest, and, setting in again from a southerly direction, the ice was once more broken up, and we were again driven upon the rocks, and a second time compelled to saw a dock for the schooner and haul her off-shore. This operation was both laborious and disagreeable, even more so than it had been on the former occasion. The ice was rotten, and so tangled up with the pressure that it was not easy to find secure footing ; and the result was that few of the party escaped with less than one good ducking. These accidents were, however, un-

---

[1] It is proper to mention here that the pendulum and magnetic observations, as well indeed as all others in physical science, were, upon my return, sent to the Smithsonian Institution at Washington, and were placed in the very competent hands of Mr. Charles A. Schott, Assistant in the United States Coast Survey, to whom I am indebted for most able and efficient cooperation, in the elaboration and discussion of my materials, preparatory to their publication in the " Smithsonian Contributions," to which source I beg to refer the reader for details.

[2] These instruments were carefully compared at every ten degrees of temperature down to —40°, and the records were subsequently referred to our "standard." a fine instrument which I had from G. Tagliabue.

7

98 DRIVEN ASHORE BY THE ICE.

comfortable rather than dangerous, as there was always help at hand.

The schooner was, for a time, in rather an alarming situation, and there were many doubts as to whether we should get her off; but not even the consciousness of this circumstance, nor the repeated plunges into the water by the giving way and tilting of the ice, could destroy the inexhaustible fund of good-humor of the ship's company. From this happy disposition I must, however, except two individuals, who were always apt to be possessed of a sort of ludicrous gravity when there was least occasion for it, and, as is usual with such persons, they were not very serviceably employed. One of them, with great seriousness and an immense amount of misdirected energy, commenced chopping into my best nine-inch hawser, that was in nobody's way; and the other, with equal solemnity, began vigorously to break up my oars in pushing off pieces of ice which were doing nobody any harm. He even tried to push the schooner off the rocks, alone and unaided, with the tide-pole, an instrument which had cost McCormick two days to manufacture. Of course, the instrument was broken; but the poor man was saved from the sailing-master's just indignation by following the fragments into the sea, where he was consoled, in the place of prompt assistance, with assurances that if he did not make haste the shrimps would be after him, and leave nothing of him but a skeleton for the Commander's collection. The temperature was not below zero, and no worse results followed our exposure than a slight pleurisy to the mate and a few twitches of rheumatism to the destroyer of my oars.

Our efforts were, however, finally rewarded with

FROZEN UP. 99

success, and the schooner was once more in safety.
The air falling calm, and the temperature going down
to 10° below zero, we were now soon firmly frozen up,
and were protected against any further accidents of
this nature, and were rejoiced to find ourselves able
to run over the bay in security. In anticipation of
this event, I had set Jensen and Peter to work making harness for the dogs, and on that day I took the
first drive with one of my teams. The animals had
picked up finely, and were in excellent condition, and
I had satisfied myself both as to their qualities and
those of their driver, Jensen. The day was indeed a
lively one to all hands. The ice having closed up
firmly with the land, the necessity no longer existed
for keeping a channel open for the boats; and the
hunters, being able now to get ashore with ease, set
off early in the morning, in great glee, after reindeer.

On the day following, the hawsers by which we had
thus far been moored to the rocks were cut out of the
ice and elevated on blocks of the same material. We
also made a stairway of slabs of this same cheap Arctic alabaster, from the upper deck down to the frozen
sea; and, a deep snow falling soon afterward, we
banked this up against the schooner's sides as a further protection against the cold.

During the next few days the teams were employed
in collecting the reindeer which had been cached in
various places, and when this labor was completed our
inventory of fresh supplies was calculated to inspire
very agreeable sensations.

The schooner being now snugly cradled in the ice,
we had no longer occasion for the nautical routine, so
I adopted a landsman's watch, with one officer and
one sailor; the sea day, which commences at noon,

102   MY DOG-TEAMS.

make some short journeys of exploration while the scrap of twilight yet remains to me, and as soon as the men were free I set them to work preparing some conveniences for camping out. I have been ready for several days, but the weather has been unfavorable for any thing more than a few hours' absence; and so our life runs on smoothly into the night.

I had to-day a most exhilarating ride, and a very satisfactory day's work. I drove up the Fiord in the morning, and have returned only a short time since. This Fiord lies directly north of the harbor, and it forms the termination of Hartstene Bay. It is about six miles deep by from two to four wide. Jensen was my driver, and I have a superb turn-out, — twelve dogs and a fine sledge. The animals are in most excellent condition, — every one of them strong and healthy; and they are very fleet. They whirl my Greenland sledge over the ice with a celerity not calculated for weak nerves. I have actually ridden behind them over six measured miles in twenty-eight minutes; and, without stopping to blow the team, have returned over the track in thirty-three. Sonntag and I had a race, and I beat him by four minutes. I should like to have some of my friends of Saratoga and Point Breeze up here, to show them a new style of speeding animals. Our racers do not require any blanketing after the heats, nor sponging either. We harness them each with a single trace, and these traces are of a length to suit the fancy of the driver — the longer the better, for they are then not so easily tangled, the draft of the outside dogs is more direct, and, if the team comes upon thin ice, and breaks through, your chances of escape from immersion are in proportion to their distance from you. The traces are all of

MY DOG-TEAMS. 103

the same length, and hence the dogs run side by side, and, when properly harnessed, their heads are in a line. My traces are so measured that the shoulders of the dogs are just twenty feet from the forward part of the runners.

The team is guided solely by the whip and voice. The strongest dogs are placed on the outside, and the whole team is swayed to right and left according as the whip falls on the snow to the one side or the other, or as it touches the leading dogs, as it is sure to do if they do not obey the gentle hint with sufficient alacrity. The voice aids the whip, but in all emergencies the whip is the only real reliance. Your control over the team is exactly in proportion to your skill in the use of it. The lash is about four feet longer than the traces, and is tipped with a "cracker" of hard sinew, with which a skilful driver can draw blood if so inclined; and he can touch either one of his animals on any particular spot that may suit his purpose. Jensen had to-day a young refractory dog in the team, and, having had his patience quite exhausted, he resolved upon extreme measures. "You see dat beast?" said he. "I takes a piece out of his ear;"—and sure enough, crack went the whip, the hard sinew wound round the tip of the ear and snipped it off as nicely as with a knife.

This long lash, which is but a thin tapering strip of raw seal-hide, is swung with a whip-stock only two and a half feet long. It is very light and is consequently hard to handle. The peculiar turn of the wrist necessary to get it rolled out to its destination is a most difficult undertaking. It requires long and patient practice. I have persevered, and my perseverance has been rewarded; and if I am obliged to turn driver on emergency, I feel equal to the task;

104   MY DOG-TEAMS.

but I fervently hope that the emergency may not
arise which requires me to exhibit my skill.

It is the very hardest kind of hard work. That
merciless lash must be going continually; and it must
be merciless or it is of no avail. The dogs are quick
to detect the least weakness of the driver, and measure him on the instant. If not thoroughly convinced
that the soundness of their skins is quite at his
mercy, they go where they please. If they see a
fox crossing the ice, or come upon a bear track, or
" wind " a seal, or sight a bird, away they dash over
snow-drifts and hummocks, pricking up their short
ears and curling up their long bushy tails for a wild,
wolfish race after the game. If the whip-lash goes
out with a fierce snap, the ears and the tails drop,
and they go on about their proper business; but woe
be unto you if they get the control. I have seen my
own driver only to-day sorely put to his metal, and
not until he had brought a yell of pain from almost
every dog in the team did he conquer their obstinacy.
They were running after a fox, and were taking us
toward what appeared to be unsafe ice. The wind
was blowing hard, and the lash was sometimes driven
back into the driver's face, — hence the difficulty.
The whip, however, finally brought them to reason,
and in full view of the game, and within a few yards
of the treacherous ice, they came first down into a
limping trot and then stopped, most unwillingly. Of
course this made them very cross, and a general fight
— fierce and angry — now followed, which was not
quieted until the driver had sailed in among them and
knocked them to right and left with his hard hickory
whip-stock. I have had an adventure with the same
team, and know to my cost what an unruly set they

AN ARCTIC TEAM.
FROM A SKETCH BY DR. HAYES.

MY DOG-TEAMS. 105

are, and how hard it is to get the mastery of them; but once mastered, like a spirited horse, they are obedient enough; but also, like that noble animal, they require now and then to have a very positive reminder as to whom the obedience is owing.

Wishing to try my hand, I set out to take a turn round the harbor. The wind was blowing at my back, and when I had gone far enough, and wanted to wheel round and return, the dogs were not so minded. There is nothing they dislike so much as to face the wind; and, feeling very fresh, they were evidently ready for some sport. Moreover, they may, perhaps, have wanted to see what manner of man this new driver was. They were very familiar with him personally, for he had petted them often enough; but they had not before felt the strength of his arm.

· After much difficulty I brought them at last up to the course, but I could keep them there only by constant use of the lash; and since this was three times out of four blown back into my face, it was evident that I could not long hold out; besides, my face was freezing in the wind. My arm, not used to such violent exercise, soon fell almost paralyzed, and the whip-lash trailed behind me on the snow. The dogs were not slow to discover that something was wrong. They looked back over their shoulders inquiringly, and, discovering that the lash was not coming, they ventured to diverge gently to the right. Finding the effort not resisted, they gained courage and increased their speed; and at length they wheeled short round, turned their tails to the wind, and dashed off on their own course, as happy as a parcel of boys freed from the restraints of the school-room, and with the wild rush of a dozen wolves. And how they danced along

106 ALIDA LAKE.

and barked and rejoiced in their short-lived liberty!

If the reader has ever chanced to drive a pair of unruly horses for a few hours, and has had occasion to find rest for his aching arms on a long, steep hill, he will understand the satisfaction which I took in finding the power returning to mine. I could again use the whip, and managed to turn the intractable team among a cluster of hummocks and snow-drifts, which somewhat impeded their progress. Springing suddenly off, I caught the upstander and capsized the sledge. The points of the runners were driven deeply into the snow, and my runaways were anchored. A vigorous application of my sinew-tipped lash soon convinced them of the advantages of obedience, and when I turned up the sledge and gave them the signal to start they trotted off in the meekest manner possible, facing the wind without rebelling, and giving me no further trouble. I think they will remember the lesson — and so shall I.

But I set out to record my journey up the Fiord. Reaching the head of it after a most exhilarating ride, we managed, with some difficulty, to cross the tide-cracks, and scrambled over the ice-foot to the land. Here we came upon a broad and picturesque valley, bounded on either side by lofty cliffs — at its further end lay a glacier, with a pool of water a mile long occupying the middle distance. This pool is fed from the glacier and the hill-sides, down which pour the waters of the melting snows of summer. The discharge from it into the sea is made through a rugged gorge which bears evidence of being filled with a gushing stream in the thaw season. Its banks are lined in places with beds of turf, (dried and hardened

MY BROTHER JOHN'S GLACIER. 107

layers of moss,) a sort of peat, with which we can readily eke out our supply of fuel. A specimen of it brought on board burns quite freely with the addition of a little grease. This pool of water, in accordance with Sonntag's wish, bears the name of Alida Lake.

The valley, which I have named "Chester," in remembrance of a spot which I hope to see again, is two miles long by one broad, and is covered in many places, especially along the borders of the lake, with a fine sod of grass, from which the wind has driven the snow and made the locality tempting to the deer. Several herds, amounting in the aggregate to something like a hundred animals, were browsing upon the dead grass of the late summer; and, forgetting for the time the object of my journey, I could not resist the temptation to try my rifle upon them. I was rewarded with two large fat bucks, while Jensen secured an equal number.

The glacier was discovered by Dr. Kane in 1855, and, being subsequently visited by his brother, who was an assistant surgeon in the United States Expedition of Search under Captain Hartstene in 1855, was named by the former, "My Brother John's Glacier." It has been christened a shorter name by the crew, and is known as "Brother John." It has frequently been seen from the hill-tops and bay by all of us, but not visited until to-day. We reached home in time for dinner, weary enough and very cold, for the temperature was several degrees below zero, and the wind was blowing sharply.

During my absence, McCormick has employed the crew in securing the boats, one of which was blown ashore and its side stove in by the violence of the gale, and in sawing out and unshipping the rudder.

108 A SURVEYOR'S CHAIN.

Hans and Peter have been setting fox-traps and shooting rabbits. The foxes, both the white and blue varieties, appear to be quite numerous, and there are also many rabbits, or rather I should say hares. These latter are covered with a long heavy pelt which is a pure white, and are very large. One caught to-day weighed eight pounds.

October 17th.

McCormick, who is general tinker and the very embodiment of ingenuity, has been making for me a surveyor's chain out of some iron rods; and a party, consisting of Sonntag, McCormick, Dodge, Radcliffe, and Starr, have been surveying the bay and harbor with this chain and the theodolite. They seem to have made quite a frolic of it, which, considering the depressed state of the thermometer, is, I think, a very commendable circumstance. Barnum and McDonald have been given a holiday, and they went out with shot-guns after reindeer. They report having seen forty-six, all of which they succeeded in badly frightening, and they also started many foxes. Charley also had a holiday, but, disdaining the huntsman's weapons, he started on a "voyage of discovery," as he styled it. Strolling down into the bay above Crystal Palace Cliffs,[1] he came upon an old Esquimau settlement, and, finding a grave, robbed it of its bony contents, and brought them to me wrapped up in his coat. It makes a very valuable addition to my ethnological collection, and a glass of grog and the promise of other holidays have secured the coöperation of Charley in this branch of science. Charley, by the way, is one of my most reliable men, and gives promise of

[1] Discovered and so named by Captain Inglefield, R. N., in August, 1852.

ESQUIMAU GRAVES. 109

great usefulness. Indeed, everybody in the vessel seems desirous of adding to my collections; but this zeal has to-day led me into a rather unpleasant embarrassment. Jensen, whose long residence among the Esquimaux of Southern Greenland has brought him to look upon that people as little better than the dogs which drag their sledges, discovered a couple of graves and brought away the two skin-robed mummies which they enclosed, thinking they would make fine museum specimens; and in this surmise he was quite right; but, unfortunately for the museum, Mrs. Hans was prowling about when Jensen arrived on board, and, recognizing one of them by some article of its fur clothing as a relative, she made a terrible ado, and could not be quieted even by Jensen's assurance that I was a magician, and would restore them to life when in my own country; so, when I learned the circumstances, I thought it right, in respect to humanity if not to science, to restore them to their stony graves, and had it done accordingly.

The Esquimau graves appear to be numerous about the harbor, giving evidence of quite an extensive settlement at no very remote period. These graves are merely piles of stones arranged without respect to direction, and in the size of the, pile and its location nothing has been consulted but the convenience of the living. The bodies are sometimes barely hidden. Tombs of the dead, they are, too, the mournful evidences of a fast dwindling race.

October 18th.

I have been well repaid for my course in re-interring the mummies; for I have won the gratitude of my Esquimau people, and Hans has brought me in their

110 PUTREFACTION AT LOW TEMPERATURES.

places two typical skulls which he found tossed among the rocks. The little shrimps are also doing me good service. They have prepared for me several skeletons of all varieties of the animals which we have captured. I first have the bulk of the flesh removed from the bones, then, placing them in a net, they are lowered into the fire-hole, and these lively little scavengers of the sea immediately light within the net, in immense swarms, and in a day or so I have a skeleton more nicely cleaned than could be done by the most skillful of human workmen.

A party brought in to-day the carcass of a reindeer which I mortally wounded yesterday, but was too much fatigued to follow. They found its tracks, and, after pursuing them for about a mile, they came upon the animal lying in the snow, dead. It is now discovered that putrefaction has rendered it unfit for use, a circumstance which seems very singular with the temperature at ten degrees below zero. A similar case is mentioned by Dr. Kane as having occurred within his own observation, and Jensen tells me that it is well known that such an event is not uncommon at Upernavik. Indeed, when the Greenlanders capture a deer they immediately eviscerate it. Puzzling as the phenomenon appears at first sight, it seems to me, however, that it admits of ready explanation. The dead animal is immediately frozen on the outside; and there being thus formed a layer of non-conducting ice, as well as the pores being closed, the warmth of the stomach is retained long enough for decomposition to take place, and to generate gas which permeates the tissues, and renders the flesh unfit for food; and this view of the case would seem to be confirmed by the fact that decomposition occurs more readily in

SONNTAG CLIMBS THE GLACIER. 111

the cold weather of midwinter than in the warmer weather of midsummer.

October 19th.

A lively party visited Chester Valley to-day. They started early with two sledges — Sonntag, with Jensen on one, Knorr and Hans on the other. Sonntag carried out the theodolite and chain to make a survey of the glacier. The others, of course, took their rifles. They saw numerous reindeer, but shot only three. One of these was a trophy of Mr. Knorr's, and had like to have cost him dearly. The poor animal had been badly wounded in the valley, and on three legs tried to climb the steep hill. Knorr, following it, reached at length within twenty yards, and brought it down with a well-directed shot; but the hunter and the victim being, unfortunately for the former, in a line, the hunter was carried off his legs, and the two together went tumbling over the rocks in a manner which, to those below, looked rather alarming. Report does not say how the boy extricated himself. It is lucky, however, that, instead of broken bones, he has only a few bruises to show for his adventure.

Sonntag, too, had his story to tell. Reaching the glacier, he ascended to its surface, after travelling two miles along the gorge made by the glacier on the one side and the sloping mountain on the other. The ascent was made by means of steps cut with a hatchet in the solid ice. The glacier was found to be crossed in places by deep narrow fissures, bridged with a crust of snow, and so completely covered as to defy detection. Into one of these, fortunately a very narrow one, the astronomer was precipitated by the giving way of the bridge, and it is probable that he would have lost his life but for a barometer which he carried

112 SEAL-HUNTING. — ESQUIMAU VILLAGE.

in his hand, and which, crossing the crack, broke the fall. The barometer was my best one, and is of course a hopeless wreck.

Carl and Christian, my two Danish recruits from Upernavik, have been setting nets for seal. These nets are made in the Greenland fashion, of seal-skin thongs, with large meshes. They are kept in a vertical position under the ice by stones attached to their lower margin; and the unsuspecting seal, swimming along in pursuit of a school of shrimps for a meal, or seeking a crack or hole in the ice to catch a breath of air, strikes it and becomes entangled in it, and is soon drowned. Most of the winter seal-fishing of Greenland is done in this manner; and it is in this that the dogs are most serviceable, in carrying the hunter rapidly from place to place in his inspection of the nets, and in taking home the captured animals upon the sledge. This species of hunting is attended with much risk, as the hunter is obliged to run out on the newly-formed ice. Jensen has enlivened many of my evenings with descriptions of his adventures upon the ice-fields while looking after his nets. On one occasion the ice broke up, and he was set adrift, and would have been lost had not his crystal raft caught on a small island, to which he escaped, and where he was forced to remain without shelter until the frost built for him a bridge to the main land. The hardihood and courage of these Greenland hunters is astonishing.

Although the wind has been blowing hard, I have strolled over to the north side of the Fiord on a visit to the Esquimau village of Etah, which is about four miles away in a northeasterly direction. The hut there, as I had already surmised, was uninhabited, but bore evidence of having been abandoned only a short

HANS AND PETER

113

time previous. This is the first time that I have seen the place since the night I passed there in December, 1854, — a night long to be remembered.

Near by the hut I discovered a splendid buck leisurely pawing away the snow and turning up the dried grass and moss, of which he was making a well-earned if not inviting meal. Approaching him on the leeward side, I had no difficulty in coming within easy range; but I felt reluctant to fire upon him. He was so intent upon his work, and seemed so little to suspect that these solitudes, through which he had so long roamed unmolested, contained an enemy, that I almost relented; and I did not pull trigger until I had aimed a third time. But, notwithstanding this irresolution, his splendid haunch now hangs in the rigging, and is set apart for some future feast; and I have no doubt that I shall then eat my share of him without once thinking that I had done a deed of cruelty.

October 20th.

I have observed for some days past decided symptoms of a rivalry existing between my two Esquimau hunters, Hans and Peter, both of whom are very serviceable to me. Peter is a very clever little fellow, and withal honest; and he has quite taken my fancy. He is a thorough-bred Esquimau, with very dark complexion, jet-black hair, which he cuts in native fashion, square across his forehead; but he keeps himself clean and neat, and is on all occasions very well behaved. Not only is he a fine hunter, but he possesses great ingenuity, and has wonderful skill with his fingers. I have before me several specimens of his handiwork in the shape of salt-spoons, paper-cutters, and other little trinkets which, with an old file, a knife, and a

8

MY ESQUIMAU PEOPLE.

piece of sand-paper, he has carved for me out of a walrus tusk. They are cut with great accuracy and taste. He is always eager to serve my wishes in every thing; and since I never allow zeal to go unrewarded, he is the richer by several red-flannel shirts, and a suit of pilot-cloth clothes. Of course, Hans is jealous. Indeed, it is impossible for me to exhibit any kindness of this sort to any of my Esquimau people without making Hans unhappy. He avoids showing his temper openly in my presence, but he gets sulky, and does not hunt, or, if ordered out, he comes home without game. He is a type of the worst phase of the Esquimau character. The Esquimaux are indeed a very strange kind of people, and are an interesting study, even more so than my dogs, although they are not so useful; and then the dog can be controlled with a long whip and resolution, while the human animal cannot be controlled with any thing. They might very properly be called a negative people, in every thing except their unreliability, which is entirely positive; and yet among themselves they exhibit the semblance of virtuous conduct, at least in this: that while in sickness or want or distress they never render voluntary assistance to each other, yet they do not deny it; indeed, the active exhibition of service is perhaps wholly unknown or unthought of amongst them; but they do the next best thing — they never withhold it From the rude hut of the hardy inhabitant of these frozen deserts the unfortunate hunter who has lost his team and has been unsuccessful in the hunt, the unprotected family who have lost their head, even the idle and thriftless, are never turned away; but they are never invited. They may come, they may use what they find as if they were members of the family,

ESQUIMAU TRAITS. 115

taking it as a matter of course; but if it were known that they were starving, at a distance, there is no one who would ever think of going to them with supplies. They are the most self-reliant people in the world. It does not appear ever to occur to them to expect assistance, and they never think of offering it.

The food and shelter which the needy are allowed to take is not a charity bestowed; the aid which the hunter gives to the dogless man who jumps upon his sledge for a lift on a journey is not a kindness. He would drop him or give him the slip if occasion offered, even if in a place from whence he could not reach his home. He would drive off and leave him with the greatest unconcern, never so much as giving him a thought. If he should change his abode, the family that had sought his protection would not be invited to accompany him. They might come if able, he could not and would not drive them away; indeed, his language contains no word that would suit the act; but, if not able to travel, they would be left to starve with as much unconcern as if they were decrepit dogs which the hunt had rendered useless.

They neither beg, borrow, nor steal. They do not make presents, and they never rob each other; though this does not hold good of their disposition toward the white man, for from him they make it a habit to filch all they can.

I cannot imagine any living thing so utterly callous as they. Why, even my Esquimau dogs exhibit more sympathetic interest in each other's welfare. They at least hang together for a common object; sometimes fighting, it is true, but they make friends again after the contest is over. But these Esquimaux never fight, by any chance. They stealthily harpoon a trouble-

116 ESQUIMAU TRAITS.

some rival in the hunt, or an old decrepit man or woman who are a burden; or a person who is supposed to be bewitched, or a lazy fellow who has no dogs, and lives off his more industrious neighbors. They even destroy their own offspring when there happen to be too many of them brought into the world, or one should chance to be born with some deformity which will make it incapable of self-support; but they never meet in open combat; at least, such are the habits of the tribes who have not yet been reached in some degree by the influences of Christian civilization, or who have not had ingrafted upon them some of the aggressive customs of the old Norsemen, who, from the ninth to the fourteenth centuries, lived and fought in Southern Greenland.

With such traits of character they are naturally disinclined to be amiable toward any one who is particularly fortunate, and it is not surprising, therefore, that Hans should be envious of Peter. Even had I given the latter no more clothing than was sufficient to cover his nakedness, it would have been all the same. Had I crowded upon Hans the best of every thing in the vessel, without respect to quantity or usefulness, it would not be more than he covets. But the fellow is especially jealous of my personal kind attentions to Peter, for he sees in that the guaranty of still further gifts.

Hans, by the way, keeps up an establishment of his own; and, having a piece of feminine humanity, he can claim the dignity of systematic housekeeping. Within the house on the upper deck he has pitched his Esquimau tent, and, with his wife and baby, half buried in reindeer-skins, he lives the life of a true native. His wife bears the name of Merkut, but is

HANS AND HIS FAMILY. 117

better known as Mrs. Hans. She is a little chubby specimen of womankind, and, for an Esquimau, not ill-looking. In truth she is, I will not say the prettiest, but the least ugly thorough-breed that I have seen. Her complexion is unusually fair, so much so that a flush of red is visible on her cheeks when she can be induced to use a little soap and water to remove the thick plaster of oily soot which covers it. This, however, rarely happens; and as for undergoing another such soaking and scrubbing as the sailors gave her on the way up from Cape York, she cannot be induced to think of it.

The baby is a lively specimen of unwashed humanity. It is about ten months old, and rejoices in the name of Pingasuk — "The Pretty One." It appears to take as naturally to the cold as ducklings to water, and may be seen almost any day crawling through the open slit of the tent, and then out over the deck, quite innocent of clothing; and its mother, equally regardless of temperature or what, in civilized phrase and conventional usage we designate as modesty, does not hesitate to wander about in the same exposed manner. The temperature, however, of the house is never very low, mostly above freezing.

My other two Esquimau hunters, Marcus and Jacob, are lodgers with the Hans family. They are a pair of droll fellows, very different from Hans and Peter. Marcus will not work, and Jacob has grown like the Prince of Denmark, "fat and scant of breath," and cannot. As for hunters, they are that only in name. They have been tried at every thing for which it was thought possible that they could be of any use and it is now agreed on all sides that they can only oe serviceable in amusing the crew and in cutting up

118 MARCUS AND JACOB.

our game; and these things they do well and cheer-fully, for out of these pursuits grows an endless opportunity to feed; and as for feeding, I have never seen man nor beast that could rival them, especially Jacob. The stacks of meat that this boy disposes of seem quite fabulous; and it matters not to him whether it is boiled or raw. The cook declares that "he can eat heself in three meals," meaning, of course, his own weight; but I need hardly say that this is an exaggeration. The steward quotes Shakespeare, and thinks that he has hit the boy very hard when he proclaims him to be a savage "of an unbounded stomach." The sailors tease him about his likeness to the animals which he so ruthlessly devours. A pair of antlers are growing from his forehead, rabbit's hair is sprouting on his distended abdomen, and birds' feathers are appearing on his back; his arms and legs are shortening into flippers, his teeth are lengthening into tusks, and they mean to get a cask of walrus blubber out of him before the spring; all of which he takes good-naturedly; but there is a roguish leer in his eye, and if I mistake not he will yet be even with his tormentors. So much for my Esquimau subjects.

October 21st.

I have had another lively race to the glacier, and have had a day of useful work. Hans drove Sonntag, and Jensen was, as usual, my "whip." We took Carl and Peter along to help us with our surveying; and, although there were three persons and some instruments on each sledge, yet this did not much interfere with our progress. We were at the foot of the glacier in forty minutes.

The dogs are getting a little toned down with use,

HABITS OF DOGS

and I have directed that their rations shall not be quite as heavy as they were. They are lively enough still, but not so hard to keep in hand.

My teams greatly interest me, and no proprietor of a stud of horses ever took greater satisfaction in the occupants of his stables than I do in those of my kennels. Mine, however, are not housed very grandly, said kennels being nothing more than certain walls of hard snow built up alongside the vessel, into which the teams, however, rarely chose to go, preferring the open ice-plain, where they sleep, wound up in a knot like worms in a fish-basket, and are often almost buried out of sight by the drifting snow. It is only when the temperature is very low and the wind unusually fierce that they seek the protection of the snow-walls.

These dogs are singular animals, and are a curious study. They have their leader and their sub-leaders — the rulers and the ruled — like any other community desiring good government. The governed get what rights they can, and the governors bully them continually in order that they may enjoy security against rebellion, and live in peace. And a community of dogs is really organized on the basis of correct principles. As an illustration, — my teams are under the control of a big aggressive brute, who sports a dirty red uniform with snuff-colored facings, and has sharp teeth. He possesses immense strength, and his every movement shows that he is perfectly conscious of it. In the twinkling of an eye he can trounce any dog in the whole herd ; and he seems to possess the faculty of destroying conspiracies, cabals, and all evil designings against his stern rule. None of the other dogs like him, but they cannot help themselves ; they

120 THE LEADER OF THE PACK.

are afraid to turn against him, for when they do so there is no end to the chastisements which they receive. Now Oosisoak (for that is his name) has a rival, a huge, burly fellow with black uniform and white collar. This dog is called Karsuk, which expresses the complexion of his coat. He is larger than Oosisoak, but not so active nor so intelligent. Occasionally he has a set-to with his master; but he always comes off second best, and his unfortunate followers are afterwards flogged in detail by the merciless redcoat. The place of Oosisoak, when harnessed to the sledge, is on the left of the line, and that of Karsuk on the right.

There is another powerful animal which we call Erebus, who governs Sonntag's team as Oosisoak governs mine, and he can whip Karsuk, but he never has a bout with my leader except at his peril and that of his followers. And thus they go along, fighting to preserve the peace, and chawing each other up to maintain the balance of power; and this is all to my advantage; for if the present relations of things were disturbed, my community of dogs would be in a state of anarchy. Oosisoak would go into exile, and would die of laziness and a broken heart, and great and bloody would be the feuds between the rival interests, led by Karsuk and Erebus, before it was decided which is the better team.

Oosisoak has other traits befitting greatness. He has sentiment. He has chosen one to share the glory of his reign, to console his sorrows, and to lick his wounds when fresh from the bloody field. Oosisoak has a queen; and this object of his affection, this idol of his heart, is never absent from his side. She runs beside him in the team, and she fights for him harder

THE QUEEN OF THE KENNEL. 121

than any one of his male subjects. In return for this devotion he allows her to do pretty much as she pleases. She may steal the bone out of his mouth, and he gives it up to her with a sentimental grimace that is quite instructive. But it happens sometimes that he is himself hungry, and he trots after her, and when he thinks that she has got her share he growls significantly; whereupon she drops the bone without even a murmur. If the old fellow happens to be particularly cross when a reindeer is thrown to the pack, he gets upon it with his forefeet, begins to gnaw away at the flank, growling a wolfish growl all the while, and no dog dare come near until he has had his fill except Queen Arkadik, (for by that name is she known,) nor can she approach except in one direction. She must come alongside of him, and crawl between his fore-legs and eat lovingly from the spot where he is eating.

So much for my dogs. I shall doubtless have more to say about them hereafter, but there is only a small scrap of the evening left, and I must go back to "My Brother John's Glacier."

Halting our teams near the glacier front, we proceeded to prepare ourselves for ascending to its surface. Its face, looking down the valley, exhibits a somewhat convex lateral line, and is about a mile in extent, and a hundred feet high. It presents the same fractured surfaces of the iceberg, the same lines of vertical decay caused by the waters trickling from it in the summer, — the same occasional horizontal lines, which, though not well marked, seemed to conform to the curve of the valley in which the glacier rests. The slope backward from this mural face is quite abrupt for several hundred feet, after which the

122 CLIMBING THE GLACIER.

ascent becomes gradual, decreasing to six degrees, where it finally blends with the *mer de glace* which appears to cover the land to the eastward.

At the foot of the glacier front there is a pile of broken fragments which have been detached from time to time. Some of them are very large — solid lumps of clear crystal ice many feet in diameter. One such mass, with an immense shower of smaller pieces, cracked off while we were looking at it, and came crashing down into the plain below.

The surface of the glacier curves gently upward from side to side. It does not blend with the slope of the mountain, but, breaking off abruptly, forms, as I have before observed, a deep gorge between the land and the ice. This gorge is interrupted in places by immense boulders which have fallen from the cliffs, or by equally large masses of ice which have broken from the glacier. Sometimes, however, these interruptions are of a different character, when the ice, moving bodily forward, has pushed the rocks up the hill-side in a confused wave.

The traveling along this winding gorge was laborious, especially as the snow-crusts sometimes gave way and let one's legs down between the sharp stones, or equally sharp ice ; but a couple of miles brought us to a place where we could mount by using our axe in cutting steps, as Sonntag had done before.

We were now fairly on the glacier's back, and moved cautiously toward its centre, fearful at every step that a fissure might open under our feet, and let us down between its hard ribs. But no such accident happened, and we reached our destination, where the surface was perfectly smooth — an inclined plain of clear, transparent ice.

SURVEYING THE GLACIER. 123

Our object in this journey was chiefly to determine whether the glacier had movement; and for this purpose we followed the very simple and efficient plan of Professor Agassiz in his Alpine surveys. First we placed two stakes in the axis of the glacier, and carefully measured the distance between them; then we planted two other stakes nearly midway between these and the sides of the glacier; and then we set the theodolite over each of these stakes in succession, and connected them by angles with each other and with fixed objects on the mountain-side. These angles will be repeated next spring, and I shall by this means know whether the glacier is moving down the valley, and at what rate.

On this, as on every other occasion when we have attempted to do any thing requiring carefulness and deliberation, the wind came to embarrass us. The temperature alone gives us little concern. Although it may be any number of degrees below zero, we do not mind it, for we have become accustomed to it; but the wind is a serious inconvenience, especially when our occupations, as in the present instance, do not admit of active exercise. It is rather cold work handling the instrument; but the tangent screws have been covered with buckskin, and we thus save our fingers from being "burnt," as our little freezings are quite significantly called.

I purpose making a still further exploration of this glacier to-morrow, and will defer until then any further description of it.

During my absence the hunters have not been idle. Barnum has killed six deer; Jensen shot two and Hans nine; but the great event has been the sailing-master's birthday dinner; and I returned on board

124 A SOCIAL RULE.

finding all hands eagerly awaiting my arrival to sit
down to a sumptuous banquet.

I have inaugurated the rule that all birthdays shall
be celebrated in this manner; and, when his birthday
comes round, each individual is at liberty to call for
the very best that my lockers and the steward's store-
room can furnish; and in this I take credit for some
wisdom. I know by experience what the dark cloud
is under which we are slowly drifting, and I know
that my ingenuity will be fully taxed to pass through
it with a cheerful household; and I know still further,
that, whether men live under the Pole Star or under
the Equator, they can be made happy if they can be
made full; and furthermore, at some hour of the day,
be it twelve or be it six, all men must "dine;" for
are they not

> " —————— a carnivorous production,
> Requiring meals, — at least one meal a day?
> They cannot live, like woodcock, upon suction;
> But, like the shark and tiger, must have prey."

And hence they take kindly to venison and such like
things, and they remember with satisfaction the ad-
vice of St. Paul to the gentle Timothy, to "use a little
wine for the stomach's sake."

McCormick was not only the subject to be honored
on this occasion, but to do honor to himself. He has
actually cooked his own dinner, and has done it well.
My sailing-master is a very extraordinary person, and
there seems to be no end to his accomplishments.
Possessing a bright intellect, a good education, and a
perfect magazine of nervous energy, he has, while
knocking about the world, picked up a smattering of
almost every thing known under the sun, from astron-
omy to cooking, and from seamanship to gold-digging.

THE SAILING-MASTER. 125

and he is something of a philosopher, for he declares
that he will have all the comfort he can get when off
duty, while he does not seem to regard any sort of
exposure, and is quite careless of himself, when on
duty; and besides, he appears to possess that highly
useful faculty of being able to do for himself any thing
that he may require to be done by others. He can
handle a marline-spike as well as a sextant, and can
play sailor, carpenter, blacksmith, cook, or gentleman
with equal facility. So much for the man; now for
his feast.

A day or so ago I found lying on my cabin-table a
neat little missive which politely set forth, that "Mr.
McCormick presents the compliments of the officers'
mess to the Commander, and requests the honor of
his company to dinner in their cabin, on the 21st instant, at six o'clock." And I have answered the summons, and have got back again into my own den
overwhelmed with astonishment at the skill of my
sailing-master in that art, the cultivation of which has
made Lucullus immortal and Soyer famous, and highly
gratified to see both officers and men so well pleased.
The bill of fare, "with some original illustrations by
Radcliffe," set forth a very tempting invitation to a
hungry man, and its provisions were generally fulfilled.
There was a capital soup — *jardinière* — nicely fla-
vored, a boiled salmon wrapped in the daintiest of
napkins, a roast haunch of venison weighing thirty
pounds, and a brace of roast eider-ducks, with currant-
jelly and apple-sauce, and a good variety of fresh vegetables; and after this a huge plum-pudding, imported
from Boston, which came in with the flames of *Otard*
flickering all around its rotund lusciousness; and then
there was mince-pie and blanc-mange and nuts and

raisins and olives and Yankee cheese and Boston crackers and coffee and cigars, and I don't know what else besides. There were a couple of carefully-treasured bottles of Moselle produced from the little receptacle under my bunk, and some madeira and sherry from the same place.

The only dish that was purely local in its character was a *mayonnaise* of frozen venison (raw) thinly sliced and dressed in the open air. It was very crisp, but its merits were not duly appreciated. The "Bill" wound up thus:—"Music on the fiddle by Knorr. Song, 'We won't go home till mornin',' by the mess. Original 'yarns' always in order, but 'Joe Millers' forbidden on penalty of clearing out the 'fire-hole' for the balance of the night."

I left the party two hours ago in unrestrained enjoyment of the evening. And right good use do they appear to be making of the occasion. The whole ship's company seem to be like Tam O'Shanter, —

"O'er a' the ills o' life victorious,"

without, however, so far as I can discover, any thing of the cause which led to that renowned individual's satisfactory state of mind. The sailors are following up their feast with a lively dance, into which they have forced Marcus and Jacob; while the officers, like true-born Americans, are making speeches. At this moment I hear some one proposing the health of "The Great Polar Bear."

CHAPTER X.

JOURNEY ON THE GLACIER — THE FIRST CAMP — SCALING THE GLACIER. — CHARACTER OF ITS SURFACE — THE ASCENT. — DRIVEN BACK BY A GALE. — LOW TEMPERATURE — DANGEROUS SITUATION OF THE PARTY — A MOON-LIGHT SCENE

NOTWITHSTANDING that we had no actual daylight even at noontime, yet it was light enough for traveling; and the moon being full, and adding its brightness to that of the retiring sun, I felt no hesitation in carrying into execution my contemplated journey upon the glacier. The severe gales appeared to have subsided, and I thought that the undertaking might be made with safety.

I could do nothing at this period that would bear directly upon my plans of exploration toward the north, and I desired to employ my time to the best advantage. The sea immediately outside of the harbor still remained unfrozen, and we were kept close prisoners within Hartstene Bay — being unable to pass around the capes which bounded it to the north and south. Both Cape Alexander and Cape Ohlsen were still lashed by the troubled sea. There was evidently a large open area in the mouth of the Sound, extending down into the "North Water." When the wind set in from that direction the ice was broken up far within the bay, to be drifted off when it changed to the eastward.

Besides this, even if the ice had closed up, so little faith had I in the autumn as a season for sledge trav-

JOURNEY ON THE GLACIER.

cling upon the sea, that I doubt if I should have attempted a journey in that quarter. In those positions most favorable to early freezing the ice does not unite firmly until the darkness has fully set in ; and traveling is not only attended with much risk, but with great loss of that physical strength so necessary to resist the insidious influences of the malady, hitherto so often fatal to sojourners in the Arctic darkness. And it has been the general judgment of my predecessors in this region, that the late spring and early summer are alone calculated for successful sledge traveling. I recall but two commanders who have sent parties into the field in the autumn, and in both of these cases the attempt was, apparently, not only useless, but prejudicial. The men were broken down by the severity of the exposure — having been almost constantly wet and always cold — and when the darkness set in they were laid up with the scurvy ; and in the spring it was discovered that the depots which they had established were, for the most part, either destroyed by bears or were otherwise unavailable.

With inland traveling the case is different. There is then no risk of getting wet, and I have not ordinarily experienced serious difficulty in traveling at any temperature, however severe, provided I could keep my party dry. Some dampness is, however, almost unavoidable even on land journeys, and this is, in truth, one of the most embarrassing obstacles with which the Arctic traveler has to contend. Even at low temperatures he cannot wholly avoid some moisture to his clothes and fur bedding, caused by the warmth of his own person melting the snow beneath him while he sleeps.

This being our first journey, of course everybody

JOURNEY ON THE GLACIER. 129

was eager to go. I had at first intended to take the dogs, with Jensen as my only companion and driver; but upon talking the matter over with that individual, (in whose judgment with respect to such things I had much confidence), I yielded to his opinion that the dogs were not available for that kind of work. I had reason afterwards to regret the decision, for it was found that they might have been used during some parts of the journey with great advantage. It occurred to me, upon subsequent reflection, that for Jensen's aspersions of the dogs an ample apology might be found in Sonntag's broken barometer.

Having concluded to make the journey with men alone, my choice fell upon Mr. Knorr, John McDonald, Harvey Heywood, Christian Petersen, and the Esquimau Peter. McDonald was one of my very best sailors — a short, well-knit fellow, always ready for work. Christian was not unlike him in make, disposition, and endurance, and, although a carpenter, was yet something of a sailor. He had lived during several years in Greenland, and had become inured to a life of exposure. Heywood was a landsman from the far-West, and had joined me from pure enthusiasm. He was full of courage and energy, and, although occupying a position in the ship's company much inferior to his deserts, yet nothing better could be done for him. He was bent upon accompanying the expedition, no matter in what capacity.[1] With Peter the reader is already acquainted.

We set out on the 22d of October, the day following the celebration which closes the last chapter. Our

---

[1] It affords me great satisfaction to learn recently that Harvey Heywood has served during the late war, in the Southwest, with great gallantry, winning for himself a commission, being attached to the engineers, on the general staff. I found him to be an excellent draughtsman.

THE FIRST CAMP.

sledge was lightly laden with a small canvas tent, two buffalo-skins for bedding, a cooking-lamp, and provisions for eight days. Our personal equipment needs but a brief description. An extra pair of fur stockings, a tin cup, and an iron spoon, per man, was the whole of it.

Our first camp was made at the foot of the glacier. The first camp of a journey anywhere in the world is usually uncomfortable enough, notwithstanding it may perhaps have its bright side; but this one, to my little party, did not appear to have any bright side at all. The temperature was —11°, and we had no other fire than what was needed in our furnace-lamp for cooking our hash and coffee. I believe no one slept. Our tent was pitched, of necessity, on a sloping hill-side, and on the smoothest bed of stones that we could find. We turned out in the moonlight and went to work.

The next journey carried us to the top of the glacier, and it was a very serious day's business. I have already described, in the last chapter, the rugged character of the gorge through which we were obliged to travel, in order to reach a point where we could scale the glacier. The laden sledge could not be dragged over the rocks and blocks of ice, and the men were therefore compelled to carry our equipments, piece by piece, on their shoulders. Reaching the spot where, with Mr. Sonntag, I had before made an ascent, we prepared to hoist the sledge.

The scenery was here quite picturesque. We were standing in a little triangular valley, with a lake in its centre. At our left rose the great glacier, and at our right a small stream of ice poured through a deep gorge. Before us stood a massive pillar of

SCALING THE GLACIER 131

sandstone rock, behind which these two streams uniting, wholly surrounded it, making it truly an island — an island in a sea of ice. The little lake exhibited a phenomenon which I found quite instructive in connection with my present journey. It had been well filled with water at the close of the thaw season, and the ice was formed upon it before the water had subsided. When the lake had drained off under the glacier the ice was left with no other support than the rocks. In many places it had bent down with its own weight, and in one instance I observed that, the pressure being finally exerted on the corners of the remaining slab, this ice, in a temperature below zero, and six inches thick, had been twisted into a shape resembling the mold-board of a farmer's plow.

The first attempt to scale the glacier was attended with an incident which looked rather serious at the moment. The foremost member of the party missed his footing as he was clambering up the rude steps, and, sliding down the steep side, scattered those who were below him to right and left, and sent them rolling into the valley beneath. The adventure might have been attended with serious consequences, for there were many rocks projecting above the snow and ice at the foot of the slope. The next effort was more successful, and the end of a rope being carried over the side of the glacier, the sledge was drawn up the inclined plane, and we started off upon our journey. The ice was here very rough and much broken, and was almost wholly free from snow.

We had not traveled long before an accident happened to me similar to that which had before occurred to Mr. Sonntag. Walking in advance of the party,

THE ASCENT.

who were dragging the sledge, I found myself, without any warning, suddenly sinking through the snow, and was only saved by holding firmly to a wooden staff which I carried over my shoulder, fearful that such a misadventure might befall me. The staff spanned the opening and supported me until I could scramble out. The crack may not have been very deep, but, not having found any support for my feet, I felt glad to have been able to postpone the solution of the interesting scientific question, as to whether these fissures extend entirely through the body of the glacier, to some future occasion.

As we neared the centre of the glacier the surface became more smooth, and gave evidence of greater security. The great roughness of the sides was no doubt due to an uneven conformation of that portion of the valley upon which the ice rested.

Journeying then about five miles, we pitched our tent upon the ice, and, turning into it, after a hearty supper of hash, bread, and coffee, we slept soundly, — being too much fatigued to give thought to the temperature, which had fallen several degrees lower than during the previous night.

On the following day we traveled thirty miles; and the ascent, which, during the last march, had been at an angle of about 6°, diminished gradually to about one third of that angle of elevation; and from a surface of hard ice we had come upon an even plain of compacted snow, through which no true ice could be found after digging down to the depth of three feet. At that depth, however, the snow assumed a more gelid condition, and, although not actually ice, we could not penetrate further into it with our shovel without great difficulty. The snow was covered with

EXCESSIVE COLD   133

ᴊugh which the foot broke at every step,
ᵢg the traveling very laborious.

twenty-five miles were made during the following day, the track being of the same character as the day before, and at about the same elevation; but the condition of my party warned me against the hazard of continuing the journey. The temperature had fallen to 30° below zero, and a fierce gale of wind meeting us in the face, drove us into our tent for shelter, and, after resting there for a few hours, compelled our return. I had, however, accomplished the principal purpose of my journey, and had not in any case intended to proceed more than one day further, at this critical period of the year.

My party had not yet become sufficiently inured to exposure at such low temperatures to enable them to bear it without risk. They were all more or less touched with the frost, and the faces of two of them had been so often frozen that they had become very painful and much swollen, and their feet being constantly cold, I was fearful of some serious accident if we did not speedily seek safety at a lower level. The temperature fell to 34° below zero during the night, and it is a circumstance worthy of mention that the lowest record of the thermometer at Port Foulke, during our absence, was 22° higher. The men complained bitterly, and could not sleep. One of them seemed likely to give up altogether, and I was compelled to send him into the open air to save himself from perishing by a vigorous walk.

The storm steadily increased in force, and, the temperature falling lower and lower, we were all at length forced to quit the tent, and in active exercise strive to prevent ourselves from freezing. To face the wind

134 A DANGEROUS SITUATION.

was not possible, and shelter was nowhere to be found upon the unbroken plain. There was but one direction in which we could move, and that was with our backs to the gale. Much as I should have liked to continue the journey one day more, it was clear to me that longer delay would not alone endanger the lives of one or two members of my party, but would wholly defeat the purposes of the expedition by the destruction of all of us.

It was not without much difficulty that the tent was taken down and bundled upon the sledge. The wind blew so fiercely that we could scarcely roll it up with our stiffened hands. The men were suffering with pain, and could only for a few moments hold on to the hardened canvas. Their fingers, freezing continually, required active pounding to keep them upon the flickering verge of life. We did not wait for neat stowage or an orderly start. Danger suggests prompt expedients.

Our situation at this camp was as sublime as it was dangerous. We had attained an altitude of five thousand feet above the level of the sea, and we were seventy miles from the coast, in the midst of a vast frozen sahara, immeasurable to the human eye. There was neither hill, mountain, nor gorge anywhere in view. We had completely sunk the strip of land which lies between the *mer de glace* and the sea; and no object met the eye but our feeble tent, which bent to the storm. Fitful clouds swept over the face of the full-orbed moon, which, descending toward the horizon, glimmered through the drifting snow that whirled out of the illimitable distance, and scudded over the icy plain; — to the eye, in undulating lines of downy softness; to the flesh, in showers of piercing darts.

JOURNEYING BY MOONLIGHT 135

Our only safety was in flight; and like a ship driven before a tempest which she cannot withstand, and which has threatened her ruin, we turned our backs to the gale; and, hastening down the slope, we ran to save our lives.

We traveled upwards of forty miles, and had descended about three thousand feet before we ventured to halt The wind was much less severe at this point than at the higher level, and the temperature had risen twelve degrees. Although we reposed without risk, yet our canvas shelter was very cold; and, notwithstanding the reduced force of the gale, there was some difficulty in keeping the tent from being blown away.

We reached Port Foulke the next evening, after a toilsome march, without having suffered any serious accident.

The latter part of the journey was made wholly by moonlight. The air was found to be quite calm when we reached the base of the glacier; and the journey down its lower face, and through the gorge, and over the valley, and across Alida Lake and the Fiord, was made in the presence of a scene which was very impressive. Sheets of drifting snow swept over the white-crested hills like insubstantial spirits flitting wildly through the night. These told that the gale yet howled above; but in our lowly shelter the air was still as a cave in the midst of winds. No cloud obscured the broad archway of the skies. The gentle stars, robed in the drapery of night, rejoiced to behold their forms in the smooth mirror of the lake. The glacier threw back the chilly moonbeams. The shadows of the dark cliffs stole into the flood of light which filled the valley. The white Fiord, dotted with islands, wound between the rugged capes, and its ice-clad waters spread out into the bay and then merged with the broad sea. In the dim distance loomed up the lofty snow-clad mountains of the west coast. Upon the sea floated a heavy bank of mist, which, slowly changing when moved by the wind, disclosed within its dark bosom the ghostly form of an iceberg; and a feeble auroral light fringed this sombre cloak of the waves. Angry flashes darted from behind this mass of impenetrable blackness, and, rushing fiercely among the constellations, seemed like fiery arrows shot up by evil spirits of another world.

CHAPTER XI.

IMPORTANT RESULTS OF THE RECENT JOURNEY — THE GLACIER SYSTEM OF GREENLAND — GENERAL DISCUSSION OF THE SUBJECT — ILLUSTRATIONS DRAWN FROM THE ALPINE GLACIERS. — GLACIER MOVEMENT — OUTLINE OF THE GREENLAND *MER DE GLACE*.

THE results of the journey recorded in the last chapter gave me great satisfaction. They furnished an important addition to the observations which I had made in former years; and I was glad to have an opportunity to form a more clear conception of the glacier system of Greenland. The journey possesses the greater value, that it was the first successful attempt which had been made to penetrate into the interior over the *mer de glace.*

Although I had, in my overland journey from Van Rensselaer Harbor with Mr. Wilson, in 1853, reached the face of the *mer de glace,* where it rested behind the lofty chain of hills which runs parallel with the axis of the continent, yet this was the first time that I had actually been upon it; and its vastness did not on the former occasion impress me as now. Even the description of the great Humboldt Glacier which I had from Mr. Bonsall, and the knowledge that I had acquired of the immense glacier discharges of the region further south, failed to inspire me with a full comprehension of the immensity of ice which lies in the valleys and upon the sides of the Greenland mountains.

Greenland may indeed be regarded as a vast reservoir

THE GLACIER SYSTEM.

of ice. Upon the slopes of its lofty hills the downy snow-flake has become the hardened crystal; and, increasing little by little from year to year and from century to century, a broad cloak of frozen vapor has at length completely overspread the land, and along its wide border there pour a thousand crystal streams into the sea.

The manner of this glacier growth, beginning in some remote epoch, when Greenland, nursed in warmth and sunshine, was clothed with vegetation, is a subject of much interest to the student of physical geography. The explanation of the phenomena is, however, greatly simplified by the knowledge which various explorers have contributed from the Alps, — a quarter having all the value of the Greenland mountains, as illustrating the laws which govern the formation and movements of mountain ice, and which possesses the important advantage of greater accessibility.

It would be foreign to the scope and design of this book to enter into any general discussion of the various theories which have been put forth in explanation of the sublime phenomena, which, as witnessed in the Alpine regions, have furnished a fruitful source of widely different conclusions. It was, however, easy to perceive in the grand old bed of ice over which I had traveled, those same physical markings which had arrested the attention of Agassiz and Forbes and Tyndall, and other less illustrious explorers of Alpine glaciers; and it was a satisfaction to have confirmed by actual experiment in the field the reflections of the study. The subject had long been to me one of great interest; and I was much gratified to be able to make a comparison between the Alpine and Greenland ice.

GLACIERS. 139

It was not difficult to read in the immense deposit over which I had walked whence came the suggestion of *dilatation* to Scheuchzer, or of *sliding* to De Saussure; or, in the steady progress of knowledge and discovery, the principles of action that are illustrated by the terms *vitrious* and *viscous* and *differential motion*, as applied to the Alpine ice by eminent explorers of later date.

The subject of Greenland ice is one about which there exists much popular misapprehension. As before stated, I do not here propose to enter into a minute discussion of the manner of its formation and movement, but will content myself with simply recognizing the fact, and with drawing such comparison as may be needful between the mountain ice of Greenland and similar deposits in other quarters of the world. Under this head I trust that the reader may find sufficient interest in the line of argument to follow me through a few pages, in a general review of the whole field. At a later period I will recur to some more specific details of information and discussion, as the narrative carries us to other objects of inquiry.

In order to make the subject clear, I cannot do better than to cite my illustrations from the region of the Alps, where, through a long period, earnest explorers have laboriously pursued their inquiries. One of the most important and gifted of these was M. Le Chanonie Rendu, Bishop of Annecy. This excellent and worthy man, and sincere devotee as well of science as of religion, died some seven years ago. A lifetime spent among the rugged crags and ice-cliffs of the Alpine Mountains had familiarized him with every phase of Nature in that region of sublimity and home of the wonderful. Professor Tyndall says truly

140   ORIGIN OF GLACIERS.

of him, that "his knowledge was extensive, his reasoning close and accurate, and his faculty of observation extraordinary;" and he early brought his splendid faculties of mind and his energy of body and profound love of truth to bear upon the elucidation of those natural phenomena which were constantly exhibited in his presence. After many years of conscientious toil, he gave to the world the results of his systematic investigations in an essay which was published in the Memoirs of the Royal Academy of Sciences of Savoy, entitled, "*Théorie des Glaciers de la Savoie.*"

I will use the information acquired from this source as the basis of my present argument, — to demonstrate, by the law as interpreted to us from the Alps by this learned priest of Annecy, how the Arctic continent receives its cloak of crystals, and how it discharges the superabundant accumulation.

Rendu first observes the piling up of the mountain snows. The snow falling upon the mountains is partly converted into water, which runs away to the river, and through the river to the sea; and is partly converted into ice. The ice thus formed Rendu estimates to equal, in the Alps, fifty-eight inches annually, — "which would make Mont Blanc four hundred feet higher in a century, and four thousand feet higher in a thousand years."

"Now it is evident," observes he, "that nothing like this can occur in Nature."

This ice must be removed by the operation of some natural cause; and observation having shown that this actually takes place, Rendu occupies himself with methods to discover how Nature has performed the task; and he comes to this very rational conclusion:

THE LAW OF CIRCULATION. 141

That the glacier and the river are in effect the same; that between them there is a resemblance so complete that it is impossible to find in the latter a circumstance which does not exist in the former; and as the river drains the *waters* which fall upon the hillsides to the ocean, so the glacier drains the *ice* which forms from the snows on the mountain-sides down to the same level:

And he closes his argument with declaring the Law:—

"The conserving will of the Creator has employed for the permanence of His work the great Law of *Circulation,* which, strictly examined, is found to reproduce itself in all parts of Nature."

And, in illustration of this law, we see that the waters circulate from the ocean to the air by evaporation, from the air again to the earth in the form of dews and rains and snows, and from the earth back again to the ocean through the great rivers which have gathered up the little streams from every hillside and valley.

Now this law of Circulation is, in the icy regions of the Alps, of the lofty Himalayas, of the Andes, of the mountains of Norway and of Greenland, the same as in the lower and warmer regions of the earth, where the rivers drain the surface-water to the sea.

A glacier is in effect but a flowing stream of frozen water; and the *river systems* of the Temperate and Equatorial Zones become the *glacier systems* of the Arctic and Antarctic.

We have now seen that a part of the snow which falls upon the mountains is converted into ice, and this ice, strange though it seems, is movable. By what exact principle of movement has not yet been

142 MOVEMENT OF THE GLACIERS.

decided to the mutual satisfaction of the learned, but it is nevertheless true. Rendu truly remarks: —

"There is a multitude of facts which would seem to necessitate the belief that the substance of glaciers enjoys a kind of ductility, which permits it to mould itself to the locality which it occupies, to grow thin, to swell and to narrow itself like a soft paste."

And this, true of the Alpine passes, is true also of the Greenland valleys. A great frozen flood is pouring down the east and west slopes of the Greenland continent; and, as in the Alps, what is gained in height by one year's freezing is lost by the downward flow of the mobile mass.

And this movement is not embarrassed by any obstacle. The lower chains of hills do not arrest it, for it moulds itself to their form, sweeps through every opening between them, or overtops them. Valleys do not interfere with its onward march, for the frozen stream enters them, and levels them with the highest hills. It heeds not the precipice, for it leaps over it into the plain below, — a giant, frozen waterfall. Winter and summer are to it alike the same. It moves ever forward in its irresistible career, — a vast, frozen tide swelling to the ocean. It pours through every outlet of the coast ranges, down every ravine and valley, overriding every impediment, grinding and crushing over the rocks; and at length it comes upon the sea. But here it does not stop. Pushing back the water, it makes its own coast line; and, moving still onward, accommodating itself to every inequality of the bed of the sea, as it had before done to the surface of the land, filling up the wide bay or fiord, expanding where it expands, narrowing where it narrows, swallowing up the islands in its slow and

FORMATION OF ICEBERGS. 143

steady course, it finally reaches many miles beyond the original shore-line.

And now it has attained the climax of its progress.

When, long ages ago, after pouring over the sloping land, it finally reached the coast and looked down the bay which it was ultimately to fill up, its face was many hundreds of feet high. Gradually it sank below the line of waters as it moved outward, and finally its front has almost wholly disappeared.

In a former chapter I have mentioned that a block of fresh-water ice floating in sea water rises above the surface to the extent of one eighth of its weight and bulk, while seven eighths of it are below the surface. The cause of this is too well known to need more than a passing explanation. Every school-boy is aware that water, in the act of freezing, expands, and that in the crystal condition fresh water occupies about one tenth more space than when in a fluid state; and hence, when ice floats in the fresh water from which it was formed, one tenth of it is exposed above, while the remaining nine tenths are beneath the surface. When this same fresh-water ice (which it will be remembered is the composition of the glacier) is thrown into the sea, the proportion of that above to that below being changed from *one* and *nine* to *one* and *seven,* is due to the greater density of the sea-water, caused by the salt which it holds in solution.

Now it will be obvious that, as the glacier continues to press further and further into the sea, the natural equilibrium of the ice must ultimately become disturbed, — that is, the end of the glacier is forced further down into the water than it would be were it free from restraint, and at liberty to float according to the properties acquired by congelation. The moment

FORMATION OF ICEBERGS.

that more than seven eighths of its front are below the water line, the glacier will, like an apple pressed down by the hand in a pail of water, have a tendency to rise, until it assumes its natural equilibrium. Now it will be remembered that the glacier is a long stream of ice, many miles in extent, and, although the end may have this tendency to rise, yet it is, for a time, held down firmly by the continuity of the whole mass. At length, however, as the end of the glacier buries itself more and more in the water, the tendency to rise becomes stronger and stronger, and finally the force thus generated is sufficient to break off a fragment, which, once free, is buoyed up to the level that is natural to it. This fragment may be a solid cube half a mile through, or even of much greater dimensions. The disruption is attended with a great disturbance of the waters, and with violent sounds which may be heard for many miles ; but, floating now free in the water, the oscillations which the sudden change imparted to it gradually subside ; and, after acquiring its natural equilibrium, the crystal mass drifts slowly out to sea with the current, and is called an ICEBERG.[1]

And thus the glacier has fulfilled its part in the great law of *Circulation* and change.

The dew-drop, distilled upon the tropic palm-leaf, falling to the earth, has reappeared in the gurgling spring of the primeval forest, has flown with the rivulet to the river, and with the river to the ocean ; has then vanished into the air, and, wafted northward by

---

[1] It was formerly supposed that the icebergs were discharged by the force of gravity, but this error, as well as the true theory of berg discharge, was pointed out by Dr. H. Rink, now Royal Inspector of South Greenland. Some fragments are, however, detached from the face of the glacier and fall into the water, but these are always necessarily of comparatively small dimensions, and can scarcely be called bergs.

THE LAW OF CIRCULATION. 145

the unseen wind, has fallen as a downy snow-flake upon the lofty mountain, where, penetrated by a solar ray, it has become again a little globule of water, and the chilly wind, following the sun, has converted this globule into a crystal; and the crystal takes up its wandering course again, seeking the ocean.

But where its movement was once rapid, it is now slow; where it then flowed with the river miles in an hour, it will now flow with the glacier not more in centuries; and where it once entered calmly into the sea, it will now join the world of waters in the midst of a violent convulsion.

We have thus seen that the iceberg is the *discharge* of the Arctic river, that the Arctic river is the glacier, and that the glacier is the accumulation of the frozen vapors of the air. We have watched this river, moving on in its slow and steady course from the distant hills, until at length it has reached the sea; and we have seen the sea tear from the slothful stream a monstrous fragment, and take back to itself its own again. Freed from the shackles which it has borne in silence through unnumbered centuries, this new-born child of the ocean rushes with a wild bound into the arms of the parent water, where it is caressed by the surf and nursed into life again; and the crystal drops receive their long-lost freedom, and fly away on the laughing waves to catch once more the sunbeam, and to run again their course through the long cycle of the ages.

And this *iceberg* has more significance than the great flood which the glacier's southern sister, the broad Amazon, pours into the ocean from the slopes of the Andes and the mountains of Brazil. Solemn, stately, and erect, in tempest and in calm, it rides the

146 BEAUTY AND GRANDEUR OF ICEBERGS.

deep. The restless waves resound through its broken archways and thunder against its adamantean walls. Clouds, impenetrable as those which shielded the graceful form of Arethusa, clothe it in the morning; under the bright blaze of the noonday sun it is armored in glittering silver; it robes itself in the gorgeous colors of evening; and in the silent night the heavenly orbs are mirrored in its glassy surface. Drifting snows whirl over it in the winter, and the sea-gulls swarm round it in the summer. The last rays of departing day linger upon its lofty spires; and when the long darkness is past it catches the first gleam of the returning light, and its gilded dome heralds the coming morn. The Elements combine to render tribute to its matchless beauty. Its loud voice is wafted to the shore, and the earth rolls it from crag to crag among the echoing hills. The sun steals through the veil of radiant fountains which flutter over it in the summer winds, and the rainbow on its pallid cheek betrays the warm kiss. The air crowns it with wreaths of soft vapor, and the waters around it take the hues of the emerald and the sapphire. In fulfillment of its destiny it moves steadily onward in its blue pathway, through the varying seasons and under the changeful skies. Slowly, as in ages long gone by it arose from the broad waters, so does it sink back into them. It is indeed a noble symbol of the Law, — a monument of Time's slow changes, more ancient than the Egyptian Pyramids or the obelisk of Heliopolis. Its crystals were dew-drops and snowflakes long before the human race was born in Eden.

The glacier by which I had ascended to the *mer de glace* furnishes a fine illustration of growth and movement as I have described it. Coming down from the

THE MER DE GLACE. 147

mer de glace in a steadily flowing stream, it has at length filled up the entire valley in which it rests for a distance of ten miles ; and its terminal face, which, as heretofore stated, is one mile across, is now two miles from the sea. The angles and measurements of October, 1860, were repeated in July, 1861, as I shall have occasion hereafter to illustrate, and the result showed the rate of progress of the glacier to be upwards of one hundred feet annually. It will thus be seen that more than a century will elapse before the front of the glacier arrives at the sea ; and since six miles must be traveled over before it reaches deep water, at least five hundred years will transpire before it discharges an iceberg of any considerable magnitude The movement of this glacier is much more rapid than others which I have explored. From "My Brother John's Glacier" the margin of the *mer de glace* sweeps around behind the lofty hills back of Port Foulke, and comes down to the sea in a discharging glacier above Cape Alexander. This has a face of two miles, and some small icebergs are disengaged from it. Thence, after surrounding Cape Alexander, embracing it as with the arm of a mighty giant, it comes again into the water on its south side ; and, continuing thence southward in a succession of broad and irregular curves, a frozen river is poured out from this great inland sea of ice through every valley of the Greenland coast from Smith's Sound to Cape Farewell, and from Cape Farewell on the Spitzbergen side northward to the remotest boundary of the explored. Northward from "My Brother John's Glacier" it makes a broad curve in the rear of the hills hitherto mentioned, and opposite Van Rensselaer Harbor it is between fifty and sixty miles from the sea, where it was reached by Mr. Wilson and myself, as before stated. Its first appearance upon the coast in that direction is at the head of Smith's Sound, in the great Humboldt Glacier, which is reputed to be sixty miles across. Beyond this it presses upon Washington Land, and thence stretches away into the region of the unknown.

CHAPTER XII.

MY CABIN — SURVEYING. — CASTOR AND POLLUX. — CONCERNING SCURVY. — DANGERS OF EATING COLD SNOW. — KNORR AND STARR. — FROST-BITES. — HANS, PETER, AND JACOB AGAIN. — COAL ACCOUNT — THE FIRES. — COMFORT OF OUR QUARTERS — THE HOUSE ON DECK — MILD WEATHER — JENSEN — MRS HANS — JOHN WILLIAMS, THE COOK — A CHEERFUL EVENING

AFTER a sound sleep had in some measure worn off the fatigues of the journey on the glacier, I returned to my diary: —

October 28th.

I am not sorry to get back again into my cosy little cabin. I never knew before what a snug home I have in the midst of this Arctic wilderness. A few days on the ice and a few nights in a tent were required to give me a proper appreciation of its comforts. Once I had begun to regard it as a dingy, musty cell, fit only for a convict. Now it is a real "weary man's rest," an oasis in a desert, a port in a storm. The bright rays of the "fine-eyed Ull-Erin" were not a more cheering guide to the love-bound Ossian than was the glimmer of this cabin-lamp as I came in last night from the cold, — trudging across the waste of snows.

The curtains which inclose what is my lounge by day and my bed by night have taken on a brighter crimson. The wolf and bear skins which cover the lounge and the floor, protecting my feet against the frost which strikes up from below, are positively luxu-

MY CABIN.

rious; the lamp, which I thought burned with a sickly sort of flame, is a very Drummond light compared with what it was; the clock, which used to annoy me with its ceaseless ticking, now makes grateful music; the books, which are stuck about in all available places, seem to be lost friends found again; and the little pictures, which hang around wherever there is room, seem to smile upon me with a sort of sympathetic cheerfulness. Rolls of maps, unfinished sketches, scraps of paper, all sorts of books, including stray volumes of the "Penny Cyclopædia" and Soyer's "Principles of Cooking," drawing implements, barometer cases, copies of Admiralty Blue Books, containing reports of the Arctic Search, track charts of all those British worthies, from Ross to Rae, who have gone in search of Sir John Franklin, litter the floor, and, instead of annoying me with their presence, as they used to do, they seem to possess an air of quiet and refreshing comfort. My little pocket-sextant and compass, hanging on their particular peg, my rifle and gun and flask and pouch on theirs, with my traveling kit between them, break the blank space on the bulk-head before me, and seem to speak a language of their own. My good and faithful friend Sonntag sits opposite to me at the table, reading. I write nestling among my furs, with my journal in my lap; and when I contrast this night with the night on the glacier summit, and listen now to the fierce wind which howls over the deck and through the rigging, and think how dark and gloomy every thing is outside and how light and cheerful every thing is here below, I believe that I have as much occasion to write myself down a thankful man, as I am very sure I do, for once at least, a contented one.

SURVEYING. 151

Sonntag has given me a report of work done during my absence, and so has McCormick. With Jensen I have had a talk about the hunt. I have dined with the officers, and all goes "merry as a marriage bell." My companions on the journey have recovered from their fatigue, and they seem none the worse for the tramp, except such of them as have been touched by the frost; and these look sorry enough. They get little consolation from their shipmates.

I am much gratified to find that every thing has gone on so smoothly while I was away. Sonntag has been twice to the glacier, and has finished the survey and made some spirited sketches. He has also done some valuable work on a base line, accurately measured upon the ice of the outer bay. This base line is 9100 feet long, and his triangulations give the following distances from the western point of Starr Island: —

To Cape Alexander, 8 nautical miles.
" " Isabella, 31 " "
" " Sabine, 42 " "

My commands respecting the hunt have been carefully observed, and numerous additions have been made to our rapidly accumulating stock of fresh food. This gives me much gratification. My experience with Dr. Kane has led me to believe that the scurvy, hitherto so often fatal to Arctic travelers, may be readily avoided by the liberal use of a fresh animal diet; and, although I have a fair supply of canned meats and a good allowance of fresh vegetables, yet I do not wish to depend wholly upon them; and, in order to make assurance doubly sure, I have endeavored to spare no pains in securing whatever game is within our reach. Accordingly I have always had a

152 CONCERNING SCURVY.

well-organized party of hunters, who are exempt from other duty, and this system I propose continuing. The result thus far has shown the correctness of my plan. A more healthy ship's company could not be desired. Not a single case of illness has yet occurred. I do not expect to have any scurvy in my party, and I am firmly impressed with the belief that at Port Foulke men might live indefinitely without being troubled with that "dread scourge of the Arctic Zone." I do not, however, wholly rely upon the hunters. The moral sentiments have much to do with health everywhere; and, with the best food in the world, unhappiness will make more than the heart sick. For my own part, I would rather take my chances against the scurvy with the herbs and the love, than with hatred and the stalled ox. Luckily my ship's company are as harmonious and happy as they are healthy, and the fault will be mine if they do not continue so

Our game-list, according to Knorr, who keeps the tally, sums up as follows: Reindeer 74, foxes 21, hares 12, seals 1, eider-ducks 14, dovekies 8, auks 6, ptarmigan 1. This includes all that has been brought on board from the beginning. Besides these substantial contributions to our winter supplies, there are some twenty or thirty reindeer cached in various places, which are available whenever we choose to bring them in. The dogs are the largest consumers.

I find McCormick suffering with a sore throat and swelled tongue, resulting from eating snow. Leaving me at the glacier, he set out to return on board, and, growing thirsty by the way, without being aware of the evil consequences likely to result therefrom, commenced eating snow to quench it. The effect of this

CASTOR AND POLLUX 153

indulgence was so to inflame the mucous membrane as, in the end, to render the thirst greater and greater the more the desire was indulged. Finally respiration became difficult and painful, and he arrived on board much exhausted. It is a good lesson for the ship's company, — a fact doubtless more consoling to me than to the sufferer.

October 29th.

I went out to-day with Mr. Sonntag to his base line, and made some further measurements. In that direction there are a couple of mammoth icebergs, which I have named "The Twins." They loom up grandly against the dark western sky. Castor carries his head 230 feet above the sea, and Pollux, though of smaller dimensions, is seventeen feet higher.

After our usual evening game of chess, we have talked over some further projects for the field. I propose a drive into the region of Humboldt Glacier, Sonntag one to Van Rensselaer Harbor. It is important that the meridian of this latter place should be connected with that of Port Foulke. I yield to Sonntag for the present, and he starts the day after to-morrow, weather permitting, — a proviso peculiarly necessary in this blustering place. There is very little light left to us, but the moon is full, and will probably serve to guide the party. There was not even the faintest streak of light to-day at three o'clock.

October 30th.

Sonntag is all ready to start. He will take two sledges, with Jensen and Hans for drivers. They are prepared for seven days' absence. I have allowed Sonntag to provide his own equipment, without interference. He has, I think, made it a little more cum-

FROST-BITES.

brous than he should, — a little too much for personal comfort, that will be dead weight. Traveling in this region is governed by very rigorous laws, and very little latitude is allowed in the choice of one's outfit. There is probably no place in the world where the traveler is compelled to deny himself so completely those little articles of convenience which contribute so much to the personal satisfaction. On shipboard he may indulge his taste for luxury to the extent of his means; but when he takes to the ice-fields and the dog-sledge he must come down to hard fare and carry nothing but what is absolutely necessary to sustain life, — and this is simply meat, bread, and coffee, or tea if he prefers it. The snow must serve for his bed, and his only covering must be what is just sufficient to keep him from freezing. Fire he cannot have, except the needful lamp to cook his food, and if he should get cold he must warm himself by exercise. During my late journey to the glacier, I carried for fuel only three quarts of alcohol and the same quantity of oil, and this was not all used.

I went this morning into the hold to look after my companions on the recent journey. They have all recovered from their little frost-bites except Christian, whose nose is as big as his fist and as red as a beet. He takes good-naturedly the jeers of his messmates. Knorr is, however, almost as badly off in the nasal region as Christian, but he has suffered no further misadventure. The nose is, indeed, a serious inconvenience to the Arctic traveler, for it insists upon exposing itself upon every occasion; and if you put it under a mask, it revenges itself by coaxing the moisture of the breath up beneath it, so that in an hour's time the intended protector becomes a worse enemy than the

KNORR AND STARR. 155

wind itself. The mask is, in a little while, but a lump of ice.

My youthful secretary, by the way, bore up bravely on the tramp. I should not have taken him but for his constant and earnest appeals. There does not appear to be much of life in him, but he has pluck, and that is an excellent substitute; and thus far this quality has carried him through My friends told me, before leaving home, that I was needlessly taking him to a very cold grave; but he does not appear inclined to fulfill their predictions, and seems likely to hold his own with the hardest-fisted sailor of the crew. He is but eighteen years old, and, except Starr, who is about the same age, is the youngest member of my party. Starr, too, is a plucky and useful boy. He got into the party against my intentions, but I am very far from sorry. Inspired with enthusiasm for Arctic adventure, he volunteered to go with me in any capacity; and, having no convenient room in the cabin, I told him that he could go in the forecastle, little dreaming that he would accept my offer; but, sure enough, he turned up the next day in sailor's rig. His bright beaver and shining broadcloth and polished pumps had given place to cap and red shirt and sea boots, and I went on board to find the metamorphosed boy of recent elegance manfully at work. Admiring his spirit, I promoted him on the spot, and sent him aft to the sailing-master, — the best I could do for him.

The rivalry between Hans and Peter waxes warmer. My sympathies go with the latter, of which I have to-day given substantial proof. Up to this time Hans has had charge of Sonntag's team, and has used it pretty much as he pleased; but he being absent this morn-

156 HANS, PETER, AND JACOB.

ing, and Jensen being off after some venison, I used Peter to drive me to the lower glacier, where I wished to make some sketches. It appears that this excited Hans' ire against poor Peter; which fact being duly reported by Jensen, I have taken the dogs from Hans and given them into Peter's exclusive charge. So one savage is pleased and the other is displeased; but we shall probably have no public exhibitions of his spleen, as I have read him a lecture upon the evil consequences arising from the display of ill-temper, which he will probably remember, — as likely, however, for evil as for good; for he is not of a forgiving disposition. Jensen tells me that "they have made friends," which probably means mischief.

Hans seems to retain the intelligence for which he was distinguished when in the *Advance*. His character has undergone but little change, and his face expresses the same traits as formerly, — the same smooth, oily voice, the same cunning little eye, the same ugly disposition. I have very little faith in him; but Sonntag has taken him into his favor, and greatly prefers him to Jensen for a dog-driver.

Peter, on the other hand, is a quiet, unobtrusive fellow, and is always ready and willing to do any thing that is required of him, even by the sailors, with whom he is very popular; and, of course, as with good-nature everywhere, he is sometimes imposed upon. Jacob is Peter's brother, and he continues to be the butt of the forecastle. The men have made a bargain with him, and, according to all accounts, it works satisfactorily. He is to wash their dishes, and they in return are to give him all the crumbs that fall from their table. On these he is growing more and more fat, and he has now greater difficulty than ever in getting about. There

COAL ACCOUNT. 157

is a beam in the fore-hold, only two feet and a half from the floor, which he can no longer climb over. His efforts to crawl under it have been not unaptly compared to those of a seal waddling over the ice about its breathing-hole. Mr. Wardle's fat boy was not more shapeless, and, like that plethoric individual, he chiefly divides his time between eating and sleeping His cheeks are puffed out in a very ridiculous manner, and altogether he answers very well the description of Mirabeau's corpulent acquaintance, who seemed to have been created for no other purpose than to show to what extent the human skin is capable of being stretched without bursting. The executive officer tells me that he sent him the other day to the upper deck to dress a couple of reindeer; but, having proceeded far enough to expose a tempting morsel, he halted in his work, carved off a slice of the half-frozen flesh, and was found some time afterwards fast asleep between the two dead animals, with the last fragment of his *bonne bouche* dangling from his lips.

November 1st.

The new month comes in stormy. The travelers were to have set out to-day, but a fierce gale detains them on board. The moon is now three days past full, and if they are delayed much longer they will scarcely have light enough for the journey.

McCormick and Dodge have set a bear-trap between the icebergs Castor and Pollux. It is a mammoth steel-trap, and is baited with venison and fastened with my best ice-anchor. I pity the poor beast that gets his foot in it.

I have been overhauling our coal account, and have regulated the daily consumption for the winter We

THE HOUSE ON DECK.

have thirty-four tons on board, and have but two fires. Two and a half buckets full a day go to the galley stove in the hold, and one and a half to the cabin; and with this consumption of fuel the people live in comfort and cook their food and melt from the ice an abundant supply of water. The ice, which is of the clearest and purest kind, comes from a little berg which is frozen up in the mouth of the harbor, about half a mile away. I have no stove in my own cabin, all the heat which I require coming to me across the companion-way through the slats of my door, from the officers' stove. The temperature in which I live ranges from 40° to 60°, and, among my furs, I lounge through the hours that I do not spend out of doors as snug and comfortable as I could wish to be. Something of my comfort is, however, due to the excess of heat of the officers' quarters. The temperature of their cabin runs sometimes to 75°, and is seldom lower than 60°, and they are at times actually sweltering. Our quarters are throughout free from dampness, and are well ventilated. A portion of the main-hatch above the men's quarters is always open, and the companion-scuttle is seldom closed. This ventilation being through the house on deck, that apartment is kept at quite a comfortable degree of warmth; and it is a very convenient medium between the lower deck and the outer air. In this house such work is performed as cannot be done below; and there, in the dim light of the signal-lamp, which hangs suspended from the main-boom, one may see almost at any time a motley group of men working or playing, as the case may be. Forward in one corner stands Hans's tent, through the slits in which come the cheerful glimmer of a lamp and the lullaby of an Esquimau mother, sooth-

COMFORT OF OUR QUARTERS 159

ing to sleep her "pretty one." On the opposite side is our butcher-shop, where are piled up a lot of frozen reindeer, awaiting Marcus and Jacob, — the butchers. Near by stands our portable forge and anvil, where McCormick is forever blowing the hot embers and pounding at nobody knows what. Dodge says "he is killing time." Under the window amidships stands the carpenter's bench and the vice, where Christian, Jensen, Peter, and Hans are always tinkering at some hunting or sledge implements, — while, mingling promiscuously on the deck, the officers and men may be seen smoking their pipes, and apparently intent only upon as little exertion and as much amusement as the Arctic night will give them. A cheerful light bursts up from below through the hatchways, bringing with it many a cheerful laugh. Around the mainmast stands our gun-rack, and near by is a neat arrangement of McCormick's where every man has a peg for his fur coat, as we do not bring these things below, on account of the great change of temperature producing dampness in them.

November 2d.

The barometer, which yesterday sank to 29.58, has been steadily rising since, and stands now at 29.98, giving us thus a reasonable assurance that the gale will come to an end by and by, and let the travelers off. The gale has made wild work with the ice, breaking it up and driving it out to the southwest until the open water is within two miles of the schooner. The "twins" are right upon the margin of it, and, were they not aground, would float away. One of Sonntag's base-line stations has drifted off, and the beartrap has followed after it, carrying away my fine ice-anchor. Strange, the loose ice has all drifted out of

160 MR. JENSEN.

sight, and not a speck is to be seen upon the unhappy waters which roll and tumble through the darkness around Cape Alexander.

The temperature during this gale has been, throughout, very mild. Although the wind was northeast, it has not been below zero at any time.

November 3d.

The travelers are off at last, and at ten o'clock this evening they disappoint me by not returning. Since it is evident that they have gone around Cape Ohlsen, which I had some reason to doubt, I see no cause why they should not reach their destination. They will have, however, cracks which have been opened by the recent gales, and doubtless heavily hummocked ice, to contend with; and I hardly know how Jensen will get on with this sort of traveling. Bad enough for those who are accustomed to it, it will be a sore trial to him. He is a splendid whip, and drives his dogs superbly when the ice is reasonably smooth, and the sledge glides glibly over it with the dogs at a gallop; but this floundering through hummocks and deep snow-drifts, where the sledge has to be lifted and is often capsized, where the dogs are continually getting into a snarl, — their traces tangled, their tempers ruffled, and a general fight resulting, — is a very different sort of business, and is what he is not used to. To get through with it one requires an almost superhuman stock of enduring patience; and if Jensen returns from this journey with a good record, I shall have no fears for him in the future. He is a very strong and able-bodied man, standing six feet in his shoes, and is of powerful muscular build. The knowledge acquired by some eight years' residence in Greenland, of hunt-

DOMESTIC FELICITY. **161**

ing, and of the Esquimau language, which he speaks like a native, and of the English which he has picked up from the British whale-ships, makes him one of the most useful members of my party.

The men have been busy sewing up seal-skins into coats, pantaloons, and boots, to complete their winter wardrobe. They have tried very hard to get Mrs. Hans to do this work for them, but the indolent creature persistently refuses to sew a stitch. She is the most obstinate of her sex; feels perfectly independent of every thing and of everybody; pouts fiercely when she is not pleased, and gets the sulks about once a fortnight, when she declares most positively that she will abandon Hans and the white men forever, and go back to her own people. She once tried the experiment, and started off at a rapid rate, with her baby on her back, towards Cape Alexander. There had evidently been a domestic spat. Hans came out of his tent as if nothing had happened, and stood at the window leisurely smoking his pipe, and watching her in the most unconcerned manner in the world. As she tripped off south I called his attention to her.

"Yes — me see."

"Where is she going, Hans?"

"She no go. She come back — all right."

"But she will freeze, Hans?"

"She no freeze. She come back by by, — you see."

And he went on smoking his pipe with a quiet chuckle which told how well he understood the whims of his beloved. Two hours afterward she came back, sure enough, very meek and very cold, for the wind was blowing in her face.

The day being Saturday, the sailors are busy by turns at the wash-tub, to have a clean turnout for

162 A CHEERFUL DAY.

Sunday, on which day, even in this remote corner of the world, everybody puts on his best, and at Sunday morning muster my people present a very neat and creditable appearance. The gray uniform which I have adopted as a dress-suit is always worn on that occasion, both by officers and men. Each officer has a sailor for a "washerwoman," and I have mine; and Knorr has just brought me in the most encouraging accounts of his skill, and as a proof of it I found on my table, when I came in out of the moonlight from a tramp to the open water, (where I had been making some observations for temperature,) a well-starched and neatly ironed cambric handkerchief, sprinkled with cologne.

The day, for some reason or other, seems to have been peculiarly bright and cheerful to everybody, and the cheerfulness runs on into the evening. I fancy that our old cook was in a more than usually good humor, and doubtless this has had something to do with it. For my own part, I must acknowledge the power of his artistic skill as affecting the moral sentiments. My walk to the open water was both cold and fatiguing. Desiring to get out as far as I could, I sprang over the loose ice-tables, and reached an iceberg near "The Twins," which I mounted; and, after digging a hole into it, found that it had a temperature only 8° lower than the temperature of the water that floated it, which was 29°. I scrambled back to the fast ice as quickly as I could, for the tide and wind, which was strong from the land, looked very much as if they intended to carry the raft out to sea.

To come back to the cook, — I was in a condition upon my return to do ample justice to a fillet of veni-

JOHN WILLIAMS, THE COOK. 163

son, garnished with currant-jelly, which was awaiting me, and upon the preparation of which the cook had evidently exhausted all his skill; and afterward Knorr made for me, with my alcohol furnace, a cup of aromatic Mocha.

And so one may find pleasure even where Bacchus and Cupid deign not to come. True, this is the region into which Apollo voluntarily wandered after the decree of Olympus made him an exile, and where the Hellenic poets dreamed of men living to an incredible age, in the enjoyment of all possible felicity; but, to say the truth, I question the wisdom of the banished god, as tradition makes no mention of a schooner, and I find that in this "Residence of Boreas" one must look out for himself pretty sharply, — poets to the contrary, notwithstanding.

The cook brought me the dinner himself. "I tinks de Commander likes dis," said he, "coming from de cold."

"Yes, cook, it is really superb. Now, what can I do for you?"

"Tank you, sar! I tinks if de Commander would only be so kind as to give me a clean shirt, I shall be very tankful. He see dis one be very dirty, and I gets no time to vash him."

"Certainly, cook, you shall have two."

"Tank you, sar!" — and he bends himself half double, meaning it for a bow, and goes back well pleased to his stove and his coppers.

Our cook is quite a character. He is much the oldest man on board, and is the most singular mixture of adverse moral qualities that I have ever chanced to meet. He makes it his boast that he has never been off the ship's deck since leaving Boston. "Vat should

I go ashore for?" said he, one day, to some of the officers who were reciting to him the wonders of the land. "Me go ashore! De land be very good place to grow de vegetables, but it no place to be. I never goes ashore ven I can help it, and please my Hebenly Fader I never vill."

I have passed an hour of the evening very pleasantly with the officers in their cabin, have had my usual game of chess with Knorr, and now, having done with this journal for the day, I will coil myself up in my nest of furs and read in Marco Polo of those parts of the world where people live without an effort, know not the use of bear-skins, and die of fever. After all, one's lines might fall in less pleasant places than in the midst of an Arctic winter.

CHAPTER XIII.

INCREASING DARKNESS — DAILY ROUTINE — THE JOURNAL — OUR HOME. —
SUNDAY — RETURN OF SONNTAG — A BEAR-HUNT. — THE OPEN WATER. —
ACCIDENT TO MR KNORR — A THAW — "THE PORT FOULKE WEEKLY
NEWS" — THE TIDE-REGISTER — THE FIRE-HOLE. — HUNTING FOXES —
PETER

THE steadily increasing darkness was driving us
more and more within doors. We had now scarcely
any light but that of the moon and stars. The hunt
was not wholly abandoned, but so few were the hours
wherein we could see that it had become unprofitable.
The gloom of night had settled in the valleys and had
crept up the craggy hills. The darkness being fairly
upon us, we had now little other concern than to live
through it and await the spring, and a return to active
life and the performance of those duties for which
our voyage had been undertaken. As a part of the
history of the expedition, I will continue to give from
my diary our course of life.

November 5th.

Our life has worked itself into a very systematic routine. Our habits during the sunlight were naturally
somewhat irregular, but we have now subsided into
absolute method. What a comfort it is to be relieved
of responsibility! How kind it is of the clock to tell
us what to do! The ship's bell follows it through the
hours, and we count its shrill sounds and thereby
know precisely how to act. The bell tells us when it
is half-past seven in the morning, and then we "turn

166   DAILY ROUTINE.

out." An hour later we breakfast, and at one o'clock we lunch. We dine at six, and at eleven we put out the lights and "turn in," — that is, everybody but the writer of this journal and the "watch." After dinner I usually join the officers at a game of whist, or in my own cabin have a game of chess with Sonntag or Knorr. One day differs very little from another day. Radcliffe shows me the record of the weather when he has made it up, in the evening; and it is almost as monotonous as the form of its presentation. The daily report of ship's duties I have from McCormick, but that does not present any thing that is peculiarly enlivening. I make a note of what is passing, in this voluminous journal, — partly for use, partly from habit, and partly for occupation. The readings of the magnetometer and the barometers and thermometers, and the tide-register, and of the growth of the ice, and all such like useful knowledge, find a place on these pages; but novelties are rare, and when they do come I set opposite to them marginal notes, that I may pick them out from time to time as one does a happy event from the memory.

The ship's duties go on thus : — After breakfast the men "turn to" under the direction of Dodge, and clear up the decks and polish and fill the lamps ; and a detail is made to go out to the iceberg for our daily supply of water. Then the fire-hole is looked after, the dogs are fed, the allowance of coal for the day is measured out, the store-room is unlocked and the rations are served ; and before lunch-time comes round the labors of the day are done. After lunch we take a walk for exercise, and I make it a rule that every one who has not been at work two hours must spend at least that much time in walking for his health.

OUR HOME. 167

For my own part I take an almost daily drive around the bay or a stroll over the hills or out upon the frozen sea. Sometimes I carry my rifle, hoping to shoot a deer or perhaps a bear, but usually I go unarmed and unaccompanied, except by a sprightly Newfoundland pup which rejoices in the name of *General*. This little beast has shared with me my cabin since leaving Boston, and has always insisted upon the choicest place. We have got to be the best of friends. He knows perfectly well when the hour comes to go out after breakfast, and whines impatiently at the door; and when he sees me take my cap and mittens from their peg his happiness is complete. And the little fellow makes a most excellent companion. He does not bore me with senseless talk, but tries his best to make himself agreeable. If in the sober mood, he walks beside me with stately gravity; but when not so inclined he rushes round in the wildest manner, — rolling himself in the snow, tossing the white flakes to the wind, and now and then tugging at my huge fur mittens or at the tail of my fur coat. Some time ago he fell down the hatch and broke his leg, and while this was healing I missed him greatly. There is excellent companionship in a sensible dog.

I try as much as a reasonable regard for discipline will allow to cultivate the social relations and usages of home. True, we cannot get up a ball, and we lack the essential elements of a successful tea-party; but we are not wholly deficient in those customs which, in the land where the loved ones are, take away so much of life's roughnesses. And these little formal observances promote happiness and peace. There is no place in the world where habits of unrestrained famil-

168 RETURN OF SONNTAG.

iarity work so much mischief as in the crowded cabin of a little vessel, nor is there any place where true politeness is so great a blessing. In short, I try to make our winter abode as cheerful as possible; and we shall need all the brightness we can get within these wooden walls, if we would not be overwhelmed with the darkness which is outside. I want my people always to feel that, from whatever hardship and exposure they may encounter, they can here find cheerful shelter from the storms, and repose from their fatigues.

As far as possible, Sunday is observed as we would observe it at home. At ten o'clock, accompanied by the executive officer, I hold an inspection of every part of the vessel, and examine minutely into the health, habits, and comforts of the whole ship's company; and immediately afterward they all assemble in the officers' quarters, where I read to them a portion of the morning service; and this is followed by a chapter from the good Book, which we all love alike, wherever we are. Sometimes I read one of Blair's fine sermons, and when meal time comes round we find it in our heart to ask a continuance of God's provident care; and if expressed in few words, it is perhaps not the less felt.

November 6th.

The travelers have returned, and, as I feared, they have been unsuccessful. Sonntag has dined with me, and he has just finished the recital of the adventures of his party.

The journey was a very difficult one. High hummocks, deep snow-drifts, open cracks, severe winds were their embarrassments; and these are obstacles not to be encountered without danger, fatigue, and frost-bites.

A BEAR HUNT. 169

They had much trouble in getting out of Hartstene Bay, the water coming almost in to the land-ice. Once outside, however, they had an easy run up the coast to Fog Inlet, where one of the sledges broke down, and they came upon open cracks which they could not pass. After repairing the sledge as well as they were able, they turned their faces homeward. When a little way above Cape Hatherton, they struck the trail of a couple of bears; and, giving chase, the animals were overtaken and captured. They proved to be a mother and her cub.

Sonntag has given me a lively description of the chase. The bears were started from the margin of a ridge of hummocked ice where they had been sleeping; and they made at once for the open cracks outside, distant about four miles. As soon as the dogs discovered the trail, they dashed off upon it into the hummocks, without waiting to be directed by their drivers, and utterly regardless of the safety of the sledges or of the persons seated upon them. The hummocks were very high, and the passages between them rough and tortuous. Had the bears kept to them they might have baffled pursuit; for the progress of the sledges was much interrupted, and the track could not always be followed. But the ridge was not above a quarter of a mile in width, and the bears, striking directly across it, evidently preferred seeking safety beyond a crack, over which they could pass by swimming.

The first plunge into the hummocks was rather exciting. Jensen's team led the way, and Hans, following after, rushed up pell-mell alongside. Jensen's sledge was nearly capsized, and Sonntag rolled off in the snow; but he was fortunate enough to catch the

170   A BEAR HUNT.

upstander, and with its aid to recover his seat. The tangled ice greatly retarded the impatient dogs, bringing them several times almost to a stand ; but their eagerness and their drivers' energy finally triumphed over all obstacles, and they emerged at length, after much serious embarrassment, upon a broad and almost level plain, where for the first time the game came in view.

The delay of the sledges in the hummocks had allowed the bears to get the start of fully a mile, and it appeared probable that they would reach the water before they could be overtaken. The dogs seemed to be conscious of this danger, as well as the hunters, and they laid themselves down to the chase with all the wild instinct of their nature. Maddened by the detention and the prospect of the prey escaping them, the blood-thirsty pack swept across the plain like a whirlwind. Jensen and Hans encouraged their respective teams by all the arts known to the native hunter. The sledges fairly flew over the hard snow and bounced over the drifts and the occasional pieces of ice which projected above the otherwise generally smooth surface.

It was a wild chase. The dogs manifested in their speed and cry all the impatience of a pack of hounds in view of the fox, with ten times their savageness. As they neared the game they seemed to Sonntag like so many wolves closing upon a wounded buffalo.

In less than a quarter of an hour the distance between pursuers and pursued was lessened to a few hundred yards, and then they were not far from the water, — which to the one was safety, to the other defeat. During all this time the old bear was kept back by the young one, which she was evidently unwilling

A BEAR HUNT. 171

to abandon. The poor beast was in agony. Her cries were piteous to hear. The little one jogged on by her side, frightened and anxious; and, although it greatly retarded her progress, yet, in full view of the danger, she would not abandon it. Fear and maternal affection appeared alternately to govern her resolution; but still she held firm to her dependent offspring. One moment she would rush forward toward the open water, as if intent only upon her own safety, — then she would wheel round and push on the struggling cub with her snout; and then again she would run beside it as if coaxingly encouraging it to greater speed. Meanwhile her enemies were rushing on and steadily nearing the game. The dogs, forgetting their own fatigue in the prospect of a speedy encounter, pressed harder and harder into their collars. The critical moment was rapidly approaching; and, to add to the embarrassments of the bruin family, the little bear was giving out.

At length the sledges were within fifty yards of the struggling animals. Leaning forward, each hunter now seized the end of the line which bound the traces together in one fastening, and slipped the knot. The sledges stopped, and the dogs, freed from the load which they had been dragging, bounded fiercely for their prey. The old bear heard the rush of her coming enemies, and, halting, squared herself to meet the assault, while the little one ran frightened round her, and then crouched for shelter between her legs.

The old and experienced leader, Oosisoak, led the attack. Queen Arkadik was close beside him, and the other twenty wolfish beasts followed in order of their speed. The formidable front and defiant roar of the infuriated monster split the pack, and they passed to

172   A BEAR HUNT.

right and left. Only one dog faced her, and he, (a young one,) with more courage than discretion, rushed at her throat. In a moment he was crushed beneath her huge paw. Oosisoak came in upon her flank, and Arkadik tore at her haunch, and the other dogs followed this prudent example. She turned upon Oosisoak, and drove him from his hold; but in this act the cub was uncovered. Quick as lightning Karsuk flew at its neck, and a slender yellow mongrel, that we call Schnapps, followed after; but the little bear, imitating the example of its mother, prepared to do battle. Karsuk missed his grip, and Schnapps got tangled among its legs. The poor dog was soon doubled up with a blow in the side, and escaped yowling from the *mêlée*. Oosisoak was hard pressed, but his powerful rival Erebus came to his relief, and led his followers upon the opposite flank, which concentrated onslaught turned the bear again in the direction of her cub in time to save it; for it was now being pulled down and worried by Karsuk and his pack. For a moment disregarding her own tormenters, she threw herself upon the assailants of the cub, and to avoid her blows they quickly abandoned their hold and enabled her once more to draw the frightened though plucky little creature under her. She had come to the rescue at the critical moment, for the poor thing was weakened with the loss of blood, and was fairly exhausted with the fight.

By this time Jensen and Hans had drawn their rifles from the sledge, and hastened on to the conflict. The dogs were so thick about the game that it was some time before they could shoot with safety. They both, however, succeeded at last in getting a fine chance at the old bear, and fired. One ball struck her

A BEAR HUNT. 173

in the mouth, and the other one in the shoulder; but neither did much harm, and brought only a louder roar of pain and anger.

, The dogs, beaten off from their attack on the cub, now concentrated upon the mother, and the battle became more fierce than ever. The snow was covered with blood. A crimson stream poured from the old bear's mouth, and another trickled over the white hair from her shoulder. The little one was torn, and bleeding from many ugly wounds. One dog was stretched out crushed and almost lifeless, and another marked the spot, where his agony was expending itself in piteous cries, with many a red stain.

Sonntag now came up with a fresh weapon. A well-directed volley from the three rifles brought her down upon her side, and the dogs rushed in upon her; but though stunned and weakened by loss of blood, yet she was not mortally hurt; and, recovering herself in an instant, she once more scattered the dogs and again sheltered her offspring. But the fate of the cub was already sealed. Exhausted by the fearful gashes and the throttlings which it had received from Karsuk and his followers, it sank expiring at its mother's feet. Seeing it fall, she forgot, for a moment, the dogs, in her affection, and, stooping down, licked its face. As if unwilling to believe it dead, she tried to coax it to rise and make a still further fight for life. But at length the truth seemed to dawn upon her, and now, apparently conscious that the cub no longer needed her protection, she turned upon her tormenters with redoubled fury, and tried to escape. Another dog was caught in the attack, and was flung howling to join the unlucky Schnapps.

For the first time she now appeared to realize that

174 THE OPEN WATER.

she was beset with other enemies than the dogs. Hans's rifle had missed fire, and he was advancing with a native spear to a hand-to-hand encounter. Seeing him approach, the infuriated monster cleared away the dogs with a vigorous dash, and charged him. He threw his weapon and wheeled in flight. The bear bounded after him, and in an instant more neither speed nor dogs could have saved him. Fortunately, Sonntag and Jensen had by this time reloaded their rifles, and, with well-directed shots, they stopped her mad career. A ball, penetrating the spine at the base of the skull, rolled her over on the blood-stained snow.

The skins being removed, and a portion of the flesh of the young bear prepared for carrying home, the dogs were allowed to gorge themselves, and the party pitched their tent and camped. The next run brought them to the vessel.

The frost has nipped Jensen a little on the nose, and Hans is touched on the cheeks; but Sonntag has come off without a scratch. They have had a very hard journey. Every thing conspired against them; and if they did not reach their destination, they are none the less entitled to great credit for their persevering efforts, continued as they were against such odds.

The existence of this open water greatly puzzles me. No such phenomenon was witnessed in 1853–55 from Van Rensselaer Harbor. Whether it extends across the Sound, or how far to the north or south, I am unable to judge. It is probably merely local, — dependent upon the currents and winds.

November 7th.

The wind is blowing fiercely from the northeast,

A BEAR HUNT.

ACCIDENT TO MR. KNORR. 175

and the temperature is 16° below zero. The effect of the gale has been to drive the ice away again from the outer bay, and we are once more within the sound of the roaring surf.

November 8th.

The air having become somewhat more quiet, I walked out to-day to the open water. Knorr accompanied me. The view from the margin of the ice was dark and fearful. Heavy mist-clouds hung over the sea. Loose ice-fields were drifting through the blackness, crashing harshly against each other, and sending the spray gleaming into the moonlight. The icebergs stood out here and there in stern defiance of the jarring elements, while the tumbling seas struck the white foam far up their lofty sides; and out of the gloom came a wail, as of

> " a thousand ghosts,
> Shrieking at once on the hollow wind."

On our way back, Knorr, who has much skill in getting himself into trouble, failed in a spring as we were making our way over some loose floes, and he plumped bodily into the sea. The accident was not less dangerous than disagreeable; for after 1 had dragged him out of the water there were almost two miles between us and the schooner. Fortunately he arrived on board after a vigorous run with nothing worse than a frozen foot, which did not, however, result in any inconvenience greater than the pain, since my former experience readily suggested the proper remedies. The frozen member was first placed in ice-cold water, the temperature of which was slowly increased from hour to hour until the flesh was completely thawed out. There was no resulting inflammation, and the foot came from the bath without even a blister.

176 A THAW.

November 10th.

We are in the midst of a regular thaw, — a thaw in November under the Pole Star, — truly a strange event to chronicle. The temperature has gone up to 11° above zero.

The cold of the last month has frescoed the house on deck with delicate frost, — the condensed moisture that escapes from below. In many places this frost is two inches thick, and now it is melting. The water drops upon the deck, and every thing thereon is soaked. We have reduced the fires and opened the windows.

November 11th.

The temperature continues to rise, and the thaw goes on. A regular shower falls upon the deck. There is a huge puddle amidships, and the drip, drip, drip is any thing but agreeable.

My journal is looking up, — two novelties in one day. First a thaw, and then a newspaper. The free press follows the flag all over the world, and the North Pole rejoices in "The Port Foulke Weekly News"

During the past week everybody has been much interested in a newspaper enterprise, bearing the above title. Thinking to create a diversion that would confound our enemy, the darkness, I proposed some time ago to the officers that we should publish a weekly paper, offering at the same time my assistance. The proposition was hailed with pleasure, and my fullest anticipations are more than realized. Mr. Dodge and Mr. Knorr undertook to act as editors, at least for the first week, and they have busied themselves gathering from cabin and forecastle whatever was likely to prove attractive, and right good success have they met with. The first number appeared to-day, and it contains

"THE PORT FOULKE WEEKLY NEWS." 177

some things that are "rich and rare," and very clever, and many of the best came from the forward part of the ship.

Its appearance makes quite an event, and, as a hygienic agent, its importance cannot be too highly estimated. The project set everybody on tip-toe of expectation, and for several days past very little else has been talked about but "the paper." All the details of its getting-up have been conducted with a most farcical adherence to the customs prevailing at home. There is a regular corps of editors and reporters, an office for "general news," an "editorial department," and a "telegraph station," where information is supposed to be received from all quarters of the world, and the relations existing between the sun, moon, and stars are duly reported by "reliable correspondents," and pictorial representations of extraordinary occurrences are also received from "our artist on the spot."

Of course, much depended upon the *eclat* with which it burst into being ; and, conscious of this important fact, the editors spared no pains to heighten public curiosity, by the issuing of "hand-bills" and "posters," and all other means known among the caterers for the popular intellectual palate. McCormick lent his assistance, and directed the preparation of a somewhat better dinner than usual ; so that, no matter what might be the merits of this eagerly expected prodigy, it was sure of a hearty reception. Mr. Knorr had charged himself with the mechanical execution, and was known to have the infant periodical in his keeping ; and accordingly, after the cloth was removed, loud calls were made for its production. While he was hauling it out from under his pillow,

178 "THE PORT FOULKE WEEKLY NEWS."

(where it had been carefully stowed out of sight until the auspicious moment should arrive,) demands were made upon him to read it aloud. This he was about to do when some one claimed that so important an event should not pass off so informally. "Agreeably to national usage, we should call a meeting, organize it by the appointment of the proper officers, and name an orator for the occasion. Then, and not until then, can it be said that we have properly inaugurated the important event which has transpired. The public of Port Foulke will not rest content with any less conspicuous mark of glorification over so momentous an occurrence as the establishment of a free press on this remote frontier of civilization."

To this proposal no objection was made, — indeed, it was received with much favor; and the meeting was accordingly organized by unanimously calling Mr. Sonntag to the "chair." After naming the requisite number of vice-presidents and secretaries, Mr. Knorr was selected orator by acclamation. And now there commenced a violent clapping of hands and a rattling of tin cups, mingled with cries of "order" and "hear, hear!" in the midst of which the orator mounted the locker and addressed his auditors as follows : —

"Fellow-citizens : — Called by the unanimous voice of this unenlightened community to inaugurate the new era which has dawned upon a benighted region, it is my happy privilege to announce that we have, at the cost of much time, labor, and means, supplied a want which has too long been felt by the people of Port Foulke. We are, fellow-citizens, no longer without that inalienable birthright of every American citizen, — a Free Press and an Exponent of Public Opinion.

"Overcome with the gravity of my situation, I find

"THE PORT FOULKE WEEKLY NEWS" 179

myself unable to make you a speech befitting the solemnity and importance of the occasion. It is proper, however, that I should state, in behalf of myself and my Bohemian brother, that, in observance of a time-honored custom, we will keep our opinions for ourselves and our arguments for the public. The inhabitants of Port Foulke desire the speedy return of the Sun. We will advocate and urge it. They wish for Light. We will address ourselves to the Celestial Orbs, and point out the opportunities for reciprocity. They are in search of happiness. We will, in pursuance of that same time-honored custom, (which I may say has made the press a power, sir, in this great and glorious nineteenth century) — we will, I say, at all times freely counsel them to the observance of both public and private virtue.

"Fellow-citizens : — This is a memorable epoch in the history of Port Foulke. We are informed that its aboriginal name is Annyeiqueipablaitah, which means, after it is pronounced, 'The Place of the Howling Winds.' On this public occasion it is proper that we should direct our thoughts to the future, especially to our sublime 'mission.' This 'Place of the Howling Winds,' you will observe, fellow-citizens, is on the remotest confines of our wide-spread country, — a country, fellow-citizens, whose vast sides are bathed by the illimitable ocean, and which stretches from the rising of the sun to the setting thereof, and from the Aurora Borealis to the Southern Cross. But why do I say the Aurora Borealis, fellow-citizens? Have we not left that vague border of the national domain far behind us? Yes, fellow-citizens! and it now devolves upon us to bring the vexed question of national boundaries, which has been opened by our enterprise, to a

180 "THE PORT FOULKE WEEKLY NEWS."

point — to a point, sir! We must carry it to the very Pole itself! — and there, sir, we will nail the Stars and Stripes, and our flag-staff will become the spindle of the world, and the Universal Yankee Nation will go whirling round it like a top.

"Fellow-citizens and friends : — In conclusion allow me to propose a sentiment befitting the occasion, — A Free Press and the Universal Yankee Nation. May the former continue in times to come, as in times gone by, the handmaiden of Liberty and the emblem of Progress; and may the latter absorb all Creation and become the grand Celestial Whirligig."

The youthful orator sat down amidst what the press would very properly designate as "tumultuous applause." He had evidently made a favorable impression as well in behalf of himself as of his paper, and we were all the more eager than ever for the reading. After the rattling of the tin cups had subsided, the reading began, and it was not interrupted except by those marks of approbation in which men are always apt to indulge when possessed of a satisfactory dinner, and are listening afterward to good stories. The only regret expressed was that it should come so quickly to an end. The expressions of approval were universal, a vote of thanks was bestowed upon the editors, the orator was toasted, and the occasion wound up in a very lively manner. Having but one copy of the paper, this was handed over to the sailors as soon as Knorr had finished reading it in the cabin, and the marks of approbation were equally reassuring from that quarter. It contains sixteen pages of closely written matter, a somewhat ambitious picture of our winter harbor, a portrait of Sir John Franklin, and a spirited likeness of the General, with his wounded paw

"THE PORT FOULKE WEEKLY NEWS." 181

in a sling. There is a fair sprinkling of "enigmas," "original jokes," "items of domestic and foreign intelligence," "personals," "advertisements," &c., &c., among a larger allowance of more pretentious effusions. Among these latter there is an illustrated prospectus by the senior editor, a poem by the steward, and a song which is addressed to the General. This last the men are now singing, and they seem to take special delight in the chorus, which runs thus: —

> "Hang up the harness and the whip,
> Put up the sledge on the ship;
> There 's no more work for poor Gen-e-ral,
> For he 's going for his wind for to slip."

I am sorry to say that the prophecy therein contained is likely to prove true, for the General is very sick. Poor fellow! he hears every word of this unpitying merriment over his misfortunes, and, could he speak, I have no doubt that he would sigh with Gray's cat, —

> "Alas! —
> A favorite has no friends!"

However, there is a verse coming, to which he is listening attentively, and the very tears mount to his eyes with this unexpected mark of sympathy. For his sake I give it a place here: —

> "Sad times there will be when the General slips his wind,
> And is gathered to his fathers down below,
> And is gone far away with his broken leg and all,
> And is buried underneath the cold snow."

November 12th.

The temperature has gone down within 4° of zero, but there is still much slush and dampness. The snow lying next the ice is filled with water, a circumstance which it is difficult to explain, since the temperature

THE TIDE-REGISTER.

has not, at any time, reached the freezing point, and the ice on which the snow rests is over three feet thick. There would appear to be a sort of an osmotic action taking place. Snow is now beginning to fall, and, as usual, it is very light and beautifully and regularly crystalized. The depth of snow which has fallen up to this time is $15\frac{1}{4}$ inches.

November 13th.

Worse and worse. The temperature has risen again, and the roof over the upper deck gives us once more a worse than tropic shower. The snow next the ice grows more slushy, and this I am more than ever puzzled to understand, since I have found to-day that the ice, two feet below the surface, has a temperature of $20°$; at the surface it is $19°$, and the snow in contact with it is $18°$. The water is $29°$.

The darkness is not yet quite absolute. With some difficulty I can still see to read ordinary print at noon.

November 14th.

The wind has been blowing for nearly twenty-four hours from the northeast, and yet the temperature holds on as before. At 10 o'clock this evening it was $4\frac{1}{2}°$. I have done with speculation. A warm wind from the *mer de glace*, and this boundless reservoir of Greenland frost, makes mischief with my theories, as facts have heretofore done with the theories of wiser men. As long as the wind came from the sea I could find some excuse for the unseasonable warmth.

I have rigged a new tide-register to-day, with the aid of McCormick, my man of all ingenious work. If it prove as effective as it is simple, I shall have a good registry of the Port Foulke tides. It is but a light

THE FIRE-HOLE. 183

rope, to one end of which is attached a heavy stone that rests firmly on the bottom of the sea. The rope comes up through the fire-hole, and passes over a pulley and down again into the water, having at this last end a ten-pound leaden weight. The pulley is attached to an oar which is supported upon two pillars made with blocks of ice. Two feet below the oar, and in close contact with the rope, there is an iron rod, and, the rope being divided into feet and tenths of a foot by little strings having "knots," the stage of the tide is read with the aid of a bull's-eye lantern, as the rod passes the strings. The only drawback is the difficulty in keeping the rope from "fouling" with the ice, as it will do if the fire-hole is not cleared at least four times an hour.

The fire-hole needs no description further than the mere mention of its name. In the event of fire occurring in the schooner, this hole is our only reliance for water, and it is therefore carefully looked after. Thus far the watch has broken it out hourly.

November 15th.

The wind has packed the snow again, and, the temperature having crawled down to zero, the dampness has almost disappeared.

I have presented Hans with a new suit of clothes and a pair of my reddest flannel shirts, thinking by making him better off than Peter to quiet his jealousy. If I have not succeeded in this, I have at least tickled his vanity, for he is a natural-born dandy, and no person on board is so fond of getting himself up as this same savage hunter. At Sunday inspection no one more delights to appear in gorgeous array. With the other Esquimaux he does not deign to asso-

184 STUDIES AND OCCUPATIONS.

ciate on terms of equality. To his finer clothes he doubtless attributes much of his personal importance; — but such things are not confined to Esquimaux.

November 16th.

McCormick has established a school of navigation, and has three good pupils in Barnum, Charley, and McDonald. There is indeed quite a thirst for knowledge in that quarter known as "Mariner's Hall," and an excellent library, which we owe to the kindness of our Boston friends, is well used. In the cabin there is a quiet settlement into literary ease. Dodge has already consumed several boxes of "Littell's Living Age" and the "Westminster Review." Knorr studies Danish, Jensen English, and Sonntag is wading through Esquimau, and, with his long, mathematical head, is conjuring up some incomprehensible compound of differential quantities. As for myself, there is no end to my occupations. The routine of our life causes me much concern and consumes much of my time. Perhaps I give myself needless anxiety about the affairs of my household, and charge myself uselessly with "that care which is the enemy of life," and which long ago disturbed the earthly career of the good old Mother Hubbard; but then I find in it my chief satisfaction, and the leisure hours are filled up pleasantly enough with a book or a walk or this journal. On me the days of darkness have not yet begun to hang heavily, but I can see weariness in the future.

November 17th.

The temperature has fallen to 10° below zero, for which we are duly thankful. Again the air sparkles with cold, and a dead calm has let the frost cover the

HUNTING FOXES. 185

whole outer bay with ice, and the crystal plain extends as far as the eye will carry over the Sound.

The tide-register works quite well, but the youngsters complain bitterly of the trouble in keeping the fire-hole clear of ice, and of reading the ice-coated knots in the darkness. Starr slipped partly into the hole to-day, and nearly ruined the instrument by grasping it for support. The readings are generally quite accurate, but to guard against serious error I have my own way of making a check upon the ice-foot. We have to-day 9 feet 7 inches between ebb and flood.

The poor foxes have become the innocent victims of a new excitement. They are very numerous, and the officers are after them with dead-falls, traps, and guns. Their skins are very fine and pretty, and make warm coats, although I do not perceive that they are used for this purpose; but they go instead into the very safest corners of their lockers. Doubtless "there's a lady in the case."

November 18th.

A calm, cold, clear, quiet day, marked by no unusual event other than the appearance of the second number of "The News." Radcliffe brought it out, and there was another bright evening in this darkness-beleaguered schooner.

November 19th.

Our quiet life has been disturbed by a mysterious event. I have often mentioned in these pages the ludicrous rivalry which grew up between the two Esquimaux, Hans and Peter. Both have been useful, but their motives have been very different. One has shown, like Mr. Wemmick, a laudable desire to get hold of "portable property" by fair means; the other

186 A RUNAWAY.

has been influenced by an envious disposition quite independent of the value attached to his gains. He is a type of a branch of the human family who cannot view with calmness the prosperity of others. Whether this feeling in Hans stopped with the emotion, or whether it has expended itself in crime, remains to be seen.

I was quietly reading on my lounge this morning at two o'clock, when the profound stillness was broken by footsteps in the companion-way. A moment afterward the steward entered without the ceremony of knocking, and stood before me with an atmosphere of alarm about him which seemed to forebode evil. While he was hesitating for speech, I inquired of him what on earth had brought him upon me at this hour. Was the ship on fire? Without heeding my question, he exclaimed, —

"Peter's gone, sir!"

"Gone! Where to?"

"Gone! Run away, sir!"

"Is that all?" and I returned to my book, and bade him go back to his bed.

"It's so, sir! He has run away, sir!"

And sure enough it was so. The earnestness of the steward's manner convinced me at length that something was wrong, and I immediately caused the ship to be searched. But Peter was nowhere to be found. His hammock had not been disturbed since it had been taken down yesterday morning, and he was evidently not in the vessel.

All hands were called, and, while I interrogated the sailors, Jensen obtained what information he could from the Esquimaux. Peter had been on board all the evening, had messed with the men, had smoked

SEARCH FOR THE FUGITIVE. 187

his pipe and drank his coffee as usual, and he appeared to be very happy and well contented. I was greatly puzzled to account for his absence. There being no moon, it seemed impossible that he should have voluntarily gone far from the vessel, and it appeared very unlikely that he would remain long absent unless some accident had overtaken him. But the vague and unsatisfactory answers given by Hans were calculated to arouse suspicion. Hans at last hinted that Peter was afraid of the men; but this was all that I could get out of him. The men declare that he has always been a great pet with them, and I cannot learn that in any instance he has been unkindly treated.

While all this cross-questioning was going on, the lamps were being prepared for a search The people were divided into seven squads, and their lights were soon seen flickering over the harbor. Two hours elapsed, and I had begun to doubt if we should make any discovery, when a signal came from McCormick, who had found fresh tracks on the south side of the harbor, and, at about two and a half miles from the schooner, he had followed them across the broken land-ice, and thence up the steep hill. At the foot of the hill a small bag, containing a few articles of clothing, was picked up, and these were quickly recognized as Peter's property. There was no longer any doubt as to the fact that the steward was right. Peter had surely run away. But what could possibly be the motive? Where had he run to? and what had he run for?

There being clearly no object in following the trail, we returned on board, very much bewildered. Nobody knew any thing about it. Marcus and Jacob declare absolute ignorance, and Hans possesses no other infor-

188 A FRUITLESS SEARCH.

mation than what he has already communicated. But nevertheless, I cannot disabuse my mind of the impression that Hans is really at the bottom of this bad business; and I have dismissed him from my cabin with the assurance that if I find him guilty of treachery toward Peter I will hang him to the yard-arm without hesitation. This he is quite competent to understand, and he declares that he will follow up Peter's tracks and bring the unhappy boy on board. Here, for the present, this painful episode in our quiet life must rest.

November 20th.

Hans, accompanied by one of the sailors, has been out for several hours trying to follow Peter's trail; but a strong wind had drifted the snow, and not a vestige of his footsteps remained. Hans came back evidently a little doubtful as to his fate; but he looked the picture of innocence itself, and did not appear to have upon his mind any other thought than that of sorrow for Peter's unhappy condition.

Where has the fugitive gone? Is he trying to reach the Whale Sound Esquimaux? From Hans's account, there are probably none nearer than Northumberland Island, a hundred miles away; and perhaps the nearest may be still fifty miles further, on the south side of the Sound. Possibly some hunters may temporarily reside on the north side, in which case only is there any chance of safety to the fugitive, should his purpose lie in that direction. It is not at all improbable that Hans has told him positively that Esquimaux are living at Sorfalik, which is not above thirty miles distant, and which place might be readily reached by him, but, without dogs, the journey further south is impracticable. It may be, however, that Hans is en-

PETER STILL ABSENT. 189

tirely innocent of all concern in this mysterious business, and that it is, as Mr. Sonntag thinks, merely an Esquimau whim, and that Peter, provoked at some slight put upon him by one of the crew, has gone off to cool his anger at Etah or in a snow hut. That Hans is guilty seems to be the general belief; and it is very easy to suppose that he has given Peter to understand that the friendly acts of the sailors only covered a hostile purpose; that he knew this because he understood English and overheard their conversation, and has thus induced the poor fellow to fly in precipitate haste from an imaginary danger. And this is the less difficult to understand, that it would be quite in keeping with Esquimau usage. With them, nothing is more likely to excite suspicion of treachery than unusual friendliness, and it is not at all improbable that Hans has first coined a lie, and then, by judiciously fanning the kindling flame with other lies and mysterious hints, he has been at last able to effect a grand *coup*, and drive the poor inoffensive lad into the darkness to seek safety at Sorfalik. Maddened with the threatening danger, he is ready for any thing, — seizes his bag and flies. Seeing our lights on the harbor, he has dropped his bag and hastened his retreating steps. Under this head I can now understand the meaning of what Jensen told me some days ago, that "they have made friends."

November 23d.

Five days have elapsed, and still Peter does not return. I have sent to the hut at Etah, but he has not been there, nor can any traces of him be discovered in the quarters of our cached deer meat. Meanwhile much snow has fallen, and a fierce gale, in which no one could live long without shelter, has been raging.

190 DRIFTING SNOW.

I have had my usual walk, notwithstanding the storm. My furs are now thrown off, and faithful old Carl is beating the snow out of them. It was pounded in by the force of the wind to the very skin, and I was one mass of whiteness. Beard and face were covered, as well as my clothing, and I was not in appearance unlike what I used to imagine Kriss Kringle might be when, "in the days of other years," I fancied him to be making his annual tour of the house-tops.

And my walk has been one of some hardship. I ventured too far out on the sea, and, miscalculating the force of the wind, I found, when I had to face it on my return, that I had before me a somewhat serious task. In the distance I could faintly distinguish the ship's light, and as blast after blast lashed my face with snow, seemingly in malicious spite, and each time with greater fury, I must confess that I more than once wished myself well out of the scrape.

In truth, I was in some danger. The frost touched my cheeks, and, indeed, I should have had no face left had I not repeatedly turned my back to the wind and revived the frosted flesh with my unmittened hand.

But now that I have got snugly stowed away in warmth, I am far from sorry for the adventure. My motive in going out was to get a full view of the storm. The snow which has lately fallen is very deep, and the wind, picking it up from hill-side and valley, seemed to fill the whole atmosphere with a volume of flying whiteness. It streamed over the mountains, and gleamed like witches' hair along their summits. Great clouds rushed frantically down the slopes, and spun over the cliffs in graceful forms of fantastic lightness, and thence whirled out over the frozen sea,

COURAGE. 191

glimmering in the moonbeams. The fierce wind-gusts brought a vast sheet of it from the terraces, which, after bounding over the schooner and rattling through the rigging, flew out over the icy plain, wound coldly around the icebergs which studded its surface, and, dancing and skipping past me like cloud-born phantoms of the night, flew out into the distant blackness, mingling unearthly voices with the roar of booming waves.

And as I think of this wild, wild scene, my thoughts are in the midst of it with my servant Peter. The stiffened ropes which pound against the masts, the wind shrieking through the shrouds, the crashing of the snows against the schooner's sides, are sounds of terror echoing through the night; and when I think that this unhappy boy is a prey to the piercing gale, I find myself inquiring continually, What could possibly have been the motive which led him thus to expose himself to its fury?

After all, what is that which we call courage? This poor savage, who would not hesitate to attack single-handed the fierce polar bear, who has now voluntarily faced a danger than which none could be more dreadful, fleeing out into the darkness, over the mountains and glaciers, and through snow-drifts and storms, pursued by fear, lacks the resolution to face an imaginary harm from his fellow-men. It seems, indeed, to be a peculiarity of uninstructed minds to dread man's anger and man's treachery more than all other evils,— whether of wild beast or storm or pestilence.

CHAPTER XIV.

MIDWINTER. — THE NIGHT OF MONTHS. — BRILLIANCY OF THE MOONLIGHT. — MILD TEMPERATURES. — REMARKABLE WEATHER. — A SHOWER. — DEPTH OF SNOW. — SNOW CRYSTALS. — AN EPIDEMIC AMONG THE DOGS. — SYMPTOMS OF THE DISORDER. — GREAT MORTALITY. — ONLY ONE TEAM LEFT. — NEW PLANS. — SCHEMES FOR REACHING THE ESQUIMAUX IN WHALE SOUND.

THE reader who has followed my diary since we entered Port Foulke will have noticed how gradually the daylight vanished, and with what slow and measured step the darkness came upon us. As November approached its close, the last glimmer of twilight disappeared. The stars shone at all hours with equal brilliancy. From a summer which had no night we had passed into a winter which had no day, through an autumn twilight. In this strange ordering of Nature there is something awe-inspiring and unreal.

We all knew from our school-boy days that, at the poles of the earth there is but one day and one night in the year; but, when brought face to face with the reality, it is hard to realize. And it is harder still to get used to. If the constant sunshine of the summer disturbed our life-long habits, the continual darkness of the winter did more. In the one case the imagination was excited by the ever-present light, inspiring action; in the other, a night of months threw a cloud over the intellect and dwarfed the energies.

To this prolonged darkness the moon gives some relief. From its rising to its setting it shines continually, circling around the horizon, never setting until

MIDWINTER. 193

it has run its ten days' course of brightness. And it shines with a brilliancy which one will hardly observe elsewhere. The uniform whiteness of the landscape and the general clearness of the atmosphere add to the illumination of its rays, and one may see to read by its light with ease, and the natives often use it as they do the sun, to guide their nomadic life and to lead them to their hunting-grounds.

The days and weeks of midwinter passed slowly away. Our experience up to this period was in many respects remarkable. Although sheltered by high lands, we were nevertheless exposed to severe and almost constant northeast winds; and although shut up in polar darkness, and hemmed in by polar ice, an open sea had thus far been within sight of us all the time, and the angry waves were often a threatening terror. Many times we had thought ourselves in danger of being cast adrift with the ice, and carried out to sea in a helpless condition.

The temperature had been strangely mild, a circumstance at least in part accounted for by the open water, and to this same cause was no doubt due the great disturbance of the air, and the frequency of the gales. I have mentioned in the last chapter a very remarkable rise in the thermometer which occurred early in November; but a still greater elevation of temperature followed a few weeks later, reaching as high as 32°, and sinking back to 15° below zero almost as suddenly as it had risen. In consequence of this extraordinary and unaccountable event, the thaw was renewed, and our former discomfort arising from the dampness on the deck and in our quarters was experienced in an aggravated degree. During two days (November 28th and 29th) we could use no other fire than what was necessary for the preparation of our meals, and for melting our necessary supply of water. To add to our astonishment, a heavy fall of snow was followed by a shower of rain, a circumstance which I had not previously witnessed in this latitude except in the months of July and August, and then scarcely more rain fell than on the present occasion. The depth of snow precipitated during this period was likewise remarkable,— the aggregate being 32 inches. In one single day 19 inches were deposited, greater by 5 inches than the entire accumlations of the winter of 1853–54 at Van Rensselaer Harbor. The total amount of snow which had fallen up to the first of December was 48 inches. Being so far north of the line of maximum snows, I was the more surprised, as my former experience appeared to have shown that the region of Smith's Sound was almost wholly free from nubilous deposits.

I was much interested at this warm period in observing how singularly perfect and beautiful were the snow crystals ; and it is a somewhat singular circumstance that the perfect crystals are only exhibited when the snow falls in a temperature comparatively mild. I have not observed them when the thermometer ranged below zero. The snow is then quite dry and hard, and does not exhibit those soft, thin, transparent flakes of the warmer air. With the aid of a magnifying glass, I was enabled to obtain very accurate sketches of a large number of them. Their form was always hexagonal, but the rays were very various in their development, although they all possessed the same radical foundation. The most perfect and full suggested a diminutive fern leaf.

As we neared the climax of the winter the satisfac-

AN EPIDEMIC AMONG THE DOGS 195

tory progress of events became disturbed by a series of misfortunes which largely influenced the destinies of the expedition, and which, by disarranging all of my plans, caused me grave embarrassments.

In a former chapter I have mentioned that a disease had been, for several years, prevailing among the dogs of Southern Greenland, and that a large proportion of these useful animals had fallen victims to it. The cause of this disease had not been determined, but I was led to believe, from what information I could obtain, that it was purely of local origin, and that, therefore, when I had removed my teams from the seat of its influence I would be freed from its dangers. Under this impression I had consumed much time at the Danish-Esquimau settlements, in picking up here and there a dog, until I had obtained thirty-six animals. Up to the first of December they remained in perfect health; and, being fed upon an abundant allowance of fresh meat, I had great confidence that I should be able to carry them through to the spring, and, when the period of my sledge explorations should arrive, that I would have four strong and serviceable teams. My fears were for a time somewhat excited by the information received from Hans, that the Esquimaux of Whale Sound and vicinity, with whom he had been living, were heavy losers by the death of a great number of their dogs, and the description which he gave of this distemper corresponded with that of Southern Greenland; but November being passed without any symptoms of the malady having made its appearance in my splendid pack, I felt hopeful that they would escape the visitation. The loss which Dr. Kane had suffered by the death of his teams was fresh in my recollection; but for this there appeared

196 AN EPIDEMIC AMONG THE DOGS.

to be a sufficient cause. Being almost wholly without fresh food of any kind, he was compelled to subsist his teams upon salt meats, which, giving scurvy to his men, could hardly be expected to act otherwise than injuriously upon the dogs, which had always before been used to a fresh diet of seal meat.

My hopeful anticipations were, however, not realized. One day early in December Jensen reported to me that one of the finest animals had been attacked with the disease, and recommended that it should be shot, to prevent the disease spreading; and this was accordingly done. A few hours afterwards another one was seized in the same manner. The symptoms were at first those of great restlessness. The animal ran several times around the ship, first one way and then the other, with a vague uncertainty in its gait, and with an alternate raising and lowering of the head and tail, every movement indicative of great nervous excitement. After a while it started off toward the mouth of the harbor, barking all the while and seeming to be in mortal dread of some imaginary object from which it was endeavoring to fly. In a little while it came back, still more excited than before. These symptoms rapidly increased in violence, the eyes became bloodshot, froth ran from the mouth, and the dog became possessed of an apparently uncontrollable desire to snap at every thing which came in its way.

The disease ran its course in a few hours. Weakness and prostration followed the excitement, and the poor animal staggered around the vessel, apparently unable to see its way, and finally fell over in a fit. After struggling for a little while in the snow, consciousness returned, and it got again upon its feet.

GREAT MORTALITY OF DOGS. 197

Another fit followed soon afterward; and then they came one after another in rapid succession, until finally its misery was relieved by death, which occurred in less than twenty-four hours from the incipience of the attack. Meanwhile I had watched it closely, hoping to discover some clew to the cause, and to establish a cure. But I could obtain no light whatever. Dissection revealed nothing. There was no apparent inflammation either of the brain, the nerve centres, the spinal cord, or the nerves themselves; and I was wholly at a loss to understand the strange phenomenon. That it was not hydrophobia was shown by the fact that the animal rather desired than shunned water. Many of the symptoms attending that disease were, however, manifested; but it did not, like hydrophobia, appear to be communicated by the bite; for those dogs which happened to be bitten were not more speedily attacked than the others.

This case had scarcely reached its fatal termination before another was reported, and it was relieved of its misery by a bullet. Seven died during four days, and I saw with consternation my fine teams melting away and my hopes endangered; and while this was in progress I could only look on and wonder and experiment, but could never stop the contagion nor arrest the evil.

Among the first dogs attacked was a superb beast that I have before named. He was the best draught animal of my best team, the second leader, — Karsuk. I have never seen such expression of ferocity and mad strength exhibited by any living creature, as he man-ifested two hours after the first symptoms were observed. Thinking that confinement might do good, and desiring to see if the disease would not wear itself

ONLY ONE TEAM LEFT.

out, I had him caught and put into a large box on the deck; but this seemed rather to aggravate than to soothe the violence of the symptoms. He tore the boards with indescribable fierceness, and, getting his teeth into a crack, ripped off splinter after splinter until he had made a hole almost large enough for his head, when I ordered him to be shot. At this moment his eyes were like balls of fire; he had broken off one of his tusks, and his mouth was spouting blood. Soon afterward another fine animal, which seemed to be perfectly well a few moments before, suddenly sprang up, dashed off with a wild yell, wheeled round the harbor, returned to the vessel, and there fell struggling in a fit. I had him tied, but he tore himself loose, and, fearful for the other dogs, he too was killed. Three others died the same day, and the deaths during the first two weeks of December were eighteen. This, with the losses before sustained, left me with only twelve animals. One week later these were reduced to nine.

The serious nature of this disaster will perhaps not at first be apparent to the reader. It will be remembered, however, that my plans of exploration for the coming spring were mainly based upon dogs as a means of transportation across the ice; and now that my teams were so much reduced (and it seemed, indeed, likely that they would all die) it became very evident that, unless I should be able to supply the loss, all of my plans would be rendered abortive.

My anxiety was fully shared by Mr. Sonntag. Having failed in all of our efforts to arrest the fatal tendency of the malady, we could only occupy ourselves with devising ways and means for remedying, in some degree, the evil, or to arrange new plans in conformity with our changed circumstances.

PLANS FOR OBTAINING DOGS.

The first expedient which suggested itself was to open communication with the Esquimaux of Whale Sound, and, in the event of this being accomplished, it was fair to suppose that some animals might be obtained from them. If we could succeed in bringing the tribe to the vessel, we might readily accomplish our wish; for, during the period that their dogs would be in our service, we could, if necessity required it, furnish them all with food, either from our stores or from the hunt.

Hans was consulted concerning the Esquimaux, and from him we learned that there was a family living on Northumberland Island, several families on the south side of Whale Sound, and possibly one or more on the north side. Northumberland Island was about a hundred miles distant as we would be obliged to travel in order to reach it, and the south side of the Sound about one hundred and fifty. That we should communicate with these people at the earliest practicable moment was a matter of the first importance. If a sufficient number of the dogs should remain alive when the moon came in December, it was arranged that Sonntag should make the journey at that period, taking a single sledge, and Hans for a driver. If the dogs should all die, then I intended to go down on foot as soon as possible, and do my best to bring all of the Esquimaux to Port Foulke and Etah, use their dogs while we needed them, and feed and clothe the people in the interval. Meanwhile, however, we could only wait through the mid-December darkness, and hope that the month would end more auspiciously than it had begun.

CHAPTER XV.

THE ARCTIC MIDNIGHT. — SONNTAG STARTS FOR WHALE SOUND. — EFFECTS OF DARKNESS ON THE SPIRITS. — ROUTINE OF DUTIES. — CHRISTMAS EVE. — CHRISTMAS DAY. — THE CHRISTMAS DINNER.

December 22d.

THE sun has reached to-day its greatest southern declination, and we have passed the Arctic Midnight. The winter solstice is to us the meridian day, as twelve o'clock is the meridian hour to those who dwell in lands where the sun comes three hundred and sixty-five times instead of once in the "revolving year."

To me these last four weeks have been eventful ones, and I hail this day with joy, and am glad to feel that we are now on the downward hill-side of the polar darkness. The death of my dogs fills me with sadness, and this sadness is doubled when I think that the disaster has sent Sonntag into the dangers of the night to remedy in season the evil.

Sonntag set out yesterday to reach the Esquimaux. We had talked the matter over from day to day, and saw clearly that it was the only thing to do. Hans told us that the Esquimaux would congregate about Cape York towards the spring, and it was evident that if we waited for daylight they would be beyond our reach. There seemed from Hans's story to be at least a reasonable probability that some of them might be at Sorfalik, or at other stations on the north side of

PREPARATIONS FOR A JOURNEY. 201

Whale Sound, and Hans had no doubt that the journey could be easily made, even if they had to travel to Northumberland Island, or beyond, to Netlik. He was eager to go, and Sonntag, impatient for the trial, was waiting only for the moon and settled weather. Hans was the only available driver, for he alone knew where to find the native villages, and three persons to one sledge was against all the canons of Arctic traveling. Although my suspicions had been aroused against him at the time of Peter's disappearance, yet nothing had been proved, and Sonntag liked him quite as well as Jensen for a driver, and still retained faith in him. To take Jensen was to incumber himself with a useless hindrance. The journey would be a rapid one, and it was important to spare all needless weight. The disease among the dogs subsided six days ago, when the last death occurred, leaving nine good animals, all of which Sonntag took with him.

But little time was required to prepare the party for the journey. Hans made for himself a buffalo bag wherein to sleep, and Sonntag carried for his own use one of bear-skin which he had brought from Upernavik. Their provisions were for twelve days, although it is not expected that they will be absent so long, for the distance can be made to Northumberland Island, if they are required to go so far, in two marches. Sonntag and myself made it in three marches in December, 1854. It is often made by the Esquimaux in one journey, and Hans seemed to look upon it as an easy and trifling task. They carried no tent, intending to rely upon the snow hut, with the construction of which Hans is, of necessity, very familiar, and Sonntag has had, in years past, much experience. The

202 SONNTAG STARTS FOR WHALE SOUND.

plan is that they are to pass over the glacier back of Cape Alexander, in case the ice should not be firm around the cape, and thence to make down the coast directly for Sorfalik. In the event of Esquimaux not being found at that place, they will cross over the Sound directly for Northumberland Island, unless they shall discover good reason for keeping along the coast twenty miles further for Peteravik.

The weather has been quite stormy up to yesterday, when it fell calm, and the thermometer stood at —21°. To-day it has grown much milder, and light snow is falling. The temperature is above zero, and every thing looks promising for the travelers. They have been absent now thirty-six hours, and have, no doubt, passed the cape and are well on the journey.

Their start occasioned much excitement, and aroused the ship's company from a lethargic disposition into which they have lately seemed inclined to fall in spite of every thing. Sonntag was in excellent spirits, and felt confident that he would soon bring the Esquimaux and dogs; and he rejoiced over the prospect of a few days of adventure. Hans was lively and eager. He cracked his whip, the dogs bounded into their collars, and were off at a full gallop. The sledge glided glibly over the snow; and, as they plunged out into the moonlight, we sent after them the true nautical "Hip, hip, hurrah!" three times repeated, and then a "tiger."

December 23d.

I had a strange dream last night, which I cannot help mentioning; and, were I disposed to superstition, it might incline me to read in it an omen of evil. I stood with Sonntag far out on the frozen sea, when suddenly a crash was heard through the darkness, and

ROUTINE OF DUTIES. 203

in an instant a crack opened in the ice between us. It came so suddenly and widened so rapidly that he could not spring over it to where I stood, and he sailed away upon the dark waters of a troubled sea. I last saw him standing firmly upon the crystal raft, his erect form cutting sharply against a streak of light which lay upon the distant horizon.

Our life moves on with unobstructed monotony. There are but few incidents to mark the progress of these tedious hours of darkness. If I have now some fears for Sonntag, yet I envy him, and cannot wonder at his eagerness to go, independent of his important object. A dash among the Esquimau villages, and a few days of combat with the storms would lift one out of the prolonged dullness of this waiting for the day. Any thing in the world is better than inaction and perpetual sameness. Rest and endless routine are our portion. The ship's duties and our social duties are performed from week to week with the same painfully precise regularity. We live by "bells," and this may be true in a double sense. "Bells" make the day, and mark the progress of time. But for these "bells," these endless "bells," I believe we should all lie down and sleep on through the eternal night, and wake not until the day dawned upon us in the long hereafter. "Bells" tell us the hours and the half hours, and change the "watch," and govern the divisons of time, as at sea. "One bell" calls us to breakfast, two to lunch, and "four bells" is the dinner summons. "Six bells" is the signal for putting out the lights, and at "seven bells" we open our eyes again to the same continuous pale glimmer of the keroscne lamp, and we awake again to the same endless routine of occupations, idleness, and *ennui*.

204 ROUTINE OF DUTIES.

The hunters continue to chase the reindeer and foxes in the moonlight, — more, however, from habit and for exercise than from any encouragement they find in success; for, even when the moon shines, they can shoot only at random. The work at the observatory goes on, and when the magnetic "term day" comes round we clamber over the ice-foot every hour, and it marks an event. The occultations of Jupiter's satellites are carefully observed through the telescope, that our chronometers may not go astray; the tide continues to rise and fall, regardless of the vast load of ice that it lifts, and indifferent as to the fact that it is watched. Dodge keeps up his ice-measurements, and finds that the crystal table has got down to our keel ($6\frac{1}{2}$ feet), so that we are resting in a perfect cradle. That the sailors may have something to do, I have given them an hour's task each day sewing up canvas bags for the spring journeys. From the officers I continue to have the same daily reports; the newspaper comes out regularly, and continues to afford amusement; the librarian hands out the books every morning, and they are well read; the officers and the men have no new means of entertainment, and usually fill up the last of the waking hours (I cannot say the evening, where there is nothing else but night) with cards and pipes. I go into the cabin oftener than I used to; but I do not neglect my chess with Knorr, and, until Sonntag left us, I filled up a portion of every evening in converse with him, and, for the lack of any thing new, we talked over and over again of our summer plans, and calculated to a nicety the measure of our labor, and the share which each would take of the work laid out.

And thus we jog on toward the spring; but each

EFFECTS OF DARKNESS. 205

hour of the darkness grows a little longer, and soaks a little more color from the blood, and takes a little more from the elasticity of the step, and adds a little more to the lengthening face, and checks little by little the cheerful laugh and the merry jest that come from the hold and cabin ; and, without being willing to confess it openly, yet we are all forced to acknowledge to ourselves that the enemy does now and then get the better of us, and that we have often to renew the resolution. The novelty of our life is exhausted, and the outside world has nothing new. The moonlight comes and goes again, and the night glistens clear and cold over the white landscape ; and the memory returns unbidden to other days that are fled and gone; and we miss in the sparkling air and the still hour of the winter night the jingling bells, and the sleigh which will always hold one more, and the wayside inn, and the smoking supper that "mine host" serves up, and the crackling blaze of country logs; and then, when we forget the moon, and the snow, and the frost, and recall the summer and the sunshine, we remember that "the seat in the shade of the hawthorn bush" is far away.

December 24th.

Christmas Eve ! What happy memories are recalled by the mention of that name ! How much of youthful promise it brings back to the weary mind and to the aching heart ! How potent is the charm, how magical the influence ! A beam of light has fallen within this little ice-bound vessel, and from the promised morn we catch the same inspiration that has come to all mankind since "that bright and lovely star" first rose to the shepherds of Judea ; for wher-

206 CHRISTMAS EVE.

ever we are on this wide, wide world, we find in the day the symbol which binds us all to one cherished hope. Gladness springs into being with the rising sun, and the Christmas bells, sending their merry voices on the wings of the returning light, encircle the earth in one continuous peal. Their chimes ring out glad tidings everywhere. The joyous music rejoices the lonely watcher on the sea, and the hunter who warms himself beside the embers of his smouldering fire; it penetrates the humble cabin of the slave and the hut of the weary emigrant; it reaches the wanderer on the steppes of Tartary, and the savage in the forest; it consoles the poor and the sorrowing, and the rich and the powerful; and to the sick and to the well alike, wherever they may be under the sun, it brings a blessed brightness; — and it gleams, too,

. . . . "on the eternal snows, beneath the Polar Star,
And with a radiant Cross it lights the Southern deep afar.
And Christmas morn is but the dawn, the herald of a day
That circles in its boundless love, no winter, no decay."

I have never seen the ship so bright and cheerful. Sundry boxes have been produced from out-of-the-way corners, and from the magical manner of their appearance one might think that Santa Claus had charged himself with a special mission to this little world, before he had begun to fill the shoes and stockings and to give marriage portions to destitute maidens, in the dear old lands where he is patron of the "Christ Kinkle Eve," and where the silver cord binding the affections is freshened once a year with the Christmas offering. The cabin-table fairly groans under a mass of holiday fare, — kindly mementos from those who are talking about us to-night around the family fire-

CHRISTMAS DAY. 207

side. Shoals of bon-bons, and "Christmas cakes" of every imaginable kind, bearing all sorts of tender mottoes, come out of their tin cases, setting off prospective indigestion against glad hearts.

Everybody has been busy to-day getting ready to celebrate the morrow and to keep the holidays. To this praiseworthy purpose I give, of course, every encouragement. The ship's stores contain nothing that is too good for the Christmas feast, which McCormick promises shall outdo that of his birthday. Unfortunately he will be unable to give it his personal attention, for he is laid up with a frosted foot which he got while hunting, in some manner known only to himself. As no one at home likes to confess that he has been run away with and thrown from his steed, so no one here cares to own to the power of Jack Frost over him. To be frost-bitten is the one standing reproach of this community.

December 26th.

Christmas has come and gone again, and has left upon the minds of all of us a pleasant recollection. To me it would have been a day of unalloyed pleasure, had it not been that my thoughts followed Sonntag, and dwelt upon the sad loss that I have suffered in the death of my dogs; for the people were gay and lively, and to see them thus is now my first concern. Aside from all sentiment connected with wishing people happy, to me it has another meaning, for it is the guaranty of health.

The ship's bell was hoisted to the mast-head, and while the bells of other lands were pealing through the sunlight, and over a world of gladness, ours sent its clear notes ringing through the darkness and the

208 CHRISTMAS DAY.

solitude. After this we met together in the cabin, and gave our thanks in our own modest way for the blessings which kind Heaven had vouchsafed us; and then each one set himself about his allotted duties. It is needless to say that these duties concerned chiefly the preparation and advancement of every thing which concerned a "Christmas dinner." The officers dressed the cabin with flags, and the sailors decorated their walls and beams with stripes of red, white, and blue flannel which was loaned to them from the ship's stores. The schooner was illuminated throughout, and every lamp was called into requisition. An extra allowance of oil was granted to the occasion, and the upper-deck was refulgent with light. Two immense chandeliers were constructed for the dinnertables, and some gold and silver paper, strings of spangles, and strips of braid, kindly presented to us by Mr. Horstmann for the winter theatricals, which have never come off, covered the wood of which they were composed, and gave them quite an air of splendor; while two dozen of spermacetti candles brilliantly illuminated the apartments in which they hung.

A short time before the dinner-hour I visited the men's quarters, at their request, and was as much gratified with the taste that they had exhibited as with the heartiness with which they entered into the spirit of the day. Every nook and corner of the hold was as clean and tidy as possible. Everybody was busy and delighted. The cook might, however, be regarded as an exception to the latter rule, for the success of everybody's projects depended upon his skill, and he was closely watched. I halted at his red-hot galley-stove, and wished him a merry Christmas. "Tank you, sar!" said he; "but I gets no time

MERRY CHRISTMAS.   209

to tink about de merry Christmas. De Commander
see dese big reindeers." And he went on vigorously
basting two fine haunches of venison which had been
carefully treasured for the occasion, and putting the
last touches to a kettle of tempting soup. Intending
encouragement, I reminded him that his labors would
be over with the serving of the dinner, when, with
that consistency for which human nature is remarkable, especially in a ship's cook, he replied, " Please
sar, so long as my Hebenly Fader gives me healt I
likes to vork."

As I passed out of the hold into the officers' cabin,
the crew sent after me three cheers, and three more
for the expedition, and I don't know how many followed afterward for a " merry Christmas " to themselves. The upper-deck was light and cheerful with
the multitude of lamps, and had been " cleared up "
with unusual care ; and from amidships every thing
had been removed. This Knorr told me was his work,
and I was informed that there was to be a " ball."
The disposition to consume oil was contagious. Even
the heathenish little wife of my absent hunter had
managed to procure an additional supply, and rejoiced
in an extra blaze in honor of the day, the meaning of
which was all Greek to her. Her hut was a cheerful
nest of furs, and little Pingasuik, with a strip of tough
seal-blubber, substituted for one of Goodyear's patent
arrangements for children's gums, was laughing and
crowing as a Christian baby would be expected to do
on this most Christian day. Jacob, fat Jacob, was
grinning in one corner. Charley told me that he began grinning early in the morning, at the prospect of
the many crumbs to come from so bounteous a feast ;
and, in order to prepare himself for the task, he had

210 AN ARCTIC BALL.

swallowed a fox which Jensen brought in from one of his traps, and which he had turned over to the boy to skin. Out on the ice I found a boisterous group engaged around two large tin kettles. They were stirring something with wooden sticks, and I found that, at 34° below zero, they were making "water ice" and "Roman punch" by wholesale. They needed no chemical compounds for their "freezer."

At six o'clock I joined the officers at dinner. Our glass and crockery has, in some mysterious manner known only to the steward, been disappearing from the time of leaving Boston, but there is plenty of tin ware to supply the deficiency, and each cup contained a boquet of flowers, cut from tissue-paper, and a mammoth centre-piece of the same materials stood under the glittering chandelier. The dinner was much enjoyed by everybody, and if we lacked the orthodox turkey, the haunch was not a bad substitute.

I remained until nine o'clock, and left the party to a merry evening. The hour for extinguishing the lights was put off at discretion; and, having myself granted this privilege, I cannot, of course, say that any of the proprieties of discipline or of ship-board life were interfered with. Rejoiced to see that the people had the spirit to be merry at all, I was only too glad to encourage them in it. Every part of the "Festival," as they facetiously call it, was conducted in a very orderly manner. The "ball" came off as promised, and when I went up, about midnight, to have a look at the merrymakers, I found Knorr, wrapped in furs, seated upon a keg, fiddling away in a very energetic manner, while Barnum and McDonald were going through a sailor's hornpipe with immense *eclat*; then Carl swung the steward round in

A PAS DE DEUX. 211

the " giddy mazes of the waltz; " and, finally, Charley set the ship shaking with laughter by attempting a *pas de deux* with Madame Hans. The old cook had crawled up the ladder from below, and, forgetting his troubles and his " reindeers," applauded the actors vociferously. But he was soon observed to be making off from the " gay and festive " scene. A dozen voices called loudly after him, —

" Hallo, cook ! — come back and have a dance ! "

" Vat for me dance, and make nonsense, ven dere be no vomens ? "

" But here 's Mrs. Hans, cook."

" Ugh ! " — and he dove below.

CHAPTER XVI.

THE NEW YEAR — LOOKING FOR SONNTAG — THE AURORA BOREALIS — A RE-MARKABLE DISPLAY — DEPTH OF SNOW. — STRANGE MILDNESS OF THE WEATHER — THE OPEN SEA — EVAPORATION AT LOW TEMPERATURES. — LOOKING FOR THE TWILIGHT. — MY PET FOX.

January 1st, 1861.

THE Christmas holidays have passed quickly away, and the year of grace eighteen hundred and sixty-one was born amid great rejoicings. We have just "rung out the Old and in the New." As the clock showed the midnight hour, the bell was tolled, our swivel gun sent a blaze of fire from its little throat into the darkness, and some fire-works went fizzing and banging into the clear sky. The rockets and blue-lights gleamed over the snow with a weird and strange light; and the loud boom of the gun and the crash of the bell echoing and reëchoing through the neighboring gorges seemed like the voices of startled spirits of the solitude.

I now look anxiously for the return of Sonntag and Hans. Indeed, I have been prepared to see them at any time within these past seven days; for although I had little expectation that they would find Esquimaux at Sorfalik or Peteravik, yet their speedy return would not have surprised me. This is the tenth day of their absence, and they have had more than ample time to go even to the south side of Whale Sound and come back again. I am the more anxious now that the moon has set, and the difficulties of traveling

LOOKING FOR SONNTAG. 213

are so greatly multiplied. However, Sonntag had an undisguised wish to remain some time among the natives, to study their language and habits, and to join them in their hunting excursions; and when he left I felt quite sure that, if a reasonable pretext could be found for absenting himself so long, we would not see him until the January moon. There is no doubt that he will remain if he finds no interest of the expedition likely to suffer in consequence.

January 5th.

I have no longer a dog. The General was the last of them, and he died two days ago. Poor fellow! I had become more than ever attached to him lately, especially since he had quite recovered from the accident to his leg, and seemed likely to be useful with the sledge after a while. It seems strange to see the place so deserted and so quiet. In the early winter I never went out of the vessel on the ice without having the whole pack crowding around me, playing and crying in gladness at my coming; now their lifeless carcasses are strewn about the harbor, half buried in snow and ice, and, if not so fearful, they are at least hardly more sightly than were those other stiff and stark and twisted figures which the wandering poets found beneath the dark sky and "murky vapors" and frozen waters of the icy realm of Dis. There was a companionship in the dogs, which, apart from their usefulness, attached them to everybody, and in this particular we all feel alike the greatness of the loss.

But it is hard to get along without a pet of some kind, and since the General has gone I have got Jensen to catch me a fox, and the cunning little creature now sits coiled up in a tub of snow in one corner of

214 THE AURORA BOREALIS.

my cabin ; and, as she listens to the scratching of my pen, she looks very much as if she would like to know what it is all about. I am trying hard to civilize her, and have had some success. She was very shy when brought in, but, being left to herself for a while, she has become somewhat reconciled to her new abode. She is about three fourths grown, weighs four and a quarter pounds, has a coat of long fine fur, resembling in color that of a Maltese cat, and is being instructed to answer to the name of *Birdie*.

January 6th.

I have often been struck with the singular circumstance that up to this time we have scarcely seen the Aurora Borealis ; and until to-day there has been no display of any great brilliancy. We have been twice favored during the past twelve hours. The first was at eleven o'clock in the morning, and the second at nine o'clock in the evening. The arch was perfect in the last case ; in the former it was less continuous, but more intense. In both instances, the direction of the centre from the observatory was west by south (true), and was 30° above the horizon. Twenty degrees above the arch in the evening there was another imperfect one, a phenomenon which I have not before witnessed. In the direction west-northwest a single ray shot down to the horizon, and there continued for almost an hour.

The infrequency of the Auroral light has been more marked here than at Van Rensselaer Harbor. We seem to have passed almost beyond it. The region of its greatest brilliancy appears to be from ten to twenty degrees further south. As at Van Rensselaer Harbor, its exhibition is almost invariably on the western sky ; and Jensen tells me that this occurs

AURORA. 215

at Upernavik, and he says also that the phenomena are there much more brilliant and of greater frequency than here.

The display of the morning was much finer than that of the evening. Indeed, I have rarely witnessed a more sublime or imposing spectacle. By the way, how strange it seems to be speaking of events happening in the morning and in the evening, when, to save your life, you could not tell without the clock by what name to call the divisions of time! We say eleven o'clock in the morning and eleven o'clock in the evening from habit; but if, by any mischance, we should lose our reckoning for twelve hours, we would then go on calling the evening morning and the morning evening, without being able to detect the error by any difference in the amount of light at these two periods of the day. But this is a digression.

To come back to the Aurora of this morning. When it first appeared I was walking out among the icebergs at the mouth of the harbor; and, although the time was so near noon, yet I was groping through a darkness that was exceedingly embarrassing to my movements among the rough ice. Suddenly a bright ray darted up from behind the black cloud which lay low down on the horizon before me. It lasted but an instant, and, having filled the air with a strange illumination, it died away, leaving the darkness even more profound than before. Presently the arch which I have before mentioned sprang across the sky, and the Aurora became gradually more fixed. The space inclosed by the arch was very dark, and was filled with the cloud. The play of the rays which rose from its steadily brightening border was for some time very

216 AURORA.

capricious, alternating, if I might be allowed the figure, the burst of flame from a conflagration with the soft glow of the early morn. The light grew by degrees more and more intense, and from irregular bursts it settled into an almost steady sheet of brightness. This sheet was, however, far from uniform, for it was but a flood of mingling and variously-tinted streaks. The exhibition, at first tame and quiet, became in the end startling in its brilliancy. The broad dome above me is all ablaze. Ghastly fires, more fierce than those which lit the heavens from burning Troy, flash angrily athwart the sky. The stars pale before the marvellous glare, and seem to recede further and further from the earth, — as when the chariot of the Sun, driven by Phæton, and carried from its beaten track by the ungovernable steeds, rushed madly through the skies, parching the world and withering the constellations. The gentle Andromeda flies trembling from the flame; Perseus, with his flashing sword and Gorgon shield, retreats in fear; the Pole Star is chased from the night, and the Great Bear, faithful sentinel of the North, quits his guardian watch, following the feeble trail. The color of the light was chiefly red, but this was not constant, and every hue mingled in the fierce display. Blue and yellow streamers were playing in the lurid fire; and, sometimes starting side by side from the wide expanse of the illumined arch, they melt into each other, and throw a ghostly glare of green into the face and over the landscape. Again this green overrides the red; blue and orange clasp each other in their rapid flight; violet darts tear through a broad flush of yellow, and countless tongues of white flame, formed of these uniting streams, rush aloft and lick

DEPTH OF SNOW. 217

the skies. The play of this many-colored light upon the surrounding objects was truly wonderful. The weird forms of countless icebergs, singly and in clusters, loomed above the sea, and around their summits the strange gleam shone as the fires of Vesuvius over the doomed temples of Campania. Upon the mountain tops, along the white surface of the frozen waters, upon the lofty cliffs, the light glowed and grew dim and glowed again, as if the air was filled with charnel meteors, pulsating with wild inconstancy over some vast illimitable city of the dead. The scene was noiseless, yet the senses were deceived, for unearthly sounds seemed to follow the rapid flashes, and to fall upon the ear like

> ———— "the tread
> Of phantoms dread,
> With banner, and spear, and flame."

January 13th.

The month of January runs on through stormy skies. The wind continues to blow as before, and the wild rush of gales fills the night with sounds of terror.

The air has been, however, for the most part, quite clear. But little snow has fallen since November. The total depth now mounts up to $53\frac{3}{4}$ inches. I am more and more struck with the difference in the atmospheric conditions of this place and Van Rensselaer Harbor. There we had rarely moisture, and gales were scarcely known. The temperatures were very low, and the winter was marked by a general calm. Here the temperatures are more mild than Parry's at Melville Island, the atmospheric disturbances have been very great, and the amount of snow has been truly surprising. There is one comfort at least in the winds. They either carry off the snow or pack it

218 EVAPORATION AT LOW TEMPERATURES.

very hard, so that we get about with as little difficulty as if we were walking upon the bare ice. It is pounded as hard as the drives in the Central Park.

All these unusual phenomena are, as has been hitherto observed, doubtless due to the close proximity of the open sea. How extensive this water may be is of course unknown, but its limits cannot be very small to produce such serious atmospheric disturbance. It seems, indeed, as if we were in the very vortex of the north winds. The poet has told us that the north winds

> "Are cradled far down in the depths that yawn
> Beneath the Polar Star;"

and it appears very much as if we had got into those yawning depths, and had come not only to the place where the winds are cradled, but where they are born.

I have been making, all the winter through, a series of experiments which give me some interesting results. They show that evaporation takes place at the very lowest temperatures, and that precipitation often occurs when the air is apparently quite clear. To determine this latter, I have exposed a number of smooth and carefully measured ice-surfaces, and have collected from them the light deposit. These accumulations, after reducing them to the standard of freshly fallen snow, amount thus far to seven eighths of an inch. To determine the evaporation, I have suspended in the open air a number of thin ice-plates, made in a shallow dish, and some strips of wet flannel. The flannel becomes perfectly dry in a few days, and the ice-plates disappear slowly and steadily. I generally weigh them every second day, and it is curious to watch my little circular disks silently melting away and vanishing "into thin air," while the thermometer is down in the zeros.

This evaporation at low temperatures is constantly taking place before our eyes, to our advantage. On wash-days the clothes are hung on lines stretched across the ship's rigging, or upon poles across the ice, as you will see on Monday afternoons in the farmhouse yards; and before the week is over the moisture has disappeared, no matter how cold it may be.

January 16th.

Our eyes now turn wistfully to the south, eagerly watching for the tip of Aurora's chariot, as the fair goddess of the morning rises from the sea to drop a ray of gladness from her rosy fingers into this long-neglected world.

It is almost a month since we passed the darkest day of the winter, and it will be a long time yet before we have light; but it is time for us now to have at noontime a faint flush upon the horizon. We find a new excitement, if such it may be called, in the impatience of expectation. Meanwhile I pet my fox.

Birdie has become quite tame, and does great credit to her instructor. She is the most cunning creature that was ever seen, and does not make a bad substitute for the General. She takes the General's place at my table, as she has his place in my affections; but she sits in my lap, where the General never was admitted, and, with her delicate little paws on the cloth, she makes a picture. Why, she is indeed a perfect little *gourmande*, well bred, too, and clever. When she takes the little morsels into her mouth her eyes sparkle with delight, she wipes her lips, and looks up at me with a *coquetterie* that is perfectly irresistible. The

220 MY PET FOX.

eagerness of appetite is controlled by the proprieties of the table and a proper self-respect; and she is satisfied to prolong a feast in which she finds so much enjoyment. She does not like highly seasoned food; indeed, she prefers to take it *au natural*, so I have a few little bits of venison served for her on a separate plate. She has her own fork; but she has not yet advanced sufficiently far in the usages of civilization to handle it for herself, so I convey the delicate morsels to her mouth. Sometimes she exhibits too much impatience; but a gentle rebuke with the fork on the tip of the nose is quite effective in restoring her patience, and saving her from indigestion.

Her habits greatly interest me. I have allowed her to run loose in my cabin, after a short confinement in a cage had familiarized her with the place; but she soon found out the "bull's-eye" over my head, through the cracks around which she could sniff the cool air; and she got into the habit of bounding over the shelves, without much regard for the many valuable and perishable articles which lay thereon. From this retreat nothing can tempt her but a good dinner; and as soon as she sees from her perch the bits of raw venison, she crawls leisurely down, sneaks gently into my lap, looks up longingly and lovingly into my face, puts out her little tongue with quick impatience, and barks bewitchingly if the beginning of the repast is too long delayed.

I tried to cure her of this habit of climbing by tying her up with a chain which Knorr made for me of some iron wire; but she took it so much to heart that I had to let her go. Her efforts to free herself were very amusing, and she well earned her freedom. She tried continually to break the chain, and, having

MY PET FOX. 221

once succeeded, she seemed determined not to be baffled in her subsequent attempts. As long as I was watching her she would be quiet enough, coiled up in her bed or her tub of snow; but the moment my eyes were off her, or she thought me asleep, she worked hard to effect her liberation. First she would draw herself back as far as she could get, and then suddenly darting forward, would bring up at the end of her chain with a jerk which sent her reeling on the floor; then she would pick herself up, panting as if her little heart would break, shake out her disarranged coat, and try again. But this she would do with much deliberation. For a moment she would sit quietly down, cock her head cunningly on one side, follow the chain with her eye along its whole length to its fastening in the floor, and then she would walk leisurely to that point, hesitate a moment, and then make another plunge. All this time she would eye me sharply, and if I made any movement, she would fall down at once on the floor and pretend sleep.

She is a very neat and cleanly creature. She is everlastingly brushing her clothes, and she bathes very regularly in her bath of snow. This last is her great delight. She roots up the clean white flakes with her diminutive nose, rolls and rubs and half buries herself in them, wipes her face with her soft paws, and when all is over she mounts with her delicate fingers to the side of the tub, looks around her very knowingly, and barks the prettiest little bark that ever was heard. This is her way of enforcing admiration; and, being now satisfied with her performance, she gives a goodly number of shakes to her sparkling coat, and then, happy and refreshed, she crawls to her airy bed in the "bull's-eye" and sleeps.

CHAPTER XVII.

THE ARCTIC NIGHT.

January 20th.

THE Morn is coming !

A faint twilight flush mounted the southern sky to-day at the meridian hour, and, although barely perceptible, it was a cheering sight to all of us.

At our usual Sunday gathering, I read from Ecclesiastes these lines : —

"Truly the light is sweet, and a pleasant thing it is for the eye to behold the sun."

And this suggested the text for our evening conversation ; and we talked long of the future and of what was to be done, with the coming again of the god of day.

We all feel now that the veil of night is lifting, that the cloud is passing away, that the heavy load of darkness is being lightened. The people have exhausted their means of amusement ; the newspaper has died a natural death ; theatricals are impossible ; and there is nothing new to break the weariness of the long hours.

But we shall soon have no need to give thought to these things. There will be ere long neither time nor occasion for amusements. The Arctic night will soon be numbered with the things of the past. We are eager that it shall have an end, and we long for the day and work.

THE ARCTIC NIGHT. 223

And say what you will, talk as you will of pluck, and manly resolution, and mental resources, and all that sort of thing, this Arctic night is a severe ordeal. Physically one can get through it well enough. We are and always have been in perfect health. I am my own "ship's doctor," and am a doctor without a patient. Believing in Democritus rather than Heraclitus, we have laughed the scurvy and all other sources of ill-health to shame. And we have laughed at the scurvy really and truly; for if it does sometimes come in, like a thief in the night, with salt rations and insufficient food, which has not been our portion, it does, too, come with despondency and the splenetic blood of an unhappy household, from which we have fortunately been exempt.

But if the Arctic night can be endured with little strain upon the physical, it is, nevertheless, a severe trial both to the moral and the intellectual faculties. The darkness which so long clothes Nature unfolds to the senses a new world, and the senses accommodate themselves to that world but poorly. The cheering influences of the rising sun which invite to labor; the soothing influences of the evening twilight which invite to repose; the change from day to night and from night to day which lightens the burden to the weary mind and the aching body, strengthening the hope and sustaining the courage, in the great life-battle of the dear home-land, is withdrawn, and in the constant longing for Light, Light, the mind and body, weary with the changeless progress of the time, fail to find Repose where all is Rest. The grandeur of Nature ceases to give delight to the dulled sympathies. The heart longs continually for new associations, new objects, and new companionships. The

224 THE ARCTIC NIGHT.

dark and drear solitude oppresses the understanding; the desolation which everywhere reigns haunts the imagination; the silence — dark, dreary, and profound — becomes a terror.

And yet there is in the Arctic night much that is attractive to the lover of Nature. There is in the flashing Aurora, in the play of the moonlight upon the hills and icebergs, in the wonderful clearness of the starlight, in the broad expanse of the ice-fields, in the lofty grandeur of the mountains and the glaciers, in the naked fierceness of the storms, much that is both sublime and beautiful. But they speak a language of their own, — a language, rough, rugged and severe.

Nature is here exposed on a gigantic scale. Out of the glassy sea the cliffs rear their dark fronts and frown grimly over the desolate waste of ice-clad waters. The mountain peaks, glittering in the clear cold atmosphere, pierce the very heavens, their heads hoary with unnumbered ages. The glaciers pour their crystal torrents into the sea in floods of immeasurable magnitude. The very air, disdaining the gentle softness of other climes, bodies forth a loftier majesty, and seems to fill the universe with a boundless transparency; and the stars pierce it sharply, and the moon fills it with a cold refulgence. There is neither warmth nor coloring underneath this etherial robe of night. No broad window opens in the east, no gold and crimson curtain falls in the west, upon a world clothed in blue and green and purple, melting into one harmonious whole, a tinted cloak of graceful loveliness. Under the shadow of the eternal night, Nature needs no drapery and requires no adornment. The glassy sea, the tall cliff, the lofty mountain, the

THE ARCTIC NIGHT. 225

majestic glacier, do not blend one with the other. Each stands forth alone, clothed only with Solitude. Sable priestess of the Arctic winter, she has wrapped the world in a winding-sheet, and thrown her web and woof over the very face of Nature.

And I have gone out often into the Arctic night, and viewed Nature under varied aspects. I have rejoiced with her in her strength, and communed with her in repose. I have seen the wild burst of her anger, have watched her sportive play, and have beheld her robed in silence. I have walked abroad in the darkness when the winds were roaring through the hills and crashing over the plain. I have strolled along the beach when the only sound that broke the stillness was the dull creaking of the ice-tables, as they rose and fell lazily with the tide. I have wandered far out upon the frozen sea, and listened to the voice of the icebergs bewailing their imprisonment; along the glacier, where forms and falls the avalanche; upon the hill-top, where the drifting snow, coursing over the rocks, sang its plaintive song; and again I have wandered away to some distant valley where all these sounds were hushed, and the air was still and solemn as the tomb.

And it is here that the Arctic night is most impressive, where its true spirit is revealed, where its wonders are unloosed to sport and play with the mind's vague imaginings. The heavens above and the earth beneath reveal only an endless and fathomless quiet. There is nowhere around me evidence of life or motion. I stand alone in the midst of the mighty hills. Their tall crests climb upward, and are lost in the gray vault of the skies. The dark cliffs, standing against their slopes of white, are the steps of a vast

226 THE ARCTIC NIGHT.

amphitheatre. The mind, finding no rest on their bald summits, wanders into space. The moon, weary with long vigil, sinks to her repose. The Pleiades no longer breathe their sweet influences. Cassiopea and Andromeda and Orion and all the infinite host of unnumbered constellations, fail to infuse one spark of joy into this dead atmosphere. They have lost all their tenderness, and are cold and pulseless. The eye leaves them and returns to earth, and the trembling ear awaits' something that will break the oppressive stillness. But no footfall of living thing reaches it; no wild beast howls through the solitude. There is no cry of bird to enliven the scene; no tree, among whose branches the winds can sigh and moan. The pulsations of my own heart are alone heard in the great void; and as the blood courses through the sensitive organization of the ear, I am oppressed as with discordant sounds. Silence has ceased to be negative. It has become endowed with positive attributes. I seem to hear and see and feel it. It stands forth as a frightful spectre, filling the mind with the overpowering consciousness of universal death, — proclaiming the end of all things, and heralding the everlasting future. Its presence is unendurable. I spring from the rock upon which I have been seated, I plant my feet heavily in the snow to banish its awful presence, — and the sound rolls through the night and drives away the phantom.

I have seen no expression on the face of Nature so filled with terror as THE SILENCE OF THE ARCTIC NIGHT.

CHAPTER XVIII.

PROLONGED ABSENCE OF MR. SONNTAG.—PREPARING TO LOOK FOR HIM.—
ARRIVAL OF ESQUIMAUX.—THEY REPORT SONNTAG DEAD.—ARRIVAL OF
HANS.—CONDITION OF THE DOGS.—HANS'S STORY OF THE JOURNEY.

A FULL month had now elapsed since Sonntag and
Hans left us, and several days of the January moonlight having passed over without bringing them back,
I had some cause for alarm. It was evident that they
had either met with an accident, or were detained
among the Esquimaux in some unaccountable manner. I therefore began to devise means for determin-
ing what had become of them. First, I sent Mr.
Dodge down to Cape Alexander to pursue the trail
and ascertain whether they had gone around or over
the cape. The sledge-track was followed for about
five miles, when it came suddenly to an end, the ice
having broken up and drifted away since December.
Dodge could now only examine the passes of the glacier; and finding there no tracks, it was evident that
the party had gone outside.

My next concern was to determine whether the
tracks reappeared on the firm ice south of the cape;
and accordingly I prepared to start with a small foot
party, and cross over the glacier. In the event of
finding tracks below Cape Alexander, my course
would then be governed by circumstances; but if the
track should not appear, it would be conclusive evidence that the party was lost, and I would proceed

ARRIVAL OF ESQUIMAUX.

south until I reached the Esquimaux, for I could no longer afford to delay communication with them. Although the temperature had now fallen to 43° below zero, yet the careful preparations which I had made for camping relieved the journey from any risks on that account The mercury froze for the first time during the winter while Dodge was absent, and I was extravagant enough to mould a bullet of it and send it from my rifle through a thick plank. Dodge, who was one of my most hardy men, returned from his twelve hours' tramp complaining that he had suffered rather from heat than cold, and he declared that, when called upon another time to wade so far through snow-drifts and hummocks, he would not carry so heavy a load of furs. In truth, both he and his two companions came in perspiring freely under their buffalo-skin coats.

My projected journey was, however, destined not to come off. The sledge was loaded with our light cargo, and we were ready to set out on the morning of the 27th, but a gale sprung up suddenly and detained us on board during that and the following day. Early in the morning of the 29th, the wind having fallen to calm, we were preparing to start. The men were putting on their furs, and I was in my cabin giving some last instructions to Mr. McCormick, when Carl, who had the watch on deck, came hastily to my door to report "Two Esquimaux alongside." They had come upon us out of the darkness very suddenly and unobserved.

Conjecturing that these people would hardly have visited us without having first fallen in with Sonntag and Hans, I at once sent the interpreter to interrogate them. He came back in a few minutes. I in-

SONNTAG'S DEATH REPORTED   229

quired eagerly if they brought news of Mr. Sonntag.
" Yes." I had no need to inquire further. Jensen's
face told too plainly the terrible truth, — Sonntag was
dead!

. I sent Jensen back to see that the wants of our
savage visitors were carefully provided for, and to
question them further. They proved to be two of my
old acquaintances, — Ootinah, to whom I was under
obligations for important services in 1854, and a
sprightly fellow, who, having had his leg crushed by
a falling stone, had since hobbled about on a wooden
one supplied to him, in 1850, by the surgeon of the
North Star, and which I had once repaired for him.
They both came on one sledge, drawn by five dogs,
and had traveled all the way through from a village,
on the south side of Whale Sound, called Iteplik, without a halt. They had faced a wind part of the way,
and were covered from head to foot with snow and
frost. Their wants were soon bountifully supplied,
and they were not slow in communicating the information which most interested me. From them I
learned that Hans was on his way to the vessel with
his wife's father and mother. Some of his dogs had
died, and he was traveling in slow and easy stages.
There being no longer any occasion for my southern
journey, the preparations therefor were discontinued.

Hans arrived two days afterward, and, much to
our surprise, he was accompanied only by his wife's
brother, a lad whom I had seen some months before
at Cape York ; but the cause of this was soon explained. His wife's father and mother, as Ootinah
informed me, had journeyed with him, but they, as
well as the dogs, had broken down, and were left behind, near the glacier, and Hans had come on for

230 HANS'S STORY.

assistance   A party was at once dispatched to bring
them in.   Hans being cold and fatigued, I refrained for
the time from questioning him, and sent the weather-
beaten travelers to get warmed and fed.

The two old people were found coiled up in a cave
dug in a snow-bank, and were shivering with the cold.
The dogs were huddled together near by, and not one
of them would stir a step, so both the animals and
the Esquimaux were bundled in a heap upon our
large ice-sledge, and dragged to the vessel.   The Esquimaux were soon revived by the warmth and good
cheer of Hans's tent, while the dogs, only five in
number, lay stretched out on the deck in an almost
lifeless condition.   They could neither eat nor move.
And this was the remnant of my once superb pack
of thirty-six, and this the result of a journey from
which I had hoped so much !   There was a mystery
somewhere.   What could it all mean ?   I quote from
my diary : —

February 1st.

Hans has given me the story of his journey, and I
sit down to record it with very painful emotions.

The travelers rounded Cape Alexander without difficulty, finding the ice solid ; and they did not halt until
they had reached Sutherland Island, where they built
a snow hut and rested for a few hours.   Continuing
thence down the coast, they sought the Esquimaux at
Sorfalik without success.   The native hut at that place
·being in ruins, they made for their shelter another
house of snow ; and, after being well rested, they set
out directly for Northumberland Island, having concluded that it was useless to seek longer for natives
on the north side of the Sound.   They had proceeded
on their course about four or five miles, as nearly as

HANS'S STORY   231.

I can judge from Hans's description, when Sonntag, growing a little chilled, sprang off the sledge and ran ahead of the dogs to warm himself with the exercise. The tangling of a trace obliging Hans to halt the team for a few minutes, he fell some distance behind, and was hurrying on to catch up, when he suddenly observed Sonntag sinking. He had come upon the thin ice, covering a recently open tide-crack, and, probably not observing his footing, he stepped upon it unawares. Hans hastened to his rescue, and aided him out of the water, and then turned back for the shelter which they had recently abandoned. A light wind was blowing at the time from the northeast, and this, according to Hans, caused Sonntag to seek the hut without stopping to change his wet clothing. At first he ran beside the sledge, and thus guarded against danger; but after a while he rode, and when they halted at Sorfalik, Hans discovered that his companion was stiff and speechless. Assisting him into the hut with all possible despatch, Hans states that he removed the wet and frozen clothing, and placed Sonntag in the sleeping-bag. He next gave him some brandy which he found in a flask on the sledge; and, having tightly closed the hut, he lighted the alcohol lamp, for the double purpose of elevating the temperature and making some coffee; but all of his efforts were unavailing, and, after remaining for nearly a day unconscious, Sonntag died. He did not speak after reaching the hut, and left no message of any kind.

After closing up the mouth of the hut, so that the body might not be disturbed by the bears or foxes, Hans again set out southward, and reached Northumberland Island without inconvenience. Much to his

232 HANS'S STORY.

disappointment, he found that the natives had recently abandoued the village at that place; but he obtained a comfortable sleep in a deserted hut, and under a pile of stones he found enough walrus flesh to give his dogs a hearty meal. The next day's journey brought him to Netlik, which place was also deserted; and he continued on up the Sound some twenty miles further to Iteplik, where he was fortunate enough to find several families residing, some in the native stone hut and others in huts of snow. Whale Sound being a favorite winter resort of the seal, the people had congregated there for the time, and were living in the midst of abundance. Hans told his story, and, delighted to hear of our being near their old village of Etah, Ootinah and he of the wooden leg put their two teams together and resolved to accompany Hans when he set out to return.

Meanwhile, however, my hunter had other projects. He was only three days from the vessel, and had he come back at once the chief purpose of the journey would still have been accomplished; but instead of doing this, he gave large rewards to two Esquimaux boys to go with his team down to Cape York. The stock of presents which Sonntag had taken for the Esquimaux all now fell to Hans, and he did not spare them. And he vows that his disposition of the property and the team was made in my interest. "You 'want the Esquimaux to know you are here. I tell them. They will come by and by and bring plenty of dogs." Why did he not go himself to Cape York? He was too tired, and had, besides, a frosted toe which he got while attending upon Mr. Sonntag.

Notwithstanding all these protestations of devotion

to my affairs, I strongly suspect, however, that certain commands were laid upon him by the partner of his tent and joys; and, if domestic secrets were not better kept than are some other kinds, I should probably discover that the journey to Cape York was made for the sole purpose of bringing up from that place the two old people who own Hans for a son-in-law. So even here under the Pole Star the daughters of Eve govern the destinies of men.

It was the old story of the borrowed horse over again. The journey was long and difficult; the dogs were over-driven and starved; and the party came back to Iteplik with only five dogs remaining of the nine with which they had set out. Four of them had broken down, and were left to die by the way.

February 2d.

Ootinah and his wooden-legged companion have left us, promising to return as soon as they have provided for their families. They carried away with them many valuable presents, and if these do not tempt their savage kindred to the ship, nothing will. They will tell the Esquimaux that I want dogs, and I have charged them to circulate the knowledge of the ample returns which I will make to the hunter who will loan or sell to me his team. But alas! dogs are scarce; most of the hunters have none to spare, and many of them are wholly destitute. I had not a bribe in the ship large enough to induce either of those who have left me to part with even one of their precious animals. Having discovered this, I could afford to be lavish with my presents, and these poor wanderers on the ice deserts probably left me quite as well off as if they had sold me their entire teams. They plead the

234 HANS'S STORY.

hunt and their families, and these are strong arguments. Needles and knives, and iron and bits of wood, will not feed wives and babies, and a hundred and fifty miles is a long way to carry a child at the breast through the cold and storms of the Arctic night, even though it be to this haven of plenty. My charity was, however, intended to cover a double purpose, — to do them a substantial service, and to stimulate as well their cupidity as that of the tribe who are sure to flock around them at Iteplik, to inspect their riches. I must own, however, that my prospects for obtaining dogs do not look encouraging. But few of the Esquimaux are likely to come so far with their impoverished teams.

Hans sticks to the story of yesterday; and, after questioning and cross-questioning him for an hour, I get nothing new. Although I have no good reason for doubting the truth of his narrative, yet I cannot quite reconcile my mind to the fact that Sonntag, with so much experience to govern him, should have undertaken to travel five miles in wet clothing, especially as he was accompanied by a native hunter who was familiar with all of the expedients for safety upon the ice-fields, and to whom falling in the water is no unusual circumstance. The sledge and the canvas apron which inclosed the cargo furnished the means for constructing a temporary shelter from the wind, and the sleeping-bag would have insured against freezing while Hans got ready the dry clothing, of which Sonntag carried a complete change. Nor can I understand how he should have lived so long and have given Hans no message for me, nor have spoken a word after coming out of the water, further than to have ordered his driver to hasten back to the snow-hut. However, it is idle to speculate about the matter; and since Hans's interests were concerned in proving faithful to the officer who, of all those in the ship, cared most for him, it would be unreasonable as well as unjust to suspect him of desertion.

CHAPTER XIX.

SONNTAG — TWILIGHT INCREASING — A DEER-HUNT — THE ARCTIC FOXES — THE POLAR BEAR — ADVENTURES WITH BEARS — OUR NEW ESQUIMAUX — ESQUIMAU DRESS — A SNOW HOUSE — ESQUIMAU IMPLEMENTS — A WALRUS HUNT

I WILL not trouble the reader with the many gloomy reflections which I find scattered over the pages of my journal during the period succeeding the events which are recorded in the last chapter. While the loss of my dogs left me in much doubt and uncertainty as to my future prospects, the death of Mr. Sonntag deprived me of assistance which was very essential to the accomplishment of some of my purposes. His familiar acquaintance with the physical sciences, and his earnest enthusiasm in every thing which pertained to physical research, both in the field and study, made him an invaluable aid, while his genial disposition and manly qualities gave him a deep hold upon my affections. Similarity of taste and disposition, equal age, a common object, and a mutual dependence for companionship, had cemented more and more closely a bond of friendship which had its origin in the dangers and fortunes of former travel.

The light was now growing upon us from day to day, and we found a fresh excitement in the renewal of the hunt. It must not, however, be supposed that, even at noon, we had yet any daylight; but there

A DEER-HUNT. 237

was a twilight, which was increasing with each successive day. The reindeer had grown very poor during the winter, and their flesh was tough and almost tasteless; but this did not discourage the hunters, and several captures were made. One day a large herd came down near the store-house, which, being reported, caused a general scramble for guns, and a rush over the hills to surround the game. The crew appeared more like boys on a holiday frolic than men catering for their mess. They made noise enough, as one would have thought, to frighten every living thing from the neighborhood; but, nevertheless, three deer were shot. The thermometer stood at 41° below zero, and, there being a light wind, the air was somewhat biting, and gave rise to numerous incidents quite characteristic of our life. The handling of the cold gun was attended with some risk to the fingers, as one can neither pull the trigger nor load with a mittened hand; and there were quite a number of slight "burns," as wounds from this cause were jestingly called. McDonald carried an old flint-lock musket, the only weapon that he could lay his hands on, and in the midst of the excitement he was heard to fire. Hurrying in that direction, Knorr eagerly inquired what he was shooting at, and where the game had gone. His answer afterward furnished us not a little amusement: "There was a monstrous big deer there half an hour ago, and had I pulled trigger when I left the ship I should have killed him. But you see the powder is so cold that it won't burn, and it takes half an hour to touch it off;" and, to prove his theory, he poured a lot of it out on the dry snow, and applied a match. His singed whiskers bore ample evidence that his theory was not founded on fact.

238   THE ARCTIC FOXES.

The hill-side seemed to be alive with foxes; and, scenting the blood of the dead deer, they flocked in from all directions. These little animals were at first quite tame, but they had been cured of their familiarity by the lessons learned from the hunters, and had to be approached with adroitness. Of both the blue and white varieties I had living specimens in my cabin. One of them was the gentle creature, named Birdie, which I have already mentioned. The other one was purely white, and did not differ from Birdie in shape, although it was somewhat larger. The fur of the latter was much more coarse than the former. Their cry was exactly the same. But, while Birdie was very docile, and had grown quite domesticated, the other was thoroughly wild and untamable. Their respective weights were $4\frac{1}{4}$ and 7 pounds. The latter was full grown and unusually large.

These two varieties of the fox, notwithstanding their many points of resemblance, are evidently distinct species. I have not known them to mix, the coat of each preserving its distinctive hue, that of the blue fox varying merely in degree of shade, while the white changes only from pure white to a slightly yellowish tinge. The term "blue," as applied to the species to which Birdie belonged, is not wholly a misnomer, for, as seen upon the snow, its color gives something of that effect. The color is in truth a solid gray, the white and black being harmoniously blended, and not mixed as in the gray fox of Northern America. Their skins are much sought after by the trappers of Southern Greenland, where the animals are rare, for the fur commands a fabulous price in the Copenhagen market.

These foxes obtain a very precarious subsistence,

THE POLAR BEAR. 239

and they may be seen at almost any time scampering over the ice, seeking the tracks of the bears, which they follow with the instinct of the jackal following the lion; not that they try their strength against these roving monarchs of the ice-fields, but, whenever the bear catches a seal, the little fox comes in for a share of the prey. Their food consists besides of an occasional ptarmigan, (the Arctic grouse,) and if quick in his spring he may be lucky enough to capture a hare. In the summer they congregate about the haunts of the birds, and luxuriate upon eggs. It is a popular belief in Greenland that they gather enormous stores of them for their winter provender, but I have never witnessed in them any such evidence of foresight.

The bears, wandering continually through the night, must needs have a hard struggle to live. During the summer, the seal, which furnish their only subsistence, crawl up on the ice, and are there easily caught; but in the winter they only resort to the cracks to breathe, and, in doing so, barely put their noses above the water, so that they are captured with difficulty. Driven to desperation by hunger, the bear will sometimes invade the haunts of men, in search of the food which their quick sense has detected. Our dogs, during the early winter, kept them from our vicinity; but, when the dogs were gone, several bears made their appearance. One of them came overland from the Fiord, and approached the store-house from behind the observatory, where Starr was engaged in reading the scale of the magnetometer. The heavy tread of the wild beast was heard through the stillness of the night, and, without much regard to the delicate organization of the instrument which he was

240 ADVENTURES WITH BEARS.

observing, the young gentleman rushed for the door, upset the magnetometer, and had nearly lost his life in his precipitate haste to get over the dangerous ice-foot, while hurrying on board to give the alarm. We sallied out with our rifles; but while Starr was fleeing in one direction, the bear had been making off in the other. I had an adventure, about this time, which, like that of Starr's, shows that the Polar bear is not so ferocious as is generally supposed; indeed, they have never been known to attack man except when hotly pursued and driven to close quarters. Strolling one day along the shore, I was observing with much interest the effect of the recent spring tides upon the ice-foot, when, rounding a point of land, I suddenly found myself confronted in the faint moonlight by an enormous bear. He had just sprung down from the land-ice, and was meeting me at a full trot. We caught sight of each other at the same instant. Being without a rifle or other means of defence, I wheeled suddenly toward the ship, with, I fancy, much the same reflections about discretion and valor as those which crossed the mind of old Jack Falstaff when the Douglas set upon him; but finding, after a few lengthy strides, that I was not gobbled up, I looked back over my shoulder, when, as much to my surprise as gratification, I saw the bear tearing away toward the open water with a celerity which left no doubt as to the state of his mind. I suppose it would be difficult to determine which was the worst frightened — the bear or I.

The additions to the Hans family furnished us as well a welcome source of amusement as of service. As I have said before, they were three in number, and bore respectively the names of Tcheitchenguak, Kab-

OUR NEW ESQUIMAUX. 241

lunet, and Angeit. This latter was the brother of Hans's wife, and his name signifies "The Catcher" — given to him, no doubt, in early infancy, from some peculiarity of disposition which he then manifested. And he was not inaptly named. The sailors took him into their favor, scrubbed and combed him, and dressed him in Christian clothing, and under their encouraging countenance he was soon found to be as full of tricks as a monkey, and as acquisitive as a magpie. He was the special torment of the steward and the cook. Driven almost to despair, and utterly defeated in every project of reform, the former finally set at the little heathen with a bundle of tracts and a catechism, while the latter declared his fixed resolve to scald him on the first favorable opportunity. "Very well, cook; but remember they hang for murder." "Den I kills him a leetle," was the ready answer.

His mother, Kablunet, proved to be a useful addition to our household. She was very industrious with her needle; and, until she became possessed, in payment for her work, of such articles of domestic use as she needed, sewed for us continually, making every sort of skin garment, from boots to coats, which belong to an Arctic wardrobe. Her complexion was quite light, as her name implied. Kablunet is the title which the Esquimaux give to our race, and it signifies "The child with the white skin;" and if the name of her husband, Tcheitchenguak, did not mean "The child with the dark skin," it ought to, for he was almost black.

The personal appearance of this interesting couple was not peculiarly attractive. Their faces were broad, jaws heavy, cheek-bones projecting like other carnivorous animals, foreheads narrow, eyes small and very

ESQUIMAU DRESS.

black, noses flat, lips long and thin, and when opened
there were disclosed two narrow, white, well-preserved
rows of polished ivory, — well worn, however, with
long use and hard service, for the teeth of the Esquimaux serve a great variety of purposes, such as softening skins, pulling and tightening cords, besides
masticating food, which I may here mention is wholly
animal. Their hair was jet black, though not abundant, and the man had the largest growth of beard
which I have seen upon an Esquimau face, but it
was confined to the upper lip and the tip of the
chin. The face of the Esquimau is indeed quite Mon-
golian in its type, and is usually beardless. In stat-
ure they are short, though well built, and bear, in
every movement, evidence of strength and endurance.

The dress of the male and female differed but little
one from the other. It consisted of nine pieces, — a
pair of boots, stockings, mittens, pantaloons, an under-
dress, and a coat. The man wore boots of bear-skin,
reaching to the top of the calf, where they met the
pantaloons, which were composed of the same materials. The boots of the woman reached nearly to the
middle of the thigh, and were made of tanned seal-
skins. Her pantaloons, like her husband's, were of
bear-skin. The stockings were of dog-skin, and the
mittens of seal-skin. The under-dress was made of
bird-skins, feathers turned inwards; and the coat,
which did not open in front, but was drawn on over
the head like a shirt, was of blue fox-skins. This coat
terminates in a hood which envelops the head as completely as an Albanian *capote* or a monk's cowl. This
hood gives the chief distinction to the dresses of the
sexes. In the costume of the man it is round, closely
fitting the scalp, while in the woman it is pointed at

A SNOW HUT. 243

the top to receive the hair which is gathered up on the crown of the head, and tied into a hard, horn-like tuft with a piece of raw seal-hide, — a style of *coiffure* which, whatever may be its other advantages, cannot be regarded as peculiarly picturesque.

Their ages could not be determined ; for, since the Esquimaux cannot enumerate beyond their ten fingers, it is quite impossible for them to refer to a past event by any process of notation. Having no written language whatever, not even the picture-writing and hieroglyphics of the rudest Indian tribes of North America, the race possesses no records, and such traditions as may come down from generation to generation are not fixed by any means which will furnish even an approximate estimate of their periods of growth, prosperity, and decay, or even of their own ages.

These old people, soon growing tired of the warmth of Hans's tent, went ashore and built a snow hut, and set up housekeeping on their own account; and living upon supplies which they got regularly from my abundant stores, and, with no need for exertion, it was perhaps not surprising that they should prove to be a very happy and contented couple. This snow-hut, although an architectural curiosity, would have excited the contempt of a beaver. It was nothing more than an artificial cave in a snow-bank, and was made thus : Right abreast of the ship there was a narrow gorge, in which the wintry winds had piled the snow to a great depth, leaving, as it whirled through the opening, a sort of cavern, — the curving snow-bank on the right and overhead, and the square-sided rock on the left. Starting at the inner side of this cavern, Tcheitchenguak began to bury himself in the snow;

TCHEITCHENGUAK "AT HOME."

very much as a prairie-dog would do in the loose soil, — digging down into the drift, and tossing the lumps behind him with great rapidity. After going downward for about five feet, he ran off horizontally for about ten feet more. This operation completed, he now began to excavate his den. His shovel was struck into the hard snow above his head, the blocks which tumbled down were cleared away, and thrown out into the open air, and in a little while he could stand upright and work; and when at length satisfied with the size of the cave, he smoothed it off all around and overhead, and came out covered with whiteness. The door-way was now fixed up and made just large enough to crawl through on all fours; the entering tunnel was smoothed off like the inside; the floor of the cave was covered first with a layer of stones, and then with several layers of reindeer-skins; the walls were hung with the same materials; two native lamps were lighted; across the door-way was suspended another deer-skin, and Tcheitchenguak and his family were "at home." I called upon them some hours afterwards, and found them apparently warm and comfortable. The lamps (their only fire) blazed up cheerfully, and the light glistened on the white dome of this novel den; the temperature had risen to the freezing point, and Kablunet, like a good housewife, was stitching away at some article of clothing; Tcheitchenguak was repairing a harpoon for his son-in-law, and Angeit, the bright-eyed pest of the galley and the pantry, was busily engaged stowing away in a stomach largely disproportionate to the balance of his body, some bits of venison which looked very much as as if they had recently been surreptitiously obtained from a forbidden corner of the steward's store-room.

ESQUIMAU PRESENTS. 245

In consideration for the kindness which I had shown these people, they gave me a set of their hunting and domestic implements, the principal of them being a lance, harpoon, coil of line, a rabbit-trap, a lamp, pot, flint and steel, with some lamp-wick and tinder. The lance was a wooden shaft, probably from Dr. Kane's lost ship, the *Advance*, with an iron spike lashed firmly to one end of it, and a piece of walrus tusk, shod with sharp iron, at the other. The harpoon staff was a narwal tooth or horn, six feet long, — a very hard and solid piece of ivory, and perfectly straight. The harpoon head was a piece of walrus tusk, three inches long, with a hole through the centre for the line, a hole into one end for the sharpened point of the staff, and at the other end it was, like the lance-head, tipped with iron. The line was simply a strip of raw seal-hide about fifty feet long, and was made by a continuous cut around the body of the seal. The rabbit-trap was merely a seal-skin line with a multitude of loops dangling from it. The lamp was a shallow dish of soft soap-stone, in shape not unlike a clam-shell, and was eight inches by six. The pot was a square-sided vessel of the same material. The flint was a piece of hard granite, the steel a lump of crude iron pyrites, the wick was dried moss, and the tinder the delicate down-like covering of the willow catkins.

Tcheitchenguak told me that he was preparing the lances for a walrus hunt, and that he and Hans intended to try their skill on the morrow. The walrus had been very numerous in the open waters outside the harbor all through the winter, and their shrill cry could be heard at almost any time from the margin of the ice. The flesh of these animals is the staple food of the Esquimaux; and although they prize the

246 A WALRUS HUNT.

flesh of the reindeer, yet it is much as we do "canvas-backs;" and, for a long and steady pull, there is nothing like the "Awak," as they call the walrus, in imitation of its cry. To them its flesh is what rice is to the Hindoo, beef to the Gouchos of Buenos Ayres, or mutton to the Tartars of Mongolia.

The proposed hunt came off successfully. Hans and the old man set out with all of their tackle in fine order, and found a numerous herd of walrus swimming near the edge of the ice. They were approached with caution, on all fours, and were not alarmed. The hunters reached within a few feet of the water. They both then lay down flat on the ice and imitated the cry of the animals of which they were in pursuit; and the whole herd was soon brought by this means within easy reach of the harpoon. Rising suddenly, Hans buried his weapon in a good-sized beast, while his companion held fast to the line and secured his end of it with the iron spike of a lance-staff, which he drove into the ice and held down firmly. The beast struggled hard to free itself, floundering and plunging like a wild bull held by a lasso, but all without avail. With every opportunity Hans took in the slack of the line and secured it, and at length the struggling prey was within twenty feet of the hunters. The lance and rifle now did their work very expeditiously; the frightened comrades of the dying animal rushed away through the waters with loud cries of alarm, their deep bass voices sounding strangely through the darkness. The edge of the ice proved to be too thin to bear the captured game, and, having secured it with a line, it was allowed to remain until the following day, when, the ice having thickened with the low temperature, the flesh was chopped out and brought in. The snow-hut now rejoiced in a supply of food and blubber sufficient to last its inmates for a long time to come; the dogs were refreshed with a substantial meal; and the head and skin were put into a barrel and labeled "Smithsonian."

CHAPTER XX.

LOOKING FOR THE SUN. — THE OPEN SEA. — BIRDS.

WHILE the days were thus running on, the sun was crawling up toward the horizon, and each returning noon brought an increase of light. I carried in my pocket at all times a little book, and early in February I began to experiment with it. When I could read the title-page at noon I was much rejoiced. By and by the smaller letters could be puzzled out; then I could decipher with ease the finest print, and the youngsters were in great glee at being able to read the thermometers at eleven and twelve and one o'clock without the lantern. On the 10th of February I made the following memorandum on the margin of my book: "Almost broad daylight at noon, and I read this page at 3 o'clock P. M." My calculations placed the sun at the horizon on the 18th.

The appearance of the sun became now the one absorbing event. About it everybody thought and everybody talked continually. No set of men ever looked more eagerly for a coming joy than did we for the promised morn, — we, half-bloodless beings, coming from the night, bleached in the long-continued lamp-light, and almost as colorless as potato-sprouts growing in a dark cellar. We all noted how to-day compared with yesterday, and contrasted it with this day a week ago. Even the old cook caught the con-

LOOKING FOR THE SUN.   249

tagion, and crawled up from among his saucepans and coppers, and, shading his eyes with his stove-hardened hands, peered out into the growing twilight. " I tinks dis be very long night," said he, "and I likes once more to see de blessed sun." The steward was in a state of chronic excitement. He could not let the sun rest in peace for an hour. He must watch for him constantly. He must be forever running up on deck and out on the ice, book in hand, trying to read by the returning daylight. He was impatient with the time. "Don't the Commander think the sun will come back sooner than the 18th?" "Don't he think it will come back on the 17th?" "Was he quite sure that it would n't appear on the 16th?" "I'm afraid, steward, we must rely upon the Nautical Almanac." "But might n't the Nautical Almanac be wrong?" — and I could clearly perceive that he thought my ciphering might be wrong too.

Meanwhile we were tormented with another set of gales, and we could scarcely stir abroad. The ice was all broken up in the outer bay, and the open sea came nearer to us than during any previous period of the winter. The ice was nearly all driven out of the bay, and the broad, dark, bounding water was not only in sight from the deck, but I could almost drop a minic-ball into it from my rifle, while standing on the poop. Even the ice in the inner harbor was loosened around the shore, and, thick and solid though it was, I thought at one time that there was danger of its giving way and going bodily out to sea.

Strange, too, along the margin of this water there came a flock of speckled birds to shelter themselves under the lee of the shore, and to warm their lit-tle feet in the waters which the winds would not let freeze. They were the *Dovekie* of Southern Greenland, — the *Uria grylle* of the naturalist. They are often seen about Disco Island and Upernavik in the winter time, but I was much surprised to find them denizens of the Arctic night so near the Pole. It was a singular sight to see them paddling about in the caves, under the ice-foot, at 30° below zero, uttering their plaintive cry, and looking for all the world like homeless children, shoeless and in rags, crouching for shelter beneath a door-stoop on a bleak December night. I wanted one of them badly for a specimen, but it would have required something stronger than the claims of science to have induced me to harm a feather of their trembling little heads.

CHAPTER XXI.

SUNRISE.

February 18th.

HEAVEN be praised! I have once more seen the sun.

Knowing that the sun would appear to-day, everybody was filled with expectation, and hastened off after breakfast to some favorite spot where it was thought that he might be seen. Some went in the right direction, and were gratified; others went in the wrong direction, and were disappointed. Knorr and others of the officers climbed the hills above Etah. Charley limbered up his rheumatic old legs, and tried to get a view from the north side of the harbor, forgetting that the mountains intervened. Harris and Heywood climbed to the top of the hill behind the harbor, and the former shook his Odd Fellow's flag in the sun's very face. The cook was troubled that he did not have a look at "de blessed sun;" but he could not gratify his wish without going upon the land, and this he could no more be induced to do than the mountain could be persuaded to come to Mahomet. He will probably have to wait until the sun steals over the hills into the harbor, which will be at least twelve days.

My own share in the day's excitement has been equal to the rest of them. Accompanied by Dodge

252 SUNRISE.

and Jensen, I set out at an early hour toward a point on the north side of the bay, from which I could command a view of the southern horizon. We had much difficulty in reaching our destination. The open water came nearly a mile within the point for which we were bound, and it was no easy task picking our way along the sloping drifts of the ice-foot. But we were at last successful, and reached our look-out station (hereafter to be known as Sunrise Point) with half an hour to spare.

The day was far from a pleasant one for a holiday excursion. The temperature was very low, and the wind, blowing quite freshly, brought the drifting snow down from the mountains, and rattled it about us rather sharply. But we were amply repaid by the view which was spread out before us.

An open sea lay at our feet and stretched far away to the front and right of us as we faced the south. Numerous bergs were dotted over it, but otherwise it was mainly free from ice. Its surface was much agitated by the winds, which kept it from freezing, and the waves were dancing in the cold air as if in very mockery of the winter. It was indeed a vast bubbling caldron, — seething, and foaming, and emitting vapors. The light curling streams of "frost smoke" which rose over it sailed away on the wind toward the southwest, and there mingled with a dark mist-bank. Little streams of young ice, as if struggling to bind the waves, rattled and crackled over the restless waters. To the left, the lofty coast mountains stood boldly up in the bright air, and near Cape Alexander the glacier peeped from between them, coming down the valley with a gentle slope from the broad *mer de glace*. The bold front of Crystal Palace Cliffs cut

SUNRISE   253

sharply against this line of whiteness, and the dark,
gloomy walls of Cape Alexander rose squarely from
the sea. Upon the crests of the silent hills, and over
the white-capped cape, light clouds lazily floated, and
through these the sun was pouring a stream of golden
fire, and the whole southern heavens were ablaze with
the splendor of the coming day.

The point of Cape Alexander lay directly south of
us, and the sun would appear from behind it at exactly the meridian hour, — rolling along the horizon,
with only half its disk above the line of waters. We
awaited the approaching moment with much eagerness. Presently a ray of light burst through the soft
mist-clouds which lay off to the right of us opposite
the cape, blending them into a purple sea and glis-
tening upon the silvery summits of the tall icebergs,
which pierced the vapory cloak as if to catch the
coming warmth. The ray approached us nearer and
nearer, the purple sea widened, the glittering spires
multiplied, as one after another they burst in quick
succession into the blaze of day ; and as this marvelous
change came over the face of the sea, we felt that the
shadow of the cape was the shadow of the night, and
that the night was passing away. Soon the dark-red
cliffs behind us glowed with a warm coloring, the hills
and the mountains stood forth in their new robes of
resplendent brightness, and the tumbling waves melted away from their angry harshness, and laughed in
the sunshine. And now the line of the shadow was
in sight. " There it is upon the point," cried Jensen.
" There it is upon the ice-foot," answered Dodge, —
there at our feet lay a sheet of sparkling gems, and
the sun burst broadly in our faces. Off went our
caps with a simultaneous impulse, and we hailed this

254 SUNRISE.

long-lost wanderer of the heavens with loud demonstrations of joy.

And now we were bathing in the atmosphere of other days. The friend of all hopeful associations had come back again to put a new glow into our hearts. He had returned after an absence of one hundred and twenty-six days to revive a slumbering world; and as I looked upon his face again, after this long interval, I did not wonder that there should be men to bow the knee and worship him and proclaim him "The eye of God." The parent of light and life everywhere, he is the same within these solitudes. The germ awaits him here as in the Orient; but there it rests only through the short hours of a summer night, while here it reposes for months under a sheet of snows. But after a while the bright sun will tear this sheet asunder, and will tumble it in gushing fountains to the sea, and will kiss the cold earth, and give it warmth and life; and the flowers will bud and bloom, and will turn their tiny faces smilingly and gratefully up to him, as he wanders over these ancient hills in the long summer. The very glaciers will weep tears of joy at his coming. The ice will loose its iron grip upon the waters, and will let the wild waves play in freedom. The reindeer will skip gleefully over the mountains to welcome his coming, and will look longingly to him for the green pastures. The sea-fowls, knowing that he will give them a resting-place for their feet on the rocky islands, will come to seek the moss-beds which he spreads for their nests; and the sparrows will come on his life-giving rays, and will sing their love songs through the endless day.

CHAPTER XXII.

SPRING TWILIGHT — ARRIVAL OF ESQUIMAUX — OBTAINING DOGS. — KALUTU-
NAH, TATTARAT, MYOUK, AMALATOK AND HIS SON — AN ARCTIC HOSPI-
TAL — ESQUIMAU GRATITUDE

My time became now fully occupied with preparations for my journey northward. The sun appearing
on the 18th, as recorded in the last chapter, rose completely above the horizon on the next day, was something higher the day following, and, continuing to
ascend in steady progression, we had soon several
hours of broad daylight before and after noon, although the sun did not for some time come in sight
above the hills on the south side of the harbor. The
long dreary night was passing away; we had with
each succeeding day an increase of light, and the
spring twilight was merging slowly into the continual
sunshine of the summer, as we had before seen the
autumn twilight pass into the continued darkness of
the winter.

The details of my preparations for traveling would
have little interest to the reader, and I pass them
over. It is proper, however, that I should recur to
the situation in which I found myself, now that the
traveling season had opened.

The dogs, five in number, which Hans brought back
from the southern journey, had recovered, and did not
appear to have been materially injured; but there
were not enough of them to furnish a serviceable

256   ARRIVAL OF ESQUIMAUX.

team for one sledge. They were therefore of little use; and it became clear that, unless I obtained a fresh supply from the Esquimaux, any plan of sledge exploration which I might form must depend wholly upon the men for its execution. Men, instead of dogs, must drag the sledges.

The Esquimaux had disappointed me by not coming up to Etah; and, February having almost passed away without bringing reinforcements from that quarter, I had quite given up the expectation of seeing them, when a party of three arrived most opportunely. This gave me new encouragement; for, although I could not hope to replace the fine teams which I had lost, yet there was still a prospect of some much-needed assistance.

The Esquimau party comprised three individuals, all of whom I had known before. Their names were Kalutunah, Tattarat, and Myouk. Kalutunah was, in 1854, the best hunter of the tribe, and was, besides, the Angekok, or priest. He was not slow to tell me that he had since advanced to the dignity of chief, or Nalegak, an office which, however, gave him no authority, as the Esquimaux are each a law unto himself, and they submit to no control. The title is about as vague as that of "Defender of the Faith;" and the parallel is not altogether bad, for if this latter did originate in a Latin treatise about the "Seven Sacraments," it was perpetuated by a sharp sword; and so the title chief, or Nalegak as they call it, is the compliment paid to the most skillful hunter, and his title is perpetuated by skill in the use of a sharp harpoon.

The excellence of Kalutunah's hunting equipments — his strong lines and lances and harpoons, his fine

ESQUIMAU TEAMS. 257

sledge and hearty, sleek dogs — bore ample evidence of the sagacity of the tribe. Tattarat was a very different style of person. His name signifies "The Kittiwake Gull," and a more fitting title could hardly have been bestowed upon him, for he was the perfect type of that noisy, chattering, graceful bird, thriftless to the last degree; and, like many another kittiwake gull or Harold Skimpole of society, he was, in spite of thieving and other arts, always "out at elbows." Myouk was not unlike him, only that he was worse, if possible. He was, in truth, one of Satan's regularly enlisted light-infantry, and was as full of tricks as Asmodeus himself.

The party came up on two sledges. Kalutunah drove one and Tattarat the other. Kalutunah's team was his own. Of the other team, two dogs belonged to Tattarat, one was borrowed, and the fourth was the property of Myouk. It is curious to observe how the same traits of character exhibit themselves in all peoples, and by the same evidences. While Kalutunah came in with his dogs looking fresh and in fine condition, with strong traces and solid sledge, the team of Tattarat was a set of as lean and hungry-looking curs as ever was seen, their traces all knotted and tangled, and the sledge rickety and almost tumbling to pieces. They had traveled all the way from Iteplik without halting, except for a short rest at Sorfalik. They declared that they had not tasted food since leaving their homes; and if the appetite should govern the belief, I thought that there was no ground for doubting, since they made away with the best part of a quarter of venison, the swallowing of which was much aided by sundry chunks of walrus blubber, before

17

KALUTUNAH.

they rolled over among the reindeer skins of Tchei-tchenguak's hut and slept.

Next morning I had Kalutunah brought to my cabin, thinking to treat him with that distinguished consideration due to his exalted rank. But caution was necessary. For a stool I gave him a keg, and I was particularly careful that his person should not come in contact with any thing else, for under the ample furs of this renowned chief there were roaming great droves of creeping things, for which no learned lexicographer has yet invented a polite name, and so I cannot further describe them. Nor can I adequately describe the man himself, as he sat upon the keg, his body hidden in a huge fur coat, with its great hood, and his legs and feet inserted in long-haired bear-skin, — the whole costume differing little from the hitherto described dress of the dark-faced Tcheitchenguak. He was a study for a painter. No child could have exhibited more unbounded delight, had all the toys of Nuremberg been tumbled into one heap before him. To picture his face with any thing short of a skillful brush were an impossible task. It was not comely like that of "Villiers with the flaxen hair," nor yet handsome like that of the warrior chief Nireus, whom Homer celebrates as the handsomest man in the whole Greek army, (and never mentions afterwards,) nor was it like Ossian's chief, "the changes of whose face were as various as the shadows which fly over the field of grass;" but it was bathed in the sunshine of a broad grin. Altogether it was quite characteristic of his race, although expressing a much higher type of manhood than usual. The features differed only in degree from those of Tcheitchenguak, heretofore described; the skin was less dark, the face broader, the cheek-bones higher, the nose flatter and more curved, the upper lip longer, the mouth wider, the eyes even smaller, contracting when he laughed into scarcely distinguishable slits. Upon his long upper lip grew a little hedge-row of black bristles, which did not curl gracefully nor droop languidly, but which stuck straight out like the whiskers of a cat. A few of the same sort radiated from his chin. I judged him to be about forty years old, and since soap and towels and the external application of water have not yet been introduced among the native inhabitants of Whale Sound, these forty years had favored the accumulation of a coating to the skin, which, by the unequal operation of friction, had given his hands and face quite a spotted appearance.

But if he was not handsome, he was not really ugly; for, despite his coarse features and dirty face, there was a rugged sort of good-humor and frank simplicity about the fellow which pleased me greatly. His tongue was not inclined to rest. He must tell me every thing. His wife was still living, and had added two girls to the amount of his responsibilities; but his face glowed with delight when I asked him about their first-born, whom I remembered in 1854 as a bright boy of some five or six summers, and he exhibited all of a father's just pride in the prospect of the lad's future greatness. Already he could catch birds, and was learning to drive dogs.

I asked him about his old rival Sipsu, who once gave me much trouble, and was an endless source of inconvenience to Kalutunah. He was dead. When asked how he died, he was a little loath to tell, but he finally said that he had been killed. He had become very unpopular, and was stabbed one night in a dark

260 A PRIMITIVE TREATY.

hut, and, bleeding from a mortal wound, had been dragged out and buried in the stones and snow, where the cold and the hurt together soon terminated as well his life as his mischief.

Death had made fearful ravages among his people since I had seen them five years before, and he complained bitterly of the hardships of the last winter, in consequence of a great deficiency of dogs, the same distemper which swept mine off having attacked those of his people. Indeed, the disease appears to have been universal throughout the entire length of Greenland. But notwithstanding this poverty, he undertook to supply me with some animals, in return for which I was to make liberal presents; and, as a proof of his sincerity, he offered me two of the four which composed his present team. From Tattarat I afterwards purchased one of his three, and for a fine knife I obtained the fourth one of that hunter's team, the property of Myouk, and the only dog that he possessed.

The hunters were all well pleased with their bargains, for they went away rich in iron, knives, and needles, — wealth to them more valuable than would have been all the vast piles of treasure with which the Inca Atahuallpa sought to satisfy the rapacious Pizarro, or the lacs of rupees with which the luckless Rajah Nuncomar strove to free himself from the clutches of the remorseless Hastings. And we had made a treaty of peace and friendship, and had ratified it by a solemn promise, befitting a Nalegak and a Nalegaksoak. The Nalegak was to furnish the Nalegaksoak with dogs, and the Nalegaksoak was to pay for them. This exceedingly simple treaty may at first strike the reader with surprise; but I feel sure

OBTAINING DOGS. 261

that that surprise will vanish when he recalls the memorable historical parallel of Burgoyne and his Hessians.

I did not tell Kalutunah that I wished only to bestow benefits upon his people, for no one is more quick to penetrate the hollowness of such declarations than the "untutored savage." He is not so easily hoaxed with philanthropic sentiment as is generally supposed, and he fully recognizes the' practical features of being expected to return a *quid pro quo.* But I did venture upon a little harmless imposition of another sort, giving him to understand that it was useless for the Esquimaux to attempt to deceive me, as I could read not only their acts but their thoughts as well ; and, in proof of my powers, I performed before him some simple sleight-of-hand tricks, and after turning up a card with much gravity told him exactly what (it was not much of a venture) Ootinah and his wooden-legged companion had stolen He was much astonished, said that I was quite right about the stealing, for he had seen the stolen articles himself, and evidently thought me a wonderful magician. He owned to me that he did something in the jugglery business himself; but when I asked him about his journeys to the bottom of the sea, in his Angekok capacity, to break the spell by which the evil spirit Torngak holds within her anger the walrus and seal, in the days of famine, he very adroitly changed the subject, and began to describe a recent bear-hunt which appeared to amuse him greatly. The wounded animal broke away from the dogs, and, making a dive at one of the hunters, knocked the wind out of the unhappy man with a blow of his fore-paw. Kalutunah laughed heartily while relating the story, and seemed to think it a capital joke

262 AN ARCTIC MICAWBER.

Our savage guests remained with us a few days, and then set out for their homes, declaring their intention to come speedily back and bring more of the tribe and dogs. I drove out with them a few miles, and we parted on the ice. When about a mile away, I observed Myouk jump from the sledge to pick up something which he had dropped. No doubt rejoiced to be rid of this extra load on his rickety sledge, Tattarat whipped up his team, and the last I saw of poor Myouk he was running on, struggling manfully to catch up; but, notwithstanding all his efforts, he was falling behind, and it is not unlikely that he was suffered to walk all the way to Iteplik.

This Myouk was the same droll creature that he was when I knew him formerly, — a sort of Arctic Micawber, everlastingly waiting for something to turn up which never did turn up; and, with much cheerfulness, hoping for good luck which never came. He recited to me all of his hardships and misfortunes. His sledge was all broken to pieces, and he could not mend it; his dogs were all dead except the one he sold to me; he had stuck his harpoon into a walrus, and the line had parted, and the walrus carried it away; he had lost his lance, and altogether his affairs were in a very lamentable state. His family were in great distress, as he could not catch any thing for them to eat, and so they had gone to Tattarat's hut. Tattarat was a poor hunter, and he made a terrible grimace, which told how great was his contempt for that doughty individual. So now he proposed, as soon as he got home, to try Kalutunah. To be sure, Kalutunah's establishment was pretty well filled already, there being not less than three families quartered there; but still, he thought there was room for one

DOMESTIC FELICITY. 263

family more. At all events, he should try it. And now would not the Nalegaksoak, — the big chief who was so rich and so mighty, be good enough to give him so many presents that he would go back and make everybody envious? Human nature is the same in the Arctic as in the Temperate zone; and, gratified with this discovery, I fairly loaded the rogue down with riches, and sent him away rejoicing. But this wife, what of her? "Oh, she's lazy and will not do any thing, and made me come all this long journey to get her some needles which she won't use, and a knife which she has no use for; and now when I go back without any dog, won't I catch it!" — and he caught hold of his tongue and pulled it as far out of his mouth as he could get it, trying in this graphic manner to illustrate the length of that aggressive organ in the wife of his bosom. "But," added this savage Benedict, "she has a ragged coat, so full of holes that she cannot go out of the hut without fear of freezing; and if she scolds me too much I won't give her any of these needles, and I won't catch her any foxes to make a new one;" — but it was easy to see that the needles would not be long withheld, and that the foxes would be caught when he was told to catch them. And so pitying his domestic misfortunes, I added some presents for this amiable creature of the ragged coat; and when he told me that she had presented him with an heir to the Myouk miseries, I added something for that, too. This little hopeful, he informed me, was already being weaned from its natural and maternal supplies, and was exhibiting great aptitude for blubber. He had called it Dak-ta-gee, which was the nearest that he could come to pronouncing Doctor Kane.

264 ESQUIMAU GRATITUDE.

Kalutunah and his companions had scarcely been gone when another sledge came, bringing two more Esquimaux, — Amalatok, of Northumberland Island, and his son. They had four dogs; and having stopped on the way to catch a walrus, part of which they had brought with them, they were much fatigued; and, having got wet in securing the prize, they were cold and a little frozen. Both were for several days quite sick in Tcheitchenguak's snow-hut, and I had at last a patient, and the snow-hut became a sort of hospital, for old Tcheitchenguak was sick too. I either visited them myself or sent Mr. Knorr twice daily; but the odor of the place becoming at length too much for that gentleman's aristocratic nose, I could no longer prescribe by proxy, and so went myself and cured my patients very speedily, winning great credit as a Narkosak, the "medicine man," in addition to being the Nalegaksoak, "the big chief." Amalatok thought at one time that he was going to die, and indeed I became sincerely alarmed about my reputation; but he came round all right in the end, and, strange though it may appear, his memory actually outlived the service long enough for him to do more than to say "Koyanak," — "I thank you;" — that is to say, as soon as he could get about he brought me his best dog, and, in token of gratitude, made me a present of it. Afterward, upon the offer of some substantial gifts, he sold me another, and he went home as rich as the party that had preceded him, and happy as Moses Primrose returning from the fair with his gross of shagreen spectacles.

And thus my kennels were being once more filled up, and my heart was rejoiced.

CHAPTER XXIII.

KALUTUNAH RETURNS. — AN ESQUIMAU FAMILY — THE FAMILY PROPERTY — THE FAMILY WARDROBE — MYOUK AND HIS WIFE — PETER S DEAD BODY FOUND — MY NEW TEAMS — THE SITUATION. — HUNTING — SUBSISTENCE OF ARCTIC ANIMALS — PURSUIT OF SCIENCE UNDER DIFFICULTIES. — KALUTUNAH AT HOME — AN ESQUIMAU FEAST — KALUTUNAH IN SERVICE — RECOVERING THE BODY OF MR SONNTAG. — THE FUNERAL — THE TOMB

KALUTUNAH came back after a few days, according to his promise, and brought along with him the entire Kalutunah family, consisting of his wife and four children. It was a regular "moving."

The chief had managed in some manner to get together another team of six good dogs, and he came up in fine style, bringing along with him on his small sledge every thing that he had in the world, and that was not much. The conveniences for life's comforts possessed by these Arctic nomads are not numerous; and it is fortunate that their desires so well accord with their means of gratifying them, for probably no people in the world possess so little, either of portable or other kind of property. The entire cargo of the sledge consisted of parts of two bear-skins, the family bedding; a half-dozen seal-skins, the family tent; two lances and two harpoons; a few substantial harpoon lines; a couple of lamps and pots; some implements and materials for repairing the sledge in the event of accident; a small seal-skin bag, containing the family wardrobe (that is, the implements for repairing it, for the entire wardrobe was on their backs);

and then there was a roll of dried grass, which they use as we do cork soles for the boots, and some dried moss for lamp-wick; and for food they had a few small pieces of walrus meat and blubber. This cargo was covered with one of the seal-skins, over which was passed from side to side a line, like a sandal-lacing, and the whole was bound down compactly to the sledge; and on the top of it rode the family, Kalutunah himself walking alongside and encouraging on his team rather with kind persuasion than with the usual Esquimau cruelty. In front sat the mother, the finest specimen of the Esquimau matron that I had seen. In the large hood of her fox-skin coat, a sort of dorsal opossum-pouch, nestled a sleeping infant. Close beside the mother sat the boy to whom I have before referred, their first-born, and the father's pride. Next came a girl, about seven years old; and another, a three year old, was wrapped up in an immense quantity of furs, and was lashed to the upstanders.

As the sledge rounded to, near the vessel, I went out to meet them. The children were at first a little frightened, but they were soon got to laugh, and I found that the same arts which win the affections of Christian babies were equally potent with the heathen. The wife remembered me well, and called me "Doc-tee," while Kalutunah, grinning all over with delight, pointed to his dogs, exclaiming with pride, "They are fine ones!" to which I readily assented; and then he added, "I come to give them all to the Nalegaksoak;" and to this I also assented.

What surprised me most with this family was their apparent indifference to the cold. They had come from Iteplik in slow marches, stopping when tired in

MYOUK AND FAMILY. 267

a snow shelter, or in deserted huts, and during this time our thermometers were ranging from 30° to 40° below zero; and when they came on board out of this temperature it never seemed to occur to them to warm themselves, but they first wandered all over the ship, satisfying their curiosity.

A few hours afterward there arrived a family of quite another description, — Myouk and his wife of the ragged coat. They had walked all the way up from Iteplik, the woman carrying her baby on her back all of these hundred and fifty miles. Myouk was evidently at a loss to find an excuse for paying me this visit; but he put a bold front on, and, like Kalutunah, discovered a reason. "I come to show the Nalegaksoak my wife and Daktagee," pointing to the dowdy, dirty creature that owned him for a husband, and the forlorn being that owned him for a father. But when he perceived that I was not likely to pay much for the sight, he timidly remarked, with another significant point, "*She* made me come," and then started off, doubtless to see what he could steal.

My arrangements were soon concluded with Kalutunah. He was to live over in the hut at Etah, to do such hunting as he could without the aid of his dogs, all of which he loaned to me; but, in any event, my stores were to be his reliance, and I bound myself to supply him with all that he required for the support of himself and his family.

On the following day the hut at Etah was cleared out and put in order, and this interesting family took up their abode there, while Myouk, as eager to place himself under the protection of a man high in favor as if his skin had been white and he knew the meaning of "public office" and lived nearer the equator,

268 PETER'S DEAD BODY.

followed the great man to his new abode, and crawled into a corner of his den as coolly as if he was a deserving fellow, and not the most arrant little knave and beggar that ever sponged on worth and industry.

Kalutunah brought a solution of the Peter mystery. As soon as the daylight began to come back, one of the Iteplik hunters, named Nesark, determined to travel up to Peteravik, and there try his fortunes in the seal hunt. Arriving at the hut (these Esquimau huts are common property) at that place, he was surprised to discover, lying on the floor, a much emaciated corpse. It was that of an Esquimau dressed in white man's clothing, and the description left no doubt that it was the body of Peter. Nesark gave it Esquimau burial. And thus, after the lapse of three months, this strange story was brought to a close; but I was still as far as ever from an explanation of the hapless boy's strange conduct.

I had now become the possessor of seventeen dogs, and awaited only one principal event to set out on a preliminary journey northward. The sea had not yet closed about Sunrise Point, and I could not get out of the bay on that side. To travel over the land was, owing to its great roughness, impracticable for a sledge, even if without cargo; and to round the Point at that season of the year, through the broken ice and rough sea, in an open boat, was, for obvious reasons, not to be thought of.

My plan had always been to set out with my principal party, when the temperature had begun to moderate toward the summer, which was likely to be about the first of April; but I had looked forward to doing some serviceable work with my dogs prior to that time. March is the coldest month of the Arctic

THE SITUATION. 269

year; but while I had no hesitation in setting out with dog-sledges at that period, the recollection of Dr. Kane's disasters were too fresh in my mind to justify me in sending out a foot party in the March temperatures.

While waiting for the frost to build a bridge for me around Sunrise Point, I was feeding up and strengthening my dogs. They soon proved to be very inferior to the animals which I had lost, and it was necessary to give them as much rest and good rations as possible. I went repeatedly to Chester Valley in pursuit of reindeer. Along the borders of the lake these beasts had flocked in great numbers during the winter, and whole acres of snow had been tossed up with their hoofs, while searching for the dead vegetation of the previous summer. The rabbits and the ptarmigan had followed them, to gather the buds of the willow-stems which were occasionally tossed up, and which form their subsistence. During one of my journeys I secured a fine specimen skin of a doe, but in order to do this I was obliged to take it off with my own hands before it should freeze. The temperature at the time was 33° below zero, and I do not ever remember to have had my regard for Natural History so severely tested.

I was exceedingly anxious to recover the body of Mr. Sonntag before I left the vessel; and, desiring to secure the assistance of Kalutunah for that purpose, I drove over to Etah a few days after he had become fixed there. I had eleven of my new dogs harnessed to the sledge, and Jensen "was himself again."

I found Kalutunah very comfortably fixed and apparently well contented. I carried with me as a present for a house-warming a quarter of a recently-captured

270 KALUTUNAH AT HOME.

deer, and a couple of gallons of oil. Observing our approach, he came out to meet us, and, some snow having drifted into the passage, he scraped it away with his foot, and invited us to enter. This we did on our hands and knees, through a sort of tunnel about twelve feet long; and thence we emerged into a dimly lighted den, where, coiled up in a nest of reindeer-skins which I had given them, was the family of the chief and the wife and baby of Myouk. Kalutunah's wife was stitching away quite swiftly at a pair of boots for my use, and I brought her some more "work," and also some presents, among which was a string of beads and a looking-glass, which much amused the children. Myouk's wife, on the other hand, was quite idle, not even looking after her child, which, startled by our approach, rolled down on the floor about our feet, and thence into the entrance among the snow which lay scattered along the passage. The poor little creature, being almost naked, set up a terrible scream, and its amiable mother, promptly seizing it by one of its legs, hauled it up and crammed into its mouth a chunk of blubber which quickly stopped its noise.

Both this woman and her husband were evidently a great annoyance to the frugal proprietors of the hut; but, with a generous practice of hospitality which I have not found elsewhere, in history or fiction, except in Cedric the Saxon, such a worthless crew are suffered to settle themselves upon a thrifty family without fear of being turned out of doors.

I sat for some time talking to Kalutunah and his industrious wife. There was not room, it was true, with so many people in the hut, to be greatly at one's ease, and I had to dodge my head when I moved, to

A MORNING CALL. 271

keep from striking the stone rafters. Besides, the smell of the place had rather a tendency to fill one's mind with longings for the open air; but I managed to remain long enough to conclude some important arrangements with my ally and his useful spouse, and then I took my leave with mutual protestations of friendship and good-will. I said to him at parting, "You are chief and I am chief, and we will both tell our respective people to be good to each other;" but he answered, "Na, na, I am chief, but you are the great chief, and the Esquimaux will do what you say. The Esquimaux like you, and are your friends. You make them many presents." I might have told him that this all-powerful method of inspiring friendship was not alone applicable to Esquimaux.

This visit was a pleasant little episode. I was much pleased at the honest heartiness with which Kalutunah entered into my plans; while the childish simplicity of his habits and the frankness of his declarations won for him a conspicuous place in my regard.

He was greatly amused with our guns, and begged for one of them, declaring that he could sit in his hut and kill the reindeer as they passed by. He would put the gun through the window, and he pointed to a hole in the wall about a foot square, where the light was admitted through a thin slab of hard snow. In the centre of it he had made a round orifice, which he said, laughingly, was for the purpose of looking out for the Nalegaksoak, — a well-turned compliment, if it did come from a savage, and all the more adroit that the orifice was really for ventilation, at least it was the only opening by which the foul air could possibly escape. Both himself and wife were highly delighted with the presents which I had brought them.

272 AN ESQUIMAU FEAST.

Although they are surrounded by reindeer, venison is a luxury which they rarely enjoy, as they possess no means of capturing the animals. They have not the bows and arrows of the Esquimaux of some other localities. Without waiting for it to be cooked, Kalutunah commenced a vigorous attack upon the raw, frozen flesh. His wife and children were not slow to follow his example, crowding round it where it lay on the dirty floor; and, without halting for an invitation, Mrs. Myouk joined in the feast. And I have never witnessed a feast which seemed to give so much satisfaction to the actors in it, not even hungry aldermen at a corporation banquet. Kalutunah was grinning all over with delight. He was eminently happy. His teeth were unintermittingly crushing the hard kernels which he chipped from the frozen "leg," and a steady stream of the luscious food was pouring down his throat. His tongue had little chance, but now and then it got loose from the venison tangle, and then I heard much of the greatness and the goodness of the Nalegaksoak. The man's enjoyment was a pleasant thing to behold.

But if the reindeer-leg gave satisfaction, the oil gave comfort. The hut was dark and chilly, not having yet become thoroughly thawed out. Kalutunah now thought that he could afford another lamp, and in a few minutes after we had entered a fresh blaze was burning in the corner. I have before explained that the Esquimau lamp is only a shallow dish, cut out of a block of soap-stone. The dried moss which they use for wick is arranged around the edge, and the blaze therefrom gives their only light and heat. Over the lamps hung pots of the same soap-stone, and into these Mrs. Kalutunah put some snow, that she

MY ESQUIMAU PEOPLE.

273

might have the water for a venison-soup, of which she invited us to stay and partake. I knew by former experience too well the nature of the Esquimau *cuisine* to make me anxious to learn further, so I plead business, and left them to enjoy themselves in their own way. How long they kept up·their feast I did not learn, but when Kalutunah came over next morning, he informed me that there was no more venison in the hut at Etah, — a hint which was not thrown away.

My Esquimau people now numbered seventeen souls; namely, six men, four women, and seven children; and they presented as many different shades of character and usefulness. The inconveniences to which they subjected us were amply compensated for by the sewing which the wives of Kalutunah and Tcheitchenguak did for us; for, in spite of all our ingenuity and patience, there was no one in the ship's company who could make an Esquimau boot, and this boot is the only suitable covering for the foot in the Arctic regions. Of the men, Hans was the most useful; for, in spite of his objectionable qualities, he was, Jensen excepted, my best hunter. Kalutunah came on board daily, and, as a privileged guest, he sought me in my cabin. My journey over to Etah made him supremely happy; for, like the sound of coming battle to the warrior who has long reposed in peace, a new life was put into him when I offered him the care of one of my newly acquired teams. He came on board the next morning and took charge of the dogs; and when, a few days afterward, I further exhibited my confidence in him by sending ·him down to Cape Alexander to see if the ice was firm, the cup of his joy was full to the brim.

274 RECOVERY OF SONNTAG'S BODY.

The report of Kalutunah being favorable, I dispatched Mr. Dodge to bring up the body of Mr. Sonntag. He took the two teams, Kalutunah driving one and Hans the other.

Mr. Dodge performed the journey with skill and energy. He reached Sorfalik in five hours, and had no difficulty in finding the locality of which they were in search, Hans remembering it by a large rock, or rather cliff, in the lee of which they had built their snow-hut. But the winds had since piled the snow over the hut, and it was completely buried out of sight. They were therefore compelled to disinter the body by laboriously digging through the hard drift; and it being quite dark and they much fatigued when the task was completed, they constructed a shelter of snow, fed their dogs, and rested. Although the temperature was 42° below zero, they managed to sleep in their furs without serious inconvenience. This was the first of Mr. Dodge's experience at this sort of camping out, and he was justly elated with the success of the experiment.

Setting out as soon as the daylight returned, the party came back by the same track which they had before pursued; but, greatly to their surprise, the tides and wind had, in the interval, carried off much of the ice in the neighborhood of the cape, so that they had before them the prospect of the very difficult task of crossing the glacier. This, not particularly embarrassing to an empty sledge, would have been exceedingly so to them. Fortunately, however, they succeeded with some risk in getting over a very treacherous place where the ice-foot, to which they were forced to adhere, was sloping, and one of the sledges had nearly gone over into the sea. Kalutunah saved it by a dexterous movement which could have been performed with safety only by one familiar, by long experience, with such dangers and expedients.

The body of our late comrade was placed in the observatory, where a few weeks before his fine mind had been intent upon those pursuits which were the delight of his life; and on the little staff which surmounted the building the flag was raised at half-mast.

The preparations for the funeral were conducted with fitting solemnity. A neat coffin was made under the supervision of Mr. McCormick, and the body having been placed therein with every degree of care, it was, on the second day after the return of Mr. Dodge, brought outside and covered with the flag, and then, followed by the entire ship's company, in solemn procession, it was borne by four of the sorrowing messmates of the deceased to the grave which had, with much difficulty, been dug in the frozen terrace. As it lay in its last cold resting-place, I read over the body the burial-service, and the grave was then closed. Above it we afterward built, with stones, a neatly shaped mound, and marked the head with a chiseled slab, bearing this inscription:—

AUGUST SONNTAG.
Died
December, 1860,
AGED 28 YEARS.

And here in the drear solitude of the Arctic desert our comrade sleeps the sleep that knows no waking in this troubled world, — where no loving hands can ever come to strew his grave with flowers, nor eyes grow dim with sorrowing; but the gentle stars, which in life he loved so well, will keep over him eternal vigil, and the winds will wail over him, and Nature, his mistress, will drop upon his tomb her frozen tears forevermore.

CHAPTER XXIV.

STARTING ON MY FIRST JOURNEY — OBJECT OF THE JOURNEY. — A MISHAP. — A FRESH START — THE FIRST CAMP — HARTSTENE'S CAIRN. — EXPLORING A TRACK — A NEW STYLE OF SNOW-HUT. — AN UNCOMFORTABLE NIGHT. — LOW TEMPERATURE — EFFECT OF TEMPERATURE ON THE SNOW — AMONG THE HUMMOCKS — SIGHTING HUMBOLDT GLACIER — THE TRACK IMPRACTICABLE TO THE MAIN PARTY — VAN RENSSELAER HARBOR. — FATE OF THE ADVANCE. — A DRIVE IN A GALE

ON the 16th of March I found myself able for the first time to get around Sunrise Point. Except during a brief interval, the temperature had now fallen lower than at any previous period of the winter; and, the air having been quite calm for two days, the ice had formed over the outer bay. This long desired event was hailed with satisfaction, and I determined to start north at once.

My preparations occupied but a few hours, as every thing had been ready for weeks past. The charge of one of the sledges was given to Jensen, the other to Kalutunah, the former having nine and the latter six dogs. One of the dogs had died and another had been crippled in a fight, thus leaving me only fifteen for service.

My object in this preliminary journey was chiefly to explore the track, and determine whether it were best to adhere to the Greenland coast, following up the route of Dr. Kane, or to strike directly across the Sound from above Cape Hatherton, in the endeavor to reach, on Grinnell Land, the point of departure

A MISHAP.

for which I had striven, without success, the previous autumn. It was evident that every thing depended upon being now able to make good what I had lost by that failure, through a chain of circumstances which I have no need to repeat, as the reader will recall the struggle which resulted in the crippling of my vessel, and which had nearly caused its total wreck among the ice-fields in the mouth of the Sound. If the state of the ice should prove favorable to a speedy crossing of the Sound to Grinnell Land, or even to securing, without much delay, a convenient point of departure on the Greenland side beyond Humboldt Glacier, I had little doubt as to the successful termination of my summer labors.

Upon reaching Sunrise Point we found the ice to be very rough and insecure, and the tide of the previous night had opened a wide crack directly off the point, which it was necessary for us to cross. This crack had been closed over but a few hours, and the dogs hesitated a moment at its margin; but Jensen's whip reassured them, and they plunged ahead. The ice bent under their weight, and, as if by a mutual understanding, the team scattered, but not in time to save themselves, for down they all sank, higgledy-piggledy, into the sea, dragging the sledge after them. Being seated on the back part of it, I had time to roll myself off, but Jensen was not so fortunate, and dogs, sledge, driver and all were floundering together in a confused tangle among the broken ice. Kalutunah, who was a few paces in the rear, coming up, we extricated them from their cold bath. Jensen was pretty well soaked, and his boots were filled with water. Being only five miles from the schooner, I thought it safest to drive back as rapidly as possible rather than

THE FIRST CAMP. 279

construct a snow-hut to shelter my unlucky driver from the cold wind which was beginning to blow. Besides, our buffalo-skins were as wet as they could be, and we should have precious little comfort on our journey if we did not return and exchange them for dry ones. The dogs, too, ran great risk of injury by being allowed to rest in their wet coats in so low a temperature. The whip was not spared, and the vessel was reached without serious consequences either to Jensen or the team. An hour or so sufficed for us to refit, when we started again; and being this time more cautious, we got around the point without further trouble.

The ice was found to be smooth and the traveling good as we moved up the coast; and, not being very heavily laden, we got on at a good pace. The snow had been packed very hard by the winds, and wherever there had been hummocks it had collected between them, so that, although the surface was somewhat rolling and uneven, yet it was as firm as a country road. Darkness coming on, (we had not yet reached the constant sunlight of summer,) we hauled in under Cape Hatherton and made our first camp.

It was a real Arctic camp; — picketing the dogs and burrowing in a snow-bank are very simple operations, and require but little time. Jensen made the burrow, and Kalutunah looked after the animals; and when all was ready we crawled in and tried our best to be comfortable and to sleep; but the recollection of the ship's bunk was too recent to render either practicable, except to Kalutunah, who did not seem to mind any thing, and snored all through the night in a most awful manner. The outside temperature was 40° below zero.

280   HARTSTENE'S CAIRN.

I was not sorry when we got under way again next morning, and we were soon warmed up with the exercise. The same condition of ice continuing after passing Cape Hatherton, we quickly reached the north horn of Fog Inlet. Here, as we approached the point, I discovered a cairn perched upon a conspicuous spot, and, not having remembered it as the work of any of Dr. Kane's parties, I halted the sledges and went ashore to inspect it. It proved to have been built by Captain Hartstene, while searching for Dr. Kane, as shown by a record found in a glass vial at its base. The record was as follows: —

"The U. S. Steamer *Arctic* touched here and examined thoroughly for traces of Dr. Kane and his associates, without finding any thing more than a vial, with a small piece of cartridge-paper with the letters 'O. K. Aug. 1853,' some matches, and a ship's rifle-ball. We go from this unknown point to Cape Hatherton for a search.

"H. J. HARTSTENE,

Lieut. Comdg. Arctic Expedition.

"8 P. M. August 16th, 1855.

"P. S. Should the U. S. bark *Release* find this, she will understand that we are bound for a search at Cape Hatherton.

"H. J. H."

I was much gratified with this discovery, for it brought to my mind the recollection of the protecting care of our government, and a gallant effort to rescue from the jaws of the Arctic ice a very forlorn party of men. I was only sorry that the author of this hastily written evidence of his spirited search had not reached Cape Hatherton some time earlier, for then we should have been saved many a hard and weary pull. The locality will hereafter be known as *Cairn Point.*

Climbing to an elevation, I had a good view of the sea over a radius of several miles. The pros-

EXPLORING A TRACK. 281

pect was not encouraging. In every direction, except immediately down the coast toward Cape Hatherton, the ice was very rough, being jammed against the shore and piled up over the sea in great ridges, which looked rather unpromising for sledges.

The view decided my course of action. Cairn Point would be my starting-place if I crossed the Sound, and a most convenient position for a depot of supplies in the event of being obliged to hold on up the Greenland coast. Accordingly, I took from the sledges all of the provisions except what was necessary for a six days' consumption, and discovering a suitable cleft in a rock, deposited it therein, covering it over with heavy stones, to protect it from the bears, intending to proceed up the coast for a general inspection of the condition of the ice on the Sound.

These various operations consumed the day; so we fed the dogs and dug into another snow-bank, and got through another night after the fashion of Arctic travelers, which is not much of a fashion to boast of. We slept and did not freeze, and more than this we did not expect.

The next day's journey was made with light sledges, but it was much more tedious than the two days preceding; for the track was rough, and during the greater part of the time it was as much as the dogs could do to get through the hummocked ice with nothing on the sledge but our little food and sleeping gear. As for riding, that was entirely out of the question. After nine hours of this sort of work, during which we made, lightened as we were, not over twenty miles, we were well satisfied to draw up to the first convenient snow-bank for another nightly burrow.

Being naturally inclined to innovation, I had busied

282   A NEW STYLE OF SNOW-HUT.

my mind all through the day, as I tumbled among the ice and the drifts, in devising some better plan of hut than the cavern arrangement of the nomadic Kalutunah. The snow-bank which I selected had a square side about five feet high. Starting on the top of this, we dug a pit about six feet long, four and a half wide, and four deep, leaving between the pit and the square side of the bank a wall about two feet thick. Over the top of this pit we placed one of the sledges, over the sledge the canvas apron used, while traveling, to inclose the cargo, and over that again we shoveled loose snow to the depth of some three feet. Then we dug a hole into this inclosure through the thin wall, pushed in our buffalo-skin bedding, and all articles penetrable by a dog's tooth and not inclosed in tin cases, (for the dogs will eat any thing, their own harness included,) then a few blocks of hard snow, and finally we crawled in ourselves. The blocks of snow were jammed into the entrance, and we were housed for the night.

Being bound on a short journey, I thought that I could afford a little extra weight, and carried alcohol for fuel, as this is the only fuel that can be used in the close atmosphere of a snow-hut. A ghastly blue blaze was soon flickering in our faces, and in our single tin-kettle some snow was being converted into water, and then the water began to hum, and then after a long while it boiled, (it is no easy matter to boil water in such temperature with a small lamp,) and we were refreshed with a good strong pint pot of tea; then the tea-leaves were tossed into one corner, some more snow was put in the tea-kettle and melted, and out of desiccated beef and desiccated potatoes we make a substantial hash; and when this was disposed of we lit

COLD LODGINGS. 283

our pipes, rolled up in our buffaloes, and did the best we could for the balance of the night.

My invention did not, however, turn out so satisfactory as was expected. The hut, if more commodious, and admitting of a little movement without knocking down the loose snow all over us, was much colder than either of our dens of the Kalutunah plan, the temperature in each of which stood about zero through the night, elevated to that degree by the heat radiated from our own persons, and from the lamp which cooked the supper. But this pit under the sledge could not be warmed above 20° below zero. No amount of coaxing could induce the thermometer to rise.

Notwithstanding all this I still adhered to my theory about snow-huts, and I very unjustly threw the blame on Jensen for carelessness in the construction; so I sent him out to pile on more snow. This did not mend matters in the least, but rather made them worse; for, through the now open doorway, what little warmth we had managed to get up made its escape; and when Jensen came back and we shut ourselves in again, the temperature was —35°, and never afterwards reached higher than —30°. Even Kalutunah was troubled to sleep, and, as he rubbed his eyes and pounded his feet together to keep them from freezing, he made a grimace which told more plainly than words in what low estimation he held the Nalegaksoak's talents for making snow-huts.

The cause of all this trouble was, however, explained next morning. The hut was well enough, and I stuck ever afterward to the plan, and even Kalutunah was compelled to own that it was the correct thing. It was perfectly tight. The thermometer

LOW TEMPERATURE.

told the story. As it hung against the snow wall I called Jensen's attention to it. The top of the delicate red streak of alcohol stood at 31° below zero.

We crawled out in the open air at last, to try the sunshine. "I will give you the best buffalo-skin in the ship, Jensen, if the air outside is not warmer than in that den which you have left so full of holes." And it really seemed so. Human eye never lit upon a more pure and glowing morning. The sunlight was sparkling all over the landscape and the great world of whiteness; and the frozen plain, the hummocks, the icebergs, and the tall mountains, made a picture inviting to the eye. Not a breath of air was stirring. Jensen gave in without a murmur. "Well, the hut must have been full of holes, after all; but I 'll fix it next time."

I brought out the thermometer and set it up in the shadow of an iceberg near by. I really expected to see it rise; but no, down sank the little red column, down, down, almost to the very bulb, and it never stopped until it had touched $68\frac{1}{2}°$ below zero, — $100\frac{1}{2}°$ below the freezing point of water.[1]

I do not recall but two instances of equally low temperature having been previously recorded, one of which, by Niveroff, at Yakoutsk, in Siberia, was —72° of the Fahrenheit scale. I am not, however, aware that any traveler has ever noted so low a temperature while in the field.

It struck me as a singular circumstance that this great depression of temperature was not perceptible to the senses, which utterly failed to give us even so much as a hint that here in this blazing sunlight we

[1] It is worthy of observation that the lowest temperature recorded at Port Foulke, during my absence, was 27° below zero.

LOW TEMPERATURE. 285

were experiencing about the coldest temperature ever recorded. But this would have held good only in the profound calm with which we were favored. At such low temperature the least wind is painful and even dangerous, especially if the traveler is compelled to face it. It is also a singular circumstance that, while the sun's rays, penetrating the atmosphere, seem to impart to it so little warmth, they are powerful enough to blister the skin, so that in truth the opposite conditions of heat — positive and negative — are operating upon the unfortunate face at one and the same time.

The effect of these low temperatures upon the snow is very striking. It becomes hardened to such a degree that it almost equals sand in grittiness, and the friction to the sledge-runner is increased accordingly. The same circumstance was noted by Baron Wrangel, but it is not new to the Esquimaux. The sledge runs most glibly when the snow is slightly wet. To obviate in some measure the difficulty thus occasioned, the native covers the sole of his runner with moisture. Dissolving in his mouth a piece of snow, he pours it out into his hand and coats with it the polished ivory sole, and in an instant he has formed a thin film of ice to meet the hardened crystals. Kalutunah stopped frequently for this purpose ; and, upon trying the experiment with my own sledge, I found it to work admirably, and to produce a very perceptible difference in the draft.

It would be needless for me to give from day to day the details of this journey. As I have said before, it was merely experimental, and it was continued until I had satisfied myself fully that the route northward by the Greenland coast was wholly impractica-

286 KALUTUNAH PUZZLED.

ble. The condition of the ice was very different from what it was in 1853–54. Then the coast ice was mainly smooth, and the hummocks were not met until we had gone from ten to twenty miles from the shore. Now there was no such belt. The winter had set in while the ice was crowding upon the land, and the pressure had been tremendous. Vast masses were piled up along the track, and the whole sea was but one confused jumble of ice-fragments, forced up by the pressure to an enormous height, and frozen together in that position. The whole scene was the Rocky Mountains on a small scale ; peak after peak, ridge after ridge, spur after spur, separated by deep valleys, into which we descended over a rough declivity, and then again ascended on the other side, to cross an elevated crest and repeat the operation. The traveling was very laborious. It was but an endless clambering over ice-masses of every form and size.

Kalutunah was much puzzled to understand my object. He had never heard of a journey into that region except to catch bears, and then only in great emergencies ; and when bear-track after bear-track was crossed without our giving chase, he became even more and more concerned. He had a double motive, — to have the sport and to see the effect of our rifles ; but none of the tracks were fresh, and the chase would have been too long to agree with my purposes. At length, however, we came to a trail evidently not an hour old, and which we might have pursued to a successful issue, for the tracks were made by a mother and a small cub. Kalutunah halted his team, and was loud in his pleadings for leave to make a dash. He argued for the sport, for the skin which would make

SIGHTING HUMBOLDT GLACIER. 287

the Nalegaksoak such a fine coat, for his wife and children, who had not tasted bear-meat for ever so long a time, and finally for his dogs. "See how unhappy they are," said he, pointing to his tired team, which seemed to possess little appreciation of the eloquence that was being wasted upon them, for they had all fallen down in their tracks as soon as we had halted the sledges. Four days of hauling through drifts and hummocks had made them care little for a bear-hunt.

Despite the difficulties of the traveling, three days more brought me within view of the great Humboldt Glacier, but the ice was becoming worse and worse, the icebergs were multiplying, my dogs were being worn out to no purpose; and much as I should have liked to continue the journey, there was no object to be gained by doing so. The ground had been covered by Dr. Kane's parties, and there was nothing to be learned further than I had experienced already, namely, that, in no event, could I get my boat to the polar sea in this direction. Whether I could do any better by the passage across the Sound to Grinnell Land remained to be seen. In any case, this last was clearly my only route.

The Humboldt Glacier was visible from the top of an iceberg. It revealed itself in a long line of bluish whiteness. Cape Agassiz, the last known point of the Greenland coast, bounded it on the right, and to the left it melted away in the remote distance. The line of its trend appeared to me to be more to the eastward than given in the original survey of Mr. Bonnsall, of Dr. Kane's expedition; and, although of little practical importance, yet this circumstance, coupled with observations hereafter to be recorded, have caused me

288 FATE OF THE "ADVANCE"

to deviate somewhat, in the small chart which accompanies this volume, from the chart of Dr. Kane.

The coast along which I had been traveling was a succession of well-remembered landmarks. The tall sandstone cliffs were as familiar as the rows of lofty warehouses and stores on Broadway. Both up and down the coast I had gone so often from Van Rensselaer Harbor that I knew every point of land, and gorge, and ravine as if I had seen them but yesterday. But when I got down into the harbor itself how changed was every thing! Instead of the broad, smooth ice over which I had so often strolled, there was but a uniform wilderness of hummocks. In the place where the *Advance* once lay, the ice was piled up nearly as high as were her mast-heads. Fern Rock was almost overridden by the frightful avalanche which had torn down into the harbor from the north, and the locality of the storehouse on Butler Island was almost buried out of sight. No vestige of the *Advance* remained, except a small bit of a deck-plank which I picked up near the site of the old Observatory. The fate of the vessel is of course a matter only of conjecture. When the ice broke up — it may have been the year we left her or years afterward — she was probably carried out to sea and ultimately crushed and sunk. From the Esquimaux I obtained many contradictory statements. Indeed, with the best intentions in the world, these Esquimaux have great trouble in telling a straight story. Even Kalutunah is not to be depended upon if there is the ghost of a chance for invention. He had been to the vessel, but at one time it was one year and then again it was another; he had carried off much wood, as many other Esquimaux had done. Another Esqui-

A DRIVE IN A GALE.

mau had seen a vessel drifting about in the North Water among the ice, and finally it was sunk in the mouth of Wolstenholme Sound. This was four summers ago. Another had seen the same vessel, but the event had happened only two years before; while still another had accidentally set fire to the brig and burned her up where she lay in Van Rensselaer Harbor. No two of them gave the same account. Indeed, one of them asserted quite positively that the vessel had drifted down into the bay below, was there frozen up the next winter, and he had there boarded her when on a bear-hunt. Kalutunah had nothing positive to say on the subject, but he rather inclined to the story of the burning.

Every object around me was filled with old associations, some pleasant and some painful. I visited the graves of Baker and the jovial cook, Pierre, and looked for the pyramid which Dr. Kane mentions as "our beacon and their tomb-stone," but it was scattered over the rocks, and the conspicuous cross which had been painted on its southern face was only here and there shown by a stone with a white patch upon it.

On our homeward journey we camped again at Cairn Point, and made there a long halt, as I desired to get another view, from a loftier position than before. Jensen was fortunate enough to shoot a deer, and our weary and battered dogs were refreshed with it. Thence to the schooner was one of the wildest rides that I remember ever to have made. A terrible gale of wind set upon us, and, with the thermometer at —52°, it carried a sting with it. The drifting snow was battering us at a furious rate; but the dogs, with their heads turned homeward, did their best, and the thirty miles were made in three and a half hours.

CHAPTER XXV.

SENDING FORWARD SUPPLIES — KALUTUNAH AS A DRIVER — KALUTUNAH CIV-
ILIZED — MR KNORR — PLAN OF MY PROPOSED JOURNEY — PREPARING TO
SET OUT — INDUSTRIOUS ESQUIMAU WOMEN — DEATH AND BURIAL OF KAB-
LUNET — THE START.

DURING the next few days the dog-sledges were going and coming between the schooner and Cairn Point continually, carrying to the latter place the stores needed, for our summer campaign. The temperature still held very low, and I did not deem it prudent to send out a foot party. I knew by former experience how important it is for a commander to keep inexperienced men under his own eye, for one frozen man will demoralize a dozen, and a frosted foot is as contagious as the small-pox.

Kalutunah's team was turned over to Mr. Knorr, and in doing this I gratified both parties and served my own interests. The novelty of serving me, and of traveling with me, had by this time worn off, and I could plainly see that the chief was quite as well satisfied to remain with his wife and babies as to trust himself to the uncertain fortunes of the ice-fields, more especially as his curiosity to see how this man that he called the big chief behaved himself had been fully gratified. The recent journey had convinced him that I was fully entitled to his respect, since I did not freeze, and altogether conducted myself as well as an Esquimau would have done under like circum-

KALUTUNAH CIVILIZED. 291

stances; and this was a great deal in his eyes. It was not difficult to perceive that Kalutunah started with me expecting to take me under his protecting wing; and if he did not have the pleasing satisfaction of seeing me groaning with the cold, at least he should have the opportunity to instruct me how to live and how to travel; but when I began to instruct him, and turned the tables on him, he was much disappointed; and when to this violation of propriety I added the still more unpardonable offense of refusing him a bear-hunt, his enthusiasm oozed out very rapidly; and if he admired the Nalegaksoak the more, he desired to follow him the less, particularly as the dangers of the service preponderated over the emoluments. Indeed, the fellow was disposed to avail himself fully of the advantages of his new situation, and I soon made up my mind that he was henceforth a pensioner upon my bounty, so I doubled his riches and made him the happiest Esquimau that ever was seen. My thoroughly energetic, daring and skillful hunter, who prided himself upon the excellence of his equipments and the abundance of his supplies, for once in his life found himself so situated that he was freed from all necessity of giving thought to the morrow. It was truly a novel sensation, and it is not surprising that he should wish to enjoy the short-lived holiday. He was greatly amused, — amused with himself, amused with the Nalegaksoak who had made him so rich and allowed him to be so lazy, and amused with the white man's dress with which he was bedecked, and in which he cut such a sorry figure. His face was never without a full-blown grin. I gave him a looking-glass, and he carried it about with him continually, looking at himself and laughing at his head with a cap on it, and

292 KALUTUNAH UNCIVILIZED.

at his red shirt which dangled beneath an old coat. It was all very fine and very wonderful. " Don't I look pretty ? " was the poser which he put to everybody.

But this pleasing state of mind into which he had been thrown by this new style of costume was doomed to be short-lived. The novelty wore off in a few days. It ceased to amuse him ; and he discovered, no doubt, that in gratifying his vanity he was vexing the flesh. One day he appeared on board in his old suit of furs. " What has become of the cap and red shirt and coat ? " " Oh ! I tumbled into the water, and my wife is drying them ! " The truth leaked out afterward that he had gone home, changed the white man's finery for the cold-resisting fox-skins, and had chucked the whole suit among the rocks

Kalutunah's team fell to Mr. Knorr from sheer necessity, since there was no one else in the ship except Hans who could handle the whip. Knorr, with commendable foresight, had commenced his exercises early in the winter, plainly foreseeing that his chances of accompanying me throughout my northern journey were not likely to be diminished by knowing how to drive dogs. The labor properly devolved upon one of the sailors ; but the field was open to all alike ; and the young gentleman, finding that official dignity stood in the way of his ambition, with a spirit which I was not slow to appreciate, did not long hesitate in his choice.

I have elsewhere mentioned that the labor of driving dogs is not an easy one. Indeed, of all the members of my party, Mr. Knorr was the only one who succeeded well. Even in Southern Greenland, among the Danes long resident there, it is rare to find a skillful driver. Neither of the sailors, Carl nor Christian,

PREPARING TO START. 293

whom I had taken from Upernavik, could throw the lash anywhere else than about their legs, or into the face of whomsoever might happen to sit upon the sledge. As for hitting a dog, they could scarcely do it by any chance.

My recent journey had decided my course of action. The last view which I had from the top of the lofty cliff behind Cairn Point convinced me that my only chance for the season was to cross the Sound from that place, for my observations up the Greenland coast had shown me, as has been already observed, the impracticability of reaching the Polar Sea by that route. McCormick had immediate charge of the work of preparation, and pushing every thing forward with his customary energy, we were ready to start before the close of March. But the temperature still continued to range too low for safety, and I only awaited a rise of the thermometer. Our little community was now full of life and business.

The Esquimaux were not an unimportant element in the hive. The most useful service came, however, from the ancient dames who presided over the domestic affairs of the snow house and the hut at Etah. They were sewing for us constantly, and were probably the first women in the world who ever grew rich

" Plying the needle and thread."

But misfortune fell at length within the snow-hut. Poor old Kablunet, the voluble and kind-hearted and industrious wife of Tcheitchenguak, took sick. Her disease was pneumonia, and it ran its course with great rapidity. All my medicines and all my efforts to save her were of no avail, and she died on the fourth day. This unhappy event had nearly de-

294   AN ESQUIMAU FUNERAL

stroyed my prestige as a Narkosak, and indeed it would have done so completely had it not been for the fortunate occurrence of an auroral display, during which time Jensen, whom my journal mentions as "a convenient and useful man," informed the Esquimaux that the white man's medicine will not operate. And thus was saved my reputation. She died at five o'clock in the evening; at six she was sewed up in a seal-skin winding-sheet, and before it was yet cold the body was carried on Hans's sledge to a neighboring gorge and there buried among the rocks and covered with heavy stones. The only evidences of sorrow or regret were manifested by her daughter, Merkut, the wife of Hans, and these appeared to be dictated rather from custom than affection. Merkut remained by the grave after the others had departed, and for about an hour she walked around and around it, muttering in a low voice some praises of the deceased. At the head of the grave she then placed the knife, needles, and sinew which her mother had recently been using, and the last sad rites to the departed savage were performed. Tcheitchenguak came over and told me that there was no longer anybody to keep his lamp burning, and that his hut was cold, and with a very sorrowful face he begged to be allowed to live with Hans. My consent given, that of Hans was not deemed necessary; and so the snow-hut became deserted, and the cheerful family that had there dispensed a rude hospitality was broken up; and the "house of feasting" had become a "house of mourning," and Tcheitchenguak had come away from it to finish alone his little remaining span of life. Old and worn down by a hard struggle for existence, he was now dependent upon a generation which cared little

THE FIELD PARTY. 295

for him, while she who alone could have soothed the sorrows of his declining years had gone away before him to the far-off island where the Great Spirit, Torngasoak the Mighty, regales the happy souls with an endless feast on the ever green banks of the boundless lake, where the ice is never seen and the darkness is never known, — where the sunshine is eternal, in the summer of bliss that is everlasting, — the Upernak that has no end.

The temperature having somewhat moderated, I determined to set out in the evening of the third of April. Although the sun had not yet reached the horizon at midnight, there was quite light enough for my purposes, and by traveling in the night instead of the day we would have greater warmth while in camp, which is really the time of greatest danger from the cold; for when on the march men have usually little difficulty in keeping warm, even at the lowest temperatures, provided there is no wind. Besides this, there is still another difficulty obviated. The constant glare of the mid-day sun is a very severe tax upon the eye, and great caution is needed to guard against that painful and inconvenient disease known as "snow-blindness.". In order to protect my men against it, as much as possible, I had supplied each of them with a pair of blue-glass goggles.

My field party consisted of every available officer and man in the schooner, twelve in number. We were all ready to start at seven o'clock; and when I joined them on the ice beside the schooner their appearance was as picturesque as it was animated. In advance stood Jensen, impatiently rolling out his long whip-lash; and his eight dogs, harnessed to his sledge, "The Hope," were as impatient as he. Next came

296 THE START.

Knorr with six dogs and the "Perseverance," to the upstander of which he had tied a little blue flag bearing this, his motto, "*Toujours prêt.*" Then came a lively group of eight men, each with a canvas belt across his shoulder, to which was attached a line that fastened him to the sledge. Alongside the sledge stood McCormick and Dodge, ready to steer it among the hummocks, and on the sledge was mounted a twenty-foot metallic life-boat with which I hoped to navigate the Polar Sea. The mast was up and the sails were spread, and from the peak floated our boat's ensign, which had seen service in two former Arctic and in one Antarctic voyage, and at the mast-head were run up the Masonic emblems. Our little signal-flag was stuck in the stern-sheets. The sun was shining brightly into the harbor, and everybody was filled with enthusiasm, and ready for the hard pull that was to come. Cheer after cheer met me as I came down the stairway from the deck. At a given signal Radcliffe, who was left in charge of the vessel, touched off the "swivel," "March," cried McCormick, crack went the whips, the dogs sprang into their collars, the men stretched their "track ropes," and the cavalcade moved off.

The events which follow I will give from my "fieldbook," trusting that the reader will have sufficient interest in my party to accompany them through the icy wilderness into which they plunged; but for this we will need a new chapter.

CHAPTER XXVI.

THE FIRST DAY'S JOURNEY. — A FALL OF TEMPERATURE — ITS EFFECT UPON
THE MEN — CAMPED IN A SNOW-HUT — THE SECOND DAY'S JOURNEY. —
AT CAIRN POINT. — CHARACTER OF THE ICE — THE PROSPECT — STORM-
STAYED — THE COOKS IN DIFFICULTY — SNOW-DRIFT — VIOLENCE OF THE
GALE — OUR SNOW-HUT

April 4th.

BURIED in a snow-bank, and not over well pleased
with my first day's work. The temperature of the air
has tumbled down to —32,° and inside the hut it is
now, two hours after entering it, a degree above zero,
and steadily rising. Three of the party succumbed to
the cold on the march, and I had much difficulty in
keeping them from being seriously frozen. We got on
finely until we reached Sunrise Point, where the ice was
very rough, and we were bothered for more than two
hours in getting over it with our long and cumber-
some boat and sledge. It was probably only a little
foretaste of what is to come when we strike across
the Sound. Once over this ugly place, we halted to
melt some water, for the men had become very warm
and thirsty. Unluckily, just at this time a smart
breeze sprung up, chilling us through and through,
for we had been perspiring freely with the violent exercise. The first cold blast put an extinguisher upon
the enthusiasm which the party had carried along
with them from the ship, and it was singular to observe the change which came over their spirits. It
was the contrast of champagne and sour cider. Some

298　THE FIRST DAY'S JOURNEY.

of them looked as if they were going to their own
funerals, and wore that "My God! what shall I do?"
look that would have been amusing enough had it not
been alarming. One of these, without sufficient energy
to keep himself in motion, crouched behind a snow-
drift, and when discovered he had squarely settled
himself for a freeze. In half an hour his inclination
would have been accomplished. When I came up to
him he said very coolly, and with a tone of resignation worthy a martyr, "I 'm freezing." His fingers
and toes were already as white as a tallow-candle.
There was no time to be lost. I rubbed a little circulation back into them, and, placing him in charge of
two men with orders to keep him moving, I saved
him from the serious consequences which would otherwise have resulted from his faint-heartedness. Without waiting for more of the coveted drops of water,
I pushed on for the first snow-bank, and got my party
out of the wind and under cover. But this was not
done without difficulty. It seemed as if two or three
of them were possessed with a heroic desire to die on
the spot, and I really believe that they would have
done it cheerfully rather than, of their own accord,
seize a shovel and aid in constructing, if not a place
of comfort, at least a place of rest and safety. This
sort of thing at the start is not encouraging, but I
cannot say that I am much surprised at it; for my
former experience has shown the hazard of exposing
men in the wind in such low temperatures. This,
however, is one of those things against which no foresight can provide. No serious consequences appear
to have resulted from the event, and the sufferers are
growing more comfortable as the temperature of the
hut rises. We have had our rude camp supper, and

AT CAIRN POINT. 299

I have started an alcohol lamp; the door is closed tightly; the party are all drawn under the sleeping-furs; the plucky ones smoke their pipes, and the balance of them shiver as if they would grow warm with the exercise. The chattering of teeth is not pleasant music.

April 5th.

Under the snow again near Cape Hatherton. Our halt at the last camp was continued for eighteen·hours, until the men had got fairly thawed out, and the wind had entirely subsided. The short march hence was made slowly and steadily, as I do not wish at first to urge upon the men too much work, nor to keep them long exposed to the cold. There are no frost-bites of consequence resulting from the exposure of yesterday. The spirits of the party have somewhat revived. The temperature has risen, and the hut is warmer than that of last night, — that is, my thermometer, hanging from the runner of the sledge over my head shows 10° above zero.

April 6th.

We have reached Cairn Point, and are comfortably housed. The men have come up to the work reasonably well. The depression of spirits which followed the blast of cold wind that overtook us above Sunrise Point has passed away, and all hands are gay and lively. I had no need to urge or instruct or use 'the snow-shovel myself at this camp. The weak in spirit have profited by their lessons, and have learned that in providing for one's comfort and safety on the ice-fields the shovel materially assists appeals to Heaven, — a very wholesome change, and, as a result of it, instead of being upward of two hours in constructing our hut, as on the first night, we have this time ac-

THE PROSPECT.

complished the task in less than one, and everybody seemed ambitious of doing the work in the shortest possible space of time.

The traveling to-day has been very fair for the dog-sledges, but very bad for the boat. It runs easily enough on the smooth surface, but dragging its long length over a snow-drift even four feet deep, or, worse still, over hummocks even half as high, is a troublesome task; and we have crossed many strips of rough ice to-day which could not be passed until we had broken a track. In consequence of this we were obliged to leave some of the load behind, especially as I wished to reach Cairn Point before camping. Knorr and Jensen had already cached one of their cargoes of March at Cape Hatherton, and this was left with it. It will cost us a day's labor to bring it up.

The difficulties in transporting the boat among the hummocks, and the very light load which either the men or dogs can carry over the broken ice, as shown by this day's experience, convince me that the boat and cargo can hardly be transported to the west coast at one journey; and I have therefore concluded to leave the boat here for the present, at least until the track is further explored, and set out with the two dog-sledges and a foot party dragging the other sledge, laden with such stores as they can carry, for a depot on Grinnell Land. I can at any time send the party back for the boat; and if it should turn out that the boat cannot be got across the Sound, then I shall, in any event, have a depot of supplies for my explorations over the ice with the dog-sledges, before the thaw of June and July shall have put an end to that species of traveling.

STORM-STAYED. 301

The track before me looks unpromising enough. After the party was housed, I climbed up to a considerable eminence, and have had the melancholy satisfaction of looking out over the ugliest scene that my eye has ever chanced to rest upon. There was nothing inviting in it. Except a few miles of what has evidently, up to a very late period of the fall, been open water, which has frozen suddenly, there is not a rod of smooth ice in sight. The whole Sound appears to have been filled with ice of the most massive description, which, broken up into a moving "pack" in the summer, has come down upon this Greenland coast with the southerly setting current, and has piled up all over the sea in a confused jumble. I know what it is from having crossed it in 1854; and if it is as bad now as then (and it appears to be much worse) there is every prospect of a severe tussle.

April 7th.

Did anybody ever see such capricious weather as this of Smith Sound? It is the torment of my life and the enemy of my plans. I can never depend upon it. It is the veriest flirt that ever owned Dame Nature for a mother.

We camped in a calm atmosphere, but in the middle of the night — bang! — down came a bugle-blast of Boreas, and then the old god blew and blew as if he had never blown in all his life before, and wanted to prove what he could do. We could hardly show our noses out of doors, and have lain huddled together in this snow den all day, — a doleful sort of imprisonment It is with much difficulty that we have got any thing to eat, and we never should if I had not turned cook myself, and shown these inno-

302   THE COOKS IN DIFFICULTY.

cents of mine how to keep the furnace-lamp from being blown out; for we can use only lard for fuel, and the smoke is so great that we cannot have the cooking done inside. It seems to me that nothing takes the wits out of a man so quickly as the cold. The cooks had not sense enough left to inclose themselves in a snow wall, and I had to teach them how to keep up the proper proportion of lard and rope-yarns in the lamp to prevent the flame from smothering on the one hand, and from being whiffed out on the other. We were more than two hours in making a pot of coffee, and came in out of the pelting snow-drift with our furs all filled with it; and now it melts, and the clothing is getting damp, for we do not change our dress when we crawl in between our buffalo-skin sheets.

April 8th.

Could any thing be more aggravating? The gale holds on and keeps us close prisoners. My people could no more live in it than in a fiery furnace. I never saw any thing like it. Last night it fell warmer, and snowed, which gave us encouragement; but the wind blew afterward more fierce than ever, and human eye never beheld such sights. There was nowhere any thing else but flying snow. The sun's face was blinded, and the hills and coast were hidden completely out of sight. Once in a while we can see the ghost of an iceberg, but that is rarely. We tried to brave it yesterday, and again to-day, for I wanted to go down to Cape Hatherton to bring up our cargo there. So we commenced tearing down the hut to get at the sledge; but ten minutes convinced me that half the party would freeze outright if we undertook to face the storm, and I sent the flock again under

IN A SNOW BANK. 303

cover, and went behind the snow wall to help the cooks with their fire.

The poor dogs were almost buried out of sight. They had all crouched together in a heap; and as the drift accumulated over them they poked their heads further and further up into it; and when I came to count them to see if any had left us and run back to the ship or been frozen to death, it was truly counting noses. There were fourteen of them.

It seems rather strange to be writing on at this rate in a snow-hut, but the truth is I have no more trouble in writing here than if I were in my cabin. The temperature has come up almost to the freezing point, and it is a great relief to write. What else should I do? I have two small books which I have brought along for just such emergencies as this, and while my companions play cards and bet gingerbread and oyster suppers and bottles of rum to be paid in Boston, I find nothing better to do than read and write; and, since I cannot remain unoccupied, but must kill time in some manner, or else sleep, suppose I describe this den in the snow-bank.

It is a pit eighteen feet long by eight wide and four deep. Over the top of said pit are placed the boat-oars, to support the sledge, which is laid across them; and over the sledge is thrown the boat's sail; and over the sail is thrown loose snow. In one end of the den thus formed there is a hole, through which we crawl in, and which is now filled up tightly with blocks of snow. Over the floor (if the term is admissible) there is spread a strip of India-rubber cloth; over this cloth a strip of buffalo-skins, which are all squared and sewed together; and over this again another just like it. When we want to sleep we

304 THIRTEEN IN A BED

draw ourselves underneath the upper one of these buffalo strips, and accommodate ourselves to the very moderate allowance of space assigned to each person as best we can. The post of honor is at the end furthest from the door; and, except the opposite end, this post of honor is the least desirable of all other places, for, somehow or other, the twelve sleepers below me manage to pull the "clothes" off and leave me jammed against the snow wall, with nothing on me but my traveling gear; for we go to bed without change of costume except our boots and stockings, which we tuck under our heads to help out a pillow, while what we call "reindeer sleeping stockings" take their place on the feet. And, furthermore, there is not much that I can say. This can hardly be called comfort I have a vague remembrance of having slept more soundly than I have done these last four nights, and of having rested upon something more agreeable to the "quivering flesh" than this bed of snow, the exact sensations communicated by which are positively indescribable,— a sort of cross between a pine board and a St. Lawrence gridiron. And yet the people are busy and merry enough. Harris, one of my most energetic and ambitious men, is sewing a patch on his seal-skin pantaloons, stopping "a hole to keep the winds away;" Miller, another spirited and careful man, is closing up a rip in his Esquimau boot; and Carl, who has a fine tenor voice, has just finished a sailor's song, and is clearing his throat for "The Bold Soldier Boy." Several packs of cards are in requisition, and altogether we are rather a jolly party,— the veriest Mark Tapleys of travelers. We are leading a novel sort of life, and I can imagine that the time will come when I shall turn over the pages of this diary

THE SOURCE OF HAPPINESS. 305

and be amused at the strangeness of the contrast of these events with the humdrum routine of ordinary existence. I have no doubt that I shall then wonder if this is not all set down in a dream, so singular will it appear; and yet so quickly do the human body and the human mind accommodate themselves to the changing circumstances of life that, in every thing we do, the events seem at the time always natural, and cause us no astonishment; still, when we review the past, we are continually amazed that we have undergone so many transformations, and can scarcely recognize ourselves in our chamelion dresses. If it should ever again be my luck to eat canvas-back at Delmonico's, I shall no doubt very heartily despise the dried beef and potato hash which now constitute, with bread and coffee, my only fare; and yet no canvas-back was ever enjoyed as much as this same hash; and no coffee distilled through French percolator was ever so fine as the pint pot which is passed along to me, smoking hot, in the morning; and the best treasures of Périgord forest were never relished more than are the few little chips of ship's biscuit which the coffee washes down. In fact, our pleasures are but relative. They are never absolute; and happiness is quite probably, as Paley has wisely hinted, but a certain state of that "nervous network lining the whole region of the præcordia;" and, therefore, since this cold pencil only gives me pain in the fingers, while nothing disturbs the harmony of the præcordia, I do not know but that I am about as well off as I ever was in my life. True, I have not the means which I expected to have for the execution of my designs, and I am beset with difficulties and embarrassments; but if happiness lies in that quarter, pleasure lies in the future, for we willingly forget the present in the anticipations, — in the delights to come from the contests and struggles ahead; and it is well that this is so; for that which we spend most time in getting is often not worth the having. The Preacher tells us that "All is vanity;" and what says the Poet? —

> "—— pleasures are like poppies spread;
> You seize the flower — its bloom is shed;
> Or like the snow-fall in the river —
> A moment white, then melts forever;
> Or like the borealis race,
> That flits ere you can point the place."

CHAPTER XXVII.

THE STORM CONTINUES — AT WORK — AMONG THE HUMMOCKS — DIFFICULTIES OF THE TRACK — THE SNOW-DRIFTS — SLOW PROGRESS.— THE SMITH SOUND ICE — FORMATION OF THE HUMMOCKS — THE OLD ICE-FIELDS GROWTH OF ICE-FIELDS — THICKNESS OF ICE — THE PROSPECT

I WILL not lay so heavy a tax upon the reader's patience as to ask him to follow the pages of my diary through the next three weeks. Diaries are of necessity so much taken up with matters that are purely personal and contain so much of endless repetition, so many events that are of daily recurrence, that it is impossible in the very nature of things that they can have much interest for anybody but the writers of them. Suffice it, therefore, to say that the storm continued with unabated violence during the day succeeding that which closed the last chapter, and it did not fairly subside until the end of the tenth day. Meanwhile, however, we were busily occupied. The storm did not keep us housed.

Our first duty was to bring up the stores left at Cape Hatherton. This accomplished, we broke up our camp and set out to cross the Sound with a moderate load, the men dragging the large sledge, while the dogs were attached as before. The wind had, fortunately, hauled more to the south, and, coming nearly on our backs, we found little inconvenience from this source. But difficulties of another kind soon gave us warning of the serious nature of the

308   DIFFICULTIES OF THE TRACK.

task which we had undertaken. By winding to the right and left, and by occasionally retracing our steps when we had selected an impracticable route, we managed to get over the first few miles without much embarrassment, but farther on the track was rough past description. I can compare it to nothing but a promiscuous accumulation of rocks closely packed together and piled up over a vast plain in great heaps and endless ridges, leaving scarcely a foot of level surface and requiring the traveler to pick the best footing he can over the inequalities, — sometimes mounting unavoidable obstructions to an elevation of ten, and again more than a hundred feet above the general level.

The interstices between these closely accumulated ice masses are filled up, to some extent, with drifted snow. The reader will readily imagine the rest. He will see the sledges winding through the tangled wilderness of broken ice-tables, the men and dogs pulling and pushing up their respective loads, as Napoleon's soldiers may be supposed to have done when drawing their artillery through the steep and rugged passes of the Alps. He will see them clambering over the very summit of lofty ridges, through which there is no opening, and again descending on the other side, the sledge often plunging over a precipice, sometimes capsizing, and frequently breaking. Again he will see the party, baffled in their attempt to cross or find a pass, breaking a track with shovel and handspike; or, again, unable even with these appliances to accomplish their end, they retreat to seek a better track; and they may be lucky enough to find a sort of gap or gateway, upon the winding and uneven surface of which they will make a mile or so

SLOW PROGRESS. 309

with comparative ease. The snow-drifts are sometimes a help and sometimes a hinderance. Their surface is uniformly hard, but not always firm to the foot. The crust frequently gives way, and in a most tiresome and provoking manner. It will not quite bear the weight, and the foot sinks at the very moment when the other is lifted. But, worse than this, the chasms between the hummocks are frequently bridged over with snow in such a manner as to leave a considerable space at the bottom quite unfilled; and at the very moment when all looks promising, down sinks one man to his middle, another to the neck, another is buried out of sight, the sledge gives way, and to extricate the whole from this unhappy predicament is probably the labor of hours; especially, as often happens, if the sledge must be unloaded; and this latter is, from many causes, an event of constant occurrence. Not unfrequently it is necessary to carry the cargo in two or three loads. The sledges are coming and going continually, and the day is one endless pull and haul. The nautical cry of the sailors, intended to inspire unison of action, mingles with the loud and not always amiable commands of Jensen and Knorr, each urging on his fatigued and toil-worn dogs

It would be difficult to imagine any kind of labor more disheartening, or which would sooner sap the energies of both men and animals. The strength gave way gradually; and when, as often happened, after a long and hard day's work, we could look back from an eminence and almost fire a rifle-ball into our last snow-hut, it was truly discouraging.

I need hardly say that I soon gave up all thought of trying to get the boat across the Sound. A hun-

310 SMITH SOUND.

dred men could not have accomplished the task. My only purpose now was to get to the coast of Grinnell Land with as large a stock of provisions as possible, and to retain the men as long as they could be of use ; but it soon became a question whether the men themselves could carry over their own provisions independent of the surplus which I should require in order that the severe labor should result to advantage. In spite, however, of every thing the men kept steadfastly to their duty, through sunshine and through storm, through cold, and danger, and fatigue.

The cause of this extraordinary condition of the ice will need but little explanation in addition to that which has been given in the preceding chapter. The reader will have no difficulty in comprehending the cause by an examination of the Smith Sound map. He will observe that the Sound is, in effect, an extensive sea, with an axis running almost east and west, and having a length of about one hundred and sixty miles and a width of eighty. The name "Sound," by which it is known, was first given to it by its discoverer, brave old William Baffin, two hundred and fifty odd years ago. The entrance from Cape Alexander to Cape Isabella is but thirty miles over, and by referring to the map it will be seen that this gateway rapidly expands into the sea to which I have invited attention, — a sea almost as large as the Caspian or Baltic, measured from the terminus of Baffin Bay to where Kennedy Channel narrows the waters before they expand into the great Polar Basin. This extensive sea should bear the name of the leader of the expedition which first defined its boundaries — I mean, of course, Dr. Kane.

Now into this sea the current sets from the Polar

DIMENSIONS OF AN ICE FIELD. 311

Basin through the broader gateway above mentioned, known as Kennedy Channel; and the ice, escaping but slowly through the narrow Sound into Baffin Bay, has accumulated within the sea from century to century. The summer dismembers it to some extent and breaks it up into fragments of varying size, which are pressing together, wearing and grinding continually, and crowding down upon each other and upon the Greenland coast, thus producing the result which we have seen.

In order fully to appreciate the power and magnitude of this ice-movement, it must be borne in mind that a very large proportion of the ice is of very ancient formation, — old floes or ice-fields of immense thickness and miles in extent, as well as of icebergs discharged from Humboldt Glacier. These vast masses, tearing along with the current in the early winter through the sea as it is closing up and new ice is making rapidly, are as irresistible as a tornado among the autumn leaves. As an illustration, I will give the dimensions of an old field measured by me while crossing the Sound. Its average height was twenty feet above the sea level, and about six by four miles in extent of surface, which was very uneven, rising into rounded hillocks as much as eighty feet in height, and sinking into deep and tortuous valleys.

To cross such a floe with our sledges was almost as difficult as crossing the hummocks themselves; for, in addition to its uneven surface, like that of a very rough and broken country, it was covered with crusted snow through which the sledge-runners cut continually, and which broke down under the foot. I estimated its solid contents, in round numbers, at

312 ORIGIN OF A FLOE.

6,000,000,000 of tons, its depth being about one hundred and sixty feet. Around its border was thrown up on all sides a sort of mountain chain of last year's ice, the loftiest pinnacle of which was one hundred and twenty feet above the level of the sea. This ice-hill, as it might well be called, was made up of blocks of ice of every shape and of various sizes, piled one upon the other in the greatest confusion. Numerous forms equally rugged, though not so lofty, rose from the same ridge, and from every part of this desolate area; and if a thousand Lisbons were crowded together and tumbled to pieces by the shock of an earthquake, the scene could hardly be more rugged, nor to cross the ruins a severer task.

The origin of such a floe dates back to a very remote period. That it was cradled in some deep recess of the land, and there remained until it had grown to such a thickness that no summer's sun or water's washing could wholly obliterate it before the winter cold came again, is most probable. After this it grows as the glacier grows, from above, and is, like the glacier, wholly composed of fresh ice, — that is, of frozen snow. It will be thus seen that the accumulation of ice upon the mountain tops is not different from the accumulation which takes place upon these floating fields, and each recurring year marks an addition to their depth. Vast as they are to the sight, and dwarfs as they are compared with the inland *mer de glace*, yet they are, in all that concerns their growth, truly glaciers — pigmy floating glaciers. That they can only grow to such great depth in this manner will be at once apparent, when it is borne in mind that ice soon reaches a maximum thickness by direct freezing, and that its growth is arrested by a natural law.

AVERAGE THICKNESS OF THE ICE. 313

This thickness is of course dependent upon the temperature of the locality; but the ice is itself the sea's protection. The cold air cannot soak away the warmth of the water through more than a certain thickness of ice, and to that thickness there comes a limit long before the winter has reached its end. The depth of ice formed on the first night is greater than on the second; the second greater than the third; the third greater than the fourth; and so on as the increase approaches nothing. The thickness of ice formed at Port Foulke was nine feet; and, although the coldest weather came in March, yet its depth was not increased more than two inches after the middle of February. In situations of greater cold, and where the current has less influence than at Port Foulke, the depth of the table will of course become greater. I have never seen an ice-table formed by direct freezing that exceeded eighteen feet. But for this all-wise provision of the Deity, the Arctic waters would, ages ago, have been solid seas of ice to their profoundest depths.

The reader will, I trust, bear patiently with this long digression; but I thought it necessary, in order that he might have a clear understanding as well of our situation as of the character of these Arctic seas; in which I shall hope that I have inspired some interest. As for ourselves, we were struggling along through this apparently impassable labyrinth, striving to reach the coast which now began to loom up boldly before us, and thence stretching away into the unknown North, there receives the lashings of the Polar Sea.

To come back to the narrative which we abandoned so suddenly. The 24th of April found us on the margin of the very floe which I have been describing, weary, worn, and much dispirited. Since we broke camp at Cairn Point, we had made in a direct line from that place not over thirty miles. The number of miles actually traveled could not be easily estimated; but it was scarcely less than five times that distance, counting all our various twistings and turnings and goings and comings upon our track. But I propose again to let my diary speak for itself; and, as on a former occasion, when the evil genius of that unhappy manuscript led it into type, we will resort to a new chapter.

CHAPTER XXVIII.

THE DIFFICULTIES MULTIPLYING — SLEDGE BROKEN. — REFLECTIONS ON THE PROSPECT. — THE MEN BREAKING DOWN. — WORSE AND WORSE. — THE SITUATION — DEFEAT OF MAIN PARTY. — RESOLVE TO SEND THE PARTY BACK AND CONTINUE THE JOURNEY WITH DOGS

April 24th.

THESE journal entries are becoming rather monotonous. I have little to set down to-day that I did not set down yesterday. There is no variety in this journeying over the same track, week in and week out, in the same endless snarl continually, — to-day almost in sight of our camp of yesterday, the sledge broken, the men utterly exhausted, and the dogs used up. We are now twenty-two days from the schooner, and have made on our course not more than an average of three miles a day. From Cairn Point we are distant about thirty miles, and our progress from that place has been slow indeed. Grinnell Land looms up temptingly above the frozen sea to the north of us, but it rises very slowly. I have tried to carry out my original design of striking for Cape Sabine, but the hummocks were wholly impassable in that direction, and I have had to bear more to the northward. The temperature has risen steadily, but it is still very low and colder than during the greater part of the winter at Port Foulke. The lowest to-day was 19° below zero, calm and clear, and the sun blazing upon us as in the early spring-time at home.

316   REFLECTIONS ON THE PROSPECT.

April 25th.

A most distressing day. The sledge was repaired in the morning with much difficulty, but not so that it held without renewal through the march. The traveling grows even worse the further we proceed. The hummocks are not heavier, but the recent snows have not been disturbed by the wind and lie loose upon the surface, making the labor of dragging the sledge much greater than before, even in those few level patches with which we have been favored since setting out in the morning.

My party are in a very sorry condition. One of the men has sprained his back from lifting; another has a sprained ancle; another has gastritis; another a frosted toe; and all are thoroughly overwhelmed with fatigue. The men do not stand it as well as the dogs.

Thus far I have not ventured to express in this journal any doubts concerning the success of this undertaking; but of late the idea has crossed my mind that the chances of ever reaching the west coast with this party look almost hopeless. The question of the boat was decided days ago, and it becomes now a very serious subject for reflection, whether it is really likely that the men can get over these hummocks to the west coast with even provisions enough to bring them back. It is almost as much as they can do to transport their own camp fixtures, which are neither weighty nor bulky.

April 26th.

The progress to-day has been even more unsatisfactory than yesterday. The men are completely used up, broken down, dejected, to the last degree. Human nature cannot stand it. There is no let up

THE SITUATION. 317

to it. Cold, penetrating to the very sources of life, dangers from frost and dangers from heavy lifting, labors which have no end, — a heartless sticking in the mud, as it were, all the time; and then comes snow-blindness, cheerless nights, with imperfect rest in snow-huts, piercing storms and unsatisfying food. This the daily experience, and this the daily prospect ahead; to-day closing upon us in the same vast ice-jungle as yesterday. My party have, I must own, good reason to be discouraged; for human beings were never before so beset with difficulties and so inextricably tangled in a wilderness. We got into a *cul de sac* to-day, and we had as much trouble to surmount the lofty barrier which bounded it as Jean Valjean to escape from the *cul-de-sac Genrot* to the convent yard. But our convent yard was a hard old floe, scarce better than the hummocked barrier.

I feel to-night that I am getting rapidly to the end of my rope. Each day strengthens the conviction, not only that we can never reach Grinnell Land, with provisions for a journey up the coast to the Polar Sea, but that it cannot be done at all. I have talked to the officers, and they are all of this opinion. They say the thing is hopeless. Dodge put it thus: " You might as well try to cross the city of New York over the house-tops!" They are brave and spirited men enough, lack not courage nor perseverance; but it does seem as if one must own that there are some difficulties which cannot be surmounted. But I have in this enterprise too much at stake to own readily to defeat, and we will try again to-morrow.

April 27th.

Worse and worse! We have to-day made but little progress, the sledge is badly broken, and I am

THE SITUATION.

brought to a stand-still. There does not appear to be the ghost of a chance for me. Must I own myself a defeated man? I fear so.

I was never in all my life so disheartened as I am to-night; not even when, in the midst of a former winter, I bore up with my party through hunger and cold, beset by hostile savages, and, without food or means of transportation, encountered the uncertain fortunes of the Arctic night in the ineffectual pursuit of succor.

Smith Sound has given me but one succession of baffling obstacles. Since I first caught sight of Cape Alexander, last autumn, as the vanishing storm uncovered its grizzly head, I have met with but ill fortune. My struggles to reach the west coast were then made against embarrassments of the most grave description, and they were not abandoned until the winter closed upon me with a crippled and almost a sinking ship, driving me to seek the nearest place of refuge. Then my dogs died, and my best assistant became the victim of an unhappy accident. Afterward I succeed in some measure in replacing the lost teams, on which I had depended as my sole reliance; and here I am once more baffled in the middle of the Sound, stuck fast and powerless. My men have failed me as a means of getting over the difficulties, as those of Dr. Kane did before me. Two foot parties sent out by that commander to cross the Sound failed. Ultimately I succeeded in crossing with dogs, but the passage was made against almost insuperable difficulties, so great that my companion, convinced that starvation and death only would result from a continuance of the trial, resolved to settle it with a Sharp's rifle ball; but the ball whizzed past my ear, and I got to the shore

MEN USED UP. 319

notwithstanding, — discovered Grinnell Land, and surveyed two hundred miles of its coast. But the ice is now infinitely worse than it was then; and I am convinced that the difficulties of this journey have now culminated and the crisis has been reached. The men are, as I have before observed, completely exhausted from the continued efforts of the past week, and are disheartened by the contemplation of the little progress that was made as well as by the formidable nature of the hummocks in front, which they realize are becoming more and more difficult to surmount as they penetrate farther and farther into them. Their strength has been giving way under the incessant and extraordinary call upon their energies, at temperatures in which it is difficult to exist even under the most favorable circumstances, each realizing that upon his personal exertions depends the only chance of making any progress, and recognizing that after all their efforts and all their sacrifices the progress made is wholly inadequate to accomplish the object in view. Besides this prostration of the moral sentiments, there is the steady and alarming prostration of the physical forces. One man is incapacitated from work by having his back sprained in lifting; another is rendered useless by having his ancle sprained in falling; the freezing of the fingers and toes of others renders them almost helpless; and the vital energies of the whole party are so lowered by exposure to the cold that they are barely capable of attending to their own immediate necessities, without harboring a thought of exerting themselves to complete a journey to which they can see no termination, and in the very outset of which they feel that their lives are being sacrificed.

It is, therefore, in consideration of the condition of

320 THE CONCLUSION.

my men, that I have been forced to the conclusion that the attempt to cross the Sound with sledges has resulted in failure; and that my only hope to accomplish that object now rests in the schooner. Having the whole of the season before me, I think that I can, even without steam, get over to Cape Isabella, and work thence up the west shore; and, even should I not be able to get as far up the Sound as I once hoped, yet I can, no doubt, secure a harbor for next winter in some eligible position. Coming to this conclusion, I have determined to send back the men, and I have given McCormick full directions what to do, in order that the vessel may be prepared when the ice breaks up and liberates her. He is to cradle the schooner in the ice by digging around her sides; repair the damage done last autumn, and mend the broken spars, and patch the sails.

For myself, I stay to fight away at the battle as best I can, with my dogs.

The men have given me twenty-five days of good service, and have aided me nearly half way across the Sound with about eight hundred pounds of food; and this is all that they can do. Their work is ended.

Although the chance of getting through with the dogs looks hopeless; yet, hopeless though the prospect, I feel that, when disembarrassed of the men, I ought to make one further effort. I have picked my companions, and have given them their orders. They will be Knorr, Jensen, and sailor McDonald,— plucky men all, if I mistake not, and eager for the journey. There are others that are eager to go with me; but, if they have courage and spirit, they have little physical strength; and, besides, more than two persons to one sledge is superfluous. And now when I think of this new trial which I shall make to-morrow, my hopes revive; but when I remember the fruitless struggles of the past few days and think of these hummocks, with peak after peak rising one above the other, and with ridge after ridge in endless succession intersecting each other at all angles and in all directions, I must own that my heart almost fails me and my thoughts incline me to abandon the effort and retreat from what everybody, from Jensen down, says cannot be done, and rely upon the schooner for crossing the Sound. But I have not failed yet! I have fourteen dogs and three picked men left to me; and now, abandoning myself to the protecting care of an all-wise Providence, who has so often led me to success and shielded me from danger, I renew the struggle to-morrow with hope and determination. Away with despondency!

CHAPTER XXIX.

THE MAIN PARTY SENT BACK — PLUNGING INTO THE HUMMOCKS AGAIN — ADVANTAGES OF DOGS. — CAMP IN AN ICE-CAVE — NURSING THE DOGS — SNOW-BLINDNESS. — A CHAPTER OF ACCIDENTS — CAPE HAWKS — CAPE NAPOLEON — STORM STAYED. — GRINNELL LAND LOOMING UP. — DISCOVERING A SOUND — RAVENOUS DISPOSITION OF DOGS — A CHEERLESS SUPPER — CAMPING IN THE OPEN AIR — PROSTRATION OF MEN AND DOGS — MAKING THE LAND AT LAST.

April 28th.

I SENT the main party back this morning. The separation was quite affecting. They were the worst used-up body of men that I have ever chanced to see. I accompanied them for a short distance, and, with much sadness, parted from them and returned to camp. Upon looking around to see what progress they were making, I observed that they had halted and were facing toward us, evidently designing to give us three parting cheers. But the case was hopeless — there was not a squeak left in them. Soon after the party had gone, we plunged again into the hummocks. We had a terrible ridge to get over, and took only half the cargo, intending to return for the balance. Knorr's sledge broke down, and it was repaired with difficulty. Jensen's sledge tumbled over a declivity which we were descending, and injured a leg of one of the dogs. The poor animal was turned loose, and has hobbled along with us to camp. We made about a mile and a half, and then turned back for the balance of the stores. This mile and a half has, by the tortuous route pursued, been prolonged

CROSSING THE HUMMOCKS.
(FROM A SKETCH BY DR. HAYES.)

SNOW BLINDNESS. 323

into near four, — making, with the three times going over it, about twelve. I have not before had so bad a day ; and yet the men could not possibly have brought their sledge through at all. The dogs climb the hummocks with the facility of the chamois mounting the Alpine crags. One advantage they possess is, that they are not so heavy as the men and do not so readily break through the crusted snow ; and then, the sledges being smaller, are more easily managed. We have reached a most formidable ridge of hummocks which we were too much exhausted to scale ; and have camped in a sort of cave made by the crowding over of some ice-tables, thus saving the labor of making a burrow ; and it came most opportunely ; for Jensen, owing to the uncertain footing, discarded his glasses, and is in consequence suffering from incipient snow-blindness, and would have been unable to assist in digging our usual nightly pit into a snow-drift. Our quarters are very tight and more than usually comfortable, — the temperature being up to within 10° of the freezing point, while, outside, it is 12° below zero.

We set out in the morning with much spirit, but are gloomy enough to-night. Such slow progress, with so much labor, is not inspiring. Sleep is our only consolation, and I am glad the temperature is sufficiently high to enable us to repose without freezing. Sleep, that has before drowned many a sorrow for many a weary and care-worn man, has drowned many a one of mine during these past twenty-five days. It is

"Tired Nature's sweet restorer,"

among these ice-deserts, even more than elsewhere ; and our sleep is truly the "sleep of the laboring

324 CANINE FEROCITY.

man." Foolish Sancho Panza! yet wise in thy folly! Mankind will long remember thee for thy sage reflection, — "Now blessings light on him that first invented sleep." I will cover myself all over with it, as thou didst; and, if I cannot find in it "heat for the cold," I will cloak with it for a few brief hours the recollection of my disappointed hopes.

April 29th.

Back again under our last night's shelter. The hummocks were much the same to-day as yesterday, and we made about the same progress — with, however, only half our stores. The load was left buried in the snow, and we returned for the balance; but, upon arriving here, the dogs were not able for the second trip. So here we are under our buffaloes once more in the ice-cave, seeking sleep. It is the best hut that I have ever had. The temperature of the air came up at noon to 4° above zero, and in the sun it was 38°. The thermometer hanging above my head in the cave now shows 31°.

April 30th.

It was all we could do to bring up the balance of our cargo to where we cached our load yesterday. I must not overtax the dogs; for, if they give out, I am done for. They are much fatigued to-night and must be nursed; so I directed Jensen to make them a warm supper of meat and potatoes and lard, and plenty of it. Nothing could exceed their ravenous hunger. The ferocity with which they tear into their food exceeds any thing that I have ever seen, and nothing escapes their sharp fangs. They eat up their harness if not closely watched, and we are obliged to bring every thing made of skin inside the hut. Several of the traces have disappeared down their rapa-

THE COAST IN VIEW. 325

cious throats; and, with these swallowings and the breakings, we are now so badly off that we must fall back upon rope to replace the skin lines. To add to our embarrassments, Jensen forgot last night to cover over his sledge, (Knorr's makes the roof of our hut,) and when we went out in the morning, the sledge was torn to pieces, the lashings were all eaten, and the pieces of the sledge were scattered over the snow all around the camp.

I have nearly eight hundred pounds of dog food, but the daily drain is very great; and this, taken in connection with the slowness of our progress, looks unpromising.

May 1st.

We found it impossible to get on to-day with even one half the cargo, and were therefore forced to make three parcels of it, — one of which I estimate that we have brought nine miles, as traveled, though probably not one third that distance in a straight line. It is impossible to describe the nature of the ice over which we have struggled. It is even worse than any thing we have encountered before. The run of to-day has brought the coast quite conspicuously in view. I am coming upon my old survey of 1854, and am not far from my return track at that time; but how different the condition of the ice! Then my principal difficulty was in the outward journey, due north from Van Rensselaer Harbor. Returning further down the Sound, near where we now are, the ice was found to be but little broken, and I crossed from shore to shore in two days.

I have now a much finer opportunity for observation than I had then, for there was on the former occasion much fog, and I was constantly snow-blind.

326 STORM-STAYED.

The coast of Grinnell Land is clearly somewhat further north than I then placed it; for we are by my observation and reckoning, within ten miles of the shore, if the map is correct. The two bold capes to which Dr. Kane applied the names Bache and Henry (the Victoria Head and Cape Albert, of Captain Inglefield) appear to be large islands, in the mouth of a sound from thirty to forty miles wide. I reserve further judgment for further observation.

Two very conspicuous headlands appear upon the coast: one, lying almost due north, stands out with a dark front, presenting a mural face at least 1500 feet high. On my former journey I gave to it the name of Louis Napoleon, in honor of the remarkable man who, as Emperor of France, was then first beginning to exhibit to the world the greatness of his powers. It stands on the north side of a very conspicuous bay. More directly in our course and nearer to us is the other bold cape, to which Dr. Kane, on my return from the survey of this coast, appended my own name; but, since there was some confusion in the maps afterward between the names Hawks and Hayes, I have discarded the latter; and this immense rock, to which Gibraltar is a pigmy, will hereafter bear the name of Cape Hawks. The whole coast before us is very bold, and the mountain-peaks loom up loftily.

May 2d.

Storm-stayed in the camp of yesterday, and miserable enough. We came back in the morning for another load, and, when ready to return, it was blowing and drifting so hard from the north that we could not face it, and so were forced to seek shelter. The rest is much needed by the dogs, and this is my only satisfaction. Our camp fixtures were all left in the

A FINE DAY'S RUN. 327

camp of last night, and we have nothing to lie upon but the snow, which is only a shade softer than ice. Out of one of our provision tins we made a kettle, and of another a lamp, and so got some supper. Jensen is still partially snow-blind, and his sufferings have not diminished. This snow-blindness is simply an inflammation of the entire eye-ball, originating in the retina in consequence of the intense light produced by the glare of the sun reflected from the universal whiteness.

May 3d.

The storm detained us in our miserable den for twelve hours. The rest did the dogs good, and we have made the cheeriest day's work yet. But, as every rose has its thorn, so every day must have its drawback. Jensen, stumbling along with his bad eyes, got his leg into a crack and gave it a severe wrench. He tells me that the leg was broken two years ago ; and the fracture having been oblique, and the parts allowed to overlap each other while healing, the union has been imperfect.

May 4th.

A fine day's run. We had some smooth ice, and got on briskly. Jensen's snow-blindness has disappeared, and our route having led us over old floes, his leg has not hurt him much and has improved. He is now digging a pit for our night shelter, and sings a Danish song as cheerily as the grave-digger in Hamlet. Knorr and McDonald are chopping up the cakes of desiccated beef for the dogs ; and the wolfish brutes fill the air with the most hideous cries. The spectral pack of the wild Hartz huntsman never split the ear of belated traveler with more awful sounds than those which come from the throats of my wild

328 THE "DELECTABLE MOUNTAINS."

beasts at this present moment. The wretches would eat us up if we gave them the least chance. Knorr stumbled among the pack yesterday, while feeding them, and, had not McDonald pounced upon them on the instant, I believe they would have made a meal of him before he could rise.

The hour is exactly midnight, and, for the first time since starting, I write in the open air. The temperature is only one degree below zero, and a more beautiful sunshine never was beheld. This vast sea of whiteness, this great wilderness of glittering peaks, possesses a stern, quiet sublimity that is wonderfully imposing. The mountains before us, unlike those of the Greenland coast, stand up in multiplied lines of heaven-piercing cones, looking like giant stacks of cannon-balls, sprinkled with snow. The midnight sun streams over them from the north, and softens their outlines through tinted vapors which float from the eastward. Oh! that I was across the barrier that separates me from that land of my desires! Those mountains are my "delectable mountains," — the fleecy clouds which rest upon them are the flocks of the "city" of my ambitious hopes — the mystic sea which I am seeking through these days of weariness and toil.

I have had some fine sights and excellent solar bearings from a position determined by solar altitude, and am now firmly convinced that a Sound opens westward from Smith Sound, overlooked by me in 1854; and that the whole coast of Grinnell Land was placed by me too far south.

May 5th.

A perfectly killing day, and I have little progress to record. Our affairs look rather blue. Jensen

A RAVENOUS PACK. 329

complains again of his leg, and was unable to proceed further when we camped. He is groaning with the pain. Knorr sticks at the work with a tenacity and spirit most admirable. He has never once confessed fatigue; and yet, to-night, after the severe labors of the day in lifting the sledge, and the endless trouble and confusion with the dogs, when I asked him if he was tired and wanted to camp, his answer was a prompt, "No, sir." And yet, when we did camp and the work was done, I found him keeled over behind a hummock, where he had gone to conceal his prostration and faintness, — but there was no faintness of the spirit. McDonald never shows eagerness for the halt, but the labor is beginning to tell upon him He has the true grit of the thorough-bred bull-dog, and holds to his work like a sleuth-hound to the scent.

Let me finish my grievances. The dogs again show symptoms of exhaustion, — my own fault, however, in some measure, for I have watched with miserly care every ounce of food; and, last night, I gave to each animal only one and a half pounds. Result — as I have stated; and, besides, to revenge themselves, they broke into Jensen's sledge, which, owing to the fatigue of everybody, was not unlashed, but covered instead with three feet of snow. The brutes scattered every thing around, tried to tear open our tin meat-cans with their wolfish fangs, and ate up our extra boots, the last scrap of skin-line that was left, some fur stockings, and made an end of Knorr's seal-skin covered meerschaum pipe, which he had imprudently hung upon the upstander. Hemp lines now make the sledge lashings and traces, and, as a consequence, the sledges are continually tumbling to pieces and the traces are constantly breaking. Another dog tore

330 A COLD SUPPER.

open a seal-skin tobacco-pouch, shook out its contents, and ate it; and another bolted our only piece of soap. This looks bad for our future cleanliness, but thirty-two days, at these low temperatures, have worn off the sharp edge of fastidiousness. At first we had always a morning wash with a handful of snow; but latterly we are not so particular, and we shall not grieve over the soap as much as we might have done some weeks ago.

Our provisions are disappearing with alarming rapidity; and yet, whenever I stint the dogs in the least, down they go. If the dogs fail me, then nothing can be done, and I am completely at fault. Two days more must surely bring us to land. We are making in for Cape Hawks, but we are compelled to own that the Cape grows from day to day very little bolder. The numerous haltings to rest the dogs, and the forced halts caused by the breaking of the sledges and traces, when I can do nothing to speed the start, give me fine opportunities for plotting the coast; and my "field-book" and "sketch-book" are both well used.

May 6th.

A most miserable day's work brought to a most miserable end. McDonald spilled our smoking-hot supper on the snow; and, as we could not afford a second allowance of fuel (lard and rope-yarns), we were in as great danger of going to bed supperless as Baillie Nicol Jarvie, at the Clachan of Aberfoil, before the red-hot coulter brought the churly Highlanders to reason; but, luckily, McDonald managed, much to our satisfaction, to scrape up the greater part of the hash along with the snow, and we ate it cold. The coffee was, however, of course, irrecoverable, and

BROKEN SLEDGES. 331

we are turning in cheerless enough in consequence. The temperature has tumbled down again to 10° below zero, and writing is not pleasant to the fingers when the thermometer behaves in this manner.

May 7th.

Another edition of all the other days. We have made but little progress, to reward us for a most energetic day's labor, and are flat down with two broken sledges. Of one a runner is split, and Jensen declares that he has mended it so often that he can mend it no more; but a few hours' sleep will sharpen his wits, I hope. We are a rather lamentable-looking set of travelers. With too little energy to build a snow hut, we have drawn the sledges together and are going to sleep on them, in the open air. The night is reasonably warm, — temperature above zero, and sleeping may be managed; but we miss the grateful warmth of the snow hut. The truth is, that the labors of the day cause us to perspire as if we were in the tropics, and hence our clothing becomes wet through and through; the coat freezes stiff and solid as sheet-iron as soon as we halt, and we experience all over the uncomfortable sensation of "packing" in wet sheets at a water-cure.

May 8th.

Battling away as before. I felt sure that we would reach the land to-day, but it appears no nearer than when we set out this morning. Sledges, harness, dogs and men are all tumbling to pieces.

May 9th.

Still battling away; but, this time, through fog and snow, bedeviled all the day in a lifeless atmosphere, thick as the gloom of Hades.

May 10th.

At the same hopeless work again; and again we go into camp among the hummocks. I dare not hope that we will reach the shore to-morrow, for I have been so often disappointed; but the shore *will* be reached some time, if there is an ounce of food left or a dog left alive to drag it with. I have settled down into a sort of dogged determination.

May 11th.

In camp at last, close under the land; and as happy as men can be who have achieved success and await supper.

As we rounded to in a convenient place for our camp, McDonald looked up at the tall Cape, which rose above our heads; and, as he turned away to get our furnace to prepare a much-needed meal, he was heard to grumble out in a serio-comic tone: "Well, I wonder if that *is* land, or only 'Cape Fly-away,' after all?"

CHAPTER XXX.

THE PROSPECT AHEAD — TO CAPE NAPOLEON — TO CAPE FRAZER — TRACES OF ESQUIMAUX — ROTTEN ICE — KENNEDY CHANNEL — MILDNESS OF TEMPER-ATURE — APPEARANCE OF BIRDS — GEOLOGICAL FEATURES OF COAST — VEGETATION — ACCIDENT TO JENSEN.

ALTHOUGH much gratified with the success which I had achieved against such desperate obstacles, yet, when I came to reflect upon my situation, in connection with the expectations which I had entertained at setting out, I had little heart to feel triumphant. The thirty-one days occupied in crossing the Sound, the failure to get the boat, or even a foot party over, had disarranged my original plans ; while the severity of the labor, and the serious and unexpected draft made upon my provisions by the extra feeding of the dogs, in order to keep up their strength, had so much reduced my resources that, for the present season, I could have little hope of making any extended exploration.   Under ordinary conditions of traveling, much less than one half the amount of food which I gave to the animals daily would have amply sufficed for their sustenance.   As it was, the eight hundred pounds of dog-food which I had when the foot party left me, was reduced by consumption and small depots for our return journey to about three hundred pounds, — in no case more than sufficient for twelve days.   The most that I could now expect to do was to explore the route to the shores of the Polar Sea, as

334 SLOWNESS OF PROGRESS.

a basis for further exploration to follow the event of my reaching the west side of Smith Sound with my vessel late in the summer; in other words, to ascertain what chance there was of carrying into effect my original design, which the circumstance of being forced into a winter harbor on the Greenland coast, instead of the coast opposite, had disturbed.

The extracts from my field diary, given in the last chapter, will have shown the reader the slowness of our progress; while a former chapter will have so far satisfied him concerning the track over which we had recently traveled as to make any review of it in this connection unnecessary. Although anticipating at the outset a grave obstacle in the hummocks, I was unprepared to encounter them in such formidable shape; and the failure of the foot party to make headway through them was a serious blow to my expectations. I had, however, prepared myself for every emergency, and looked forward to making up what I had lost by remaining in Smith's Sound another year.

The journey across the Sound from Cairn Point was unexampled in Arctic traveling. The distance from land to land, as the crow flies, did not exceed eighty miles; and yet, as hitherto observed, the journey consumed thirty-one days, — but little more than two miles daily. The track, however, which we were forced to choose, was often at least three times that of a straight line; and since almost every mile of that tortuous route was traveled over three and often five times, in bringing up the separate portions of our cargo, our actual distance did not probably average less than sixteen miles daily, or about five hundred miles in all, between Cairn Point and Cape Hawks. The last forty miles, made with dog-sledges alone, oc-

WADING THROUGH DEEP SNOW. 335

cupied fourteen days — a circumstance which will of itself exhibit the difficult nature of the undertaking, especially when it is borne in mind that forty miles to an ordinary team of dogs, over usually fair ice, is a trifling matter for five hours, and would not fatigue the team half so much as a single hour's pulling of the same load over such hummocks as confronted us throughout this entire journey.

In order to obtain the best result which the Esquimau dog is capable of yielding, it is essential that he shall be able to trot away with his load. To walk at a dead drag is as distressing to his spirits and energies as the hauling of a dray would be to a blooded horse; and he will much more readily run away with a hundred pounds over good ice than to pull one-fourth of that weight over a track which admits only of a slow pace.

We did not halt longer at Cape Hawks than was needful to rest the teams, when we commenced our journey up the coast. The first day's march carried us across the wide bay between Capes Hawks and Napoleon. We were rejoiced to find ourselves now, for the first time, able to carry our cargo all at one load; and yet the traveling was far from good. Owing to the conformation of the coast, the bay had been sheltered from the winds, and the snows of the winter, in consequence. lay loose upon the surface of the ice. We had, however, no alternative but to cross the bay, for to go outside was to plunge again into the hummocks. The snows had accumulated to the depth of more than two feet, through which the wading was very toilsome. The sledge cut in to the cross-ties, and the dogs sank to their bellies; and, to make the matter worse, Jensen's leg gave out so that it

KENNEDY CHANNEL.

became necessary to transfer a part of his load to Knorr's sledge, in order that he might ride. Not wishing to be detained by this circumstance, I put a belt across McDonald's shoulders, took one myself, and gave one to Knorr, and we each pulled, I dare say, as much as the best dog in the team.

On the second day's march the ice was found to be jammed in a terrible manner upon Cape Napoleon, so that we were quite unable to reach the shore at that place, and were forced to hold out into the Sound and become once more entangled among the hummocks. A thick fog, completely veiling the land, coming upon us from the north, and a shower of snow following after, caused us so much bewilderment that we were obliged to camp and await better weather.

The land-ice was reached next morning, and during that day we made a brisk run to the north side of Cape Frazer — the first time that we had struck a trot since leaving Cairn Point. Our camp was made near the furthest point reached by me in 1854.

We were now within Kennedy Channel, which I had before barely entered. The ice in the entrance of the Channel was much like that of the Sound below; so that we were obliged to adhere to the land-ice, even while crossing Gould Bay,[1] which lies between Capes Leidy and Frazer, and which I once thought would furnish a good winter harbor. Indeed, this was the bay which it was my aim to reach with my vessel the previous autumn. The little flag-staff, which I had before planted at this place, was discovered, still standing erect among the rocks; but not a vestige of the flag remained. The winds had whipped it entirely away.

[1] So named in honor of Dr. B. A. Gould, of Cambridge.

TRACES OF ESQUIMAUX. 337

While rounding the head of Gould Bay, I observed that, as at Port Foulke, Van Rensselaer Harbor, and indeed in almost every bay of the Greenland coast which I have visited above Cape York, the land rises with a gentle slope, broken into steppes of greater or less regularity, — a series of terraced beaches, the highest of which I estimated to be from one hundred and twenty to one hundred and fifty feet above the sea. To these terraces I shall have occasion hereafter to refer, and will not now longer detain the reader than merely to observe that they indicate a consecutive elevation of the two coasts. I also found in that Bay the remains of an Esquimau camp. The marks were quite unmistakable in their character although of very ancient date. The discovery was the more gratifying, that it confirmed the native traditions which had been recited to me by Kalutunah. They were a single circle of heavy stones lying upon the shingly terrace. The circle was about twelve feet in diameter, and is such as may be seen in all places where Esquimaux have been in the summer time. The stones answer the purpose of securing the lower margin of their seal-skin tent; and, when they break up camp, the skins are drawn out, leaving the stones in the situation above described.

The journey of the next day was the most satisfactory of any that had been made, yet it had its drawbacks. As we proceeded, we began to experience in even a greater degree than in Smith Sound the immense force of ice-pressure resulting from the southerly set of the current. Every point of land exposed to the northward was buried under ice of the most massive description. Many blocks from thirty to sixty feet thick, and of much greater breadth, were

22

338 ROTTEN ICE.

lying high and dry upon the beach, pushed up by the resistless pack even above the level of the highest tides. The first embarrassment to our progress occasioned by this cause occurred soon after setting out from our camp above Cape Frazer, and being wholly unable to pass it, we were obliged to take once more to the ice-fields. But this was a matter not easily accomplished. The tide was out, apparently at full ebb, and the land-ice formed a wall, down which we were obliged to scramble. By lashing the two sledges together we made a ladder, and thus secured our own descent; while the dogs were lowered by their traces, and the cargo piece by piece with a line. The field-ice was, however, found to be, in addition to its roughness, in many places very rotten and insecure, so that after one of the teams had broken through and was rescued not without difficulty, we found ourselves compelled to haul in shore and take once more to the land-ice. Being thenceforth under the necessity of following all the windings of the shore line, our distance was at least doubled, and when we hauled up for the night both ourselves and the dogs were very weary.

Although much exhausted with the day's journey, I availed myself of the time consumed by my companions in preparing the camp and supper to climb the hill-side for a view. The air was quite clear, and I commanded an uninterrupted horizon to the eastward. The ice was much less rough than that which we had crossed in Smith Sound, owing to the old floes having been less closely impacted while that part of the sea was freezing up during the last autumn or winter. Hence, there was much more new ice. It was evident that the sea had been open to a very

MILDNESS OF TEMPERATURE. 339

late period; and, indeed, like the water off Port Foulke, had not closed up completely until the spring. I was much surprised to see the ice so thin and washed away thus early in the season. Small patches of open water were visible at points where the conformation of the coast warranted the conclusion that an eddy of the current had operated upon the ice more rapidly than in other places

I was struck with the circumstance that no land was visible to the eastward, as it would not have been difficult through such an atmosphere to distinguish land at the distance of fifty or sixty miles. It would appear, therefore, that Kennedy Channel is something wider than hitherto supposed. To the northeast the sky was dark and cloudy, and gave evidence of water; and Jensen, who watched the rapid advance of the season with solicitude, was not slow to direct my attention to the "water-sky."

The temperature of the air was strangely mild, and indeed distressingly so for traveling, although it possessed its conveniences in enabling us to sleep upon our sledges in the open air with comfort. The lowest temperature during the day was 20°; while, at one time, it rose to the freezing-point, — the sun blazing down upon us while we trudged on under our heavy load of furs. The day seemed really sultry. To discard our furs and travel in our shirt-sleeves was of course our first impulse; but to do so added to the load on the sledges, and it was of the first importance that the dogs should be spared every pound of unnecessary weight; so each one carried his own coat upon his back, and perspired after his own fashion.

This unseasonable warmth operated greatly to our disadvantage. The snow became slushy, and with so

340 APPEARANCE OF BIRDS.

great a distance of ice between us and Port Foulke, -Jensen, whose experience in the rapid dissolution of ice about Upernavik, at the same season of the year, had brought him into many serious difficulties, kept a sharp eye open upon our line of retreat. But danger from a general break-up I did not consider as likely to come for at least a month. Yet the spring (if such it might be called) was approaching rapidly, as was shown by the appearance of birds. As I stood upon the hill-side some little snow-buntings came chirping about me, and a burgomaster-gull flew over our heads wheeling his flight northward He seemed to have caught the sound of tumbling seas, and was leading his mate, who came sailing along after him with modest mien, to a nuptial retreat on some wave-licked island; and he screamed as if he would inquire, were we too bound on the same errand. A raven, too, came and perched himself upon a cliff above our camp, and croaked a dismal welcome, or a warning. One of these birds had kept us company through the winter, and this one looked very much as if he was bent upon adhering to my fortunes; though, I suppose, in truth, he was only looking for crumbs He stuck by us for several days, and always dropped down into our abandoned camp as soon as we were on our way.

The coast along which we were now traveling possessed much interest. It presented a line of very lofty cliffs of silurian rocks [1] — sandstone and lime-

[1] At Capes Leidy, Frazer, and other points of the coast I subsequently obtained a considerable collection of fossils, — all of which were forwarded to the Smithsonian Institution, at Washington, soon after my return home. Unhappily, the finest of them were lost after having been sent from Philadelphia, but a sufficient number of specimens were found among the geological collections to enable Prof. F B. Meek, to whom I intrusted them, to establish some interesting points of comparison. In a short paper

GEOLOGICAL FEATURES OF COAST.   341

stone — much broken down by the wasting influences of the winter frosts and summer thaws. Behind these cliffs the land rose into lofty peaks, such as I have before described. Upon the sides of these peaks the snow rested, clothing them with a uniform whiteness; but nowhere was there any evidence of mountain-ice. Along the entire coast of Grinnell Land no glacier appears, presenting thus a striking contrast to Greenland and the land on the south side of the Channel which I discovered while crossing Smith Sound — the Ellesmere Land of Captain Inglefield.

During this day's journey I had discovered numerous traces of the former presence of Esquimaux. They were similar to those which I had before found in Gould Bay. I also picked up some fossils at Cape Frazer and other places, which clearly exhibited the character of the rock. There were but few traces of vegetation in those places where the land had been bared of snow by the winds. A willow stem (probably, *salix arctica*), a single specimen of a dead saxifrage (*saxifraga oppositifolia*), and a tuft of dried grass (*festuca ovina*), were all that I found.

published in Silliman's Journal, for July, 1865, Prof. Meek enumerates and describes twelve species. Some of the specimens were imperfect, and their specific character could not be determined. The list is as follows : —

1. *Zaphrentis Hayesii.*
2. *Syringopora* * * * *.
3. *Favosites* * * * *.
4. *Strophomena Rhomboidalis.*
5. *Strophodonta Headleyana.*
6. *Strophodonta Beckii.*
7. *Rhynchonella* * * * *.
8. *Cœlospira concava.*
9. *Spirifer* * * * *.
10. *Loxonema Kanei.*
11. *Orthoceras* * * * *.
12. *Illænus* * * * *.

Prof. Meek makes this observation : — " From the foregoing list, it is believed that geologists will agree that the rocks at this highest locality at which fossils have ever been collected, belong to the Upper Silurian era. The most remarkable fact, however, is, that they are nearly all very closely allied to, and some of them apparently undistinguishable from species found in the Catskill shaly Limestone of the New York Lower Helderberg group."

342 ACCIDENT TO JENSEN.

If fortunate in point of distance accomplished, yet the day was not all that I had hoped. The land-ice was exceedingly rough, and it was not without much difficulty that we effected a passage around some of the points. In one of our most difficult encounters of this nature, Jensen slipped, and again injured his leg, and afterwards sprained his back while lifting his sledge. In consequence of these accidents our progress was much retarded during the following day, and involved me again in serious embarrassment. My diary thus sums up our situation : —

May 15th.

Jensen, my strongest man and the one upon whose physical endurance I have always relied most confidently, is not only fatigued but completely broken down. He lies on the sledge, moaning and groaning with pain from a sprained back and his injured leg ; and what to do with him I do not see. He appears to be unable to go further, and the only question concerning him seems to be, how he is to be got home. With anything like a fair field, I ought to reach about lat. 83°, but the loss of Jensen's muscular strength is damaging to me. The track has been execrable to-day ; and yet, all things considered, we have done very well. We have made, at the least, twenty miles. McDonald is pretty well used up, and Knorr is quite as bad, if he could be got to own it. Jensen's sufferings have naturally affected his spirits ; and with these long hundreds of miles lying behind us, it is perhaps not surprising that his only present expectation will be realized, if his bones are left to bleach among these barren rocks. What I shall do to-morrow, the morrow must determine. Thanks to careful nursing, I have yet my dogs in fair condition ; and that is the best part of the battle.

CHAPTER XXXI.

A NEW START —SPECULATIONS —IN A FOG —POLAR SCENERY.—STOPPED BY ROTTEN ICE —LOOKING AHEAD.—CONCLUSIONS —THE OPEN SEA —CLIMAX OF THE JOURNEY —RETURNING SOUTH

THE unexpected breaking down of my strong man, Jensen, was a misfortune only one degree less keenly felt than the previous failure of the foot party, and it troubled me much; for, while I lost the services of a stout arm and an active body, I was naturally anxious about his safety. With a helpless man on my hands, and with four hundred and fifty miles of rough ice between me and the schooner, and with but scant depots of provision by the way, calculated only for a journey with empty sledges, I must own that I was somewhat perplexed.

When the morning came, Jensen was found to have improved but little and was scarcely able to move. I promptly determined to leave him in charge of McDonald, and to push on with Knorr alone. Lest accident from rotten ice (the only one that I had to fear) should befall me, I left with McDonald five dogs, with directions to await us as many days, and then make the best of his way back to Port Foulke.

Our simple breakfast over, I was once more plunging through the hummocks, making my last throw. Our track lay across a bay so deep that the distance would be more than quadrupled if we followed its tortuous windings of the shore upon the land-ice.

344 IN A FOG.

My purpose now was to make the best push I could, and, traveling as far as my provisions warranted, reach the highest attainable latitude and secure such a point of observation as would enable me to form a definite opinion respecting the sea before me, and the prospects of reaching and navigating it with a boat or with the schooner. I had already reached a position somewhat to the northward of that attained by Morton, of Dr. Kane's expedition, in June, 1854, and was looking out upon the same sea from a point probably about sixty miles to the northward and westward of Cape Constitution, where, only a month later in the season, his further progress was arrested by open water.

It only remained for me now to extend the survey as far to the north as possible. By the judicious husbanding of my resources I had still within my hands ample means to guarantee a successful termination to a journey which the increasing darkness and extent of the water-sky to the northeast seemed to warn me was approaching its climax.

Our first day's journey was not particularly encouraging. The ice in the bay was rough and the snow deep, and, after nine hours of laborious work, we were compelled . to halt for rest, having made, since setting out, not more than as many miles. Our progress had been much retarded by a dense fog which settled over us soon after starting, and which, by preventing us from seeing thirty yards on either side, interfered with the selection of a track; and we were, in consequence, forced to pursue our course by compass.

The fog clearing up by the time we had become rested. and the land being soon reached, we pursued

POLAR SCENERY. 345

our way along the ice-foot with much the same fortune as had befallen us since striking the shore above Cape Napoleon. The coast presented the same features — great wall-sided cliffs rising at our left, with a jagged ridge of crushed ice at our right, forming a white fringe, as it were, to the dark rocks. We were, in truth, journeying along a winding gorge or valley, formed by the land on one side and the ice on the other; for this ice-fringe rose about fifty feet above our heads, and, except here and there where a cleft gave us an outlook upon the sea, we were as completely hemmed in as if in a cañon of the Cordilleras. Occasionally, however, a bay broke in upon the continuity of the lofty coast, and as we faced to the westward along its southern margin, a sloping terraced valley opened before us, rising gently from the sea to the base of the mountains, which rose with imposing grandeur. I was never more impressed with the dreariness and desolation of an Arctic landscape. Although my situation on the summit of the Greenland *mer de glace*, in October of the last year, had apparently left nothing unsupplied to the imagination that was needed to fill the picture of boundless sterility, yet here the variety of forms seemed to magnify the impression on the mind, and to give a wider play to the fancy; and as the eye wandered from peak to peak of the mountains as they rose one above the other, and rested upon the dark and frost-degraded cliffs, and followed along the ice-foot, and overlooked the sea, and saw in every object the silent forces of Nature moving on through the gloom of winter and the sparkle of summer, now, as they had moved for countless ages, unobserved but by the eye of God alone, I felt how puny indeed are all men's works and

346 QUITTING THE LAND-ICE.

efforts; and·when I sought for some token of living
thing, some track of wild beast, — a fox, or bear, or
reindeer, — which had, elsewhere, always crossed me
in my journeyings, and saw nothing but two feeble
men and our struggling dogs, it seemed indeed as if
the Almighty had frowned upon the hills and seas.

Since leaving Cairn Point we had looked most
anxiously for bears; but although we had seen many
tracks, especially about Cape Frazer, not a single ani-
'mal had been observed. A bear, indeed, would have
been a godsend to us, and would have placed me
wholly beyond anxiety respecting the strength of the
dogs, as it would not only have put new life into
them, but would have given them several days of
more substantial rations than the dried beef which
they had been so long fed upon.

After a ten hours' march, we found ourselves once
more compelled to camp; and four hours of the following day brought us to the southern cape of a bay
which was so deep that, as in other cases of like ob-
struction, we determined to cross over it rather than
to follow the shore line. We had gone only a few
miles when we found our progress suddenly arrested.
Our course was made directly for a conspicuous headland bounding the bay to the northward, over a strip
of old ice lining the shore. This headland seemed to
be about twenty miles from us, or near latitude 82°,
and I was very desirous of reaching it; but, unhappily, the old ice came suddenly to an end, and after
scrambling over the fringe of hummocks which mar-
gined it, we found ourselves upon ice of the late winter. The unerring instinct of the dogs warned us of
approaching danger. They were observed for some
time to be moving with unusual caution, and finally

Mt. Murchison.   Church's Pk.   C. Lieber.   Mt. Parry.   C. Eugénie.   C. Frederick VII.   C. Union.

THE SHORES OF THE POLAR SEA.

FROM A SKETCH BY DR. HAYES.

STOPPED BY ROTTEN ICE. 347

they scattered to right and left, and refused to proceed further. This behavior of the dogs was too familiar to me to leave any doubt as to its meaning; and moving forward in advance, I quickly perceived that the ice was rotten and unsafe. Thinking that this might be merely a local circumstance, resulting from some peculiarity of the current, we doubled back upon the old floe and made another trial further to the eastward. Walking now in advance of the dogs they were inspired with greater courage. I had not proceeded far when I found the ice again giving way under the staff, with which I sounded its strength, and again we turned back and sought a still more eastern passage.

Two hours consumed in efforts of this kind, during which we had worked about four miles out to sea, convinced me that the ice outside the bay was wholly impassable, and that perseverance could only end in disappointment; for if we happened to break through, we should not only be in great jeopardy but would, by getting wet, greatly retard, if not wholly defeat our progress to the opposite shore. Accordingly we drew back toward the land, seeking safety again upon the old floe, and hauling then to the westward, endeavored to cross over further up the bay; but here the same conditions existed as outside, and the dogs resolutely refused to proceed as soon as we left the old ice. Not wishing to be defeated in my purpose of crossing over, we held still further west and persevered in our efforts until convinced that the bay could not be crossed, and then we had no alternative but to retreat to the land-ice and follow its circuit to our destination.

With the view of ascertaining how far this course

348 VIEW FROM THE CLIFF.

was likely to carry us from a direct line, I walked, while the dogs were resting, a few miles along the shore until I could see the head of the bay, distant not less than twenty miles. To make this long *détour* would occupy at least two if not three days, — an undertaking not justified by the state of our provisions, — and we therefore went into camp, weary with more than twelve hours' work, to await the issue of further observation on the morrow.

Surprised at the condition of the ice in the bay, I determined to climb the hill above the camp, with the view of ascertaining the probable cause of our being thus baffled ; and to ascertain if a more direct route could not be found further to the eastward than that by the land-ice of the bay ; for it was now clear that it was only possible to continue our journey northward in one or the other of these directions. The labors of the day made it necessary, however, that I should procure some rest before attempting to climb the hill to such an elevation as would enable me to obtain a clear view of the condition of the ice to the opposite shore.

After a most profound and refreshing sleep, inspired by a weariness which I had rarely before experienced, to an equal degree, I climbed the steep hill-side to the top of a ragged cliff, which I supposed to be about eight hundred feet above the level of the sea.

The view which I had from this elevation furnished a solution of the cause of my progress being arrested on the previous day.

The ice was everywhere in the same condition as in the mouth of the bay, across which I had endeavored to pass. A broad crack, starting from the middle of the bay, stretched over the sea, and uniting

VIEW FROM THE CLIFF. 349

with other cracks as it meandered to the eastward, it expanded as the delta of some mighty river discharging into the ocean, and under a water-sky, which hung upon the northern and eastern horizon, it was lost in the open sea.

Standing against the dark sky at the north, there was seen in dim outline the white sloping summit of a noble headland, — the most northern known land upon the globe. I judged it to be in latitude 82° 30', or four hundred and fifty miles from the North Pole. Nearer, another bold cape stood forth; and nearer still the headland, for which I had been steering my course the day before, rose majestically from the sea, as if pushing up into the very skies a lofty mountain peak, upon which the winter had dropped its diadem of snows. There was no land visible except the coast upon which I stood.

The sea beneath me was a mottled sheet of white and dark patches, these latter being either soft decaying ice or places where the ice had wholly disappeared. These spots were heightened in intensity of shade and multiplied in size as they receded, until the belt of the water-sky blended them all together into one uniform color of dark blue. The old and solid floes (some a quarter of a mile, and others miles, across) and the massive ridges and wastes of hummocked ice which lay piled between them and around their margins, were the only parts of the sea which retained the whiteness and solidity of winter.

I reserve to another chapter all discussion of the value of the observations which I made from this point. Suffice it here to say that all the evidences showed that I stood upon the shores of the Polar Basin, and that the broad ocean lay at my feet: that

THE JOURNEY ENDED.

the land upon which I stood, culminating in the distant cape before me, was but a point of land projecting far into it, like the Ceverro Vostochnoi Noss of the opposite coast of Siberia; and that the little margin of ice which lined the shore was being steadily worn away; and within a month, the whole sea would be as free from ice as I had seen the north water of Baffin Bay, — interrupted only by a moving pack, drifting to and fro at the will of the winds and currents.

To proceed further north was, of course, impossible. The crack which I have mentioned would, of itself, have prevented us from making the opposite land, and the ice outside the bay was even more decayed than inside. Several open patches were observed near the shore, and in one of these there was seen a flock of *Dovekie*. At several points during our march up Kennedy Channel I had observed their breeding-places, but I was not a little surprised to see the birds at this locality so early in the season. Several burgomaster-gulls flew over head, making their way northward, seeking the open water for their feeding grounds and summer haunts. Around these haunts of the birds there is never ice after the early days of June.

And now my journey was ended, and I had nothing to do but make my way back to Port Foulke. The advancing season, the rapidity with which the thaw was taking place, the certainty that the open water was eating into Smith Sound as well through Baffin Bay from the south, as through Kennedy Channel from the north, thus endangering my return across to the Greenland shore, warned me that I had lingered long enough.

PLANTING THE FLAG. 351

It now only remained for us to plant our flag in token of our discovery, and to deposit a record in proof of our presence. The flags [1] were tied to the whip-lash, and suspended between two tall rocks, and while we were building a cairn, they were allowed to flutter in the breeze; then, tearing a leaf from my note-book, I wrote on it as follows: —

> " This point, the most northern land that has ever been reached, was visited by the undersigned, May 18th, 19th, 1861, accompanied by George F. Knorr, traveling with a dog-sledge. We arrived here after a toilsome march of forty-six days from my winter harbor, near Cape Alexander, at the mouth of Smith Sound. My observations place us in latitude 81° 35', longitude 70° 30', W. Our further progress was stopped by rotten ice and cracks. Kennedy Channel appears to expand into the Polar Basin , and, satisfied that it is navigable at least during the months of July, August, and September, I go hence to my winter harbor, to make another trial to get through Smith Sound with my vessel, after the ice breaks up this summer.
>
> "I. I. HAYES.
>
> " *May 19th,* 1861."

This record being carefully secured in a small glass vial, which I brought for the purpose, it was deposited beneath the cairn; and then our faces were turned homewards. But I quit the place with reluctance.

---

[1] These were a small United States flag (boat's ensign), which had been carried in the South Sea Expedition of Captain Wilkes, U. S N., and afterwards in the Arctic Expeditions of Lieut. Comg. DeHaven and Dr. Kane; a little United States flag which had been committed to Mr. Sonntag by the ladies of the Albany Academy ; two diminutive Masonic flags intrusted to me, — one by the Kane Lodge of New York, the other by the Columbia Lodge of Boston; and our Expedition signal-flag, bearing the Expedition emblem, the Pole Star — a crimson star, on a white field — also a gift from fair hands. Being under the obligation of a sacred promise to unfurl all of these flags at the most northern point attained, it was my pleasing duty to carry them with me — a duty rendered none the less pleasing by the circumstance that, together, they did not weigh three pounds.

It possessed a fascination for me, and it was with no ordinary sensations that I contemplated my situation, with one solitary companion, in that hitherto untrodden desert; while my nearness to the earth's axis, the consciousness of standing upon land far beyond the limits of previous observation, the reflections which crossed my mind respecting the vast ocean which lay spread out before me, the thought that these ice-girdled waters might lash the shores of distant islands where dwell human beings of an unknown race, were circumstances calculated to invest the very air with mystery, to deepen the curiosity, and to strengthen the resolution to persevere in my determination to sail upon this sea and to explore its furthest limits; and as I recalled the struggles which had been made to reach this sea, — through the ice and across the ice, — by generations of brave men, it seemed as if the spirits of these Old Worthies came to encourage me, as their experience had already guided me; and I felt that I had within my grasp "the great and notable thing" which had inspired the zeal of sturdy Frobrisher, and that I had achieved the hope of matchless Parry.

CHAPTER XXXII.

THE OPEN POLAR SEA — WIDTH OF THE POLAR BASIN. — BOUNDARIES OF THE POLAR BASIN — POLAR CURRENTS — POLAR ICE — THE ICE-BELT — ARCTIC NAVIGATION AND DISCOVERY — THE RUSSIAN SLEDGE EXPLORATIONS — WRANGEL'S OPEN SEA — PARRY'S BOAT EXPEDITION — DR KANE'S DISCOVERIES — EXPANSION OF SMITH SOUND — GENERAL CONCLUSIONS DRAWN FROM MY OWN DISCOVERIES AND THOSE OF MY PREDECESSORS

LET us pause here a few moments, in order that we may take a brief survey of the Polar Basin and arrive at a correct understanding of what is meant by the term, "OPEN POLAR SEA," so often used.

By referring to the circumpolar map, the reader will be able to form a more accurate judgment than he could from the most elaborate description. He will observe that about the North Pole of the earth there is an extensive sea, or, more properly, ocean, with an average diameter of more than two thousand miles. He will observe that this sea is almost completely surrounded by land, and that its shores are, for the most part, well defined, — the north coasts of Greenland and Grinnell Land, which project farthest into it, being alone undetermined. He will note that these shores occupy, to a certain extent, a uniform distance from the Pole, and are everywhere within the region of perpetual frost. He will remember that they are inhabited everywhere by people of the same race, to whom the soil yields no subsistence, who live exclusively by hunting and fishing, and confine their dwelling-places either to the coast or to the banks of

354 BOUNDARIES OF THE POLAR BASIN.

the rivers which flow northward. He will observe that the long line of coast which gives lodgment to these Arctic nomads is interrupted in three principal places; and that through these the waters of the Polar Sea mingle with the waters of the Atlantic and Pacific Oceans, — these breaks being Baffin Bay, Behring Strait, and the broader opening between Greenland and Nova Zembla; and if he traces the currents on the map and follows the Gulf Stream as it flows northward, pouring the warm waters of the Tropic Zone through the broad gateway east of Spitzbergen and forcing out a return current of cold waters to the west of Spitzbergen and through Davis Strait, he will very readily comprehend why in this incessant displacement of the waters of the Pole by the waters of the Equator the great body of the former is never chilled to within several degrees of the freezing-point; and since it is probably as deep, as it is almost as broad, as the Atlantic between Europe and America, he will be prepared to understand that this vast body of water tempers the whole region with a warmth above that which is otherwise natural to it; and that the Almighty hand, in the all-wise dispensation of His power, has thus placed a bar to its congelation; and he will read in this another symbol of Nature's great law of circulation, which, giving water to the parched earth and moisture to the air, moderates as well the temperature of the zones — cooling the Tropic with a current of water from the Frigid, and warming the Frigid with a current from the Tropic.[1]

[1] The temperature of the air at the North Pole has furnished a fruitful theme of speculation, both in connection with the influence of the sea and of the sun I have before me a highly instructive paper on the climate of the North Pole, read before the Royal Geographical Society of London,

POLAR CURRENTS. 355

Bearing these facts in mind, the reader will perceive that it is the surface-water only which ever reaches so low a temperature that it is changed to ice ; and he will also perceive that when the wind moves the surface-water, the particles which have become chilled by contact with the air mingle in the rolling waves with the warm waters beneath, and hence that ice can only form in sheltered places or where the water of some bay is so shoal and the current so slack that it becomes chilled to the very bottom, or where the air over the sea is uniformly calm. He will remember, however, that the winds blow as fiercely over the Polar Sea as in any other quarter of the world ; and he will, therefore, have no difficulty in comprehending that the Polar ice covers but a small part of the Polar water ; and that it exists only where it is nursed and protected by the land. It clings to the coasts of Siberia, and springing thence across Behring Strait to America, it hugs the American shore, fills the narrow channels which drain the

April 10th, 1865, by W. E. Hickson, Esq., from which I extract the following : —

"It had always been supposed that the immediate areas of the Poles must be the coldest regions of the globe, because the farthest points from the equator. Hence the argument that the higher the latitude the greater must be the difficulties and dangers of navigation Quite an opposite opinion, however, had begun to prevail among meteorologists on the publication, in 1817, of the Isothermal system of Alexander Von Humboldt, which showed that distance from the equator is no rule for cold, as the equator is not a parallel of maximum heat The line of maximum heat crosses the Greenwich meridian, in Africa, fifteen degrees north of the equator, and rises, to the eastward, five degrees higher, running along the southern edge of the Desert of Sahara. In 1821, Sir David Brewster pointed out, in a paper on the mean temperature of the globe, the probability of the thermometer being found to range ten degrees higher at the Pole than in some other parts of the Arctic Circle. No new facts have since been discovered to invalidate this conclusion — many, on the contrary, have come to light tending to confirm it."

THE ICE-BELT.

Polar waters into Baffin Bay through the Parry Archipelago, crosses thence to Greenland, from Greenland to Spitzbergen, and from Spitzbergen to Nova Zembla, — thus investing the Pole in an uninterrupted land-clinging belt of ice, more or less broken as well in winter as in summer, and the fragments ever moving to and fro, though never widely separating, forming a barrier against which all the arts and energies of man have not hitherto prevailed.

If the reader would further pursue the inquiry, let him place one leg of a pair of dividers on the map near the North Pole (say in latitude 86°, longitude 160° W.), and inscribe a circle two thousand miles in diameter, and he will have touched the margin of the land and the mean line of the ice-belt throughout its wide circuit, and have covered an area of more than three millions of square miles.

Although this ice-belt has not been broken through, it has been penetrated in many places, and its southern margin has been followed, partly along the waters formed near the land by the discharging rivers of the Arctic water-sheds of Asia and America, and partly by working through the ice which is always more or less loosened by the summer. It was in this manner that various navigators have attempted the northwest passage; and it was after following the coast line from Behring Strait to Banks Land, and then pushing through the broken ice that Sir Robert McClure finally succeeded in effecting this long-sought-for passage — not, however, by carrying his ship completely through, but by traveling over the winter ice three hundred miles to Wellington Channel, whence he returned home through Baffin Bay in a ship that had come from the eastward. And it was in this

ICE NAVIGATION. 357

same manner that Captain Collinson, passing from west to east, reached almost to the spot where perished Franklin, who had entered the ice from the opposite direction. And it is thus, also, that the Russians have explored the coasts of Siberia, meeting but two insurmountable obstacles to the navigation from the Atlantic to the Pacific side, namely, Cape Jakan, against which the ice is always jammed, and which Behring tried in vain to pass, and Cape Ceverro Vostochnoi, which the gallant young Lieutenant Prondtschikoff made such heroic efforts to surmount. And it was by the same method of navigation that the Amsterdam pilot, earnest old William Barentz, strové, in 1598, to find by the northeast a passage to Cathay.

The efforts to break through the belt, with the expectation of finding clear water about the Pole, have been very numerous, and they have been made through every opening from the southern waters to the Polar Sea. To follow the history of those various attempts would not fall within my present purpose. It is but a long record of defeat, so far as concerned the single object of getting to the Pole. Cook, and all who have come after him, have failed to find the ice sufficiently open to admit of navigation northward from Behring Strait, as Hudson and his followers have through the Spitzbergen Sea; and all the efforts through Baffin Bay have been equally futile. The most persevering attempts to break through the ice-belt have been made to the west of Spitzbergen, and in this quarter ships have approached nearer to the Pole than in any other. The highest well-authenticated position achieved by any navigator was that of Scorsby, who reached latitude 81° 30.′

358 WRANGEL'S OPEN SEA.

although it is claimed that Hudson had gone still further; and if the stories which Daines Barrington picked up from the fishermen of Amsterdam and Hull are to be relied on, then the old Dutch and English voyagers have gone even beyond this, seeking new fishing-grounds and finding everywhere an open sea. There is, however, as before observed, no well-authenticated record of any ship having attained a higher latitude than that of Scorsby.

Failing to get through the ice, explorers have next tried to cross it with sledges. In this the Russians have done most. Many enterprising officers of the Russian service, using the dog-sledges of the native tribes inhabiting the Siberian coast, have, in the early spring, boldly struck out upon the Polar Sea. Most conspicuous among them was Admiral Wrangel, then a young lieutenant of the Russian Navy, whose explorations, continued through several years, showed that, at all seasons of the year, the same condition of the sea existed to the northward. The travelers were invariably arrested by open water; and the existence of a *Polynia* or open sea above the New Siberian Islands, became a fact as well established as that the rivers flow downward to the sea.

Sir Edward Parry tried the same method above Spitzbergen, using, however, men instead of dogs for draft, and carrying boats for safety in the event of the ice breaking up. Parry traveled northward until the ice, becoming loosened by the advancing season, carried him south faster than he was traveling north; and after a while it broke up under him, and set him adrift in the open sea.

Next came Captain Inglefield's attempt to get into this circumpolar water through Smith Sound; and

KANE'S OPEN SEA. 359

then Dr. Kane's. The latter's vessel could not be forced further into the ice than Van Rensselaer Harbor; and, like the Russians, he continued the work with sledges. After many embarrassments and failures in his attempts to surmount the difficulties presented by hummocked ice of the Sound, one of his parties succeeded finally in reaching the predicted open water; and, to quote Dr. Kane's words, "from an elevation of five hundred and eighty feet, this water was still without a limit, moved by a heavy swell, free of ice, and dashing in surf against a rock-bound shore." This shore was the shore of the land which he named Washington Land.

Next, after Dr. Kane's, came my own undertaking; and the last chapter leaves me with my sledge upon the shores of that same sea which Dr. Kane describes, about one hundred miles to the north and west of the point from which one of his parties looked out upon the iceless waters. My own opinion of what I saw and of the condition of this sea, which Wrangel found open on the opposite side from where I stood, and which Kane's party had found open to my right, and which Parry's journey showed to be open above Spitzbergen, may be inferred from what I have already briefly stated, and may be more briefly concluded.

The boundaries of the Polar Basin are sufficiently well defined to enable us to form a rational estimate of the unknown coast-lines of Greenland and Grinnell Land, — the only parts of the extensive circuit remaining unexplored. The trend of the northern coast-line of Greenland is approximately defined by the reasonable analogies of physical geography; and the same process of reasoning forbids the conclusion

360 EXPANSION OF SMITH SOUND.

that Grinnell Land extends beyond the limit of my explorations. I hold, as Inglefield did before me, that Smith Sound expands into the Polar Basin. Beyond the narrow passage between Cape Alexander and Cape Isabella, the water widens steadily up to Cape Frazer, where it expands abruptly. On the Greenland side the coast trends regularly to the eastward, until it reaches Cape Agassiz, where it dips under the glacier and is lost to observation. That cape is composed of primitive rock, and is the end of a mountain spur. This same rock is visible at many places along the coast, but is mostly covered with the deposit of sandstone and greenstone, which forms the tall cliffs of the coast-line, until it crops out about thirty miles in the interior into a mountain chain, which, (in company with Mr. Wilson), I crossed, in 1853, to find the *mer de glace* hemmed in behind it. Further to the north the *mer de glace* has poured down into the Polar Sea, and pushing its way onward through the water, it has at length reached Washington Land, and swelled southward into Smith Sound. That the face of Humboldt Glacier trends more to the eastward than is exhibited on Dr. Kane's chart, I have shown; and that Washington Land will be found to lie much farther in the same direction, I have sufficient grounds for believing. According to the report of Morton, it is to be inferred that this island is but a continuation of the same granitic ridge which breaks off abruptly at Cape Agassiz, and appears again above the sea at Cape Forbes, in a line conformable with the Greenland range. It is probable then that at some remote period this Washington Land stood in the expansion of Smith Sound, washed by water on every side. — that lying to the

THE OPEN POLAR SEA. 361

eastward being now supplanted by the great glacier of Humboldt; that lying to the westward now bearing the name of Kennedy Channel.

With the warm flood of the Gulf Stream pouring northward, and keeping the waters of the Polar Sea at a temperature above the freezing point, while the winds, blowing as constantly under the Arctic as under the Tropic sky, and the ceaseless currents of the sea and the tide-flow of the surface, keep the waters ever in movement, it is not possible, as I have before observed, that even any considerable portion of this extensive sea can be frozen over. At no point within the Arctic Circle has there been found an ice-belt extending, either in winter or in summer, more than from fifty to a hundred miles from land. And even in the narrow channels separating the islands of the Parry Archipelago, in Baffin Bay, in the North Water, and the mouth of Smith Sound, — everywhere, indeed, within the broad area of the Frigid Zone, the waters will not freeze except when sheltered by the land, or when an ice-pack, accumulated by a long continuance of winds from one quarter, affords the same protection. That the sea does not close except when at rest, I had abundant reason to know during the late winter; for at all times, as this narrative frequently records, even when the temperature of the air was below the freezing point of mercury, I could hear from the deck of the schooner the roar of the beating waves.

It would be needless for me to detain the reader with the conclusions to be drawn from the condition of the sea as observed by me at the point from which the last chapter left us returning, as the facts speak for themselves. It will not, however, be out of place

362 THE OPEN WATER.

to observe that no one whose eye has ever rested upon the Arctic ice or witnessed the changes of the Arctic seasons, could fail to realize that in a very short time, as the summer advanced, the open water would steadily eat its way southward, through Kennedy Channel, into Smith Sound.

CHAPTER XXXIII.

ON BOARD THE SCHOONER — REVIEW OF THE JOURNEY. — THE RETURN DOWN KENNEDY CHANNEL — A SEVERE MARCH IN A SNOW-STORM. — ROTTEN ICE — EFFECTS OF A GALE. — RETURNING THROUGH THE HUMMOCKS — THE DOGS BREAKING DOWN. — ADRIFT ON A FLOE AT CAIRN POINT — THE OPEN WATER COMPELS US TO TAKE TO THE LAND. — REACHING THE SCHOONER. — PROJECTING A CHART. — THE NEW SOUND — MY NORTHERN DISCOVERIES

PORT FOULKE, June 3d.

BACK again on board the schooner after two months' toiling and journeying on the ice.

Since I left her deck on the 3d of April, I have traveled not less than 1300 miles, and not less than 1600 since first setting out in March. I am somewhat battered and weather-beaten, but a day or so of rest and civilized comfort, the luxury of a wash and a bed, and of a table covered with clean crockery filled with the best of things that my old Swedish cook can turn out, are wondrously rejuvenating, — potent as the touch of Hebe to the war-worn Iolas.

Affairs seem to have gone on well at the schooner. Radcliffe has given me his report, and it is satisfactory. McCormick has presented a full history of events since leaving me among the hummocks; but I refrain now from recording them until I have set down some of the leading incidents of my journey, while they are yet fresh in my mind. Besides, McCormick tells me that he is unable to repair the schooner that she may be ice-worthy; and, as I am unwilling to accept this conclusion without a further

364 REVIEW OF THE JOURNEY.

examination than I have yet been able to make, I postpone any further allusion to the matter. To confess the truth, the last days of the homeward journey used us all up pretty thoroughly; and, although the confined atmosphere of the cabin is oppressive to me after so long an exposure in the open air, yet the doctor (which is my *doppelganger*) warns me to keep to this lounge for a day or so. I am not, however, forbidden to write.

I have returned well satisfied that Kennedy Channel is navigable; and it remains only to be proven whether Smith Sound will open sufficiently to permit a passage through. With steam, I should have no doubt whatever of my ability to force it; with sails, of course, the effort is filled with greater uncertainty; and yet, I think, the chances are with me.

I am fully convinced that a route to the Pole, — a route, certainly, not wholly unobstructed by ice, yet free enough at least for steam navigation, is open every summer from Cape Frazer; and if I can pull through to that point, then I shall have accomplished the full measure of my desires. In truth, this is the real difficulty. My views of the whole matter will be set down here on the spot as opportunity offers from day to day. To-morrow, I hope to be sufficiently recovered from the fatigues of the journey to begin the discussion of my materials, and the projection of my chart.

And now, with a heart filled with thankfulness to that Great Being who suffereth not even a sparrow to fall to the ground without His notice, I have here the happiness to record that in these two months of perilous traveling, He has spared me and every member of my party from serious accident or permanent injury.

THE RETURN. 365

June 4th.

I have worked up some of my sights, and rudely sketched in the coast-line of my track-chart. It makes a respectable show for our summer's sledging. Since the middle of March, I have covered the entire ground gone over by Dr. Kane's various parties, except the coast of Washington Land, and have extended the former surveys considerably to the north and west. But the important additions which I have been enabled to make to the geographical knowledge of the region I regard as of secondary interest to the circumstance that my journey has shown the practicability of this route into the Polar Basin.

My return southward from the shores of the Polar Sea is not recorded in my field-diary. There is no record after we had turned our faces homeward. That water-soaked and generally dilapidated-looking book, which now lies open on the table before me, breaks off thus : —

"Halted in the lee of a huge ice-cliff, seeking shelter from a fierce storm that set upon us soon after we started south. We have made about ten miles, and have from forty to fifty yet to make before we reach Jensen. We have given the dogs the last of our food. It is snowing and blowing dreadfully."

The storm continued with unabated violence through the next day; and as the wind shrieked along the tall cliffs, carrying with it the drifting snow, I thought that I had scarcely ever seen or heard any thing more dismal. Unable to bear the chilliness of our imperfect shelter, (we had no means of making a snow-hut,) we pushed on, wading through deep drifts in addition to climbing the rocks and masses of ice, which, in going north, had

366 LONG AND WEARY MARCH

everywhere more or less embarrassed our progress.
The snow-drifts were often so deep that the dogs' had
much trouble in wading through them, and it was
all that they could do to drag the now quite empty
sledge. After a time they became so much exhausted
that it was with the utmost difficulty that we could
force them forward. The poor beasts fell in their
tracks the moment the whip ceased to be applied. I
had never before seen them so much broken. To
halt was of little use, as rest, without food, would
do harm rather than good ; and as we had no shelter, and in the item of food were as badly off as the
dogs, there was nothing for us to do but to hold on
and get through to Jensen's camp, or perish in the
storm. Fortunately, the wind was at our backs.

We kept on in our winding course through the
pelting snow, and reached, finally, the north side of
the bay above Jensen's camp ; and then the hardest
part of the journey was to come. The tramp across
that bay comes back to me now as the vague recollection of some ugly dream. I scarcely remember
how we got through it. I recall only an endless
pounding of the dogs, who wanted to lie down with
every step, the ceaseless wading, the endless crunch
of the wearied feet breaking through the old snow-
crust, the laborious climbing over hummocks, the
pushing and lifting of the sledge, — and, through the
blinding snow, I remember, at length, catching sight
of the land and of hearing the cry of Jensen's dogs ;
and then of crawling up the ice-foot to his snow-hut.
Through all these last hours, we were aware of a desire to halt and sleep ; and it is fortunate for us that
we did not lose consciousness of its dangers.

Without waiting to be fed, the dogs tumbled over

A LAST LOOK. 367

on the snow the moment they were left to themselves; and we, dragging ourselves inside the hut which McDonald had made to shelter his sick companion, fell into a dead, dead sleep. Jensen noted the time. We had been twenty-two hours on the way, since leaving our shelter beneath the ice-cliff.

When we awoke, the storm had died away, and the sun was shining brightly. McDonald had looked after the dogs, and had ready for us a hot pot of coffee and an abundant breakfast, which thirty-four hours' fasting had prepared us fully to appreciate. Refreshed by this, I climbed the hill-side for a last look at the sea which we were leaving. The gale had told somewhat upon it. The dark water-sky to the northeast had followed us down the coast, the wind had acted upon the open places in the ice, and the little waves had eaten away their margins, and magnified them greatly, while many of the old floes had finally yielded to the immense pressure of the wind, and had moved in their winter moorings, tearing up the rotten ice about them. Several cracks had opened almost to the shore, and the "hinge" of the ice-foot had mainly tumbled away.

Jensen was better, but still moved with much difficulty and pain. By sitting on the sledge, however, he thought that he should be able to drive his dogs; so I gave Knorr our entire cargo. This cargo was now reduced to small dimensions, and consisted of nothing but our buffalo-skins, rifle, my instruments, and a few geological specimens. Our food was consumed to the last pound, and hence we must go supperless if we did not reach our next cache. where, if the bears should not have discovered it, we had one meal buried under a heap of stones.

368 THE SHORE-ICE

June 5th.

I resume the narrative.

The march to the cache was a very tedious one, but we took it leisurely, and got through with it in sixteen hours, to find our food unmolested. The repeated halts to rest the dogs gave me abundant leisure to search among the limestone cliffs for further fossil remains, and my exertions were rewarded with a valuable collection. It is, perhaps, too much to say that they are fossils of the Silurian era, from a hasty examination; but I think it more than probable.

I had also opportunity to measure some of the masses of ice which had been forced upon the shore. In many places these masses were crowded together, forming an almost impassable barrier. In other places the ice-foot had been torn through, and in one spot a table sixty feet in thickness and forty yards across had been crowded on the sloping shore, pushing up the loose, rocky *débris* which lay at the base of the cliffs; and when the pack that had caused the disturbance had drifted away, this fragment was left with its lower edge above the tide. Around it were piled other masses; and, in order to pass it, we were obliged to climb far up the hill-side.

Our next day's journey was even more difficult, as we became entangled among deep snow-drifts below Cape Frazer, and, on account of the rotten condition of the ice lining the shore, we could not take to the ice-fields. We tried twice, and came near paying dearly for the experiment. One of the teams got in bodily, and was extricated with difficulty; while, on the other occasion, I, acting in my usual capacity of pilot, saved myself from a cold bath with my ice-pole, which, plunging through the rotten ice and disappear-

SIGHTING GREENLAND. 369

ing out of sight, gave me timely warning; so we put back again to the more secure land-ice.

In the bay below Cape Napoleon we found, on the following day, secure footing, and reached Cape Hawks without difficulty, in two more marches. Thence we proceeded to follow our outward track through the hummocks. The sledges being now light, and Jensen having so far improved as to be able to walk, we experienced less embarrassment than on our outward journey; but the dogs were now in a very different condition, and lightness of load leveled not the hummocks and made not the steep places smooth, nor the ice less sharp, nor the snow-crusts less treacherous. The task was wearisome and exhausting to the last degree, — a hard struggle, destructive to the energies of men and dogs alike.

Some snow had fallen, but, fortunately, the wind had drifted it from our tracks in many places, and we found our way to the small provision caches which we had left going north, and, luckily, they had all escaped the observation of the bears except one; but, having made a good march on the first day from Cape Hawks, we picked up the first cache we came to, and thus saved a day's food, — a piece of good fortune which we had not counted upon.

The coast of Greenland rose at length into view, and, steadily rising day by day, we came within sight of Cairn Point; but, for some time previous, we were warned of the rapid advance of the season by the dark water-sky which lay before us, showing that the open water extended up to the Point, for which we were shaping our course. On the north side of it, however, the ice appeared to be solid. Thinking that we could make the land in that direction, we pushed

24

ADRIFT ON AN ICE-RAFT.

on, picking our way over the rough and thicker ice, and avoiding the younger ice, which was everywhere porous, and occasionally worn completely away. At length, when about a mile from land, we came upon a crack, which had opened not more than a foot. Crossing this, we held in directly for the Point, but, unfortunately, the wind was blowing heavily down the Sound; and, as we neared the land, we found that the water had eaten in between the ice and the shore, obliging us to keep up the coast. To our horror and dismay, we now discovered that the crack which we had crossed had opened at least twenty yards, and we were adrift upon an ice-raft in an open sea, without power to help ourselves.

The movement of the ice was slow. After waiting a short time, irresolute as to what course we should pursue, it was observed that the outer end of the loosened floe was moving, while the inner edge was almost stationary, owing to a small iceberg, which, being aground and fastened to the floe itself, formed a pivot about which we were revolving. If this berg held, it was evident that the floe would strike the land, and we approached nearer to its margin.

The event which we had so eagerly desired now happened; and, dashing forward when the collision came, we managed to get upon the land-ice. The tide, being at full flood, facilitated the undertaking. The contact did not long continue. The rotten edge of the floe broke loose from the little berg which had given us this most fortunate assistance, and we were not sorry to see the ice-raft drifting away without us.

By this time, the dogs had become more broken. They had borne up admirably during the journey

TAKING TO THE LAND. 371

north, but the scant rations which we had left behind for the return journey were found to be insufficient to support their strength, especially as they had, for some time, Jensen's additional weight to carry. One of them gave out completely, and died in a fit, during the first day's journey in the hummocks; two others followed soon afterward; while another, having become unable either to pull or follow, was shot. Much to my surprise, as soon as the bullet struck the animal, wounding him but slightly and causing him to set up a terrible cry, his companions in the team flew upon him and tore him to pieces in an instant, and those who were lucky enough to get a fragment of him were tearing the flesh from his bones almost before the echo of his last howl had died away in the solitude.

The sea below Cairn Point was filled with loose ice, evidently broken adrift by a very recent gale. By keeping to the land-ice we managed to work our way down the coast, and got around Cape Hatherton; but, below this, the ice-foot, too, was gone, thus obliging us to take to the land. To cross the mountains with our sledges was, of course, impracticable; so we were compelled to abandon them until such time as we could come for them in a boat.

The land journey was very tedious and tiresome, exhausted and foot-sore as we were already; but we managed better than the dogs. Most of them sneaked away as soon as loosened from the sledges, and would not follow us; and when sought for could not be found. I did not feel apprehensive for them, as I supposed they merely needed rest, and would follow our tracks to the vessel. Three of them only stuck to us. One is the noble old beast,

372 A NEW SOUND.

Oosisoak; another is his brave queen, Arkadik; and the third Nenook, the finest of Kalutunah's dogs. Three others have come in since; but four are yet missing. I have sent out to seek them, without success. I much fear that they will not have strength to drag themselves on board.

And so my journey ended. If it has had its disappointments, it has had, too, its triumphs and successes. It was unfortunate that I did not get the boat over the Sound, together with a good supply of provisions; but, failing in this, the failure of the foot-party was of little moment. No amount of assistance could, with sledges alone, have helped me further north; or, if I had got further, could have ever got me back again.

June 8th.

I have finished the plotting of my chart, and I find, as I have already had occasion to observe, that the coast-line from Cape Sabine to Cape Frazer differs somewhat from that shown from my journey in 1854, which was made under the embarrassments of partial snow-blindness and a vapory atmosphere. The most important feature in connection with this old survey is the fact that the Sound opening westward from Smith Sound, above Cape Sabine, formerly escaped my observation. The existence of this Sound was abundantly confirmed during my return journey; and my materials, now reduced and put on paper, give me the correct conformation of the coast. The Sound is somewhat wider than Smith Sound, narrowing, however, steadily, from a broad entrance, something like Whale Sound. Whether it continues to the westward, parallel with Jones and Lancaster Sounds, separating the Ellesmere Land, of Ingle-

NOMENCLATURE. 373

field, from the Grinnell Land of my former exploration, of course, remains to be proven; but, that such is the fact, I have no doubt.

I give to this Sound the name of my vessel The first conspicuous Cape which appears on its south side I name Cape Seward, and the most remote point of visible land lying beyond it, Cape Viele. The three last conspicuous Capes on the north side I name as follows: the most westerly, Cape Baker; that next to it, Cape Sawyer; and the third, Cape Stetson. The apparently deep indentations of the coast which lie between these bold headlands are designated as Joy Bay and Peabody Bay. The two large islands lying in the mouth of the Sound I have distinguished as Bache Island and Henry Island. Eastward of Cape Stetson I have applied such names as seemed to me appropriate to distinguish the prominent landmarks; but it is unnecessary to mention them here, as the map tells its own story. In those parts of the coast which were plotted by Dr. Kane from my old survey, I have endeavored to adhere, as far as practicable, to his nomenclature; and such parts of the shores of Kennedy Channel as were seen by Morton alone, I have, for the most part, simply applied Dr. Kane's names, without inquiring very particularly as to their corresponding places on the two maps. I think this course, in the main, preferable to that somewhat confusing system which deprived Captain Inglefield of the benefits of his survey of Smith Sound; and I have, besides, the additional satisfaction of joining Dr. Kane in paying respect to many distinguished men of science, dead and living, and among them to none that contribute more gratification than that of M. de la Roquette, Vice-President of the Geographical Soci-

374   NOMENCLATURE.

ety of Paris; and to Sir Roderick Murchison, President of the Royal Geographical Society, London, and Dr. Norton Shaw, its Secretary. The coast-range, which forms such a conspicuous feature of Grinnell Land, I have followed Dr. Kane in designating as Victoria and Albert Mountains.

The highest point attained by me I have called Cape Lieber; a remarkable peak rising above it, Church's Monument; and the Bay, which lies below it, is named in respectful remembrance of Lady Franklin. The conspicuous headland which I vainly attempted to reach, on the last day of my northward journey, I have named Cape Eugénie, thinking, in this manner, to express my high appreciation of the many acts of kindness to this expedition and to myself which I owe to French citizens, by remembering their Empress. Another prominent headland appearing beyond it I designate as Cape Frederick VII., in honor of the King of Denmark, to whose subjects in Greenland I am indebted for so many serviceable attentions. And to the noble headland which, in faint outline, stood against the dark sky of the open sea — the most northern known land upon the globe — I name Cape Union, in remembrance of a compact which has given prosperity to a people and founded a nation. In naming the bay which lies between Cape Union and Cape Frederick VII., I am desirous of expressing my admiration of Admiral Wrangel, whose fame in connection with Arctic discovery is equaled by that of Sir Edward Parry only. And the lofty peak which overlooks the Polar Sea from behind Cape Eugénie, I name Parry Mountain. With this eminent explorer I will now divide the honors of extreme northern travel; for, if he has carried the

British flag upon the sea nearer to the North Pole than any flag had been carried hitherto, I have planted the American flag further north upon the land then any flag has been planted before. The Bay between Capes Frederick VII. and Eugénie I name in honor of the distinguished geographer, Dr. Augustus Peterman; and two large bays lower down the coast I call, respectively, after Carl Ritter and William Scorsby.

In plotting my survey I have been a little puzzled with the Washington Land of Dr. Kane's map, and I am much tempted to switch it off twenty miles to the eastward; for it is not possible that Kennedy Channel can be less than fifty miles wide; and, since I believe that Smith Sound expands into the Polar Basin, I must look upon Washington Land merely as an island in its centre, — Kennedy Channel lying between it and Grinnell Land on the west, and Humboldt Glacier filling up what was once a channel on the right.

CHAPTER XXXIV.

INSPECTION OF THE SCHOONER. — METHOD OF REPAIRING. — THE SERIOUS NATURE OF THE INJURY. — THE SCHOONER UNFIT FOR ANY FURTHER ICE-ENCOUNTERS. — EXAMINATION OF MY RESOURCES. — PLANS FOR THE FUTURE.

THE extracts from my journal quoted in the preceding chapter will have sufficed to give the reader an understanding of the results of my spring and summer sledging, and he will have perceived that they were regarded by me as having laid down a correct basis for future exploration. With the character of the Smith Sound ice I had become more familiar, and the accurate determination of the coast-lines enabled me more readily to calculate upon the influence of the summer drift; while the rotten state of the ice in Kennedy Channel, even at so early a period of the season as May, and the existence of open water beyond it, left no doubt upon my mind as to the practicability of getting a vessel through under ordinarily favorable conditions of the season.

It will be perceived, therefore, that my future course was dependent upon the condition of the schooner.

Although I have not made more than a passing allusion to the report of Mr. McCormick as to the damage sustained by the vessel, yet the reader will have gathered from my journal that it caused me much anxiety. I was too much prostrated after my return

INSPECTION OF THE SCHOONER. 377

from the journey to make, during the first few days, that thorough inspection which was needed to form a correct judgment. I was consoled, however, in some measure for the delay, by realizing the necessity of writing up the occurrences of my return journey, while they were fresh in my mind, and of defining on my chart the observations and geographical discoveries which I had made.

These duties performed, and my strength sufficiently restored to justify me in leaving my cabin, I made a careful examination of the schooner and the means which had been adopted for repairing her. These means were altogether unexceptionable, and reflected much credit upon Mr. McCormick and also upon the mate, Mr. Dodge, who had given him zealous assistance.

McCormick had begun by digging the ice away from the bows down to the very keel, thus exposing all the forward part of the vessel as completely as if she lay in a dry-dock. The damage proved to have been even greater than we had anticipated, and it seemed remarkable that the forward planks and timbers had not opened to such a degree as to let the water through in torrents and sink us at once. The heads of the planks which were let into the stem were all started; the outer planking was loose and gaping open; the iron sheathing of the cut-water and bows was torn and curled up as if it had been pine-shavings; the stem-post was started, and the cut-water itself was completely torn away.

By dint of much earnest exertion and the use of bolts and spikes, — by replacing the torn cut-water, careful calking, and renewal of the iron plates, — it seemed probable that the schooner would be sea-

REPAIRING THE SCHOONER.

worthy; but I was forced to agree with my sailing-master, that to strike the ice again was sure to sink her.

The stern of the schooner had been dry-docked in the same manner as the bows; and it was found that the severe wrench which she had got off Littleton Island had started the stern-post, upon which hangs the rudder; and the rudder itself had been twisted off, — the pintles having been snapped asunder as if they had been made of pipe-clay. This accident to the rudder had been quite unavoidable, for we were so situated at the time of its occurrence that we could not avail ourselves of the facilities with which we were provided for unshipping it.

McCormick had succeeded in getting in some stout screw-bolts, and had managed, by an ingenious device, in hanging the rudder in such a manner that we could rely upon it to steer the schooner; but it would not bear contact with the ice, or another wrench, and it could not be unshipped. The schooner's sides were much torn and abraided, but no material damage seemed to have been done which was not repaired with some additional spikes to secure the started planks, and a general calking to close the seams.

I felt much disappointment at the turn of affairs. It seemed very probable that, in view of the crippled condition of the schooner, the project of getting into Kennedy Channel and of navigating the Polar Sea with her would have to be abandoned for the present, and that I had now no chance for another year but with boat and sledge. In this direction there was nothing to give encouragement. To transport a boat across such ice as that of Smith Sound was wholly impracticable, and I was now more poorly off

MY RESOURCES. 379

for dogs than before. Only six animals survived the late journey. Of these one died after a few days, apparently from sheer loss of vitality ; and one was returned to Kalutunah.

Under these circumstances, it became a matter for serious reflection, whether it were not wiser to return home, refit, add — what was of much consequence — steam-power to my resources, and come back again immediately. Once at Cape Isabella with a proper vessel, I was fully persuaded that I could get into the northern water, and find a free route to the Pole, although it might be a hard struggle and somewhat hazardous. The chances of success would be greatly enhanced by *steam*.

On the other hand, by remaining, I could not clearly see my way to accomplish any thing more of northern discovery than had been accomplished already ; and I was now called upon to consider whether my time and means could be employed to better advantage by promptly returning to refit than to postpone that inevitable result to another year. The responsibilities of the expedition had been wholly assumed by myself; and, from the time of leaving Boston until I should have completed the exploration which I had undertaken, I proposed to make the costs which, hitherto, various associations and individuals had shared with me, now exclusively my own. I was, therefore, compelled to husband my resources and to act with caution and deliberation.

I will not now detain the reader with the full details of my plans for the future, arranged to meet this new exigency ; suffice it here to observe that, after taking Jensen and Kalutunah into my counsels, I was fully convinced that, by bringing out two ships,

PLANS FOR THE FUTURE.

— mooring one of them in Port Foulke, and pushing north with the other, — a practicable scheme of exploration could be inaugurated, and that its success as well as safety would be secured. To this end, I proposed to myself to establish a permanent hunting station or colony at Port Foulke; to collect about that place all of the Esquimaux;[1] organize a vigorous hunt; and make that hunt yield whatever was essential for sustaining indefinitely an extended system of exploration toward the North Pole. In the practicability of establishing such a station, Jensen, whose experience in the Greenland colonies was extensive, fully agreed with me, and he was much delighted with the plan, accepting without hesitation my proposal to make him superintendent of it; Kalutunah was overjoyed with the prospect of bringing all of his people together; and, in this aspect alone, the scheme possessed much that was to me personally gratifying. My intercourse with this fast-dwindling race had caused me to feel a deep interest in them and to sympathize with their unhappy condition. The hardships of their life were telling upon them sadly, and, if not rescued by the hand of Christian philanthropy and benevolence, in less than half a century these poor wanderers of the icy sea will have all passed away.

My plans for the future did not, however, assume definite shape at the period of which I write, nor could they until the schooner should be set free.

---

[1] The Esquimaux may, to a limited extent, be even made available in exploration, as has been shown by the experience of Mr. C F Hall, who is now, with no other reliance than the natives, energetically pushing his discoveries westward from Repulse Bay.

CHAPTER XXXV.

THE ARCTIC SPRING — SNOW DISAPPEARING — PLANTS SHOW SIGNS OF LIFE — RETURN OF THE BIRDS. — CHANGE IN THE SEA — REFITTING THE SCHOONER. — THE ESQUIMAUX — VISIT TO KALUTUNAH — KALUTUNAH'S ACCOUNT OF THE ESQUIMAU TRADITIONS — HUNTING-GROUNDS CONTRACTED BY THE ACCUMULATION OF ICE — HARDSHIPS OF THEIR LIFE — THEIR SUBSISTENCE — THE RACE DWINDLING AWAY — VISIT TO THE GLACIER — RE-SURVEY OF THE GLACIER — KALUTUNAH CATCHING BIRDS — A SNOW-STORM AND A GALE. — THE MID-DAY OF THE ARCTIC SUMMER.

HAVING determined to be guided by circumstances, as set forth in the last chapter, I had now only to await the breaking up of the ice and the liberation of the schooner, — an incident which I could not anticipate wholly without anxiety, owing to our exposure to the southwest rendering the disruption liable to come in the midst of a heavy swell from the sea that would set us adrift in a rolling pack.

The spring had already fairly set in when I returned from the north, and each day added to the encroachment of the water upon the ice. A wonderful change had taken place since my departure in April The temperature had risen steadily from 35° below zero to as many degrees above it; the wintery cloak of whiteness which had so long clothed the hills and valleys was giving way under the influence of the sun's warm rays; and torrents of the melted snow were dashing wildly down the rugged gorges, or bounding in cascades from the lofty cliffs; and the air was everywhere filled with the pleasing roar of falling waters. A little lake had formed in a basin be-

THE ARCTIC SPRING.

hind the Observatory, and a playful rivulet gurgled from it over the pebbles down into the harbor, wearing away the ice along the beach, and the banks of the lake and stream were softened by the thaw, and, relieved of their winter covering, were, thus early in June, showing signs of a returning vegetation ; the sap had started in the willow-stems, while ice and snow yet lay around the roots, and the mosses, and poppies, and saxifrages, and the cochlearia, and other hardy plants, had begun to sprout; the air was filled with the cry of birds, which had come back for the summer ; the cliffs were alive with the little auks ; flocks of eider ducks swept over the harbor in rapid flight, seemingly not yet decided which of the islands to select for their summer home ; the graceful terns flitted, and screamed, and played over the sea ; the burgomaster-gulls and the ger-falcons sailed about us with solemn gravity ; the shrill *"Ha-hah-wee"* of the long-tailed duck was often heard, as the birds shot swiftly across the harbor ; the snipe were flying about the growing fresh-water pools; the sparrows chirped from rock to rock; long lines of cackling geese were sailing far overhead, winging their way to some more remote point of northness; the deep bellow of the walrus came from the ice-rafts, which the summer had set adrift upon the sea ; the bay and the fiord were dotted over with seal, who had dug through the ice from beneath, and lay basking in the warm sun; and the place which I had left robed in the cold mantle of winter was now dressed in the bright garments of spring. The change had come with marvelous suddenness. The snow on the surface of the ice was rapidly melting ; and, whenever we went outside of the ship, we waded through slush. The ice itself was decaying

REFITTING THE SCHOONER. 383

rapidly, and its sea-margin was breaking up The "Twins" had been loosened from their bonds and had floated away; and a crowd of icebergs, of forms that were strange to us, had come sailing out of the Sound in stately and solemn procession, wending their way to the warmer south — their crystals tumbling from them in fountains as they go.

Every thing about me gave warning that I had returned from the north in the nick of time.

McCormick had been at work as well on the inside as on the outside of the vessel. The temporary house had been removed from the upper deck, and the decks, and bulwarks, and cabins, and forecastle had been furbished up; and, after all this spring house-cleaning, the little schooner looked as neat and tidy as if she had never been besmeared with the soot and lamp-smoke of the long winter. The men were setting up the rigging; the bow-sprit, and jib-boom, and foretop-mast had been repaired; the yards had been sent aloft; the masts were being scraped down; and a little paint and tar fairly made our craft shine again. The sailors had moved from the hold to their natural quarters in the forecastle; and Dodge was busy getting off and stowing away the contents of the store-house, except such articles as I had proposed leaving behind, which were carefully deposited in a fissure of a rock, and covered over with heavy stones.

The Esquimaux still hung round us. Tcheitchenguak had set up a tent on the terrace, and had for a companion a new-comer, named Alatak, and for house-keeper a woman, who appeared to have a roving commission, without special claim on anybody, and whom I had seen before at Booth Bay, where she figured

384   A CHIEF WAXED FAT.

among my companions as "The Sentimental Widow."
Hans had gone, with his family, up to Chester Valley,
where he was catching auks by hundreds, and living
in the seal-skin tent that he brought from Cape York.
Angeit still prowled round the galley and pantry,
and continued, alternately, to annoy and amuse the
cook and still stoutly to resist the steward's efforts at
conversion.   Kalutunah, my jolly old chief, held on
at Etah, and looked to my abundant commissariat
and fruitful bounty as the source of all human bliss.
He had grown so rich that he did not know where to
put all his wealth; and when I went over to Etah to
look after him, I found him waxing fat on laziness,
and stupid with over-feeding. I discovered him lounging behind a rock, basking in the warm sunshine, like
the monk in the "Monastery," sitting before the fire,
"thinking of nothing."   He was much rejoiced at
seeing me again, asked me many questions about my
journey, and where I had been; said that he had
never been so happy in all his life before; and he
stole the thoughts, if not the Spanish, of honest Sancho, in his emphatic declaration, "You have filled my
belly, and therefore have won my heart."   I was sorry
to have but one dog to restore to him of the eight
with which he had supplied me; but he declared himself satisfied.   He appeared, at first, strongly to fear
that, in returning his dog, I was withdrawing my support, and was much gratified when I told him to come
over and get as much food as he could carry away.
  Kalutunah's first question was, whether I had found
any Esquimaux. Before starting, I had frequently
spoken to him concerning the extension of his people
to the north, and he recited to me a well-established
tradition of the tribe, that the Esquimaux once ex-

TRACES OF ESQUIMAUX. 385

tended both to the north and the south; and that, finally, the tribe now inhabiting the coast from Cape York to Smith Sound were cut off by the accumulation of ice as well above as below them; and he believed that Esquimaux were living at this present time in both directions. That there was once no break in the communication between the natives of the region about Upernavik, along the shores of Melville Bay, there can be no doubt; and Kalutunah appeared to think that the same would hold good in the opposite direction. The ice has accumulated in Smith Sound as it has in Melville Bay; and what were evidently once prosperous hunting-grounds, up to the very face of Humboldt Glacier, are now barren wastes, where living thing rarely comes. At various places along the coast Dr. Kane found the remains of ancient huts; and lower down the coast, toward the mouth of the Sound, there are many of more recent date. Near Cairn Point there is a hut which had been abandoned but a year before Dr. Kane's visit, in 1853, and has not been occupied since. In Van Rensselaer Harbor there were several huts which had been inhabited by the last generation.

The simple discovery of traces of Esquimaux on the coast of Grinnell Land was not altogether satisfactory to Kalutunah, for he had confidently expected that I would find and bring back with me some living specimens of them; but he was still gratified to have his traditions confirmed, and he declared that I did not go far enough or I should have found plenty of natives; for, said he, in effect, "There are good hunting-grounds at the north, plenty of musk-ox (oomemak), and wherever there are good hunting-grounds, there the Esquimaux will be found."

THE ESQUIMAUX.

Kalutunah grew more sad than I had ever before seen him, when I spoke to him of the fortunes of his own people. "Alas!" said he, "we will soon be all gone." I told him that I would come back, and that white men would live for many years near Etah. "Come back soon," said he, "or there will be none here to welcome you!"

To contemplate the destiny of this little tribe is indeed painful. There is much in this rude people deserving of admiration. Their brave and courageous struggles for a bare subsistence, against what would seem to us the most disheartening obstacles, often being wholly without food for days together and never obtaining it without encountering danger, makes their hold on life very precarious. The sea is their only harvest-field; and, having no boats in which to pursue the game, they have only to await the turning tide or changing season to open cracks, along which they wander, seeking the seal and walrus which come there to breathe. The uncertain fortunes of the hunt often lead them in the winter time to shelter themselves in rude hovels of snow; and, in summer, the migrating water-fowl come to substitute the seal and walrus, which, when the ice-fields have floated off, they can rarely catch.

From the information which I obtained through Hans and Kalutunah, I estimated the tribe to number about one hundred souls, — a very considerable diminution since Dr. Kane left them, in 1855. Hans made for me a rude map of the coast from Cape York to Smith Sound, and set down upon it all of the villages, if by such name the inhabited places may be called. These places are always close by the margin of the sea. They rarely consist of more than one

SCIENTIFIC COLLECTIONS.

387

hut, and the largest village of but three. Of the nature of these habitations the reader will have already gathered sufficient from my description of Kalutunah's den at Etah.

Awaiting the thawing out of the schooner, I could only employ my time in the immediate vicinity of Port Foulke with such work as I found practicable. The pendulum experiments of the previous autumn were repeated, and several full sets of observations were made for the determination of the magnetic force. The survey of the harbor and the bay was completed; the terraces were leveled and plotted; and the angles on "My Brother John's Glacier" were renewed. In all of these labors I found an intelligent and painstaking assistant in Mr Radcliffe. This gentleman also labored assiduously with the photographic apparatus; and, through his patient coöperation, I was finally enabled to secure a large number of reasonably good pictures. Some valuable collections of natural history were also made, and in this department I had much useful assistance from Mr. Knorr and Mr. Starr. The ice in the harbor offered them a fine opportunity as the cracks opened, and their labors were rewarded with one of the finest collections of marine invertebrata that has been made from Arctic waters.[1] My

[1] I am indebted to Dr. William Stimpson for a careful examination and comparison of this collection, the results of which were published by him in the "Proceedings" of the Academy of Natural Sciences of Philadelphia, for May, 1863 The collection contains little that is wholly new; but, as Dr. Stimpson has remarked, "They possess great interest from having been found, in great part, in localities much nearer the Pole than any previous expeditions have succeeded in reaching on the American side of the Arctic Circle. They include some species hitherto found only on the European side; and, we may add, the number of species collected by Dr. Hayes is greater than that brought back by any single expedition which has yet visited these seas, as far as can be judged by published ac-

388　　AN ENLIVENING SCENE.

journey to the glacier occupied me a week. We pitched our tent near Alida Lake, and went systematically to work to measure and photograph our old acquaintance of the last autumn.

We arrived at the lake in the midst of a very enlivening scene. The snow had mainly disappeared from the valley, and, although no flowers had yet appeared, the early vegetation was covering the banks with green, and the feeble growths opened their little leaves almost under the very snow, and stood alive and fresh in the frozen turf, looking as glad of the spring as their more ambitious cousins of the warm south. Numerous small herds of reindeer had come down from the mountains to fatten on this newly budding life. Gushing rivulets and fantastic waterfalls mingled their pleasant music with the ceaseless hum of birds, myriads of which sat upon the rocks of the hill-side, or were perched upon the cliffs, or sailed through the air in swarms so thick that they seemed like a dark cloud passing before the sun. These birds were the hitherto mentioned little auk (*uria allœ*), and are a water-fowl not larger than a quail. The swift flutter of their wings and their constant cry filled the air with a roar like that of a storm advancing among the forest trees. The valley was glowing with the sunlight of the early morning, which streamed in over the glacier, and robed hill, mountain, and plain in brightness.

Hans had pitched his tent at the further end of the lake, and Kalutunah came up with Myouk and Ala-

counts" The collection embraces, of *Crustacea*, 22 species, *Annelida*, 18 species; *Mollusca*, 21 species; *Echinodermata*, 7 species; *Acalephæ*, 1 specie; and, besides these, a considerable number of *Nudibranchiata*, *Actinæ*, etc., which cannot well be determined from alcoholic specimens.

GLACIER MOVEMENT. 389

tak, and joined him. Jensen quickly shot a deer, and Hans brought us some auks; and, before going to work, we drew around a large rock, of which we made a table, and partook of a substantial dinner of Carl's preparation, washing it down with purest water from the glacier, while listening to the music of gurgling streams and the song of birds.

The face of the glacier had undergone much change. Blocks of immense size had broken from it, and lay strewn over the valley at its base; while the glacier itself had pressed down the slope, crowding rocks, and snow, and the *débris* of ice before it in a confused, wave-like heap. The progress toward the sea had been steady and irresistible.

The journey to the top of the glacier was much more difficult than in the previous autumn, the snow having in a great measure melted away, exposing the rocks, and embarrassing us in the ascent of the glacier's side, as well as of the gorge. Every thing was wet and mucky, overhead as well as under foot. The glacier-surface was shedding water from every side, like the roof of a house in a February thaw; and the little streams which flowed down its side, joining the waters of the melting snow, trickled underneath the glacier and reappeared in rushing torrents in the valley below from the glacier front; and thence poured into the lake, and from the lake to the sea.

I was fortunate in finding my stakes all standing; and, having brought up the theodolite, I repeated the angles which, with Sonntag, I had taken the previous October. These angles, when afterwards reduced, exhibited a descent of the centre of the glacier, down the valley, of ninety-six feet.

Chester Valley has in former times been quite a re-

THE MUSK-OX.

sort of the Esquimaux. We found there several old ruins of huts, some of them with bones strewn about them, which showed that they were not of very ancient date. Among these bones, which were mostly of the walrus, seal, and bears, I found a part of the head of a musk-ox, and in such a position as appeared to render it probable that the animal of which it had formed a part had been the food of the former inhabitants of the ruin. Upon referring the matter to Kalutunah, he told me that the musk-ox was supposed to have been once numerous along the entire coast, and that they are still occasionally seen. No longer ago than the previous winter, a hunter of Wolstenholme Sound, near a place called Oomeak, had come upon two animals and killed one of them. It would seem from this circumstance that the musk-ox is not yet extinct in Greenland, as naturalists have supposed.

One day of my stay in the valley was occupied with running a set of levels down from the foot of the glacier to the sea, by which I found the former to be ninety-two feet above the latter; and another day was passed in hunting.

It would be impossible to convey an adequate idea of the immense numbers of the little auks which swarmed around us. The slope on both sides of the valley rises at an angle of about forty-five degrees to a distance of from three hundred to five hundred feet, where it meets the cliffs, which stand about seven hundred feet higher. These hill-sides are composed of the loose rocks which have been split off from the cliffs by the frost. The birds crawl among these rocks, winding far in through narrow places, and there deposit each a single egg and hatch their young,

AUK-CATCHING.

secure from their enemy, the foxes, which prowl round in great numbers, ever watching for a meal.

Having told Kalutunah that I wanted to accompany him and help him at auk-catching, that worthy individual came to my tent early one morning, much rejoiced that the Nalegaksoak had so favored him, and, bright and early, hurried me to the hill-side. The birds were more noisy than usual, for they had just returned in immense swarms from the sea, where they had been getting their breakfast.[1] Kalutunah carried a small net, made of light strings of seal-skin knitted together very ingeniously. The staff by which it was held was about ten feet long. After clambering over the rough, sharp stones, we arrived at length about half-way up to the base of the cliffs, where Kalutunah crouched behind a rock and invited me to follow his example. I observed that the birds were nearly all in flight, and were, with rare exceptions, the males. The length of the slope on which they were congregated was about a mile, and a constant stream of birds was rushing over it, but a few feet above the stones; and, after making in their rapid flight the whole length of the hill, they returned higher in the air, performing over and over again the complete circuit. Occasionally a few hundreds or thousands of them would drop down, as if following some leader; and in an instant the rocks, for a space of several rods, would swarm all over with them, — their black backs and pure white breasts speckling the hill very prettily.

[1] The food of the little auk, as indeed the food of all of the Arctic water-fowl, consists of different varieties of marine invertebrata, chiefly *crustacea*, with which the Arctic waters abound. It is owing to the riches of the North water in these low forms of marine life that the birds flock there in such great number during the breeding season, which begins in June and ends in August.

392 AUK-CATCHING.

While I was watching these movements with much interest, my companion was intent only upon business, and warned me to lie lower, as the birds saw me and were flying too high overhead. Having at length got myself stowed away to the satisfaction of my savage companion, the sport began. The birds were beginning again to whirl their flight closer to our heads, — so close, indeed, did they come that it seemed almost as if I could catch them with my cap. Presently, I observed my companion preparing himself as a flock of unusual thickness was approaching; and, in a moment, up went the net; a half dozen birds flew bang into it, and, stunned with the blow, they could not flutter out before Kalutunah had slipped the staff quickly through his hands and seized the net; with his left hand he now pressed down the birds, while with the right he drew them out, one by one; and, for want of a third hand, he used his teeth to crush their heads. The wings were then locked across each other, to keep them from fluttering away; and, with an air of triumph, the old fellow looked around at me, spat the blood and feathers from his mouth, and went on with the sport, tossing up his net and hauling it in with much rapidity, until he had caught about a hundred birds; when, my curiosity being amply satisfied, we returned to camp and made a hearty meal out of the game which we had bagged in this novel and unsportsman-like manner. While an immense stew was preparing, Kalutunah amused himself with tearing off the birds' skins, and consuming the raw flesh while it was yet warm.

Our stay at the glacier was brought suddenly to an end by a violent storm of wind and snow, and both ourselves and our Esquimau companions were forced

HURRICANE. 393

to seek other shelter. The storm came from the north-east, and the first mischief done was to pick Hans's tent up and carry it off down the valley like a balloon, and finally to drop it in the lake. Without waiting long to lament over the unhappy circumstance, the whole Esquimau party set out for Etah. As they passed our tent, Kalutunah stopped a moment at the door, and despite the fierce wind and the snow which covered him all over, he still bore the same imperturbable grin. "You should have seen Hans's tent!" said he; and the old fellow fairly shook with laughter, as he recalled the ridiculous scene of the suddenly unhoused party and their vanishing tent tearing away toward the lake. But his satisfaction reached its climax when he informed us that it was going to blow harder, and that our turn would come directly. Sure enough it was as the savage had predicted; for, soon afterward, we heard a great noise, — the photographic tent had given way, the instruments and plates were scattering over the stones, the glasses were being all crushed up into little bits; and, while we were springing up to go out and save the wreck, our windward guys gave way, and our canvas protection following the example of Hans's seal-skins, left us standing in the very jaws of the storm. As may be supposed, we did not delay long in finding our way back on board.

I found the schooner in a somewhat critical situation. The spars had been sent aloft and caught the wind, and the vessel being still firmly locked in the ice, the masts were subjected to a dangerous strain. I thought, at one time, that they would be carried bodily out of the schooner, and had guys fastened to the mast-heads and secured to stakes driven in the ice to windward. The loose ice was all blown out of

394 MID-SUMMER.

the bay, the icebergs were driven out of sight, and the open water was not more than a quarter of a mile distant from us.

The sun reaching its greatest northern declination on the 21st, we were now in the full blaze of summer. Six eventful months had passed over since the Arctic midnight shrouded us in gloom, and now we had reached the Arctic mid-day. And this mid-day was a day of wonderful brightness. The temperature had gone up higher than at any previous time, marking, at meridian, 49°, while in the sun the thermometer showed 57°. The barometer was away up to 30.076, and a more calm and lovely air never softened an Arctic landscape.

Tempted by the day, I strolled down into the valley south of the harbor. The recent snow had mostly disappeared, and valley and hill-side were speckled with a rich carpet of green, with only here and there a patch of the winter snow yet undissolved,— an emerald carpet,. fringed and inlaid with silver and sprinkled over with fragments of a bouquet, — for many flowers were now in full bloom, and their tiny faces peeped above the sod. A herd of reindeer were browsing on the plain beneath me, and some white rabbits had come from their hiding-places to feed upon the bursting willow-buds. New objects of interest led me on from spot to spot — babbling brooks, and rocky hill-sides, and little glaciers, and softening snow-banks, alternating with patches of tender green — until, at length, I came to the base of a lofty hill, whose summit was surmounted with an imposing wall which overlooked the sea, seemingly a vast turreted castle, guarding the entrance to the valley. I thought of my late comrade, and named it Sonntag's

Monument. Passing this, I climbed to a broad plateau, probably five hundred yards above the sea; and keeping along this toward Cape Alexander, came at length upon a deep gorge at the bottom of which flowed a stream, some ten yards over, which came from the melting snows of the mountains and the *mer de glace*. Descending into this ravine I followed its rough banks until they came abruptly to the tall cliff of the coast, over which the water leaped wildly down into a deep and picturesque glen, which it filled with a cloud of its own spray. The spot figures in my diary as Little Julia's Glen and Fall.

CHAPTER XXXVI.

THE ARCTIC SUMMER — THE FLORA. — THE ICE DISSOLVING. — A SUMMER STORM OF RAIN, HAIL, AND SNOW — THE TERRACES — ICE ACTION. — UPHEAVAL OF THE COAST — GEOLOGICAL INTEREST OF ICEBERGS AND THE LAND-ICE — A WALRUS HUNT — THE "FOURTH" — VISIT TO LITTLETON ISLAND — GREAT NUMBERS OF EIDER-DUCKS AND GULLS — THE ICE BREAKING UP — CRITICAL SITUATION OF THE SCHOONER. — TAKING LEAVE OF THE ESQUIMAUX. — ADIEU TO PORT FOULKE

THE reader will have observed the marvelous change that had come over the face of Nature since the shadow of the night had passed away. Recalling those chapters which recount the gloom and silence of the Arctic night, — the death-like quiet which reigned in the endless darkness, — the absence of every living thing that could relieve the solitude of its terrors, — he will perhaps hardly have been prepared to see, without surprise, the same landscape covered with an endless blaze of light, the air and sea and earth teeming with life, the desert places sparkling with green, and brightening with flowers, — the mind finding everywhere some new object of pleasure, where before there was but gloom. The change of the Arctic winter to the Arctic summer is indeed the change, from death to life ; and the voice which speaks to the sun and the winds, and brings back the joyous day, is that same voice which said

" She is not dead, but sleepeth," —

and the pulseless heart was made to throb again, and the bloom returned to the pallid cheek.

THE ARCTIC SUMMER. 397

There is truly a rare charm in the Arctic summer, especially if watched unfolding from the darkness, and followed through the growing warmth, until the snows are loosened from the hills and the fountains burst forth, and the feeble flower-growths spring into being, and the birds come back with their merry music; and then again as it passes away, under the dark shadow of a sunless sky, — the fountains sealing up, the hill-sides and valleys taking on again the white robes of winter and the stillness of the tomb, the birds in rapid flight with the retreating day, and the mantle of darkness settling upon the mountains, and overspreading the plain.

To describe the summer as I have before described the winter, and to attempt fully to picture in detail those features which give it such a striking contrast to the winter as is not seen in any other quarter of the world, would too far prolong this narrative; and I will therefore content myself with selecting from my diary such extracts as will show the progress of the season, and those occupations of myself and associates that bore upon the purposes which we had mainly in view.

June 22d.

It is just six months since I wrote, "The sun has reached to-day its greatest southern declination, and we have passed the Arctic midnight;" and now the sun has reached its greatest northern declination, and we have passed the Arctic noonday. Constant light has succeeded constant darkness, a bright and cheerful world has banished a painful solitude; —

"The winter is past and gone; the flowers appear on the earth; the time of the singing of birds is come;"

and the long night which the glad day has succeeded is remembered as a strange dream.

ARCTIC FLORA.

June 23d.

A bright day, with the thermometer at 47°, and light wind from the south. I have been out with my young assistants collecting plants and lichens. The rocks are almost everywhere covered with the latter, — one variety, orange in color, grows in immense patches, and gives a cheerful hue to the rocks, while another, the *tripe de roche*, which is still more abundant, gives a mournful look to the stony slopes which it covers. I have brought in a fine assortment of flowers, and it seems as if the plants are now mostly in bloom. They have blossomed several days earlier than at Van Rensselaer Harbor in 1854. I have had a bouquet of them in my cabin for many days past, and from the banks of the little lake behind the Observatory I can always replenish it at will.[1]

[1] Not wishing to interrupt the text with details which would have little interest for the general reader, I give here the complete flora (so far as a most persistent effort could make it so) of the region northward from Whale Sound. Most of the plants were found at Port Foulke. My collections numbered several thousand specimens, which my kind friend, Mr. Elias Durand, of Philadelphia, was good enough to assist me in arranging, and afterward to classify in a paper for the "Proceedings" of the Academy of Natural Sciences of Philadelphia, from which I give the following list: —

1. *Ranunculus nivalis.*		16. *Lychnis apetala.*	
2. *Papaver nudicaule.*		17. *Lychnis panciflora.*	
3. *Hesperis Pallasii.*		18. *Dryas integrifolia*	
4. *Draba Alpina.*		19. *Dryas octopetala.*	
5. *Draba corymbosa.*		20 *Potentilla pulchella.*	
6. *Draba hirta.*		21. *Potentilla nivalis.*	
7. *Draba glacialas.*		22. *Alchemilla vulgaris.*	
8. *Draba rupestris.*		23 *Saxifraga oppositifolia.*	
9. *Cochlearia officinalis.*		24 *Saxifraga flagellaris.*	
10. *Vesicaria Arctica.*		25. *Saxifraga cæspitosa.*	
11. *Arenaria Arctica.*		26. *Saxifraga rivularis.*	
12 *Stellaria humifusa.*		27. *Saxifraga tricuspidata.*	
13 *Stellaria Stricta.*		28. *Saxifraga cornua.*	
14. *Cerastium Alpinum.*		29. *Saxifraga nivalis*	
15. *Silene acaulis.*		30. *Leontodon palustre.*	

SUMMER SHOWERS.

399

June 25th.

A rainy day for a novelty. Nearly an inch of water has fallen already, and it still continues to patter upon the deck. I was out completing my geological collections when the shower began, and not only got thoroughly soaked, but had like to have got killed into the bargain; for, in attempting to cross a small glacier which lay on the side of a hill, my feet flew up in consequence of the water making it more slippery, and I slid down over the ice and the stones which stuck up through it, and was finally landed among the rocks below with many bruises and not much clothing

The thermometer has stood at 48°, and the continuance of the warmth since the 20th, together with this "gentle rain from heaven," is telling upon the ice. It is getting very rotten, and the sea is eating into it rapidly. The "hinge" of the ice-foot is tumbling to pieces, and we have trouble in getting ashore.

June 26th.

Our summer shower has changed its complexion, and the "gentle rain" is converted into hail and snow, quite as unseasonable as it is disagreeable. The white snow with which a fierce wind has bespattered the

31. *Campanula linifolia.*
32. *Vaccinium uliginosum.*
33. *Andromeda tetragona.*
34. *Pyrola chlorantha.*
35. *Bartsia Alpina.*
36. *Pedicularis Kanei.*
37. *Armeria Labradorica.*
38. *Polygonum viviparum.*
39. *Oxyria didyma.*
40. *Empetrum nigrum*
41. *Betula nana.*
42. *Salix Arctica.*
43. *Salix herbacea.*
44. *Luzula* (too young)
45. *Carex rigida.*
46. *Eriophorum vaginatum.*
47. *Alopecurus Alpinus.*
48. *Glyceria Arctica.*
49. *Poa Arctica.*
50. *Poa Alpina.*
51. *Hierocloa Alpina.*
52. *Festuca ovina.*
53. *Lycopodium annotinum.*

400 A SUMMER STORM.

cliffs gives a very un-June-like aspect to the prospect from the deck. The wind is southerly, and the waves, coming into the bay with no other resistance than that given by a few icebergs, begin to shake the ice about the schooner, and we can see the pulsations of the seas in the old fire-hole. I should not much relish seeing the ice crumbling to pieces about us in the midst of such a storm.

June 27th.

The storm continues, — occasional rain, mixed up with a great deal of hail. The scene from the deck, to seaward, was so wild that I was tempted to the nearest island, (the only one of the three not in open water,) to get a better view of it. I had much trouble facing the wind, and was nearly blown into the sea, and the hail cut the face terribly. The little flowers, which had been seduced by the warm sun of last week into unveiling their modest faces, seemed shrinking and dejected.

I was, however, repaid for some discomfort by the scene which I have brought back in my memory, and which is to go down on a sheet of clean white paper that is now drying on a drawing-board which I owe to McCormick's ingenuity. I have not seen the equal of this storm except once — a memorable occasion — last year, when we were fighting our way into Smith Sound. The wind seemed, as it did then, fairly to shovel the water up and pitch it through the air, until it had to stop from sheer exhaustion, and then I could see away off under a dark cloud a vast multitude of white specks creeping from the gloom, and moving along in solid phalanx, magnifying as they came. and charging the icebergs, hissing over their very summits, or breaking their heads upon the islands, or

FRESH EGGS. 401

wreaking their fury on the ice of the harbor, into which their Titan touch opened many a gaping wound.

June 28th.

The storm subsiding this morning, a party got a boat over the ice into the water, and, pulling to the outer island, brought back the first fresh eggs of the season. Those of the little tern or sea-swallow are the most delightful eggs that I have ever tasted. Those of the eider-duck are, like the eggs of all other duck, not very palatable. Knorr lit upon a patch of cochlearia which had just sprouted up around the bird-nests of the last year, and no head of the first spring-lettuce was ever more enjoyed. I had a capital salad. The islands promise to give us all the eggs we want, and we shall have little more trouble in getting them than a housewife who sends to the farm-yard. The ducks have plucked the first instalment of down from their breasts, and Jensen has brought in a good-sized bagful of it. The poor birds have been, I fear, robbed to little purpose, and will have to pick themselves again. Jensen tells me that, upon the islands near Upernavik, where he has often gone for eider-down, the male bird is sometimes obliged to pluck off his handsome coat, to help out his unhappy spouse, when she has been so often robbed that she can pluck no more of the tender covering for her eggs from her naked breast.

June 30th.

Another rain-storm, during which half an inch of water has fallen. The temperature has gone down to 38°. The ice is loosening, and threatens to break up bodily.

402 UPHEAVAL OF THE GREENLAND COAST.

July 2d.

I have been occupied during the past two days with running a set of levels from the harbor across to the fiord and with plotting the terraces. These terraces are twenty-three in number and rise very regularly to an altitude of one hundred and ten feet above the mean tide-level. The lowest rises thirty-two feet higher than the tide, but above this they climb up with great regularity. They are composed of small pebbles rounded by water action.

Of these terraces I have frequently made mention in this journal, and their existence in all similar localities has been before remarked. They have much geological interest, as illustrating the gradual upheaval of that part of Greenland lying north of latitude 76°; and the interest attaching to them is heightened when viewed in connection with the corresponding depression which has taken place, even within the period of Christian occupation, in southern Greenland. These evidences of the sinking of the Greenland coast from about Cape York, southward, are too well known to need any comment in this place; but I may dwell, for a few moments, upon the evidences of rising of the coast here and northward. At many conspicuous points, where the current is swift and the ice is pressed down upon the land with great force and rapidity, the rocks are worn away until they are as smooth and polished as the surface of a table, — a fact which may at any time be observed by looking down through the clear water. This smoothness of the rock continues above the sea, to an elevation which I have not been able with positive accuracy to determine in any locality, but having a general correspondence to the height of the terraces at

GEOLOGICAL CHANGES.

Port Foulke, which, as before observed, rise one hundred and ten feet above the sea-level. At Cairn Point the abrasion is very marked, and, where the polished line of syenitic rock leaves off and the rough rock begins, is quite clearly defined. This same condition also exists at Littleton Island (or, rather, McGary Island, which lies immediately outside of it) to an almost equally marked degree. I have before mentioned the evidences of a similar elevation of the opposite coast found in the terraced beaches of Grinnell Land.

It is curious to observe here, actually taking place before our eyes, those geological events which have transpired in southern latitudes during the glacier epoch, not only in the abrasion of the rock as seen at Cairn Point and elsewhere, but in the changes which they work in the deeper sea. In this agency the ice-foot bears a conspicuous influence. This ice-foot is but a shelf of ice, as it were, glued against the shore, and is the winter-girdle of all the Arctic coasts. It is wide or narrow as the shore slopes gently into the sea or meets it abruptly. It is usually broken away toward the close of every summer, and the masses of rock which have been hurled down upon it from the cliffs above are carried away and dropped in the sea, when the raft has loosened from the shore and drifted off, steadily melting as it floats. The amount of rock thus transported to the ocean is immense, and yet it falls far short of that which is carried by the icebergs; the rock and sand imbedded in which, as they lay in the parent glacier, being sometimes sufficient to bear them down under the weight until but the merest fragment rises above the surface. As the berg melts, the rocks and sand fall to the bottom of the ocean; and, if the place of their deposit should one day rise

404 A WALRUS HUNT.

above the sea-level, some geological student of future ages may, perhaps, be as much puzzled to know how they came there as those of the present generation are to account for the boulders of the Connecticut valley.

July 3d.

I have had a walrus hunt and a most exciting day's sport. Much ice has broken adrift and come down the Sound, during the past few days; and, when the sun is out bright and hot, the walrus come up out of the water to sleep and bask in the warmth on the pack. Being upon the hill-top this morning to select a place for building a cairn, my ear caught the hoarse bellowing of numerous walrus; and, upon looking over the sea I observed that the tide was carrying the pack across the outer limit of the bay, and that it was alive with the beasts, which were filling the air with such uncouth noises. Their numbers appeared to be even beyond conjecture, for they extended as far as the eye could reach, almost every piece of ice being covered. There must have been, indeed, many hundreds or even thousands.

Hurrying from the hill, I called for volunteers, and quickly had a boat's crew ready for some sport. Putting three rifles, a harpoon, and a line into one of the whale-boats, we dragged it over the ice to the open water, into which it was speedily launched.

We had about two miles to pull before the margin of the pack was reached. On the cake of ice to which we first came, there were perched about two dozen animals; and these we selected for the attack. They covered the raft almost completely, lying huddled together, lounging in the sun or lazily rolling and twisting themselves about, as if to expose

A WALRUS HUNT. 405

some fresh part of their unwieldy bodies to the warmth, — great, ugly, wallowing sea-hogs, they were evidently enjoying themselves, and were without apprehension of approaching danger. We neared them slowly, with muffled oars.

As the distance between us and the game steadily narrowed, we began to realize that we were likely to meet with rather formidable antagonists. Their aspect was forbidding in the extreme, and our sensations were perhaps not unlike those which the young soldier experiences who hears for the first time the order to charge the enemy. We should all, very possibly, have been quite willing to retreat had we dared own it. Their tough, nearly hairless hides, which are about an inch thick, had a singularly iron-plated look about them, peculiarly suggestive of defense; while their huge tusks, which they brandished with an appearance of strength that their awkwardness did not diminish, looked like very formidable weapons of offense if applied to a boat's planking or to the human ribs, if one should happen to find himself floundering in the sea among the thick-skinned brutes. To complete the hideousness of a facial expression which the tusks rendered formidable enough in appearance, Nature had endowed them with broad flat noses, which were covered all over with stiff whiskers, looking much like porcupine quills, and extending up to the edge of a pair of gaping nostrils. The use of these whiskers is as obscure as that of the tusks; though it is probable that the latter may be as well weapons of offense and defense as for the more useful purpose of grubbing up from the bottom of the sea the mollusks which constitute their principal food. There were two old bulls in the herd who appeared

406   A WALRUS HUNT.

to be dividing their time between sleeping and jamming their tusks into each other's faces, although they appeared to treat the matter with perfect indifference, as they did not seem to make any impression on each other's thick hides. As we approached, these old fellows — neither of which could have been less than sixteen feet long, nor smaller in girth than a hogshead — raised up their heads, and, after taking a leisurely survey of us, seemed to think us unworthy of further notice; and, then punching each other again in the face, fell once more asleep. This was exhibiting a degree of coolness rather alarming. If they had showed the least timidity, we should have found some excitement in extra caution; but they seemed to make so light of our approach that it was not easy to keep up the bold front with which we had commenced the adventure. But we had come quite too far to think of backing out; so we pulled in and made ready for the fray.

Beside the old bulls, the group contained several cows and a few calves of various sizes, — some evidently yearlings, others but recently born, and others half or three quarters grown. Some were without tusks, while on others they were just sprouting; and above this they were of all sizes up.to those of the big bulls, which had great curved cones of ivory, nearly three feet long. At length we were within a few boats' lengths of the ice-raft, and the game had not taken alarm. They had probably never seen a boat before. Our preparations were made as we approached. The walrus will always sink when dead, unless held up by a harpoon-line; and there were therefore but two chances for us to secure our game — either to shoot the beast dead on the raft, or to

A WALRUS HUNT. 407

get a harpoon well into him after he was wounded, and hold on to him until he was killed. As to killing the animal where he lay, that was not likely to happen, for the thick skin destroys the force of the ball before it can reach any vital part, and indeed, at a distance, actually flattens it; and the skull is so heavy that it is hard to penetrate with an ordinary bullet, unless the ball happens to strike through the eye.

To Miller, a cool and spirited fellow, who had been after whales on the "nor-west coast," was given the harpoon, and he took his station at the bows; while Knorr, Jensen, and myself kept our places in the stern-sheets, and held our rifles in readiness. Each selected his animal, and we fired in concert over the heads of the oarsmen. As soon as the rifles were discharged, I ordered the men to "give way," and the boat shot right among the startled animals as they rolled off pell-mell into the sea. Jensen had fired at the head of one of the bulls, and hit him in the neck; Knorr killed a young one, which was pushed off in the hasty scramble and sank; while I planted a minie-ball somewhere in the head of the other bull and drew from him a most frightful bellow, — louder, I venture to say, than ever came from wild bull of Bashan. When he rolled over into the water, which he did with a splash that sent the spray flying all over us, he almost touched the bows of the boat and gave Miller a good opportunity to get in his harpoon, which he did in capital style.

The alarmed herd seemed to make straight for the bottom, and the line spun out over the gunwale at a fearful pace; but, having several coils in the boat, the end was not reached before the animals began to rise, and we took in the slack and got ready for what was

408   A WALRUS HUNT.

to follow. The strain of the line whipped the boat around among some loose fragments of ice, and the line having fouled among it, we should have been in great jeopardy had not one of the sailors promptly sprung out, cleared the line, and defended the boat.

In a few minutes the whole herd appeared at the surface, about fifty yards away from us, the harpooned animal being among them. Miller held fast to his line, and the boat was started with a rush. The coming up of the herd was the signal for a scene which baffles description. They uttered one wild concerted shriek, as if an agonized call for help; and then the air was filled with answering shrieks. The "huk! huk! huk!" of the wounded bulls seemed to find an echo everywhere, as the cry was taken up and passed along from floe to floe, like the bugle-blast passed from squadron to squadron along a line of battle; and down from every piece of ice plunged the startled beasts, as quickly as the sailor drops from his hammock when the long-roll beats to quarters. With their ugly heads just above the water, and with mouths wide open, belching forth the dismal "huk! huk! huk!" they came tearing toward the boat.

In a few moments we were completely surrounded, and the numbers kept multiplying with astonishing rapidity. The water soon became alive and black with them.

They seemed at first to be frightened and irresolute, and for a time it did not seem that they meditated mischief; but this pleasing prospect was soon dissipated, and we were forced to look well to our safety.

That they meditated an attack there could no longer be a doubt. To escape the onslaught was im-

A WALRUS HUNT.

A WALRUS HUNT. 409

possible. We had raised a hornet's nest about our ears in a most astonishingly short space of time, and we must do the best we could. Even the wounded animal to which we were fast turned upon us, and we became the focus of at least a thousand gaping, bellowing mouths.

It seemed to be the purpose of the walrus to get their tusks over the gunwale of the boat, and it was evident that, in the event of one such monster hooking on to us, the boat would be torn in pieces and we would be left floating in the sea helpless. We had good motive therefore to be active. Miller plied his lance from the bows, and gave many a serious wound The men pushed back the onset with their oars, while Knorr, Jensen, and myself loaded and fired our rifles as rapidly as we could. Several times we were in great jeopardy, but the timely thrust of an oar, or the lance, or a bullet saved us. Once I thought we were surely gone. I had fired, and was hastening to load; a wicked-looking brute was making at us, and it seemed probable that he would be upon us. I stopped loading, and was preparing to cram my rifle down his throat, when Knorr, who had got ready his weapon, sent a fatal shot into his head. Again, an immense animal, the largest that I had ever seen and with tusks apparently three feet long, was observed to be making his way through the herd with mouth wide open, bellowing dreadfully. I was now as before busy loading; Knorr and Jensen had just discharged their pieces, and the men were well engaged with their oars. It was a critical moment, but, happily, I was in time. The monster, his head high above the boat, was within two feet of the gunwale, when I raised my piece and fired into his mouth. The dis-

410   A WALRUS HUNT.

charge killed him instantly, and he went down like a stone.

This ended the fray. I know not why, but the whole herd seemed suddenly to take alarm, and all dove down with a tremendous splash almost at the same instant. When they came up again, still shrieking as before, they were some distance from us, their heads all now pointed seaward, making from us as fast as they could go, their cries growing more and more faint as they retreated in the distance.

We must have killed at least a dozen, and mortally wounded as many more. The water was in places red with blood, and several half-dead and dying animals lay floating about us. The bull to which we were made fast pulled away with all his might after the retreating herd, but his strength soon became exhausted; and, as his speed slackened, we managed to haul in the line, and finally approached him so nearly that our rifle-balls took effect, and Miller at length gave him the *coup de grace* with his lance We then drew him to the nearest piece of ice, and I had soon a fine specimen to add to my Natural History collections. Of the others we secured only one; the rest had died and sunk before we reached them.

I have never before regarded the walrus as a really formidable animal; but this contest convinces me that I have done their courage great injustice. They are full of fight, and, had we not been very active and self-possessed, our boat would have been torn to pieces, and we either drowned or killed. A more fierce attack than that which they made upon us could hardly be imagined, and a more formidable looking enemy than one of these huge monsters, with his immense tusks and bellowing throat, would be difficult to find.

THE "GLORIOUS FOURTH." 411

Next time I try them I will arm my boat's crew with lances. The rifle is a poor reliance, and, but for the oars, the herd would have been on top of us at any time.

July 4th.

The "glorious Fourth" gives us a sorry greeting — rain and hail and snow are unusual accompaniments to this national holiday. The thermometer has gone down almost to the freezing point ; but, nevertheless, we have fired our salute, and have displayed our bunting, as in duty bound. Thanks to the hunters, we have had a good dinner of venison and birds, winding up with a cochlearia salad ; and if we lacked the oration, we did not the less turn our thoughts to the ever dear land, where all are gay, — all alike forgetting for the time their differences of party creeds and party interests, unite together under the nation's broad banner, to hail the returning dawn of its wonderful career, and to drink bumpers to fraternal union. God bless the day !

July 7th.

I have been up to Littleton Island for three days, watching the ice, hunting, etc. We caught another walrus and had another fight, but this time we had fewer enemies, and drove them off very quickly.

Littleton and McGary Islands are literally swarming with birds, chiefly eider-ducks and burgomasters. There was no end to the number that could have been shot. The eggs have nearly all chicks in them, but fortunately we have already collected from the islands of the harbor a good supply. I found a flock of brant-geese, but could not discover their nests. The burgomaster-gulls are very numerous, but there were no ivory or other gulls, as I had hoped to find. They do not appear to come so far north.

412   PREPARATIONS FOR DEPARTURE.

The open water has made still further inroads upon the ice. The islands are all now in the open sea, and it is but a few rods from the ship to its margin. The ice still clings tightly to the schooner, notwithstanding all our efforts to free her. In anticipation of a southerly swell setting into the harbor and breaking the ice, I have had the men at work for several days sawing a crack across the harbor from the vessel's forefoot in the one direction, and from the stern-post in the other. The ice is now only $4\frac{1}{2}$ feet thick.

The sails are all bent on, the hawsers are brought on board, our depot ashore is completed, and we are ready for any fortune. If blown with the ice out to sea, we are fully prepared.

Upon the hill-top of the north side of the harbor we have constructed a cairn, and under it I have deposited a brief record of the voyage. The Observatory I leave standing, and Kalutunah engages that the Esquimaux will not disturb it during my absence. All of them who have been here are so amply enriched that I think I ought to rely upon their good faith; yet the wood will be valuable to them, and these poor savages are not the only people who find it hard to resist temptation.

July 9th.

I have paid another visit to Chester Valley, and have bade adieu to "Brother John." If the latter continues to grow until I come again, the stakes which I have stuck into its back will show some useful results. The valley was clothed in the full robes of summer The green slopes were sparkling with flowers, and the ice had wholly disappeared from Alida Lake. Jensen shot some birds and tried hard to catch a deer, and while thus engaged I secured a yellow-winged butterfly, and — who would believe it ? — a mosquito. And these I add to an entymological collection which already numbers ten moths, three spiders, two humble-bees, and two flies, — a pretty good proportion of the genus *Insecta* for this latitude, 78° 17′ N., longitude 73° W.

July 10th.

A heavy swell is setting into the harbor from the southwest. There has evidently been a strong southerly wind outside, although it has been blowing but lightly here. The ice has been breaking up through the day, and crack after crack is opening across the harbor. If it lasts twelve hours longer we will be liberated. It is a sort of crisis, and may be a dangerous one. The crashing of the ice is perfectly frightful. The schooner still holds fast in her cradle.

July 11th.

We have passed through a day of much excitement, and are yet not free from it. The seas continuing to roll in, more cracks opened across the harbor, until the swell at length reached the vessel. Late this afternoon, after more than thirty-six hours of suspense, the ice opened close beside us, and after a few minutes another split came diagonally across the vessel. This was what I had feared, and it was to prevent it that I had sawed across the harbor. The ice was, however, quickly loosened from the bows, but held by the stern, and the wrenches given the schooner by the first few movements made every timber of her fairly creak again ; but finally the sawed crack came to the rescue, and, separating a little, the schooner gave a lurch to port, which loosened the ice from under the counter, and we were really afloat, but grinding most uncomfortably, and are grinding still.

414 WAITING FOR A WIND.

July 12th.

The swell has subsided, the storm clouds have cleared away, and the tide is scattering the ice out over the sea. We are fairly and truly afloat, and once more cannot leave the deck without a boat.. It is just ten months to a day since we were locked up, during which time our little craft has been a house rather than a ship. We are glad to feel again the motion of the sea; and "man the boat" seems a novel order to give when one wants to go ashore. We await only a wind to send us to sea.

July 13th.

Still calm, and we are lying quietly among the ice which so lately held us prisoners. I have been ashore, taking leave of my friends the Esquimaux. They have pitched their tents near by, and, poor fellows! I am truly sorry to leave them. They have all been faithful, each in his way, and they have done me most important service. The alacrity with which they have placed their dogs at my disposal (and without these dogs I could have done absolutely nothing) is the strongest proof that they could give me of their devotion and regard; for their dogs are to them invaluable treasures, without which they have no security against want and starvation, to themselves and their wives and children. True, I have done them some good, and have given them presents of great value, yet nothing can supply the place of a lost dog; and out of all that I obtained from them, there were but two animals that survived the hardships of my spring journey. These I have returned to their original owners. I have given them high hopes of my speedy return, and in this prospect they appear to take consolation.

ADIEU TO PORT FOULKE. 415

It is sad to reflect upon the future of these strange people; and yet they contemplate a fate which they view as inevitable, with an air of indifference difficult to comprehend. The only person who seemed seriously to feel any pang at the prospect of the desolation which will soon come over the villages, is Kalutunah. This singular being — a mixture of seriousness, good-nature, and intelligence — seems truly to take pride in the traditions of his race, and to be really pained at the prospect of their downfall. When I took his hand to-day and told him that I would not come ashore any more, the tears actually started to his eyes, and I was much touched with his earnest words, — it was almost an entreaty, — "Come back and save us." Save them I would and will, if I am spared to return; and I am quite sure that upon no beings in the whole wide world could Christian love and Christian charity more worthily fall.

July 14th.

Moving out to sea under full sail, with a light wind from the eastward. We make little progress, but are able to pick our way among the loose ice. As we pass along, I see shoals of old tin cans, dead dogs, piles of ashes, and other debris of the winter, floating on ice-rafts upon the sea, — relics of the ten months which are gone, with all its dreary and all its pleasant memories. As I retreated from the deck, I saw the Esquimaux standing on the beach, gazing after us; the little white Observatory grew dim in the distance; and I have come below with a kindly "Adieu, Port Foulke," lingering on the lip.

CHAPTER XXXVII.

LEAVING PORT FOULKE — EFFORT TO REACH CAPE ISABELLA — MEET THE PACK AND TAKE SHELTER AT LITTLETON ISLAND — HUNTING — ABUNDANCE OF BIRDS AND WALRUS — VISIT TO CAIRN POINT — REACHING THE WEST COAST. — VIEW FROM CAPE ISABELLA — PLANS FOR THE FUTURE — OUR RESULTS — CHANCES OF REACHING THE POLAR SEA DISCUSSED — THE GLACIERS OF ELLESMERE LAND

THE schooner glided gently out to sea, but the wind soon died away and the current carried us down into the lower bay, where we moored to a berg, and I went ashore and got some good photographs of Little Julia's Glen and Fall, Sonntag's Monument, Crystal Palace Glacier, and Cape Alexander.

Although doubtful as to the prospect ahead, I was determined not to quit the field without making another attempt to reach the west coast and endeavor to obtain some further information that might be of service to me in the future. I had still a vague hope that, even with my crippled vessel, some such good prospect might open before me as would justify me in remaining. Accordingly, as soon as the wind came, we cast off from the friendly berg, and held once more for Cape Isabella. The wind rose to a fresh breeze as we crawled away from the land, and the schooner, as if rejoiced at her newly acquired freedom, bounded over the waters with her old swiftness. But, unhappily, a heavy pack lay in our course, through which, had the schooner been strong, a passage might have been forced; but as it could not be done without frequent

AT LITTLETON ISLAND. 417

collisions with the ice, the intention was not entertained. The pack was not more than ten miles from the Greenland shore, and I therefore put back to Littleton Island, and from that point watched the movements of the ice.

We found a convenient anchorage between Littleton and McGary Islands, and we reached it just in time; for a severe gale, with thick snow, set in from the northward as I had anticipated from the appearance of the sky, and held for several days. Meanwhile the people amused themselves with hunting. A herd of deer was discovered on Littleton Island, and the walrus were very numerous. Four of the latter were captured, — this time, however, not from a boat, but by Hans, in the true Esquimau style. They came along the shore in great numbers, lying upon the beach in the sun; where Hans approached them stealthily, and got fast to them one by one with his harpoon. The line being secured to a rock, the animals were held until they were exhausted, and then drawn in, when they soon became a prey to the rifles. Wishing to obtain a young one for a specimen, I joined the hunters; and, selecting from the herd which lay upon the rocks one to suit my purposes, I fired upon and killed it. The others plunged quickly into the water. The mother of the dead calf was the last to leave the rock, and seemed to do so very reluctantly. In a few moments she came to the surface, and, wheeling around, discovered the young one still lying upon the rock. Finding that it did not answer to her cries, she rushed frantically into the face of danger, and in full view of the cause of her woes, (for I had approached very near the spot,) the unhappy creature, intent only upon rescuing her offspring, drew herself out of the

418   AT CAPE ISABELLA.

water, crying piteously all the while, and, crawling around it, pushed it before her into the sea. I endeavored first to frighten her off, and then tried to arrest her, and save my specimen, with a fresh bullet; but all to no effect. Although badly wounded, she succeeded in her purpose, and, falling upon the dead calf with her breast, carried it down with her, and I saw them no more. I have never seen a stronger or more touching instance of the devotion of mother to its young, among dumb animals, and it came from a quarter wholly unexpected.

Having leisure while the snow-storm lasted, I went up to Cairn Point to see how the ice appeared from that place. After waiting there for a day, the atmosphere cleared up, and I could see with much distinctness to Cape Isabella. The line of the solid ice extended in a somewhat irregular curve up the Sound from that cape to a few miles above Cairn Point. The sea thence down into the North Water was filled with a loose pack.

The day after my return we put to sea. The pack being now much scattered, we entered it and penetrated to the margin of the fast ice without difficulty. In two days we reached the coast near Gale Point, about ten miles below Cape Isabella. Thence to the cape I went in a whale-boat; but the cape itself could not be passed; so we hauled into the first convenient bight, and climbed the hill. The view convinced me, if I was not convinced already, of the folly of attempting any thing further with the schooner. I no longer hesitated, even in thought. My opinions were thus recorded at the time : —

"I am fully persuaded, if there still remained a

RESULTS OF THE VOYAGE. 419

lingering doubt, of the correctness of my decision to return home, and come out next year strengthened and refitted with steam. If my impulses lead me to try conclusions once more with the ice, my judgment convinces me that it would be at the risk of every thing. As well use a Hudson-river steamboat for a battering-ram as this schooner, with her weakened bows, to encounter the Smith Sound ice.

"I have secured the following important advantages for the future, and, with these I must, perforce, rest satisfied, for the present : —

"1. I have brought my party through without sickness, and have thus shown that the Arctic winter of itself breeds neither scurvy nor discontent.

"2. I have shown that men may subsist themselves in Smith Sound independent of support from home.

"3. That a self-sustaining colony may be established at Port Foulke, and be made the basis of an extended exploration.

"4. That the exploration of this entire region is practicable from Port Foulke, — having from that starting-point pushed my discoveries much beyond those of my predecessors, without any second party in the field to coöperate with me, and under the most adverse circumstances.

"5. That, with a reasonable degree of certainty, it is shown that, with a strong vessel, Smith Sound may be navigated and the open sea reached beyond it.

"6. I have shown that the open sea exists.

"And now, having proven this much, I shall return to Boston, repair the schooner, get a small steamer, and come back as early next spring as I can. The schooner I will leave at Port Foulke; and, remaining there only long enough to see the machinery set in motion for starting the hunt, collecting the Esquimaux, and establishing the discipline of the colony, I will seek Cape Isabella, and thence steam northward by the route already designated. If I cannot reach the open sea in one season, I may the next; in any event, I shall always have at Port Foulke a productive source of food and furs, and a vessel to carry them to Cape Isabella, upon which I may fall back; and if I need dogs, they will be reared at the colony in any numbers that may be required. Besides, if in this exploration I should be deficient in means, and the expedition should be hereafter left entirely to its own resources, a sufficient profit may be made out of the colony in oils, furs, walrus ivory, eider down, etc., to pay at least a very considerable proportion of the wages of the employés, beside subsisting them. The whole region around Port Foulke is teeming with animal life, and one good hunter could feed twenty mouths. Both my winter and summer experience proves the correctness of this opinion. The sea abounds in walrus, seal, narwhal, and white whale; the land in reindeer and foxes; the islands and the cliffs, in summer, swarm with birds; and the ice is the roaming-ground of the bears."

Thus much for the future; let me now come back to the present.

Inglefield has very correctly exhibited the expansion of Smith Sound, as I have had most excellent opportunity for observing, both in my passage over, and from Cape Isabella. He has placed some of the capes too far north, and his local attraction, probably,

CAPE ISABELLA. 421

has caused a slight error in the axis of the Sound. His Victoria Head is the eastern cape of my Bache Island, and his Cape Albert is the eastern cape of Henry Island.

The view up the Sound from Cape Isabella was truly magnificent. The dark, wall-sided coast, rendered more dark in appearance by the contrast with the immense cloak of whiteness that lay above it, was relieved by numerous glaciers, which pour through the valleys to the sea. The *mer de glace* is of great extent, and, rising much more rapidly and being more broken, gives a picturesque effect not belonging to the Greenland side, and adds much to the grandeur of its appearance. The mountains are lofty, and are everywhere uniformly covered with ice and snow; and the glacier streams which descend to the sea convey the impression almost as if there had once been a vast lake on the mountain-top, from which the overflowing waters, pouring down every valley, had been suddenly congealed.

Off Cape Sabine there are two islands, which I name Brevoort and Stalknecht; and another, midway between them and Wade Point, which I name Leconte. A deep inlet running parallel with the Cadogen Inlet of Captain Inglefield, fringed all around with glaciers set into the dark rocks like brilliants into a groundwork of jet, opens between Wade Point and Cape Isabella. I leave the naming of it until I see whether Inglefield has not a bay set down there, as I have not with me the official map of his explorations.

Cape Isabella is a ragged mass of Plutonic rock, and looks as if it had been turned out of Nature's laboratory unfinished and pushed up from the sea while it was yet hot, to crack and crumble to pieces

A "DIAMOND OF THE DESERT."

in the cold air. Its surface is barren to the last degree; immense chasms or cañons cross it in all directions, in which there was not the remotest trace of vegetation, — great yawning depths with jagged beds and crumbling sides, — sunless as the Cimerian caverns of Avernus.

As I clambered over crag after crag, I thought that I had not in the summer-time anywhere lit upon a place so devoid of life; but, as if to compensate for this barrenness, or through some freak of Nature, a charming cup-like valley nestled among the forbidding hills, and upon it I stumbled suddenly. Balboa could hardly have been more surprised when he climbed the hills of Darien and first saw the Pacific Ocean. It was truly a "Diamond of the Desert," and the little hermitage in the wilderness of Engadi was not a more pleasing sight to the Knight of the Couchant Leopard than was this to me.

The few hardy plants which I had found in all other localities had failed to find a lodgment upon the craggy slopes of this rough cape, and the rocks stood up in naked barrenness, without the little fringe of vegetation which usually girdles them elsewhere; but down into this valley the seeds of life had been wafted; the grass and moss clothed it with green; and the poppies and buttercups sprinkled it over with leaves of gold. In its centre reposed a little sparkling lake, like a diamond in an emerald setting — a little "charmed sea," truly,

"Girt by mountains wild and hoary;"

and weird and wonderful as any that ever furnished theme for Norland legend.

From the lower margin of this lake a stream

A GLACIER GROTTO. 423

rushed in a series of cascades through a deep gorge to the sea, and from the valley a number of little rivulets gurgled among the stones, or wound gently through the soft moss-beds. Tracing one of these to its source, I came upon a glen which was terminated abruptly by a glacier, appearing at a little distance like a draped curtain of white satin drawn across the narrow passage, as if to screen some sacred chamber of the hills. As I approached nearer this white curtain assumed more solid shape, and I observed that a multitude of bright fountains fluttered over it. Near. its centre a narrow Gothic archway led into a spacious grotto filled with a soft cerulean light, fretted with pendants of most fantastic shape and of rare transparency, which were reflected, as in a silver mirror, on the still surface of a limped pool, from which gushed forth a crystal rivulet, pure and sparkling as the cypress-embowered waters that laved the virgin limbs of the huntress-queen.

While peering into the deep recesses of this wonderful cave, so chaste and exquisite, where solitude appeared to dwell alone and undisturbed except by the soft music of streams, I became suddenly conscious of having been enticed into danger, Actæon-like, unawares. A mass of ice broke from the glacier front and, splitting into numerous fragments, the shower came crushing down upon the rocks and in the water near me, and sent me flying precipitately and with my curiosity still unsatisfied.

Returning to the lake, I followed around its green border, plucking, as I went, a nosegay of bright flowers, which have so pleasing an association that they will not find place in the "botanical collections," but, rather, in another collection, — mementos, if less

424 TRACES OF ESQUIMAUX.

prized, more cherished; and the recollection which I shall carry with me of this charming valley, and the silvery lake, and the gushing rivulets, and the grottoed glacier, will be enhanced when I name them in remembrance of the fairest forms that ever flitted across the memory of storm-beaten traveler, and the fairest fingers that ever turned Afghan wool into a cunning device to brighten the light of a dingy cabin!

Upon going ashore at Gale Point, I discovered traces of Esquimaux much more recent than those at Gould Bay and other places on the shores of Grinnell Land. Indeed they were of such a character as to cause me strongly to suspect that the shore is at present inhabited. The cliffs are composed of a dark sandstone which, to the northward of the Point, breaks suddenly away into a broad plain that slopes gently down to the water's edge. This plain is about five miles wide, and is bounded at the north much as at the south, by lofty cliffs, which rise above the primitive rocks back of Cape Isabella. The plain was composed of loose shingle, covered over in many places with large patches of green, through which flowed a number of broad streams of water. These streams sprang from the front of a glacier which bulged down the valley from the *mer de glace*. It was about four miles from the sea, and bounded the green and stony slope with a great white wall several hundred feet high, above which the snow-covered steep of the *mer de glace* led the eye away up to the bald summits of the distant mountains. As I looked up at this immense stream of ice it seemed as if a dozen Niagaras had been bounding together into the

THE MER DE GLACE. 425

valley and were frozen in their fall, and the discharging waters of the river below had dried up, and flowers bloomed in the river-bed. My journal compares it to a huge white sheet, hung upon a cord stretched from cliff to cliff.

CHAPTER XXXVIII.

LEAVING SMITH SOUND. — CROSSING THE NORTH WATER. — MEETING THE PACK. — THE SEA AND AIR TEEMING WITH LIFE. — REMARKABLE REFRACTION. — REACHING WHALE SOUND. — SURVEYING IN A BOAT. — THE SOUND TRACED TO ITS TERMINATION. — MEETING ESQUIMAUX AT ITEPLIK. — HABITS OF THE ESQUIMAUX. — MARRIAGE CEREMONY. — THE DECAY OF THE TRIBE. — VIEW OF BARDEN BAY. — TYNDALL GLACIER.

THE ice coming in at length with an easterly wind, and being unable to find any harbor (Cadogen Inlet was completely filled with ice), we had no alternative but to stand away to the south ; and this we did at a fortunate moment, for the ice crowded in against the shore with great rapidity ; and, had we waited longer, we should have been unable to escape, and would have been driven upon the beach by the irresistible pack.

We carried the wind along with us down the coast until we reached below Talbot Inlet, when we came upon a heavy pack, and held our course for Whale Sound, which I was desirous of exploring. Passing close to the land, I had an excellent opportunity for observing the coast and perfecting the chart, especially of Cadogen and Talbot Inlets, both of which were traced around their entire circuit. The coast is everywhere bristling with glaciers. A large island lies below Talbot Inlet, inside of the Mittie Island of Captain Inglefield, and not before laid down.

Skirting the northern margin of the ice, we made a course to the northeastward, across the

A RARE DAY. 427

North Water, through one of the most charming days that I have spent under the Arctic skies. There was but the feeblest "cat's-paw" to ruffle the sea, and we glided on our way over the still waters through a bright sunshine. The sea was studded all over with glittering icebergs and bits of old floes, and here and there a small streak of ice which had become detached from the pack. The beasts of the sea and the fowls of the air gathered around us, and the motionless water and the quiet atmosphere were alive. The walrus came snorting and bellowing through the sea as if to have a look at us; the seals in great numbers were continually putting up their cunning heads all around the vessel; the narwhal in large schools, "blowing" lazily, thrust their horns out of the sea, and their dappled bodies followed after with a graceful curve, as if they enjoyed the sunshine and were loathe to quit it; great numbers of white whale darted past us; the air and the icebergs swarmed with gulls; and flocks of ducks and auks were flying over us all the time. I sat upon the deck much of the day, trying, with indifferent success, to convey to my portfolio the exquisite green tints of the ice which drifted past us, and watching a most singular phenomenon in the heavens. These Arctic skies do sometimes play fantastic tricks, and on no occasion have I witnessed the exhibition to such perfection. The atmosphere had a rare softness, and throughout almost the entire day there was visible a most remarkable mirage or refraction, — an event of very frequent occurrence during the calm days of the Arctic summer. The entire horizon was lifting and doubling itself continually, and objects at a great distance beyond it rose as if by strange enchantment and stood suspended

428 ARCTIC MIRAGE.

in the air, changing shape with each changing moment. Distant icebergs and floating ice-fields, and coast-lines and mountains were thus brought into view; sometimes preserving for a moment their natural shapes, then widening or lengthening, rising and falling as the wind fluttered or fell calm over the sea. The changes were as various as the dissolving images of a kaleidoscope, and every form of which the imagination could conceive stood out against the sky. At one moment a sharp spire, the prolonged image of a distant mountain-peak, would shoot up; and this would fashion itself into a cross, or a spear, or a human form, and would then die away, to be replaced by an iceberg which appeared as a castle standing upon the summit of a hill, and the ice-fields coming up with it flanked it on either side, seeming at one moment like a plain dotted with trees and animals; again, as rugged mountains; and then, breaking up after a while, disclosing a long line of bears and dogs and birds and men dancing in the air, and skipping from the sea to the skies. To picture this strange spectacle were an impossible task. There was no end to the forms which appeared every instant, melting into other shapes as suddenly. For hours we watched the "insubstantial pageant," until a wind from the north ruffled the sea; when, with its first breath, the whole scene melted away as quickly as the "baseless fabric" of Prospero's "vision;" and from watching these dissolving images, and wooing the soft air, we were, in a couple of hours, thrashing to windward through a fierce storm of rain and hail, under close-reefed sails.

We had some ugly knocking about and some narrow escapes in the thick atmosphere, before we reached Whale Sound. A heavy pack, apparently hanging upon the Carey Islands, drove us far up the North Water; and, to get to our destination, we were obliged to hold in close to Hakluyt Island Here, the air having fallen calm, I pulled ashore; and, when we set out to return, we found ourselves enveloped in a fog which caused us some alarm. Observing its approach, we pulled to catch the schooner before the dark curtain closed upon us, but were overtaken when almost a mile away. Having no compass we became totally ignorant of which way to steer; and, although we heard the ship's bell and an occasional discharge of guns to attract our attention, yet, so deceptive is the ear where the eye is not concerned in guiding it, that no two of us caught the sound from the same direction; so we lay on our oars, and trusted to fortune. After a while, a light wind sprung up; and the schooner, getting under way, by the merest chance bore right upon us, and came so suddenly in view out of the dark vapors that we had like to have been run down before we could get headway on the boat.

We had much difficulty, owing to the fogs, current, and icebergs, in getting up Whale Sound; but, after much patient perseverance, we arrived at length in Barden Bay, and came to anchor off the native settlement of Netlik.

The settlement was found to be deserted. The fog lifting next day, disclosing much heavy ice, among which it would be dangerous to trust the schooner, I took a whale-boat and pulled up the Sound.

The Sound narrows steadily until a few miles beyond Barden Bay, where the coasts run parallel until the waters terminate in a deep bay or gulf, to which

430   AN ESQUIMAUX VILLAGE.

I gave the name of the enterprising navigator, Captain Inglefield, who first passed the entrance to it. The coast on the north side runs much further south than appears on the old charts; and two conspicuous headlands, which Inglefield mistook for islands, I have designated on my chart by the names which the supposed islands have on his. A cluster of islands at the farther end of the gulf I called Harvard Islands, in remembrance of the University at Cambridge, to members of whose faculty I am indebted for many courteous attentions while fitting out in Boston ; and a range of noble mountains which rise from the head of the gulf and with stately dignity overlook the broad *mer de glace*, holding the vast ice-flood in check, I named the Cambridge Hills.

On the south side of the Sound, toward which the Harvard Islands seem to trend, there are two prominent capes which I named respectively Cape Banks and Cape Lincoln ; [1] while two deep bays are designated as Cope's Bay and Harrison Bay. Another, on the north side, I called Armsby Bay.

I had to regret that I could not reach the further end of the gulf. The ice for about twenty miles remained quite solid and impenetrable, so that I was obliged to draw back. Skirting along the southern coast we came upon the village of Itiplik and found it inhabited by about thirty people. They were living in seal-skin tents, three in number, and were overjoyed to see us. Near by, there was a rookery of auks similar to that near Port Foulke, which, together with the seal and walrus that were observed to

---

[1] In honor of His Excellency N P. Banks, Governor of Massachusetts, and of His Honor F. W. Lincoln, Mayor of Boston, at the time of my sailing, in 1860.

ESQUIMAU STATISTICS.

be very numerous in all parts of the Sound, furnished them ample subsistence. There were in all nine families, but there was no family that consisted of more than four persons, — the parents and two children. The largest family that I have seen among them was that of Kalutunah. Hans told me of several families of three children ; and Tattarat, now a lonely widower, lives on Northumberland Island, near the auk-hill of that place, with three orphans ;, and his wife bore him a fourth, which disappeared in some mysterious manner soon after its mother died and while it was yet a babe at the breast.

With the aid of Hans, I endeavored to get at a correct estimate of the whole tribe, and, commencing with Cape York, took down their names. In this community there can be no domestic secrets, and everybody knows all about everybody else's business, — where they go for the summer, and what luck they have had in hunting, — and talk and gossip about it and about each other just as if they were civilized beings, having good names to pick to pieces. But I strongly suspect that Hans grew tired of my questioning and cross-questioning, and stopped short at seventy-two. I have good reason to believe, however, that the tribe numbers more nearly one hundred. I obtained a complete list of the deaths which had taken place since Dr. Kane left them, in 1855. They amounted to thirty-four ; and, during that time, there had been only nineteen births.

Their marriage engagements are, of necessity, mere matters of convenience. Their customs allow of a plurality of wives ; but among this tribe, even if there were sufficient women, no hunter probably could support two families. The marriage arrange-

432 ESQUIMAU MARRIAGE CEREMONY.

ment is made by the parents, and the parties are fitted to each other as their ages best suit. When a boy comes of age, he marries the first girl of suitable years. There is no marriage ceremony further than that the boy is required to carry off his bride by main force ; for, even among these blubber-eating people, the woman only saves her modesty by a sham resistance, although she knows years beforehand that her destiny is sealed and that she is to become the wife of the man from whose embraces, when the nuptial day comes, she is obliged by the inexorable law of public opinion to free herself if possible, by kicking and screaming with might and main until she is safely landed in the hut of her future lord, when she gives up the combat very cheerfully and takes possession of her new abode. The betrothal often takes place at a very early period of life and at very dissimilar ages. A bright-looking boy named Arko, which means "The spear thrower," who is not over twelve years of age, is engaged to a girl certainly of twenty, named Kartak, "The girl with the large breasts." Why was this ? I inquired. "There is no other woman for him." I thought he looked rather dubious of his future matrimonial prospects when I asked him how soon he proposed to carry off this big-breasted bride. Two others, whom I judged to be about ten years each, were to be married in this romantic style as soon as the lover had caught his first seal. This, I was told, is the test of manhood and maturity.

I talked to the oldest hunter of the tribe, an ancient, patriarchal-looking individual named Kesarsoak, — " He of the white hairs," — about the future of the tribe. The prospect to him was the same as to Kalu-

TYNDALL GLACIER.

433

tunah, — " Our people have but a few more suns to live !" Would they all come up to Etah if I should return, and stay there, and bring guns and hunters? His answer was a prompt, " Yes " He told me, as Kalutunah had done before, that Etah was the best hunting-place on the coast, only the ice broke up so soon and was always dangerous ; while Whale Sound was frozen during nearly all the year, and gave the hunters greater security.

After returning to the schooner, I pulled up into Barden Bay, taking with me the magnetic and surveying instruments and facilities for completing my botanical and other collections, and for photographing the fine scenery of the bay. Landing on its north shore, we found the hill-side covered in many places with a richer green sward than I had ever seen north of Upernavik, except once on a former occasion at Northumberland Island. The slope was girdled with the same tall cliffs which everywhere meet the eye along this coast ; and the same summer streams of melted snow tumbled over them, and down the slope from the mountain sides. The day was quite calm and the sky almost cloudless. The sun shone broadly upon us, and the temperature was 51°. Immense schools of whales and walrus, with an occasional seal, were sporting in the water ; flocks of sea-fowl went careering about the icebergs and through the air, and myriads of butterflies fluttered among the flowers ; while from the opposite side of the bay an immense glacier,[1] whose face was almost buried in the sea, carried the eye along a broad and winding valley, up steps of ice of giant height, and over smooth plains of whiteness, around the base of the hills, until

[1] I have named this glacier in honor of Professor John Tyndall.

28

434 TYNDALL GLACIER.

at length the slope pierced the very clouds, and, re-appearing above the curling vapors, was lost in the blue canopy of the heavens.

Three glaciers were visible from my point of ob-servation, — a small one, to the right, barely touching the water, and hanging, as if in suspensive agony, in a steep declivity; another, at the head of the bay, was yet miles away from the sea; while before us, in the centre of the bay, there came pouring down the rough and broken flood of ice before alluded to, which, bulging far out into the bay, formed a coast-line of ice over two miles long.

The whole glacier system of Greenland was here spread out before me in miniature. A lofty mountain-ridge, like a whale's back, held in check the expanding *mer de glace*, but a broad cleft cut it in twain, and the stream before me had burst through the opening like cataract rapids tumbling from the pent-up waters of a lake. The sublimity and picturesqueness of the scene was greatly heightened by two parallel rocky ridges, whose crests were to the left of the glacier. These crests are trap-dykes, left standing fifty feet perhaps above the sloping hill-side below them, by the wasting away of the sandstone through which they have forced their way in some great convulsion of Nature.

On the day following, I visited this glacier and made a careful examination of it, pulling first along its front in a boat and then mounting to its surface.

It would be difficult to imagine any thing more startling to the imagination or more suggestive to the mind than the scene presented by this two miles of ice coast-line, as I rowed along within a few fathoms of it. The glacier was broken up into the most sin-gular shapes, and presented nothing of that uniformity

GOTHIC GLACIER.

usual to the glacier's face. It was worn and wasted away until it seemed like the front of some vast incongruous temple, — here a groined roof of some huge cathedral, and there a pointed window or a Norman doorway deeply molded; while on all sides were pillars round and fluted, and pendants dripping crystal drops of the purest water, and all bathed in a soft, blue atmosphere. Above these wondrous archways and galleries there was still preserved the same Gothic character, — tall spires and pinnacles rose along the entire front and multiplied behind them, and new forms met the eye continually. The play of light and the magical softness of the color of the sea and ice was perfectly charming, as the scene I have heretofore described among the icebergs. Strange, there was nothing cold or forbidding anywhere. The ice seemed to take the warmth which suffused the air, and I longed to pull my boat far within the openings, and paddle beneath the Gothic archways. The dangers from falling ice alone prevented me from entering one of the largest of them.

Pulling around to the west side of the glacier, I clambered up a steep declivity over a pile of mud and rock, which the expanding and moving ice had pushed out from its bed. Once at the top of this yielding slope, the eye was met by a perfect forest of spires; but it was not easy to get on the glacier itself. Along its margin, half in mud and rock and half in ice, a torrent of dirty water came tearing along at a furious pace, disclosing the laminated structure of the ice in a very beautiful manner; and this was not easily crossed. At length, however, I came to a spot where the chief feeder of this rushing stream branched off at right angles, coming from the glacier itself, and I

GLACIER STREAM.

had no difficulty in wading across above the junction of the two arms. Following thence up the eastward branch as it dashed wildly down in a succession of cataracts, cutting squarely across the laminæ or strata (which lay at an angle of about 35°), I came at length to a place where the ice was much disturbed, and rose by broken steps from the plain on which I stood to the height of about one hundred and fifty feet, and right out from this wall came the rushing torrent, hissing and foaming from a monstrous tunnel, to which the Croton Aqueduct would be a pigmy. It was a strange sight. The ice was perfectly pure and transparent; and yet, out of its very heart, was pouring the muddy stream of which I have made mention, and which, although the comparison is rather remote, reminded me of the image which Virgil draws of the Tiber, when Æneas first beheld its turbid waters, pouring out from beneath the bright and lovely foliage which overspread it.

The tunnel out of which the waters poured was about ten yards wide and as many high, the supporting roof being composed of every form of Gothic arch, fretted and fluted in the most marvelous manner, and pure as the most stainless alabaster; yet the distant effect within the tunnel was quite different, — the dark stream beneath being reflected above; and truly, if I might be allowed to paraphrase a line of Dryden, —

"The muddy bottom o'er the arch was thrown."

I clambered within this tunnel as far as I could, along a slippery shelf above the tumbling waters, until the light was almost shut out behind me, but far enough to perceive that, on my right hand, other tunnels dis-

CLIMBING THE GLACIER. 437

charged into this main sewer, as the underground culverts which drain into the main artery the refuse of a city.

Returning to the open air, I pursued my way up the glacier for a couple of miles further, and discovered that this stream had its origin in the mountain on the right, where the melting snows rolled over the rocky slope, evidently by a newly formed channel, for the water was tearing through moss-beds and deposits of sand and silt, and, rushing thence on the glacier, tumbled headlong hundreds and hundreds of feet, down into a yawning chasm. This chasm or crevasse no doubt extended to the bottom of the glacier, and the water, after winding along the rocky bed under the ice, finally has found its way into the cracks formed by the ice in its descent over a steep and rugged declivity, and has slowly worn away the tunnels or culverts which I have described.

I had now come to the gorge in the mountain through which the glacier descends to the sea. The view of the glacier from the margin is, at this point, somewhat like what I fancy the *mer de glace* at Tréla-porte, in the Alps, would be if the Grande Jorasse and Mont Tacul, and the other mountains which form the cradle for the *glacier de Léchaud* and the *glacier du Géant*, and their tributaries, were all leveled. Instead of the variety disclosed in the Alpine view, the eye lights here upon one expanding stream instead of many streams, which narrows as it approaches the pass until it is about two miles over; thence descending the steep declivity to the sea, breaking up as it moves over the rougher places in the manner before described.

In all my glacier experience I had not seen any

thing so fully exhibiting the principles of glacier movement or so forcibly illustrating the river-like character of the crystal stream. To scale the glacier further was not in my power; but the eye climbed up, step by step, through the mountain-pass to the giddy summit, and as the imagination wandered from this icy pinnacle over sea and mountain, it seemed to me that the world did not hold any more impressive evidence of the greatness and the power of the Almighty hand; and I thought how feeble were all the efforts of man in comparison. As I turned away and commenced my descent, I found myself repeating these lines of Byron, penned as his poet-fancy wandered up the ice-girdled steeps and over the ice-crowned summits of the Alps:—

" . . . . . . these are
The palaces of Nature, whose vast walls
Have pinnacled in clouds their snowy scalps,
And throned Eternity in icy halls
Of cold sublimity."

TYNDALL GLACIER—WHALE SOUND
(FROM A PHOTOGRAPH BY DR. HAYES.)

CHAPTER XXXIX.

HOMEWARD BOUND. — ENTERING MELVILLE BAY. — ENCOUNTER WITH A BEAR. — MEETING THE PACK. — MAKING THE " SOUTH WATER " — REACHING UPER- NAVIK — THE NEWS — TO GOODHAVEN. — LIBERALITY OF THE DANISH GOV- ERNMENT AND THE GREENLAND OFFICIALS — DRIVEN OUT OF BAFFIN BAY BY A GALE. — CRIPPLED BY THE STORM AND FORCED TO TAKE SHELTER IN HALIFAX — HOSPITABLE RECEPTION. — ARRIVAL IN BOSTON — REALIZE THE STATE OF THE COUNTRY. — THE DETERMINATION — CONCLUSION

MY story is soon ended. Having completed the exploration of Whale Sound, we tripped our anchor and stood southward. The heavens were bright and the air soft with a summer warmth; and as we glided down the waveless waters, all sparkling with icebergs, watching the scene of our adventures slowly sinking away behind us under the crimson trail of the midnight sun, it seemed truly as if smooth seas and gentle winds had come to invite us home.

But this repose of the elements was of short duration. A dark curtain rose after a while above the retreating hills, and sent us a parting salute, in the shape of a storm of snow and wind, so that we were soon obliged to gather in some of our canvas, and keep a sharp look-out.

My purpose was to reach the "West Water," by making a course toward Pond's Bay, then round the "middle ice" to the southward, and make an easterly course for the Greenland coast.

The atmosphere cleared up at length, but the wind held on fiercely. Being from the north-northeast, it seemed to me then to favor an easterly rather than a

440   ENCOUNTER WITH A BEAR.

westerly passage ; so, having reached a little below the latitude of Cape York, on the meridian of 73° 40′ without discovering any signs of ice, I changed my original purpose, and, altering the course of the schooner, struck directly across Melville Bay for Upernavik. The result proved the prudence of this change. In twenty-four hours we ran down nearly two degrees of latitude, and hauled in seven degrees of longitude, finding ourselves at noon of August 10th in latitude 74° 19′, longitude 66°, without having encountered any ice seriously to trouble us. The air still holding clear, we had no difficulty in avoiding the bergs.

The sea had by this time become very angry, and I was almost as anxious as I had been the year before, when entering the bay from the south. The atmosphere was, however, perfectly clear.

While bounding along, logging ten knots an hour, we almost ran over an immense polar bear, which was swimming in the open water, making a fierce battle with the seas, and seemingly desirous of boarding us. He was evidently much exhausted, and, seeing the vessel approach, doubtless had made at her in search of safety. The unhappy beast had probably allowed himself to be drifted off on an ice-raft which had gone to pieces under him in the heavy seas. Although these polar bears are fine swimmers, I much feared that the waves would in the end prove too much for this poor fellow, as there was not a speck of ice in sight on which he could find shelter. As we passed, he touched the schooner's side, and Jensen, who had seized a rifle, was in the act of putting an end to his career, when I arrested his hand. The beast was making such a brave fight for his life that I would not see him shot, more especially as the waves were running too high

RECROSSING MELVILLE BAY. 441

to lower a boat for his carcass, without a risk which the circumstances did not warrant.

The presence of this bear warned me that the pack could not be very remote, and accordingly we shortened sail, and I took my old station aloft on the foreyard. Sure enough the pack was there, as was soon evidenced by an "ice-blink," and in a little while we were close upon it. Hauling by the wind, we skirted its margin for some time without discovering any termination to it; and, the ice appearing to be very loose and rotten, I stood away again on our southerly course, and entered the first favorable lead. It was something of a venture, as we could not, although the ice was wholly different from that of Smith Sound, owing to the condition of the schooner's bows, strike it with safety. Luckily the wind favored us, and the schooner answering her helm promptly, we managed to avoid the floes for about twelve hours, at least without a thump of any serious consequence, at the end of which time the wind had fallen to calm; and this continuing for some time, with the temperature several degrees below freezing, new ice was formed more than half an inch thick, all over the sea.

A light and fair breeze springing up again, we were once more under way, crunching through this crystal sheet much to the damage of the schooner's sides, where there was no iron, and very embarrassing to our progress, for we were often absolutely stuck fast. We were glad enough when the breeze stiffened and knocked the ice to pieces, giving us a free passage into the "East Water."

We made land on the morning of the 12th, and found it to be the Horse's Head. The pack was now far behind us, and our southern passage through Mel-

442   NEWS FROM HOME.

ville Bay had been made in about five hours less time than our northern.

From the Horse's Head we jogged on through a foggy atmosphere with occasional thick squalls of snow and light variable winds, until after three days' groping we found ourselves again at anchor in Upernavik harbor.

While the chain was yet clicking in the hawse-hole, an old Dane, dressed in seal-skins, and possessing a small stock of English and a large stock of articles to trade, pulled off to us with an Esquimau crew, and, with little ceremony, clambered over the gangway. Knorr met him, and, without any ceremony at all, demanded the news.

"Oh! dere 's plenty news."

"Out with it, man! What is it?"

"Oh! de Sout' States dey go agin de Nort' States, and dere 's plenty fight."

I heard the answer, and, wondering what strange complication of European politics had kindled another Continental war, called this Polar Eumæus to the quarter-deck. Had he any news from America?

"Oh! 't is 'merica me speak! De Sout' States, you see? dey go agin de Nort' States, you see? and dere 's plenty fight!"

Yes, I did see! but I did not believe that he told the truth, and awaited the letters which I knew must have come out with the Danish vessel, and which were immediately sent for to the Government-House.

It proved that letters had been brought for us by our old friend, Dr. Rudolph, who had returned a few weeks before from Copenhagen, and who kindly brought them aboard himself as soon as he knew of our arrival, and almost before my messenger had reached the shore.

THE REBELLION. 443

These and some files of papers, and the Doctor's memory, gave us the leading occurrences which had taken place at home up to near the end of March, 1861. We learned of the inauguration of the new President and of the leading events following his election, but of the startling incidents of a later period we were ignorant. We could not apprehend that war had actually broken out. We knew only of the intrigues for a division of the States and of the acts looking to that design. We learned that suspicion on the one hand, and treason on the other, ruled the hour; that threats of violence and irresolute counsels had thrown society into a ferment; and that the national safety was imperiled; but we knew not of the firing on Fort Sumter, nor of the bloody wound which the Nation had received at Bull Run; nor that a vast army for the protection of the Capital and the defense of the Government was then growing up on the banks of the Potomac. We little thought, that in every city, and town, and hamlet, the occupations of peace had already given place to the passionate excitements of war; that a cry of indignation and anger had gone up throughout the land against men who, pledged to protect the national flag and the national name, had abandoned and repudiated them; or, that under the banner of States' rights and under the impulse of ambition, a powerful party had boldly bid defiance to the Federal power and declared their purpose to break the Federal compact. And, even had we heard these things, it would have been difficult for us to have thus suddenly realized that, in a single year, human folly and human madness had so completely got the better of right and reason.

I occupied myself while the schooner lay at Upernavik with visiting a magnificent glacier nine miles wide, which discharges into a fiord named Aukpadlatok, about forty miles from the town. Near this glacier there is a hunting-station of the same name which is superintended by a Dane, called Philip, who lives there in the enjoyment of peace and plenty, with an Esquimau wife and a large family of children, among whom are four full-grown half-breed boys, — the best hunters, I was told, north of Prüven. My surveys detained me several days at Philip's hut, and, before I left, I had made full arrangements with himself and his seal-skin-coated boys and his wife and daughters, to make sledges, for which I gave them abundant materials, and fur-clothing, and skin-lines; and I engaged them to rear and accumulate dogs for me, that I might be well supplied when I came back the next year.

After leaving Upernavik, light and baffling winds kept us at our old trade of dodging the icebergs for four days, at the end of which time we were at anchor in Goodhaven, and I was enjoying, as I was sure to do, the courteous hospitality of my old friend, Inspector Olrik.

This settlement is situated on the south side of Disco Island, and takes its name from the excellence of the harbor, which is completely land-locked. It is the principal colony of North Greenland, and, being the residence of the Viceroy or Royal Inspector, has attached to it an air of importance not belonging to the other stations.

Mr. Olrik exhibited to me an order from his Government, commanding the Greenland officials to give attention to my requirements, and offering me at the same time as well his official as personal good offices.

LEAVING GREENLAND. 445

Being on my way home, I had little occasion to avail myself of this gracious act of the Danish Government; but I informed the Inspector of my future purposes and signified to him my desire to avail myself of its privileges next year. I am glad of an opportunity publicly to express my admiration of the conduct of the Danish Government toward the Arctic expeditions of whatever nationality; and in my own case it was the more personally gratifying, and the more highly appreciated, that I had no "Department" orders wherewith to back up my claims to consideration.

From the Chief Trader, Mr. Anderson, as well as from the Inspector, I had much kindly assistance in perfecting my collections and in completing my series of photographic views, and I found myself so agreeably as well as profitably occupied that I was truly loath to quit the good harbor; but it was necessary for me to be hastening home, as the nights were growing dark, and I did not wish to be caught among the icebergs without some sunlight to guide me; so, when the first fine wind came, I huddled my collections aboard, bade good-by, saluted the Danish ensign for the last time, and — well, we did over again what we had done a dozen times before — dove into a villainous fog-bank, out of which came a rush of wind that sent us homeward a little faster than we cared to go.

It was a regular equinoctial storm, and, from the time of leaving Disco until we had passed Newfoundland, it scarcely once relaxed its grip of us. We were blown out through Davis Strait even more fiercely than we had been blown in. At one time we were beset with a perfect hurricane, and how the

446 . FLYING BEFORE THE GALE.

schooner staggered through it was little short of a miracle. Ulysses could hardly have had a worse dusting, when his stupid crew let loose all the winds which Æolus had so kindly bagged up for him. Every stitch of canvas was ripped up but the little rag of a top-sail, under which we scudded before the gale through four days, running down in one four-and-twenty hours two hundred and twenty miles of latitude. The seas which came tumbling after us, each one seemingly determined to roll over the poop, were perfectly frightful; especially when one looked aloft and saw the little patch of canvas threatening every moment to give way, and heard the waters gurgling under the counter as the stern went down and the bows went up, while a very Niagara was roaring and curveting after us, as if maddened with defeat, and with each new effort the more determined to catch the craft before she should mount the crest ahead. But she slipped from under every threatening danger as gracefully, if not as

"Swift, as an eagle cleaving the liquid air,"

and, leaving the parted billows foaming and roaring behind her, passed on triumphant and unharmed.

When off Labrador, the wind hauled suddenly to the westward, and we had to give up the chase, and get the schooner's head to it. McCormick had managed to patch up the foresail, and, getting a triangular piece of it rigged for a storm-sail, we proposed to heave her to. There did not appear to be much chance of a successful termination to this new venture, but it was clearly this or nothing. The sail was set and the determination come to just in time, for we shipped a terrible sea over the quarter, the schooner

CRIPPLED BY THE STORM. 447

gave a lurch to leeward, and then righted so suddenly that the little topsail which had done us such good service went into ribbons, the top-mast cracked off at the cap, and crash went the jib-boom right away afterward. "Hard a-lee!" was rather a melancholy sort of order to give under the circumstances, and, as was to be expected, when the helm went down we were thrown into the trough of the next sea, where we were caught amidships by the ugliest wave that I ever happened to look upon, and down it thundered upon us, staving in the bulwarks, sweeping the decks from stem to stern, and carrying every thing overboard, our water-casks included. The schooner shivered all over as if every rib in her little body was broken, and for a moment I felt sure that she was knocked over on her beam ends; but the craft seemed to possess more lives than a cat, and, righting in an instant, shook herself free of the water, took the next wave on the bow, rose to it nobly, and then shot squarely into the wind's eye. "Bravely done, little lady!" was McCormick's caressing approval of her good behavior.

We lay hove to for three days, at the end of which time we found ourselves drifted from our course two hundred miles. Meanwhile, there had been a good deal of alarm caused by the loss of our water-casks. We had an extra cask or so in the hold, but these could not be got up without removing the mainhatch, an effort not to be thought of, as the decks were flooded and the vessel would be swamped; so I at once set myself to work to remedy the evil, and succeeded perfectly. With a tea-kettle for a retort and a barrel for a condenser, I managed to distil water enough for the entire ship's company: and, in less

448 RECEPTION IN HALIFAX.

than three hours after the disaster, all alarm vanished when it was known that a stream of pure water was trickling from this novel contrivance in the officers' cabin, at the rate of ten gallons a day.

The damaged condition of the schooner compelled us, when off Nova Scotia, to make a port as speedily as possible, and accordingly we put into Halifax. Our reception there was most gratifying, and among a people famed for hospitality we had abundant reason to rejoice over the ill winds which had blown us so much good. The admiral of Her Britannic Majesty's fleet, then in Halifax Harbor, generously tendered the use of the Government conveniences for repairing my crippled vessel; and from the officers of Her Majesty's civil service and of the squadron and garrison; from the Mayor and many other citizens of Halifax, — most especially from the Medical Society, — the Expedition received attentions which exhibited not less a friendliness of disposition for ourselves than respect for the flag under which our explorations had been made.

Up to the time of our arrival at Halifax we had, of course, no further news than what reached us at Upernavik We had scarcely dropped our anchor before a a citizen of the town and a countryman of my own, neither of whom was long a stranger to my friendship or my gratitude, hurried off to give us greetings, and to bring the news. They had picked up some files of New York papers on the way, and we soon learned of the terrible struggle that had been going on for many months. Although not wholly unprepared for this by the intelligence received at Upernavik, yet we had confidently cherished the expectation that hostilities had been averted by wise and prudent counsellors.

ARRIVAL IN BOSTON.

The shock was to us such as those who had watched at home the progress of events from day to day could, perhaps hardly realize. The first intelligence I had of the war was the account of the Bull Run battle, next I heard of the firing on Sumter, and then of the riots in Baltimore, and the destruction of Norfolk Navy-Yard, and the capture of Harper's Ferry; and then followed an account of the universal arming and volunteering.

We remained at Halifax not longer than was necessary to complete the repairs of the schooner, when we again put to sea, and in four days made the Boston Lights. We picked up a pilot out of the thickest fog that I have ever seen south of the Arctic Circle, and with a light wind stood into the harbor. As the night wore on the wind fell away almost to calm; the fog thickened more and more, if that were possible, as we sagged along over the dead waters toward the anchorage. The night was filled with an oppressive gloom. The lights hanging at the mast-heads of the vessels which we passed had the ghastly glimmer of tapers burning in a charnel-house. We saw no vessel moving but our own, and even those which lay at anchor seemed like phantom ships floating in the murky air. I never saw the ship's company so lifeless, or so depressed even in times of real danger.

The sun was beginning to pour into the atmosphere a dim light when we let go our anchor; but it did not seem that we were at home, or that a great city lay near by. No one was anxious to go ashore. It appeared as if each one anticipated some personal misfortune, and wished to postpone the shock foreboded by his fears. I landed on Long Wharf, and found my way into State Street. Two or three figures were moving through the thick vapors, and their solemn foot-fall broke the worse than Arctic stillness. I reached Washington Street, and walked anxiously westward. A news-boy passed me. I seized a paper, and the first thing which caught my eye was the account of the Ball's Bluff battle, in which had fallen many of the noblest sons of Boston; and it seemed as if the very air had shrouded itself in mourning for them, and that the heavens wept tears for the city's slain.

I was wending my way to the house of a friend, but I thought it likely that he was not there. I felt like a stranger in a strange land, and yet every object which I passed was familiar. Friends, country, every thing seemed swallowed up in some vast calamity, and, doubtful and irresolute, I turned back sad and dejected, and found my way on board again through the dull, dull fog.

The terrible reality was now for the first time present to my imagination. The land which I had left in the happy enjoyment of peace and repose was already drenched with blood; a great convulsion had come to scatter the old landmarks of the national Union, and the country which I had known before could be the same no more. Mingled with these reflections were thoughts of my own career. To abandon my pursuits; to give up a project in which I had expended so much time and means; to have nipped, as it were, in the very bud, a work upon which I had set my heart, and to which I had already given all the early years of my manhood; to sacrifice all the hopes and all the ambitions which had encouraged me through toil and danger, with the promise of the fame to follow the successful completion of a great object; to abandon an

THE DETERMINATION. 451

enterprise in which I had aspired to win for myself an honorable place among the men who have illustrated their country's history and shed lustre upon their country's flag, were thoughts which first seriously crossed my mind while returning on board, carrying in my hand the bloody record of Ball's Bluff. In the face of the startling intelligence which had crowded upon me since reaching Halifax, and which had now culminated; in the face of the duty which every man owes, in his own person, to his country when his country is in peril, I could not hesitate. Before I had reached my cabin, while our friends were yet in ignorance of our presence in the bay, I had resolved to postpone the execution of the task with which I had charged myself; and I closed as well the cruise as the project, by writing a letter to the President, asking for immediate employment in the public service, and offering my schooner to the government for a gun-boat.

Five years have now elapsed since the schooner *United States* crept to anchorage through the murky vapors of Boston Harbor. The terrible struggle then first realized by me, as at hand, is now over, and has become an event of history. The destinies of individuals are ever subordinate to the public weal; and in the presence of great social and political revolutions, when ideas are fringed with bayonets, and great interests are in conflict. men have little leisure for the consideration of questions of science, or of remote projects unconnected with the national safety.

Therefore it is that the further exploration of the Arctic regions was lost sight of by me during the past

452 PLANS POSTPONED, NOT ABANDONED.

few years The facilities which I had acquired, and the advantages which I had gained, have been in a great measure sacrificed since my return to Boston in October, 1861, and I cannot therefore speak with confidence as to the time when the exploration will be renewed. The scheme has not, however, been abandoned, nor are my views in any respect changed I still contemplate the execution of my original design, and hope at an early day to carry into effect the plan of discovery indicated in the concluding chapters of this narrative. It is still my wish to found at Port Foulke such a colony as I have hitherto described, and, with a corps of scientific associates, to make that the centre of a widely extended system of exploration. The value of such a centre will be evident to every instructed mind without illustration, and the availability of the situation is shown by the experience of my own party. The project has the more interest at this time in connection with the effort by way of the Spitzbergen Sea, contemplated by the Prussian government, the inception of which is due to the eminent geographer, Dr. Augustus Petermann. As with my own enterprise, that of Dr. Petermann has temporarily given place to the necessities of war; but I have been informed that the expedition is contemplated for the coming spring. The organization of this expedition is founded upon, I think, a correct assumption that the Open Sea and the North Pole may be reached with steam-vessels by pushing through the ice-belt to the west and north of Spitzbergen. This route possesses some advantages over that of Smith Sound, while it has some disadvantages. The temporary colonization at Port Foulke gives to the Smith Sound route its chief claim over the other, to the consideration of the explorer.

ADVANTAGES OF ARCTIC EXPLORATION. 453

It is not needful that I should here demonstrate the advantages to be derived from a continuation of the line of exploration which I have indicated;—the age in which we live has too much profited by researches into every department of science, which, not immediately prosecuted with the view to practical advantage, have, by a steady enlargement of the boundaries of human knowledge, promoted the interests of commerce, of navigation, of the arts, and of every thing which concerns the convenience and the comfort and the well-being of mankind. In truth, civilization has profited most by those discoveries which possessed at the outset only an abstract value, and excited no interest beyond the walls of the academy. The vast system of steam communication, which weaves around the world its endless web of industry, began in the apparently useless experiments of a thoughtful boy with the lid of his mother's tea-kettle; that wonderful net-work of wires which spreads over the continents and underlies the seas, and along which the thoughts of men fly as with the wings of light, results from the accidental touching of two pieces of metal in the mouth of Volta; the lenses of the mammoth telescope of Lord Rosse, which reduced to practical uses the celestial mechanism, came from observing the magnifying powers of a globule of water; the magnetic needle which guides the navies of the world to their distant destinations, succeeds the casual contact of a piece of loadstone and a bit of steel: everywhere, indeed, we witness the same constant growth from what seemed unprofitable beginnings;— the printing-press, the loom, the art of solar painting, all sprang from the one same source, — from minds intent only upon interrogating Nature, and revealing her mysteries, without knowledge of the good to come therefrom. The progress of scientific discovery is indeed the progress of the human race, and the question, *Cui bono?* is now no longer asked of him who would reveal hidden truths. Wherever men have sought wider fields of gain, or power, or usefulness, there has been science in the midst of them, — guiding, supporting, and instructing them. Wherever men have sought to plant, among barbarous peoples, the emblem of the only true religion, there has she gone before, — opening the gates and smoothing the pathway. She has lifted the curtain of ignorance from the human mind, and Christianity, following her advancing footsteps, has banished from the West the ancient superstitions, and the dark Pantheism of the East and the Fetich worship of the savage tribes are passing away. The light of science and the gospel of our Christian faith have moved hand in hand together through the world, and, overriding the barriers of custom, have, with unselfish zeal, steadily unfolded to the human understanding the material interests which concern this life, and to the human soul the sacred truths of Revelation which concern the life to come.

PAGE 101-102 MISSING
INUM SOUL 113→, 256
DOGS 102-55, 119→, 213, 240
WALRUS p. 405

The Open Polar Sea: A Narrative Of A Voyage Of Discovery Towards The North Pole, In The Schooner "united States"

Hayes, I. I. (Isaac Israel), 1832-1881

Nabu Public Domain Reprints:

You are holding a reproduction of an original work published before 1923 that is in the public domain in the United States of America, and possibly other countries. You may freely copy and distribute this work as no entity (individual or corporate) has a copyright on the body of the work. This book may contain prior copyright references, and library stamps (as most of these works were scanned from library copies). These have been scanned and retained as part of the historical artifact.

This book may have occasional imperfections such as missing or blurred pages, poor pictures, errant marks, etc. that were either part of the original artifact, or were introduced by the scanning process. We believe this work is culturally important, and despite the imperfections, have elected to bring it back into print as part of our continuing commitment to the preservation of printed works worldwide. We appreciate your understanding of the imperfections in the preservation process, and hope you enjoy this valuable book.